The
Genesis
of Ethics

The
Genesis
of Ethics

On the Authority
of God as the
Origin of
Christian Ethics

ESTHER D. REED

DARTON·LONGMAN+TODD

First published in 2000 by
Darton, Longman and Todd Ltd
1 Spencer Court
140–142 Wandsworth High Street
London SW18 4JJ

ISBN 0–232–52352–5

A catalogue record for this book is available from the British Library.

Designed by Sandie Boccacci
Phototypeset in 11/13¾pt Minion by Intype London Ltd
Printed and bound in Great Britain by
Redwood Books, Trowbridge, Wiltshire

Contents

Preface

This book is an enquiry into the theological principles of Christian ethics. It argues that 'the genesis of ethics' is found in the authority of God. At a time when, for many, the authority of God is the problem of Christian ethics, not its answer, this book offers an answer to the moral challenge from Nietzsche, post-Christian feminists et al., that confession of the authority of God is harmful to the human condition. It does so by drawing on biblical and traditional resources and by allowing doctrines of the Trinity, creation, salvation, ecclesiology and eschatology to provide working theological axioms. *The Genesis of Ethics* argues that the authority of God has nothing to do with the authoritarianism, patriarchy and legalism with which it is sometimes associated. Rather, Christian ethics finds its 'genesis' in the authority of God because God is the Author of all creation (Latin *auctor*, meaning originator or author, and *augere*, meaning to increase), and because the Word of God reveals the truth about God and humanity. The book identifies Christian ethics with the dynamic of human response to God's revelation in Christ, and explores tensions that sometimes arise between freedom in the Spirit and the teaching authority of the church.

It is assumed throughout the book that Christian ethics is the discipline which deals with the living of Christian life and comprises the study of Christian ethos (Greek *ethos*, meaning custom or character) in relationship to belief and doctrine. Christian living flows from belief in Christ, participation in the life of the church, the sacraments, prayer and fellowship. It concerns learning to live according to the 'mind of Christ' (Phil. 2:5) and as 'the body of Christ' (1 Cor. 12:27; Eph. 4:12; Col. 1:18), and involves the articulation and application of Christian belief and doctrine in specific situations. It is assumed that Christian ethics is different from all other ways of doing ethics because it refers everything to God revealed in Jesus Christ, because it pays close and careful attention to what the bible says – in full awareness of the polyphony of its witness to God's salvation, and because it requires knowledge of the critical spirit of the church, sometimes called 'tradition'. This said, what it means to live a Christian life in the face of rapid technological change and the unbridled ideologies of the free market, and in a pluralist culture, is often not clear. Hence the need for detailed and careful examination of the theological principles of Christian life which inform moral decision-making. Christian ethics is not a set of moral absolutes. Nor is it solely the responsibility of the clergy or 'professionals'. Yet the theology underlying any response to new situations must be sound and adequate to the task.

For this reason, the book attempts to point to a vision of God's goodness (Lk. 18:19) and to expound something of what it means to be created in the image of God (Gen. 1:27) – not least the capacity for making moral judgements and the vocation to union with God through life in Christ. It contemplates the theological truth that the Word of God became truly human in order that humans might share in the divine life, and considers why and how the incarnation reveals to us both the authority and goodness of God. In particular, it invites reflection upon why and how, in assuming human flesh, Jesus Christ embodied true humanity, calling all humanity to union (*henosis*) with God and to deification (*theosis*). It invites reflection upon why and how life in the Spirit is inherently communal and never private or solitary, why and how Christian ethics is ecclesial.

Acknowledgements

Quotations from the Bible are from the *New Revised Standard Version* (*NRSV*), copyright © 1989, Division of Education of the National Council of the Churches of Christ in the United States of America, and the *Revised English Bible*, copyright © 1989 Oxford University Press and Cambridge University Press.

Abbreviations

ANF   *The Ante-Nicene Fathers: Translations of the Writings of the Fathers down to AD 325*, ed. Alexander Roberts and James Donaldson (Edinburgh: T. & T. Clark)

NPNF   *The Nicene and Post-Nicene Fathers of the Christian Church*, ed. Philip Schaff (Edinburgh: T. & T. Clark)

Introduction

The Problem of Authority in a Season of Disenchantment

A criticism frequently heard against the Christian church is that
it lacks the authority necessary to help individuals cope with
contemporary spiritual, social and personal problems. Science,
through technology, has altered human life radically in most of its
aspects, such that traditional theological pronouncements can seem
largely irrelevant. As a television cynic once remarked, 'My neighbour doesn't have an ox or a donkey for me to covet!'[1] Add to this
the fact that institutionalised Christianity is often perceived as
morally bankrupt because of the prejudice it has sanctioned
throughout its history against so-called 'heretics', women, persons
of other faiths, homosexuals and many others, and its claims to
authority in the present day sound increasingly hollow.[2] Even when
people consult recognised Christian leaders or churches, the advice
given can differ markedly. Old divisions between conservative
absolutism and liberal wishy-washyness confuse the casual inquirer.
Some bishops believe that the days are long gone when theological
absolutes were of any use to Christian people.[3] Others hold fast to
the ancient foundations of the church, but seek to apply Christian
teaching in ways that seem out of touch with where people are.

1. Cited by Paul Davies, *God and the New Physics* (London: Penguin, 1983/1990),
p. 2.
2. Such charges are made by, for example, Hermann Bondi, who takes the
example of the European witch-craze to support his accusation that organised
religion has had a perverting influence on otherwise decent human behaviour.
See 'Religion is a good thing' in R. Duncan and M. Weston-Smith (eds), *Lying
Truths* (Oxford: Pergamon Press, 1979).
3. Richard Holloway, *Dancing on the Edge* (London: Fount, 1997), *passim.*

In this climate, it is tempting for Christian theologians to settle for a dogmatic minimalism that allows study of Christian ethics to be separated from serious theological and interdisciplinary reflection, or built upon shallow foundations. It is easy to get a case of theological jitters, or opt for a 'safe', 'vote-winning' option to advertise Christianity as a form of therapy that induces some vague feeling of well-being, or a placebo that anaesthetises us to life's troubles. It is even more enticing, perhaps, to slip into extreme forms of individualism in which spirituality is privatised, its criteria are pragmatic, and discourse about God reveals only what is hidden and internal to the heart. The individual must, as part of a linguistically formed world, work to create spiritual meaning and truth. This sounds like hubris, although its proponents claim that it is simply recognition of the radically linguistic and, therefore, intrinsically subjective flux that is the spiritual life of the individual. Many are tempted by the non-objectivity of this kind of spirituality and ethics, not least because it frees the individual from the strictures of institutionalised religion and leaves them able to follow the message of Jesus like a New-Age traveller. To do any of these, however, is to risk making God the vehicle for personal preferences and the justification for individual outlooks or lifestyles. Even if one manages to resist these temptations, it is easy to succumb to a season of disenchantment that erodes one's energy for criticism and innovation. If one listens for too long to theorists such as Hannah Arendt, who asserted in 1958 that the 'holy trinity' of religion, authority and tradition has been wrecked (Luther had destroyed the power of religion and the authority of the church, and Hobbes had undermined tradition), one becomes accustomed to a depression and stasis.[4] Old vocabularies seem to be exhausted, but new concepts and words not yet available.

What is clear is that many think that traditional sources and

---

4. Hannah Arendt, 'What is Authority?' in Carl J. Friedrich (ed.), *Authority, NOMOS 1* (Cambridge: Harvard University Press, 1958), p. 105.

orders of authority have lost (or are in the process of losing) their significance. Alasdair MacIntyre analysed the problem from the perspective of moral philosophy in *After Virtue*, and observed: 'it [is] no longer possible to appeal to moral criteria in a way that it had been possible in other times and places – *and* [this is] a moral calamity'.[5] Some social theorists dub this kind of contemporary phenomenon 'detraditionalisation', by which they typically imply that our age has moved beyond tradition and no longer accepts moral values or life-practices because they are part of an established and/or timeless order. Paul Heelas refers to a 'loss of faith in once familiar landmarks, in long-standing values, more specifically in religion . . . in the family . . . in the monarchy and in the political system'.[6] As he makes plain, this radical 'loss-of-tradition thesis' has its rivals; some theorists operate with a less bleak portrayal of tradition and do not think that we are witnessing the crumbling of belief in foundational morality.[7] Yet 'detraditionalisation' takes many forms. There has been a loss of faith not only in the church, but also in long-standing values associated with the family, marriage, the monarchy, membership of political parties, etc. The churches are not alone in having been affected by the shift of authority from 'without' to 'within'.[8]

The resulting uncertainty and confusion has led some to lament severance of ethics and moral discourse from its philosophical and theological roots. Gillian Rose, for example, was wary of the 'unabated search for a *new ethics*' which takes as its method only

5. Alasdair MacIntyre, *After Virtue: A Study in Moral Theory*, 2nd edition (London: Duckworth, 1981), p. ix.

6. Paul Heelas, 'Introduction: Detraditionalization and its Rivals' in Paul Heelas et al. (eds), *Detraditionalization* (Oxford: Blackwell, 1996), p. 1.

7. Compare Zygmunt Bauman's bleak portrayal of the loss of the traditional with Paul Morris's glimpsing of 'Community beyond Tradition' in Heelas et al., *Detraditionalization*, chs 3 and 12 respectively.

8. See Paul Heelas, 'Introduction: Detraditionalization and its Rivals' in Heelas et al., *Detraditionalization*, pp. 1–20.

the overcoming of tradition.[9] In particular, she criticised neo-pragmatist forms of new ethics that eschew any theory of justice that is dependent on the metaphysics of objective truth and independent of language.[10] She was aware of trends towards conceding that individuals no longer have any option other than to handle moral problems locally, without recourse to clear and rational bases for ethics and moral discourse.[11] She knew that, for some, moral philosophy is no longer possible on the basis of universal moral codes and rules of conduct based on reason and/ or tradition, and that the reasons for this trend are far from trivial. For Zygmunt Bauman, for example, atrocities in the twentieth century are proof of the inadequacy of modern approaches to moral reason, and he urges their abandonment; the Holocaust exposed complicity between 'the rationality of evil' and 'the evil of rationality'.[12] If modern creeds of rationality have been – and still sometimes are – confused with 'the calculus of self-preservation', then we can no longer trust the 'Certainty and Truth of Reason' that characterised modernity.[13] If Bauman is correct, then we are witnessing an unrestrained relativism of values which robs moral principles of their meaning and force. Jean Baudrillard writes, 'Properly speaking there is now no law of value, merely a sort of *epidemic of value* ... a haphazard proliferation and dis-

---

9. Gillian Rose, *Mourning Becomes the Law* (Cambridge: CUP, 1997), p. 1.

10. Rose, *Mourning*, p. 5.

11. Consider Zygmunt Bauman's observation: '[T]he postmodern mind does not expect any more to find the all-embracing, total and ultimate formula of life without ambiguity, risk, danger and error, and is deeply suspicious of any voice that promises otherwise.' Zygmunt Bauman, *Postmodern Ethics* (Oxford: Blackwell, 1993), p. 245.

12. Z. Bauman, *Modernity and the Holocaust* (Cambridge: Polity Press, 1989), esp. ch. 8.

13. G. W. F. Hegel speaks about the 'Certainty and Truth of Reason' as that which is integrally bound to the unfolding development of the self, and also world history. See G. W. F. Hegel, *Phenomenology of Spirit*, trans. A. V. Miller (Oxford: OUP, 1977), §231f.

persal of value. We should really no longer speak of "value" at all, for this kind of propagation or chain reaction makes all valuation impossible.'[14] We are experiencing 'despairing rationalism without reason'.[15]

In this kind of intellectual milieu it is not clear where disciplinary boundaries lie or what of western philosophical tradition can bear reinvestigation. It is not clear that there can be any rational basis for being moral. There are no objectively moral or immoral acts because, so the argument goes, there are no value-free judgements that are not culturally or ideologically conditioned. Morality is humanly constructed and local. Ethicists should learn to acknowledge and cultivate difference. There are some, of course, who reintroduce reason, discourse and communicative action, and are less despairing of the relationship between reason and morality. Reason, writes Agnes Heller, 'is the remedy against self-deception'.[16] It encompasses language, argumentation, knowledge, truth, and is 'certitude incarnate'.[17] As a defender of the modern project, she rejects what postmodernists accept and contrasts the laissez-faire of pragmatism-based everyday thinking with the republic of reason in which each person has an equal share. While the degree of continuity and/or discontinuity between the so-called modern and postmodern eras is debatable, and the kinds of reason enacted in both are various, she is one who rejects the 'end of reason' slogan and seeks to reintroduce its powers. Jürgen Habermas is another who has faith in reason, as he struggles to hold on to the baby that he thinks postmodernists, like Zygmunt Bauman and Richard Rorty, pour out with the bath

---

14. Jean Baudrillard, 'After the Orgy' in *The Transparency of Evil* (London and New York: Verso, 1993), p. 7.
15. The postmodern condition has been described by Gillian Rose as 'despairing rationalism without reason'. Rose, *Mourning*, p. 7.
16. Agnes Heller, *A Philosophy of History in Fragments* (Oxford: Blackwell, 1993), p. 93.
17. Heller, *A Philosophy of History*, p. 95.

water. His reintroduction of reason is in discursive form, the central tenet being that moral-practical questions can be decided in a rational manner. Discourse ethics are, he thinks, about the employment of practical reason in such a way that good judgements can be made about pragmatic, ethical and moral matters.[18] Universalisation functions as a rule of argumentation through which moral norms are established and conflicts settled.

What are we to make of all this? To paraphrase the title of Alasdair MacIntyre's now famous book, the authority of reason is far from clear because we must ask: Whose sources of authority? Which method of justification? If Baudrillard and Bauman are correct, then the philosophy of the modern era culminates in self-deception and suicides at the threshold of universal truth. If we commend Jürgen Habermas's theory of discourse ethics, then we tend towards the location of morality in the procedures of argumentation, which, while having enormous benefits that warrant serious investigation, is no guarantee of protection against ideological distortion, or the hidden domination of some discourse participants over others. Procedures themselves do not contain wisdom. Yet the perceived breakdown of rationality, or, at least, the gap between its legitimate and illegitimate authority, renders problematic any ethical endeavour based upon metaphysics. Ethics and metaphysics are, according to Gillian Rose's diagnosis, two halves of an integral freedom that don't add up.[19] Ethics and moral discourse have been severed from their philosophical and theological roots. This is evident in many standard ethical textbooks which conclude that no single theory will explain the nature

---

18. According to Habermas, the pragmatic refers to assessments as to 'What ought I (we), to do?' taken on the basis of empirical data. The moral judgement involved refers to assessments as to 'What ought I (we), to do?' taken in the knowledge that others will be affected by my decision, and that my action should be just. See Jürgen Habermas, *Justification and Application: Remarks on Discourse Ethics* (Cambridge: Polity Press, 1993), ch. 1.

19. Rose, *Mourning*, p. 9.

of moral thinking because none can do justice to the complexities of everyday life. They present the strengths and weaknesses of major ethical arguments: usually intuitionism, utilitarianism, deontology, natural law, etc., and often decide that no related moral theory is adequate to the task.[20] Calculations about utility often exclude the value of social solidarity, thus leaving the interests of the minority at risk in the hands of the majority. Deontological theorists are forced to admit that moral principles frequently conflict, with the result that principles are treated as little more than empty words thrown up on the beach of pragmatism.[21] There is no way of resolving conflicts between different ethical systems because there are no shared grounds upon which further argument could be based. When the question 'Is this good?' does not yield a direct answer, moral choices become arbitrary affirmations of one's own values and cultural experiences.

The season of disenchantment that results from even this sketch of our contemporary ethico-philosophical context can erode our energy for criticism and innovation. One senses an impending long period of reaction and inaction because, as George Steiner contends, 'there is no adequate answer to the question of the frailty of culture'.[22] Yet if we are not to give up on the task of

---

20. See, for example, Mel Thompson, *Teach Yourself Ethics* (London: Hodder Headline, 1994), pp. 212ff.

21. In medical ethics, for example, the Beauchamp and Childress mantra, 'autonomy, beneficence, non-maleficence and justice', has served well as an instrument of thought in so far as it helps in the articulation of common, basic prima facie moral commitments and concerns. It fails, however, to provide ways to explore the historical, cultural, personal and social factors that influence the choice, formation or interpretation of such principles. It provides a framework within which to share moral thoughts, but contains little that a theologian or philosopher might recognise as argument. See R. Gillon, *Philosophical Medical Ethics* (Chichester: Wiley, 1986), and T. L. Beauchamp and J. F. Childress, *Principles of Biomedical Ethics* (Oxford: OUP, 1994).

22. George Steiner, *In Bluebeard's Castle* (London and Boston: Faber & Faber, 1971), esp. p. 69, although the whole of his essay 'In a Post-culture' is relevant.

Christian ethics and moral reason, then we must 'stay in the fray' and seek the wisdom we need for the problems of the day.[23] For a Christian moral theologian, this means approaching such problems from the perspective of the Christian gospel, that is, from a perspective which assumes that if Christians have anything worth contributing to contemporary ethical and moral debate then it will stem in some way from Jesus Christ's revelation to us of the truth of humanity in relationship to God. As Oliver O'Donovan observes: 'Christian ethics must arise from the gospel of Jesus Christ. Otherwise it could not be *Christian* ethics.'[24] The work of Christian ethics and moral theology has to do with discernment of the truth of the gospel itself.[25] It is about both the 'what' and the 'so what' of God's revelation in human form and the calling of the church today.

The task is not easy in the present cultural context where many claim that traditional Christian beliefs have disintegrated into absurdity. Academic discussion about detraditionalisation accords with anecdotal evidence about the improbability that a young person leaving school will know the Lord's prayer or be able to rehearse the parable of the Good Samaritan. '[T]he signs of the times' are read by Grace Davie when she observes that religion is now more often about believing than belonging.[26] Privatised forms of religion appear to be more popular than the mainstream de-

---

23. Gillian Rose, *Love's Work* (London: Chatto & Windus, 1995), p. 125. Rose finishes this book with the lovely words: 'I will stay in the fray, in the revel of ideas and risk; learning, failing, wooing, grieving, trusting, working, reposing – in this sin of language and lips.'

24. Oliver O'Donovan, *Resurrection and Moral Order* (Leicester and Grand Rapids, MI: Inter-Varsity Press and Eerdmans, 1986), p. 11.

25. This was also argued by Enda McDonagh in 'The Natural Law and the Law of Christ' in Gordan R. Dunstan (ed.), *Duty and Discernment* (London: SCM, 1975), ch. 5.

26. Grace Davie, *Religion in Britain since 1945: Believing without Belonging* (Oxford and Cambridge, MA: Blackwell, 1994).

nominations.[27] The market place for spirituality is de-monopolised and, while the churches and denominations have far from disappeared, their social distribution has become narrower.[28] Institutional religion appears to be in decline and traditional authorities are no longer recognised. Social anthropologists tell us that the influence of Christianity in societal life is waning. Historians shame us with accounts of how twentieth-century church life in western Europe has been tainted by hypocrisy and complicity with secular powers in their quests for domination. Psychologists recount numerous reasons why Christianity is something to be scared of because of the self-loathing and abjection that it can evoke in persons who confuse the practice of religion with sacred horror.[29] So, why bother with Christian ethics and moral theology? Would it not be better to concede that there is nothing especially moral about Christianity, or especially Christian about morality, and to concentrate one's efforts on 'spirituality for the individual'? Given the appalling record of the church as regards moral hypocrisy, and the fact that the church has more often been like the figure of 'the Grand Inquisitor' than 'the Good Samaritan', would it not be shrewder to omit the church from our considerations?[30]

Seeking the Wisdom We Need

Martha Nussbaum writes in her book *Love's Knowledge* of the need to confront each new thing and situation resourcefully. She is interested in how, in the dialogue between philosophy and

---

27. See Paul Heelas et al., *Religion, Modernity and Postmodernity* (Oxford: Blackwell, 1998).
28. This is argued by Thomas Luckman, 'The Privatization of Religion and Morality' in Heelas et al., *Detraditionalization*, ch. 5.
29. Julia Kristeva, *Powers of Horror* (New York: Columbia University Press, 1984), p. 210.
30. This is Helen Oppenheimer's pertinent question in *The Character of Christian Morality* (London: The Faith Press, 1965), p. 19.

literature, certain texts and ideas are considered as serious candidates for truth.[31] 'What parts of oneself, what method, what writing should one choose then? What is, in short, love's knowledge – and what writing does it dictate in the heart?'[32] The Christian theologian (i.e., the person who prays to, thinks and talks about, and worships God) who seeks the necessary wisdom for Christian living in the present day faces similar questions. Theology, in its many varieties and tangled relations to love's knowledge of God, expresses different senses of what matters and different ways of caring about what happens in the future. In this book, I consider aspects of the relationship between Christian theology and ethics that will inform our debate if Christian people are to keep open to, and ready for, the new things of the gospel.

This task is not as easy as might be expected because, as Jürgen Moltmann notes, many of the familiar patterns of Christian ethics have almost ceased to rest on any christological or trinitarian foundations:

> The ethics of natural law, the secular ethics of the Lutheran doctrine of the two kingdoms, the ethics of 'orders' – whether it be the orders of creation, the orders of preservation, or the orders based on the covenant with Noah – are all conceived without a specific basis in any Christology.[33]

When the christological, soteriological and eschatological dimensions of Christian ethics are neglected, a gap opens up between Christian tradition and contemporary culture, and the church loses its power to illuminate the issues of the day. Thus, the Christian ethicist needs to keep asking Bonhoeffer's question: Who is Jesus Christ for us today? How do we keep before us the 'moral image of Christ' as a check for our actions? In other words, what

---

31. Martha Nussbaum, *Love's Knowledge* (Oxford: OUP, 1990), pp. 3–10.
32. Nussbaum, *Love's Knowledge*, p. 4.
33. Jürgen Moltmann, *The Way of Jesus Christ: Christology in Messianic Dimensions* (London: SCM, 1990), p. 117.

is it about the incarnation of the Word of God that allows us to generate an ethics and moral theory in which Jesus Christ is the touchstone for conduct and a check for our consciences? How does God's revelation in human form affect our understanding of what is, and is not, authoritative when moral decisions have to be made? What it is about the incarnation of the Word of God that is normative for the Christian community, and that gives freedom and the power to act in accordance with divine will? Why does God's revelation in human form affect our perception of the aim and means of human life? What shapes Christian morality in interaction with the Christian hope of union (*henosis*) with God and deification (*theosis*)? These questions are important because, while Christian moral theologians are not obliged to sort out the mess that is the contemporary ethical and moral scene, we are responsible within given historical contexts for rethinking and distinguishing the main elements of Christian moral theology, and for addressing the problem of authority on distinctively theological grounds.

The Genesis of Ethics

With this in mind, the argument of this book can be summarised as follows. The genesis of Christian ethics is found in the authority of God. For many, the authority of God is the problem of Christian ethics, not its answer. Indeed, it may yet prove to be that, if authority is associated in Christian theory and polity with authoritarianism, patriarchy and legalism. This book argues, however, that God's authority can be equated with divine grace, and it is here that we find the generative principles of Christian ethics. Christian ethics finds its genesis in the authority of God because God is the author of all creation (Latin *auctor*, meaning originator or author, and *augere*, meaning to increase). The existence of all creation is inseparably bound to the free, creative will of God. We have life because God gave it to us – the character and quality of this life being determined by the structural conditions which God built into creation, the effects of sin, and divine providence. A central task of Christian ethics is to locate questions of truth and moral freedom within this relationship of creator to created. Only in this way can we consider the relationship between ethics and the truth of human existence. Using Mikhail Bakhtin's idea of authoring, I argue in Chapter 1 that the genesis of ethics is found in the authority of God because God enables human life and delights in its creation.[34]

However, Christian ethics cannot be constructed from talk about God (the Father) alone. It is ultimately soteriological and, therefore, has to be discussed with reference to the economy of the Trinity, the work of the incarnate Word of God and the Spirit of God in history. Christian ethics is soteriological because it is the response in freedom of human persons to the divine work of salvation. Christian ethics is eschatological because salvation leads to perfection and eternal life in communion and relationship with God. The task of Christian ethics concerns the human adventure of freedom in movement towards this goal. Not confined to the categories of law, punishment, or even the promise of eternal life, the task of Christian ethics includes wider questions about what can be known of God in Jesus Christ and the human vocation to union with God through life in Christ. It follows that the authority of God's Word is supreme in Christian ethics. However – and of central importance to this book – this authority is not of a controlling or hegemonic kind but of the dialogic, answerable kind, which draws human persons into relationship. Even after the fall, God acted out of love for humanity in sending his Son for the salvation of the world (Jhn 3:16). By assuming our human nature, the incarnate Word, a divine person, became what we are so that we might be deified. Christian ethics concerns the dynamic

---

34. Mikhail Bakhtin (1895–1975) is a Russian scholar whose contribution to literary and critical theory in the West is considerable. This book allows the provocation entailed in his writing to draw out the significance of 'authoring' and 'kenosis' in a Christian understanding of authority.

of human response in personal freedom to that communication of divine love. By employing Mikhail Bakhtin's ideas, in so far as they are influenced by Orthodox Christianity, I explore in Chapter 2 how God's Word is answerable in ways that involve a paradigmatic openness to the other, sensitivity to their anticipated and actual response, self-giving and change. Of central and ontological importance is that God's work of salvation is established in human nature at the incarnation of the Word; the incarnate Word is God's call to all persons to 'perfect union with God'.[35] The incarnation is a communication-event in which the truth of humanity is revealed and affirmed. Through the operation of the Holy Spirit, the Word of God becomes incarnate as the quintessential utterance of love, revealing humanity's full potential for life and destiny as given in Christ. This communication-event is not one-way. God's Word is born into dialogue in the sense that it anticipates an answer. God's Word calls us to life, and the way we answer with our lives is the stuff of Christian ethics and moral theology.

In Chapter 3 we think about how this answering is enabled by the Holy Spirit's moment-by-moment application of salvation and deification to our persons. God's authority does not destroy personal, moral freedom but enables and fulfils it. As persons created 'in the image of God' who is Trinity, human beings are relational beings, whose true mode of existence is freedom and love (1 Cor. 14:1). Christian ethics – or the Christian ethos – is characterised by moral freedom in the Spirit. The Holy Spirit floods the hearts of all believers with the love of God (Rom. 5:5), makes the body of every believer a temple of the Holy Spirit (1 Cor. 6:19), and blesses each person with gifts for some useful purpose (1 Cor. 12:7). However, we must reckon with the reality of sin. One of the effects of the fall was to fragment human existence in such a way that authentic personal existence was reduced to autonomous individualism. This means that a clear conceptual distinction is needed

---

35. See Vladimir Lossky, *The Mystical Theology of the Eastern Church* (London: James Clarke, 1957), p. 98.

between the freedom of individuals who seek autonomy and self-gratification, and the freedom of persons who seek fulfilment of their God-given potential in Christ in communion with God and others. Arguably, the majority of secular ethics is concerned more with the autonomy of the individual than with attaining to full personhood or the quality of communion between persons. Moral freedom is often equated with social utility, the right to choose, or the universalisable validity of the freedom of the 'I'. By contrast, Christian ethics distinguishes clearly between the concept of the individual and that of the person. As Adam and Eve became subject to a variety of natural instincts and impulses which limited their existence (Gen. 3:16–21), so the individual is defined by a quest for autonomy which results in various biological, social and cultural constraints and by the need for self-preservation. Drawing again on biblical and traditional resources, I maintain that Christian ethics asserts the differences between the moral freedom of the individual and that of true personhood restored in baptism and nurtured by the Holy Spirit. The work of Mikhail Bakhtin provides expression for these truths in terms of the 'polyphony' of many voices enjoying full and authentic personal existence. I use his notion of 'polyphony' to describe a way of talking about self-expression though utterance and testimony, answerability to God and to one another. It is very different from 'heteroglossia', understood as the conflicting voices of individuals subject to the necessities associated with mortality.

All this raises questions, however, about the teaching authority of the church. When does moral freedom in Christ fall into moral licence? Is there a tension between freedom in Christ bestowed in baptism and the role of the church as moral guide and teacher? How is the church to exercise authority in ways that promote the growth of personal freedom in Christ while preventing its teaching authority from becoming authoritarian? How is the exercise of authority in the church to mirror the authority of God without confusing confidence in the Spirit and monologistic control? Working with an understanding of the church as body of Christ,

I maintain that persons are restored to the freedom of personhood in the image of God within the church because it is here that they are grafted into Christ. However, the challenge for the church is not to undermine its vocation by imposing codes of human behaviour enforced by impersonal mechanisms of power. This challenge is considered in Chapter 4 with reference to frequently used – but often problematic – symbols of the teaching authority of the church, notably 'deposit of faith', 'guardianship', and 'handing on'. I argue that the teaching authority of the church with respect to ethics cannot – or, at least, should not – be made to fit any secular category, but that its apostolic character should be preserved because the church is sent by Jesus Christ with the good news of God's love for the life of the world and its salvation. There is need for caution, however, because this message of good news is not an object-like treasure or quasi-financial deposit but the person of Jesus Christ who calls us to recognise sin and allow God to restore in us the freedom of personhood. Consequently, there is no room in the church's ethic for abstract theoretical principles or legalistic axioms, though there is need for properly derived theological principles and normative standards.

Finally, the book considers dimensions of the church's ethic that follow more immediately from contemplation of the life and ministry of Jesus Christ. According to Eusebius of Caesarea and successive traditions of the church, there were three dimensions to the mission of Jesus Christ: prophetic, priestly and royal.[36] Chapter 5 is structured according to these dimensions of Jesus Christ's ministry and suggests that they are also the dimensions of the church's life and ethos. As a prophet, Jesus Christ taught humankind the truth of God, being himself the truth of God incarnate. As a priest, he offered himself 'for the life of the world', redeeming us from the curse of death through his sacrifice on the cross. As 'king', Jesus Christ came to announce and to establish

---

36. Eusebius of Caesarea, *Church History*, Bk X, 'Panegyric on the Splendor of Affairs', ch. 4 in *NPNF* Second Series, Vol. 1, pp. 370–378.

the reign of God and to win victory over the powers of evil. He
ascended into heaven, to share the glory of God, until his coming
again. There is much about this threefold construal of Christ's
ministry – especially as continued by the church – that is problematic, not least its male-dominated language. As a theologian with
gospel-inspired feminist principles, I am aware of reasons to be
cautious of a too-easy reclamation of traditional resources and of
problematic links between knowledge and power. Feminists are
well aware that Christian tradition has not been socially neutral
but has functioned to legitimise dominant power relationships,
reconstructing supposedly authentic pasts in the present.[37] At the
very least, we must suspect that narrative histories are influenced
by dominant power groups, and that these groups construe the
factual and symbolic content of corporate memory to legitimise
their control of the balance of power. This said, I argue that careful
reconsideration of the priestly, royal and prophetic dimensions of
the church's ethos is of contemporary benefit in Christian ethics.
Paul begged the saints at Ephesus to lead a life worthy of their
calling 'for we are what he has made us' (paraphrasing Eph.
2:8–10). Everything about their ethic (*ethos*) possessed semiotic
value and was productive of meaning about life in Christ. Thus
we consider how the church is called to participate in the priestly,
royal and prophetic ministries of Christ, and the nature of the
relationship between the ministry of Christ and the ethical life of
the church.

Of course, Christian ethics deals not only with origins but also
with eschatology, and the word 'genesis' should not detract from

---

37. Elizabeth A. Johnson's feminist theological reading of the communion of
saints is just one illustration of the point. For many centuries, she argues, 'the
communion of saints has been structured according to the social system of
patronage, taken from earth and writ large in heaven'. God has been imagined
as a monarch ruling in splendour, surrounded by hosts of courtiers who are
ranked in descending order of importance. Elizabeth A. Johnson, *Friends of God
and Prophets: A Feminist Theological Reading of the Communion of Saints*
(London: SCM, 1998), p. 2.

Christian confession that the true nature of things belongs to their future within divine providence. Christian ethics, like all aspects of Christian theology, is properly characterised by the eschatological hope of union with God in the age to come. The resurrection is God's pledge to us of the final victory of life over death and good over evil, and, because of this, Christian ethics is rooted as much in the future as it is in the past. Christian ethics is directed and shaped by this hope. Its goal is *theosis*, or achieving our potential in Christ, and its task concerns imitative incarnations in daily life of what we know in Jesus Christ of divine love.[38] For this reason, I define 'ethics' with reference to the aim of the Christian life, construed in terms of Jesus' injunction as recorded in Matthew's gospel: 'Be perfect, therefore, as your heavenly Father is perfect' (Matt. 5:48).[39] I use the term 'morality' for the articulation of this aim in norms within specific historical contexts.[40] Morality (cf. L. *moralis*, from *mor-*, *mos* custom) is the personal response in freedom to existence as given by God; our existential answer to God's invitation to personal communion with Godself.

---

38. See Anthony M. Coniaris, *Achieving Your Potential in Christ: Theosis* (Minneapolis: Light and Life Publishing Co., 1993).

39. These definitions are similar to those of Paul Ricoeur, *Oneself as Another* (Chicago: UCP, 1992), p. 170.

40. Following Paul Ricoeur, I assume that ethics has primacy over morality in the sense that the norm is that through which the aim is actualised. The ethical aim is, so to speak, required to pass through the sieve of the norm, in processes of testing and application (pp. 170–171.) The definition of the terms 'Christian ethics' and 'moral theology' is notoriously tricky. In general terms, the discipline of ethics tends to be more descriptive than that of morality because it discerns the principles and values that determine moral decisions. In Christian ethics, however, there are such close links between the relating of theological principles and the ends that direct the moral life that the two are closely interrelated.

Chapter One

The Authority
of God:
God as Author

Divine Authority and Christian Ethics

This chapter offers a way of thinking about divine authority as a starting point for Christian ethical reflection. It argues that 'the genesis of ethics' can, and should, be traced to the authority of God because God is the author of the heavens and the earth (Gen. 1:1) and of our salvation (Jon. 2:9; Lk. 1:69; Heb. 5:9). Thus understood, the authority of God has nothing to do with the authoritarianism, patriarchy and legalism with which it is often associated. Rather, it concerns the personal being and free creative decision of God to bring new life into being. This chapter considers biblical witness to God/the author, especially God's aesthetic reaction to creation and conferring of blessing upon it. It explores how God's authoring-authority both sets limits to the kind of existence enjoyed by humanity and gives a value-and-meaning structure to creation/the work as a whole.[1] There will always be problems with finding reverent and useful ways for humans to speak about the authority of God, because God transcends all human reality and is without limit. This said, the argument is that all creation has its origin in God and that, because of this, creation has worth, human beings can find meaning and truth in relationship with God, and moral norms can reflect the structure of the good as revealed in the persons of the Trinity. The working

---

1. M. M. Bakhtin, *Art and Answerability* (Austin, TX: University of Texas Press, 1990), p. 194.

assumption is that Christian ethics is a derivative discipline which is 'dependent for its first principles on the truths of doctrine'.[2] Christian confession of God the source or *Arche* of all life and good determines Christian ethics as life-affirming, characterised by delight, and providing a basis from which to speak about universal moral standards.

Defining authority

The word authority has several etymological roots. Edward Said provides helpful information about this in *Beginnings: Intention and Method*:

> *Authority* suggests to me a constellation of linked meanings: not only, as the OED tells us, 'a power to enforce obedience', or 'a derived or delegated power', or 'a power to influence action', or 'a power to inspire belief', or 'a person whose opinion is accepted'; not only those, but a connection as well with *author* – that is, a person who originates or gives existence to something, a begetter, beginner, father or ancestor, a person also who sets forth written statements. There is still another cluster of meanings: *author* is tied to the past participle of *auctus* of the verb *augere*; therefore *auctor*, according to Eric Partridge, is literally an increaser and thus a founder. *Auctoritas* is production, invention, cause, in addition to meaning a right of possession. Finally, it means continuance, or a causing to continue. Taken together these meanings are all grounded in the following notions: (1) that of the power of an individual to initiate, institute, establish – in short, to begin; (2) that this power and its product are an increase over what had been there previously; (3) that the individual wielding this power controls its issue and what is derived

2. Stanley S. Harakas, 'Human Rights: An Eastern Orthodox Perspective', *Journal of Ecumenical Studies*, Vol. 19, No. 3 (1982), p. 23.

therefrom; (4) that authority maintains the continuity of its course.[3]

This etymological information reminds us that, while the word authority is today readily associated with the power to enforce obedience, to influence action or belief, it has additional associations with 'authoring' and 'increasing', 'initiating' and 'establishing'. Thus, even before looking at biblical associations of divine authority with creating (Hebrew *bara*), speaking (Hebrew *'amr*) and forming (Hebrew *ysr*), self-emptying (Greek *kenosis*), and creative decision (Greek *exousia*), we are reminded that the English word 'authority' can be variously defined and interpreted. In ordinary parlance, and not only in Christian theology, the understanding and practice of authority is not necessarily about the enforcement of absolutes or control. Too often, however, this etymological information does not spring readily to mind and we think more immediately of authority as the exercise of legal power or right, of power – possibly derived from a particular office or status – exercised over someone or something. Jesus promised his disciples nothing of what the world typically regards as authority, i.e., authority as supremacy (Mk 10:35–45), only the ability to live without honour, prestige and security. There is a qualitative difference between his exercise of authority and those who 'lord it over' others. His authority was not about the power or right to enforce obedience but something closer to the Greek *exousia*, which implies strength, or the liberty or power to act, the freedom to exercise an inward force or faculty expressed by *dunamis*.[4]

---

3. Edward Said, *Beginnings: Intention and Method* (New York: Basic Books, 1975), p. 83.

4. G. Abbott-Smith, *A Manual Lexicon of the New Testament* (Edinburgh: T. & T. Clark, 1981), distinguishes between authority as the liberty or power to act (1 Cor. 9:12; 2 Thess. 3:9; Jn 10:18; 1 Cor. 9:4, 5; Rom. 9:20; Rev. 22:14) and authority as the power of right (Matt. 21:23; Mk 11:28; Lk. 20:2), e.g. Messianic authority (Matt. 9:6; Mk 2:10); apostolic authority (2 Cor. 10:8); or the authority of government (Matt. 8:9, 28:18). We are concerned primarily with the former, ▷

Reasons for Speaking about God's Authority

Before proceeding, however, let's ask ourselves why we want to consider this topic. What is our motivation? Early church fathers warned their readers frequently against idle speculation that pondered what God is and how God is, reminding them of the limits of human nature, and the fact that they could know nothing of the divine nature except that which is revealed: 'who aspires to know the unknown will not always arrive at truth, but may also conceive of falsehood itself as truth'.[5] There are things about the nature of God that we cannot know, so there is no point commencing our study in the hope that, at its completion, we shall be able to say to ourselves: 'Got it!' We shall never have the authority of God within the compass of our understanding, so it is unlikely that our study will be a neat one with a series of answers to an orderly set of questions. If the motivation for our study is the security of knowledge, or mental tidiness, then we are likely to be disappointed. Early church fathers also remind us that any discussion of authority can quickly become a cover for the furtherance of personal or partisan interests. Envy, writes Gregory of Nyssa, is the result of closing one's eyes to the good, and is a road which leads to many evils.[6] Be mindful, he urges, of the distinction between the carnal and spiritual disposition of the soul.[7] Authority is a subject amenable to the passion of envy, and can easily be dragged away from all that is good in the direction of vice, not virtue. Theologians are not exempt from the temptations of envy and pride, even when busying themselves with

---

although consideration will be given to points of tension in the practice of church life between the two definitions.

5. Gregory of Nyssa, *Answer to Eunomius*, Bk II, *NPNF* Second Series, Vol. V, p. 260.

6. Gregory of Nyssa, *The Great Catechism*, *NPNF* Second Series, Vol. V, pp. 480–481. According to Gregory, the devil first fell away from God's goodness in a passion of envy.

7. Gregory of Nyssa cites 1 Cor. 2:15.

speaking about God. Gregory of Nyssa's word of caution is still apposite: 'For the object to be aimed at, in questions respecting God, is not to produce a dulcet and melodious harmony of words, but to work out an orthodox formula of thought whereby a worthy conception of God may be ensured.'[8]

If our motivation is to work out a worthy conception of God within the limits of Christian orthodoxy, then we must give some consideration to what Christian orthodoxy is. For the early church, orthodoxy was rarely, if ever, understood as merely 'right faith' or 'right thinking', but was closely linked to right living and the kind of adoration of God which took over all one's faculties.[9] Orthodoxy was never confined to intellectual activity but was about how the whole of human living was informed by knowledge and the grace of God. It did, however, involve consideration of the conditions under which Christians may discuss the authority of God. Christian theology is far from uniform but certain doctrinal views give it distinctive shape and are of lasting and central importance to the theological task. Again, Gregory of Nyssa helps us by offering a concise statement of Christian orthodoxy as it concerns the authority of God:

> Now the main point of Christian orthodoxy (*eusebias*) is to believe that the Only-begotten God, Who is the truth and the true light, and the power of God and the life, is truly all that He is said to be ... that He is God and the truth, that is to say, God in truth, ever being what He is conceived to be and what He is called, Who never at any time was not, nor ever will cease to be, Whose being, such as it is essentially,

---

8. Gregory of Nyssa, *Answer to Eunomius*, Bk II, *NPNF* Second Series, Vol. V, p. 263.

9. William Moore and Henry Austin Wilson write in a footnote to Gregory of Nyssa's observation: 'Piety is a devout life joined with *a right faith* (Œcumenius on 1 Tim. IV). Piety is the looking up to the one only God, Who is believed to be and is the *true* God, and the life in accordance with this ... the *science* of adoration.'

is beyond the reach of the curiosity that would try to comprehend it.[10]

Such knowledge of God – i.e., that God was never brought into existence, produced or evolved, and is rightly called the maker and creator of the whole universe – is given through the gift of faith. It does not comprise mere precepts which are understood intellectually, but involves the whole person caught up in the worship of God. Orthodoxy is more than right thinking; it is also right faith and right living.

Gregory of Nyssa's summary of Christian orthodoxy implies that, in some important respects, Christian theology cannot have too high and exalted an understanding of the authority of God. God is 'the Maker of all things visible and invisible' (Job 38–41; Ps. 100:3; Is. 45:11–12), who has the power to judge the earth (Ps. 93; Ps. 98:9; Lk. 12:5; Rev. 14:19–20) and to do as willed with creation (Rom. 9:21). Despite its unpopular tenor, traditional Christian confession is of an autonomous creator who transcends history and all human ideology, and whose power is, and will be, displayed in every sphere of creation (Rev. 7). God is the first cause of all things who cannot properly be spoken of in any category familiar to humans, e.g., genus, species, individuality or number.[11] God is without beginning or end and is worthy of such praise as humans are capable of giving.[12] As creatures of God, humans are radically different to God. Despite some contemporary trends in theology, they are not co-creators or co-redeemers unless it be clear that they cannot create or redeem in any way comparable to that of God:

---

10. Gregory of Nyssa, *Answer to Eunomius*, Bk II, *NPNF* Second Series, Vol. V, p. 251.

11. Clement of Alexandria, *The Stromata or Miscellanies*, Bk V, ch. XII, *ANF*, Vol. II, pp. 463–464.

12. Augustine, *On the Psalms* in *NPNF* First Series, Vol. VIII, pp. 624–625 (Ps. 35:3).

For God creates, and to create is also ascribed to men [*sic*] . . .
Yet does God create as men do? . . . Perish the thought; we
understand the terms in one sense of God, and in another
of men. For God creates, in that He calls what is not into
being, needing nothing thereunto; but men work with
existing material . . . God is self-existent, enclosing all things,
and enclosed by none; within all according to His own goodness and power, yet without all in His proper nature.[13]

As Athanasius is at pains to emphasise, the difference between
Creator and created is not to be misrepresented by the creature
with ideas that make humanity the pattern for thinking about
God. Such ideas are laughable and will always be disrupted by the
clear-sightedness of biblical witness and Christian confession.

Nor is it only early church fathers who guide us in these matters.
Shall we, asks Calvin, 'distinguish between right and wrong by
that judgement which has been imparted to us, and neglect to
acknowledge that there is a judge in heaven? Shall we think ourselves the inventors of so many arts and useful things that God
may be defrauded of his praise . . .?'[14] God is author without
origin, whose intention in creating can alone give meaning to
existence. For Calvin, if God governs all creation it is preposterous
to enjoy the gifts of creation without acknowledging the creator.
If God is the creator of all that is, and if humans have the
natural capacity to acknowledge this, then they ought at least to
contemplate God in the works of creation and acknowledge his
governance.[15] He warns against any suppression of God's name

---

13. Athanasius, *De Decritu or Defence of the Nicene Definition*, ch. III §11, *NPNF*
Second Series, Vol. IV, p. 157.
14. John Calvin, *Institutes of the Christian Religion* (Philadelphia: Westminster
Press, 1960), Bk I, ch. V, §5.
15. 'Let us therefore remember, whenever each of us contemplates his own nature,
that there is one God who so governs all natures that he would have us look
unto him, direct our faith to him, and worship and call upon him.' Calvin,
Institutes, Bk I, ch. V, §6.

and talks about God's authority in the language of governance, lordship, rule, majesty and command, etc. Yet for Calvin – one of the most zealous maintainers of the God's sovereign authority – God is the author who ceaselessly calls into question all human authority.[16] Christian orthodoxy requires that we make this kind of confession of the authority of God a starting point, and that we hold fast to other ecumenically agreed teaching about the mysteries of salvation and divine grace.

---

16. It is worth noting that, for Calvin, nothing lay outside the scope of God's providential grace, including the proper function of authority in society, the reason being that God's sovereignty extended over all creation. Thus he commended the authority of magistrates, believing them to have been appointed by God and, therefore, to be held in honour (Rom. 13:1 *Institutes*, Bk IV, ch. X, §5). God rules by the authority of his Word but states need to be governed; the laws of a nation can be used piously before God as they are rightly administered (*Institutes*, Bk IV, ch. XX, §4). There are differences between the exercise of authority in civil and ecclesial communities so that they should not be confused or mingled. The reign of God cannot be understood in terms of any earthly governance because it does not consist in earthly forms of jurisdiction. Yet the different kinds of authority are not antithetical. According to Calvin, good human government 'affords a certain forecast' of the blessings yet to come (*Institutes*, Bk IV, ch. XX, §2). Magistrates 'have a mandate from God, have been invested with divine authority, and are wholly God's representatives' (Bk IV, ch. XX, §4). The authority of a magistrate, however, should never lead one away from recognition of the authority of God. A similar point can be made with reference to Augustine who, using arguments about the human rational soul, links talk of authority with the benefits of ordered harmony. In *City of God*, Bk XIX, ch. 17 he writes: 'the earthly city, whose life is not based on faith, seeks earthly peace and in doing so establishes a fixed harmony of its citizens in authority and obedience so as to provide a kind of orderly alignment of human wills in things pertaining to this mortal life' (*NPNF* First Series, Vol. II, p. 412). This passage is profoundly problematic in that it advocates the obedience of wives to husbands as the basis of domestic peace and ordered harmony in civil life, and includes slavery within the God-ordained law of nature which preserves human freedom. However, the underlying argument is that the maintenance of earthly peace is to be desired, and that the just and kindly exercise of authority is in accordance with the judgement of God.

Reconsidering God's Authority: 'God as Author'

God's authorship of creation and salvation rarely forms the basis for contemporary discussions of divine authority and Christian ethics. This said, there is established precedent in Christian tradition for speaking about God as author of creation and salvation. Major figures witness eloquently and movingly to the unique nature of God's authorship. God, writes Augustine, is the author of truth and felicity, and it is fitting for Christian people to entrust themselves to this God, by whose power and judgement earthly kingdoms are founded and maintained.[17] As the author of life, God has freed the human race from guilt and death.[18] As the author of beauty, God has created good things (e.g., fire and wind, the swift air, the circle of the stars, and the violent water) for our delight.[19] Yet the etymological links that exist in English between 'authoring' and 'authority' are rarely explored. Nor is it popular these days – for reasons outlined in the Introduction – to link the generative principles in Christian ethics and moral theology to discussions of divine authority. In this chapter, however, I argue that biblical witness to God's authorship of creation and salvation is the necessary ground from which we can speak of divine authority, and that this is, in turn, the 'genesis' of Christian ethics and moral theology. The source or 'genesis' of Christian ethics and moral theology is given in the authority of God to which the bible and Christian tradition give testimony.

Using metaphorical language

This said, we must be clear about the kind of language employed when speaking about 'God as author'. To say that God 'authors', i.e., to use author as a verb, is to say that God causes to be, gives

---

17. See Augustine, *Confessions,* Bk XII, ch. XXV, *NPNF* First Series, Vol. I, and *City of God,* Bk IV, *passim, NPNF* First Series, Vol. II.
18. Augustine, *On the Trinity,* Bk XIII, ch. 18, *NPNF* First Series, Vol. I, p. 180.
19. Augustine, *On the Trinity,* Bk XV, ch. 3, §5, *NPNF* First Series, Vol. I, p. 201.

origin to, gives rise to, gives occasion to, brings to pass, produces or creates. Something comes into existence or happens when God authors it. There is nothing metaphorical about the fact of God's authoring of creation and salvation because when God speaks and acts something happens: 'God said, "Let there be light"; and there was light' (Gen. 1:3); 'the Lord saved Israel that day from the Egyptians' (Exod. 14:30); God 'sent his Son as the Saviour of the world' (1 Jn 4:14). Biblical testimony is to the efficacy of God's Word and the reality of salvation. To refer to 'God as author', however, is to cease speaking about God as the subject of a verb and to make a statement about the God who authors. To move from saying 'God authors' to saying 'God is author' is to derive a noun from a verb and to use that noun as a name for God. To say 'God authors' is to be concerned with the action of God and with the changes that result from this action. To refer to 'God as author' is to speak of God's character and being from what we know of God's actions. Thus, in Acts 3:15, Peter preached to those who killed 'the author of life' (*archegos zoes*; cf. Acts 5:31) because he believed that Christ, the Son of God, had caused the world to come into existence. Similarly, the writer to the Hebrews refers to Christ as 'the author' (*archegos* Heb. 2:10 and 12:2) or pioneer of salvation because Christ had once and for all removed sin by the sacrifice of himself (Heb. 9:26), and leads believers to faith as Moses led God's people out of slavery. The word 'author' is used as a name and can be traced to the actions that gave rise to it.

In no instance is there an exact match between a noun and the subject to which it refers. Every noun characterisation of God has a metaphorical dimension to it because human language can only approximate to the reality of God. The noun may refer to actions performed by a subject but, in the human act of referring to the subject of an action, meanings are transferred that both do and do not refer specifically to that action. As Walter Brueggemann emphasises, we need to take seriously both the 'is' and 'is not' utterance that metaphor allows: 'Metaphors are nouns that function . . . in order to give access to the Subject of verbs, who is endlessly elusive.'[20] Metaphors give rise to variant meanings because their 'is' quality varies according to different users and interpreters; different contexts give rise to different orientations of sense. This is consistent with Paul Ricoeur's explanation of the function of metaphor as creating new meanings within new socio-historical contexts while also acquiring particular sense according to given frameworks of reference.[21] The word 'author' may have conjured up very different social expectations in Stalinist Russia than in the present-day advanced capitalist environment of the USA. The original writer of a manuscript in the second century AD may have had a very different self-understanding to that of many who call themselves authors today. Hence Ricoeur emphasises less the ability of the hearer or reader to create new worlds of meaning than the world of meaning in which the metaphor unfolds: 'The meaning is not something hidden but something disclosed . . . Interpretation thus becomes the apprehension of the proposed worlds which are opened up by the non-ostensive references of the text.'[22] Meaning is not something to be created or uncovered but is revealed; it lies not behind the words but in front of them. Therefore, in theological usage, any sense which emerges from a metaphor for God should be tested and interpreted with reference to other metaphors and biblical ways of speaking because lack of congruence with other biblical witness would be cause for concern. Nevertheless, because metaphors give rise to different meanings in different contexts they tend to resist reification into sense-orientations that are fixed and absolute.

This ability of metaphors to give rise to variant meanings is both a blessing and a curse. Christian feminists have exposed how

---

20. Walter Brueggemann, *Theology of the Old Testament: Testimony, Dispute, Advocacy* (Minneapolis: Fortress Press, 1997), esp. p. 230.

21. See Paul Ricoeur, 'Metaphor and the Central Problem of Hermeneutics' in *Hermeneutics and the Human Sciences*, trans. John B. Thompson (Cambridge: CUP, 1981), ch. 6.

22. Ricoeur, *Hermeneutics*, p. 177.

metaphors of God as King, Warrior and Father (supposing 'Father' to be a metaphor) with associated anthropomorphic language of governance, lordship, rule, majesty and command, etc., have had an alienating effect on many people's Christian devotion, and how cultural stereotypes concerning male authority have perverted confession of divine authority. Thus Elisabeth Schüssler Fiorenza argues that scripture, tradition, theology and Christology must be examined critically to distinguish whether they further oppression or emancipation in the church; they must be 'tested for their ideological-political functions in legitimating or subverting kyri-archal structures and mind-sets of domination'.[23] Rebecca Chopp laments how the sin of patriarchy in the church, and elsewhere, has 'raped' women and defiled their relationship with God.[24] Her work on theological education is aimed at establishing women as subjects of theological education, so that they can name God in the midst of their everyday experience without being drawn into language systems that reflect problematic forms of social hierarchy. Much more could be said on this subject.[25] For the moment, let's note that feminist theologians have done the church great service in challenging Christian people to recognise that they can never take for granted that metaphorical interpretations of the authority of God – especially when taken to justify forms of ecclesial practice – will either reflect the wide range of biblical metaphors used of God, or be congruent with biblical testimony to God as lover of justice, giver of strength and peace, fighter against oppression, etc. Human ability to understand and interpret the authority of

---

23. Elisabeth Schüssler Fiorenza, *Jesus: Miriam's Child, Sophia's Prophet* (London: SCM, 1994), p. 49.

24. Rebecca Chopp, *Saving Work: Feminist Practices of Theological Education* (Louisville, KY: Westminster John Knox Press, 1995), pp. 54–60.

25. For a useful summary of feminist discussion of gender and the churches, see Elaine Graham, *Making the Difference: Gender, Personhood and Theology* (London: Mowbray, 1995), ch. 2. For a feminist discussion of new possibilities for spiritu-ality in the church of today, see Mary Grey, *Beyond the Dark Night: A Way Forward for the Church?* (London: Mowbray, 1997).

God is fallible and – as feminists make us aware – no study, interpretation or exercise of authority is value-free or socially neutral.[26] Whether we like it or not, social standing, employment status, gender, nationality and other personal and corporate experiences affect our perspective on the subject of divine authority and use of metaphorical language. There is no guarantee that human understanding and interpretation of metaphors for divine authority will accord fully with biblical testimony.[27]

Exposing the contextual nature of much traditional language for God is no longer a radical fringe activity. Less prolific, however, have been attempts to find language to express the authority of God for our own age. Christian orthodoxy will, I believe, always centre around confession of God who 'presides over the system and working of the things that are' and who is 'Maker and the Framer of the universe'.[28] This does not prevent us, however, from seeking fresh ways of expressing our faith in God. 'We are fully justified', writes Gregory of Nyssa, 'in allowing the use of . . . fresh applications of words in respect to all things that can be named, and to God himself.'[29] Indeed, Gregory expects believers to

---

26. As G. W. F. Hegel wrote: 'The idea which a man has of God corresponds with that which he has of himself, of his freedom'. G. W. F. Hegel, *Lectures on the Philosophy of Religion*, trans. E. B. Speirs and J. Burdon Sanderson (London: Routledge, 1962), Vol. I, p. 79. Cited by Gillian Rose, *Hegel contra Sociology* (London: Athlone, 1981), p. 92, from which I paraphrase the question above.

27. See David Nicholls, *Deity and Domination* (London: Routledge, 1989), *passim*.

28. Gregory of Nyssa continues the first of these declarations: 'His existence is without cause, while to all else he is the Cause of being . . . He is that which has no generation or beginning, no corruption, no turning backward, no diminution of supremacy . . . He is that in which evil finds no place, and from which no good is absent.' Gregory of Nyssa, *Answer to Eunomius*, Bk II, *NPNF* Second Series, Vol. V, p. 264. Calvin affirms: 'No one will weigh God's providence properly and profitably but him who considers that his business is with his Maker and the Framer of the universe and with becoming humility submits himself to fear and reverence.' Calvin, *Institutes*, Bk I, ch. XVII, §2.

29. Gregory of Nyssa, *Answer to Eunomius*, Bk II, *NPNF* Second Series, Vol. V, p. 265.

experience the operations of God in their lives differently and, therefore, to name God differently. We cannot know anything of the nature of God that is not revealed by God: 'There is no faculty in human nature adequate to the full comprehension of the divine essence.'[30] Human faculties are limited, whereas God, who is 'bounded only by infinity', is ineffable and incomprehensible by reason, and what we do understand is grasped by faith.[31] God is, however, the author of our faculties of investigation. Intelligence is a gift of God and each person may use that ability to speak of God.[32] More than this, each person may, with due reverence, express the divine nature with a variety of names that concur with their experience of God; we cannot conceive what is unknown, but we can use a variety of concepts and terms when expressing divine authority.

In the following 'experiment', I consider God's authority in terms of God's activity of authoring, not least the authoring of creation, and use the metaphor 'God as author'. The experimental part of the exercise lies not in speaking about God as author per se. There are, as we have seen, biblical references to divine 'authoring'. There are also several references to God as author in patristic texts, of which the following are but a few. Irenaeus writes in *Against the Heresies* that God was the former and author of the world, and of the angels.[33] In his *Exhortation to the Heathen*, Clement of Alexandria refers to Christ as the 'Author of all blessings to us', by whom we are sent on our way to eternal life.[34] Origen named the Trinity the 'author of all things', including the

---

30. Gregory of Nyssa, *Answer to Eunomius*, Bk II, *NPNF* Second Series, Vol. V, p. 257.

31. 'For ourselves, "through faith we understand that the worlds were framed by the word of God", as said the Apostle.' Gregory of Nyssa, *Answer to Eunomius*, Bk II, *NPNF* Second Series, Vol. V, p. 258.

32. Gregory of Nyssa, *Answer to Eunomius*, Bk II, *NPNF* Second Series, Vol. V, p. 263.

33. Irenaeus, *Against Heresies*, Bk II, ch. II, §3, *ANF*, Vol. I, p. 361.

34. Clement of Alexandria, *Exhortation to the Heathen*, ch. I, *ANF*, Vol. II, p. 173.

human faculty of free will.[35] He uses the terms 'author', 'creator' and 'maker' synonymously, urging his readers to worship the 'one Author of one effect', i.e., God who holds the whole universe together in harmony.[36] Augustine spoke in *On Christian Doctrine* of God as the author and governor of time.[37] In his *Confessions*, he acknowledges: 'Thou art the Author and Creator of all ages . . . For there was no "then" when time was not.'[38] The experimental part of this exercise lies not in casting divine authority in terms of God as author, but in making trial of ideas about authorship developed in literary theory and by Mikhail Bakhtin in particular. I suggest that exploration of the connections between authoring and authority can provide ways of speaking that are not impossibly immobilised by bad human experiences of human authority as authoritarian and conflictual. Reflection on God's authorship and authoring can lead us to new perceptions of divine authority that are not shaped and constrained by societal standards of 'correctness' (as important as these may be at times), but that inform the task of Christian ethics. The work of Mikhail Bakhtin helps in this process because he breaks out of certain limited concepts of authoring in ways that help us to reinterpret neglected aspects of Christian tradition, paying close attention to constitutive features of the act of authoring as only a literary theorist is able.

In identifying the authoring-authority of God as a foundation for the doing of Christian ethics, I am arguing that Christian ethics is an essentially theological task. God is the absolute or final authority simply because God is God. However, confession of divine authority does not equate to unthinking obedience on the part of human beings. Far from being repressive, disabling, and

---

35. Origen, *De Principiis*, Bk I, ch. VI, II, Bk II, ch. VI, §3, *ANF*, Vol. IV, pp. 242 and 282.

36. Origen, *De Principiis*, Bk III, ch. V, § 1–4, *ANF*, Vol. IV, pp. 340–342; *Against Celsus*, Bk I, ch. 23, *ANF*, Vol. IV, pp. 405–406.

37. Augustine, *On Christian Doctrine*, Bk II, ch. 28, §44, *NPNF*, Vol. II, p. 549.

38. Augustine, *Confessions*, Bk XI, ch. XIII, *NPNF*, Vol. I, p. 167.

incompatible with human well-being, the authority of God/the author is affirming of human freedom, enabling of and conducive to human well-being. In *Godless Morality*, Richard Holloway equates confession of divine authority with 'the type of consciousness that wants to be commanded to perform extreme acts of obedience by an absolute authority whose attractiveness lies in its very refusal to explain itself'.[39] He cites with approval Nietzsche's critique of Christianity as inculcating a slave morality of obedience and 'denial of the life-force'.[40] By contrast, I argue that a proper confession of divine authority does not imply blind compliance to rules and demands operated by the church as mechanisms of control. Confession of divine authority is not intrinsically oppressive. Rather, if God's authority is that of author, then Christian ethics will be biased towards the affirmation of life, its enhancement, transmission, protection and healing, as well as the avoidance of harm. Christian ethics is no set of rules or mindset to be assimilated but is characterised by qualities that become incorporated into Christian ways of living and form patterns of freedom and love. Mikhail Bakhtin helps us to elaborate this in so far as he provokes us into thinking about the quality of relationship that pertains between God/the author and ourselves, and why and how this supports various dimensions of the ethical life.

Drawing on the thought of Mikhail Bakhtin

As a literary theorist and not a theologian, there is a risk that Bakhtin's work may confuse as much as illuminate a theological search for, and statement of, the authorship of God. There are limits to Bakhtin's usefulness, not least that his work centres around the form of the novel and gives relatively little consideration to the role of the reader in the relationship between author and hero. However, as Martha Nussbaum writes with respect to

---

39. Richard Holloway, *Godless Morality: Keeping Religion Out of Ethics* (Edinburgh: Canongate, 1999), p. 7.
40. Holloway, *Godless Morality*, p. 19.

certain elements of human life, so also with respect to certain aspects of human talk about the divine: 'the terms of the novelist's art are alert winged creatures, perceiving where the blunt terms of ordinary speech, or of abstract theoretical discourse, are blind, acute where they are obtuse, winged where they are dull and heavy'.[41] Briefly stated, I suggest that Bakhtin's ideas about authoring can help us to explore connections between divine authority and our being created in the image of God with the capacity for communion with God and for creativity. He is not usually acknowledged to be a Christian theorist, though recent scholarship has demonstrated convincingly that his work is thoroughly informed by Christian principles and meaning.[42] One of a group of thinkers who addressed philosophical, linguistic and literary issues raised by the Russian revolution, Bakhtin pre-dated recent discussion about the reader's response to a text and was more interested in the formal aspects of the authoring process than in the creation of the meaning of a text by the reader. Discussion centres more around the form of the novel than the relationship between author and reader. Our particular interest is with his understanding of authoring as a relationship of trust which is open to the future and in which the author's privilege is not of a controlling and hegemonic kind, but of a different, life-giving and dialogic kind.

Creating not Created

Bakhtin writes most clearly about authoring in an essay entitled 'Author and Hero in Aesthetic Activity' included in *Art and Answerability* and *Problems of Dostoevsky's Poetics*, and we shall

---

41. Martha Nussbaum, *Love's Knowledge* (Oxford: OUP, 1990), p. 5.
42. For a useful introduction to his life and work, see Katerina Clark and Michael Holquist, *Mikhail Bakhtin* (Harvard: HUP, 1986). For Bakhtin's influence by and use of Christian themes and motifs, see Ruth Coates, *Christianity in Bakhtin: God and the Exiled Author* (Cambridge: CUP, 1999).

confine ourselves to these works. In the latter, Bakhtin talks about how the astonishing independence of Dostoevsky's characters is achieved by 'specific artistic means', including the very structure of the novel, all of which are dependent on the creative will of the author.[43] As author, Dostoevsky wills to create a novel of the kind that allows heroes (i.e. main characters) genuine freedom, and does this by building freedom (albeit a relative freedom) into the text. In a summary statement, he writes:

> Thus the freedom of a character is an aspect of the author's design. A character's discourse is created by the author, but created in such a way that it can develop to the full its inner logic and independence as *someone else's discourse*, the word of the *character himself*. As a result it does not fall out of the author's design, but only out of a monologic authorial field of vision. And the destruction of this field of vision is precisely a part of Dostoevsky's design.[44]

Dostoevsky's writings leave the impression that one is not dealing with a single author-artist but with a plurality of independent and valid voices. The authorial point of view is not single, fixed or monologic, but multiple, dynamic and polyphonic, almost creating chaos and lack of direction because many different voices coexist and interact.[45] An author can, he argues, create a genuinely dialogical text in which voices other than that of the author are heard and in which heroes are neither effectively silenced nor is their speech predetermined. This is effected by means of certain generic and compositional features which allow Dostoevsky to win an authorial position from which he writes a genuinely polyphonic novel.

---

43. M. M. Bakhtin, *Problems of Dostoevsky's Poetics*, ed. and trans. Caryl Emerson (Minnesota: UMP, 1984), p. 13.

44. Bakhtin, *Problems of Dostoevsky's Poetics*, p. 65.

45. Bakhtin, *Problems of Dostoevsky's Poetics*, esp. pp. 5–9.

> In Dostoevsky's polyphonic novel we are dealing not with
> ordinary dialogic form, that is, with an unfolding of material
> within the framework of its own monologic understanding
> and against the firm background of a unified world of objects.
> No, here we are dealing with an ultimate dialogicality, that
> is, a dialogicality of the ultimate whole ... By this means a
> new authorial position is won and conquered, one located
> above the monological position.[46]

The heroes' freedom is built into the design and form of the novel,
the novel being about the heroes' ideas and discourse rather than
those of the author. The author yields up their monologic field of
vision, their particular and authoritative way of viewing things, in
favour of allowing the heroes to live independently. Other structural features are also significant, such as representing every
thought as the position of a personality; ideas are never left
abstract but are always embodied.[47] Each 'I' in the novel was
allowed to develop as a subject, or person with an authentic
reality.[48] The logical links in each novel are made within the limits
of individuals' consciousnesses and nothing happens which makes
sense for, or is directed only by the author; decisions and choices
are made within the heroes' fields of vision. The novel is never
given a single field of vision but has as many fields of vision are
there are heroes and ideas.[49] In these ways Dostoevsky's novels
have an ultimate dialogicality and are never tied to a unified
perspective. The author sustains the consistency and wholeness of
the text while providing the structural condition whereby it is
genuinely polyphonic. The author's privilege is not controlling
or hegemonic. A novel can contain disparate and contradictory

---

46. Bakhtin, *Problems of Dostoevsky's Poetics*, p. 18.
47. Bakhtin, *Problems of Dostoevsky's Poetics*, p. 9.
48. Bakhtin, *Problems of Dostoevsky's Poetics*, p. 11.
49. Bakhtin, *Problems of Dostoevsky's Poetics*, p. 16.

utterances; heroes are not only objects of the author's attention but subjects of their own discourse.[50] [51]

The truly creative author, says Bakhtin, experiences the product of their labour *in the product* and not in the experience of their own creating: 'The actual work of creation *is* experienced, but this experiencing neither hears nor sees itself; it sees and hears only the product that is being created or the object to which it is directed.'[52] In this sense, the author is *for* the product; the creative event is influenced more by the product created than by the author's self-reflection on the creative process.[53] This allows

---

50. Bakhtin, *Problems of Dostoevsky's Poetics*, pp. 5–9.

51. This stands in sharp contrast to Roland Barthes's later observation that writing is 'the destruction of every voice, of every point of origin' other than that of the author. (Roland Barthes, 'The Death of the Author' in *Image – Music – Text*, trans. and ed. Stephen Heath (London: Fontana 1977)). Barthes argued that the language of 'author' had died the same death as language of 'God', and that this happened at the time when the language of 'reader' came to birth, famously linking the death of the author with the refusal of divine unilateral determinism: 'We know now that a text is not a line of words releasing a single "theological" meaning (the "message" of the Author-God) but a multi-dimensional space in which a variety of writings, none of them original, blend and clash.' Since Barthes, the pendulum has swung back somewhat. Some now think that the Barthes-inspired 'death of the author' controversy has been given an overly literal interpretation in academic circles, becoming 'a gloriously baroque meditation' on the language-centred nature of a text rather than representing the actual demise of the concept of the author. See Seán Burke, *The Death and Return of the Author* (Edinburgh: EUP, 1998) and *Authorship: From Plato to the Postmodern: A Reader* (Edinburgh: EUP, 1995), esp. pp. x and 69. We cannot pursue this matter here. Suffice it to say that Bakhtin provides few points of entry into this discussion.

52. Bakhtin, *Art and Answerability*, p. 7.

53. Its obvious manifestations lie in how the hero's life unfolds in a variety of ways, including 'many grimaces, random masks, wrong gestures, and unexpected actions', through which the author struggles to achieve a stable image of the hero. The less obvious manifestations often concern the author's struggles with aspects of their own character, which becomes especially evident in biography, and with the problem of type as a form of the author/hero interrelationship. Bakhtin, *Art and Answerability*, p. 6.

Bakhtin to think (albeit indirectly) of the text as graced, and of grace as the basis of the relationship between the author and the hero. The world of the hero is bestowed as a gift, and their existence is a 'beautiful given'. The relationship between author and hero cannot go beyond the bounds of the given; the 'outside-ness' of the author creates the possibility of their relationship. But this is a relationship in which 'grace' is bestowed by the author in order that the hero can live to the full: 'From within itself, a lived life can express itself in the form of an action, a confession-as-penitence, an outcry; absolution and grace descend upon it from the Author.'[54] The transcendence of God/the author is the fundamental condition for the movement of relationship with creation/the hero, though it is not a one-way relationship because it is characterised by mercy and bounds of trust.[55] A life lived from itself, he says, cannot attain to the ultimate. What really matters comes to us from outside as gift. This is true of relationships between persons/heroes, and it is true of relationships between persons and God: 'An ultimate issue out of itself is not *immanent* to a lived life: it descends upon a life-lived-from-within as a gift from the self-activity of another – from a self-activity that *comes to meet* my life from *outside* its bounds.'[56] God/the author cannot be reduced to creation/the product. However, divine condescension is not of the kind which flattens or patronises the recipient. There is no annihilation or humiliation of the other. Rather, 'trust in God is an immanent constitutive moment of pure self-

---

54. Bakhtin, *Art and Answerability*, p. 79.
55. It is worth noting that, for Bakhtin, the relationship between God/the author and creation/the hero is not dialectical, at least in an Hegelian or Marxist sense. It does not have to do with the resolution of contradiction or the overcoming of alienation; it does not proceed by way of negation, and is not speculative. Also, as Morson and Emerson note, it is not contained 'within a single consciousness' or monologic view. Gary Saul Morson and Caryl Emerson, *Mikhail Bakhtin: Creation of a Prosaics* (Stanford, CA: Stanford University Press, 1990), pp. 55–56.
56. Bakhtin, *Art and Answerability*, p. 79.

consciousness and self-expression.'[57] Authority implies a relationship of trust which is open to the future and in which the created, as well as the creator, are responsible for their creativity.

In 'Author and Hero in Aesthetic Activity', Bakhtin is interested in the living relationship between author and hero (i.e., main character/s). He is concerned with what he calls the 'necessary foundation' of this relationship, and with the particulars of it as worked out in diverse novels by many different authors. His work raises the following questions. What kinds of relationship occur between author and hero? How are these relationships structured? How does the author react to the hero, and what do we learn about the author as person?[58] In addressing these questions, it is important to bear in mind that there are differences between how Bakhtin casts the author–hero relationship in 'Author and Hero in Aesthetic Activity' and in *Problems of Dostoevsky's Poetics*. Briefly stated, the former assumes an imbalance of power between author and hero; the dominant motif is of the author as radically 'other' and 'outside' of the text. The latter adopts a more kenotic theology in which the 'otherness' of God/the author is immanent in the text and hidden, as if the author were an equal participant in dialogue with self-realising heroes. Coates argues that, at least in Bakhtin's opinion, this difference represents progress in his work from a less adequate to a more adequate understanding. It is certainly true that the author–hero relationship receives different

---

57. Bakhtin, *Art and Answerability*, p. 144.
58. In approaching Bakhtin's answers to these questions, I share Ruth Coates's assumption that there is a Christian framework to his early aesthetics, especially as outlined in 'Author and Hero in Aesthetic Activity'. She argues convincingly, as does Alexandar Mihailovic in *Corporeal Words: Mikhail Bakhtin's Theology of Discourse* (Evanston, IL: Northwestern University Press, 1997), that a Christian understanding of God, Christology, incarnation and transcendence inform every page of Bakhtin's work. His work evolves in such a way that different aspects of Christian truth inform different essays and articles, but Christianity is the 'organising centre' of most, if not all, of his contributions to literary theory. Coates, *Christianity in Bakhtin*, *passim*.

emphasis. The author writes the hero into existence, and there is a sense in which the author 'intonates', i.e., pronounces or performs, every aspect of the hero's life and action.[59] Just as God is transcendent in relation to creation, so the author is always 'outside' the novel, and cannot be rendered immanent to it. Bakhtin is convinced, however, that the relationship between author and hero, creator and created, is more complex. What interests him particularly is how this principled starting point – which he calls 'necessary principle' – is the basis for creative and productive relationship between author and hero. Just as God is the creator of all that is, so the author writes the hero into existence. Without the author's act the hero would not exist. Yet in his view, this is far from a complete representation of the whole relationship of author and hero in many novels; there is much more to be said about the relationship between the two.

In 'Author and Hero in Aesthetic Activity', Bakhtin casts the relationship between author and hero in aesthetic terms – in the sense that he considers the author's reaction to a work as a whole – and explores how the author responds to the whole meaning evinced by the hero. To use his words, he is interested in the 'comprehensive reaction of the author to the hero'; the unitary reaction of the author to the whole of the hero's life, actions, thoughts, feelings etc.[60] This relationship has a productive and constructive character because it is founded on 'necessary principle' regarding the character of authorial activity. In essence, this means that the author-as-creator is always external to the work created.[61] As Gary Saul Morson and Caryl Emerson explain: 'the author-as-creator is a crea*ting*, not a crea*ted*, thing; he [*sic*]

---

59. See 'Author and Hero in Aesthetic Activity', note 5 by Vadim Liapunov in Bakhtin, *Art and Answerability*, p. 232.
60. Bakhtin, *Art and Answerability*, p. 5.
61. For commentary on this, see Morson and Emerson, *Mikhail Bakhtin*, pp. 429–432.

represents, but is not himself represented.'[62] The author alone sustains the unity of the work because only the author knows all the heroes both individually and collectively and how each participates in the work as a whole. The author alone sees it as their creation and is uniquely active in giving form and existence to it. The author brings the work into being and assesses its reality and significance in relation to their creative intent. The author/artist is situated outside the work and, while not indifferent to it, occupies what Bakhtin calls 'an essential axiological position'.[63] The author holds the work together as a unity, individualises and concretises it, makes it an object of cognition and renders it physical, identifies and evaluates its reality.

Without pushing the correspondence between God/the author and created/the hero too far, we can observe that, for Bakhtin, the author is 'without image', and that no constructed image can convey their nature.[64] For Bakhtin, as for Christian theology, the author's involvement in the creative process is qualitatively different to that of any other party. He never settles for a view of the author as the Absolute who exercises, or transmits, direct disposition over humanity, to the extent that humanity/the hero is denied scope for self-realisation and development. Of course, there is nothing new for theologians in the idea that God is creating and not created, 'outside' of creation/the novel and not immanent to it, and 'without image'. Yet at a time when we are challenged to defend the morality of confessing divine authority, it might be that Bakhtin's use of literary and theological categories and terms can illuminate our task.

62. Morson and Emerson, *Mikhail Bakhtin*, p. 430.
63. M. M. Bakhtin, 'Supplement: The Problem of Content, Material, and Form in Verbal Art' in *Art and Answerability*, p. 282.
64. Morson and Emerson, *Mikhail Bakhtin*, p. 430.

'God Saw'

Bakhtin's interest in the aesthetic nature of the relationship between author and hero leads him to explore two interrelated areas: how the author reacts to the work produced; and how this reaction shapes the relationship between author and hero/creator and created. For Bakhtin, an aesthetic relationship involves more than the author looking at completed work as if it were 'any ol' object'. A work of art is more than a 'thing' that may or may not have utility. In one sense it is a material thing, but it also has form and content which have been actualised by the author's relationship to it. It is an 'aesthetic object', i.e., a material object that exists in a peculiar relationship to its author. As such, a work of art has structure or composition. He refers to 'the sum total of the factors that produce an artistic impression'; that which gives it order, wholeness and value.[65] It exists for the author as something unique and unrepeatable; it *is* something for its author other than simply a material thing whose material form looks and/or

---

65. Bakhtin, 'Supplement: The Problem of Content', p. 267. Words like 'order', 'wholeness' and 'value' are associated by Bakhtin with 'architectonic forms', by which he means the very essence of aesthetic appreciation or that which both gives and orders aesthetic meaning. Architectonic forms are different to compositional forms and belong to different planes of understanding. Compositional forms are understood by Bakhtin teleologically and are subject to a purely technical evaluation (see p. 270). For instance, a straight line can be judged to be either straight or not straight according to an agreed standard; artistic performances can be compared and judged by experts trained to evaluate the elements that comprise it. Architectonic forms have to do with values on a larger scale which are also distinctive to aesthetic appreciation. They are not to be reduced to technique but have to do with the ordering of all technical and compositional matters into an artistic whole or single event. Equivalent to what might be termed 'first philosophy', architectonic forms deal with causes and principles and what makes it possible for aesthetics to bring concepts like order, wholeness and value into relationship with particular works. When an author signs a work, or acknowledges it as their own and becomes answerable for it, they render that work available for judgement according to both kinds of forms.

feels in particular ways. Thus aesthetic analysis is incomplete unless it includes both how the work looks and/or feels, etc., *and* what it is for the artist.[66]

For Bakhtin, an author's 'seeing' of a work involves both the evaluative and the responsible or answerable aspects of a relationship. When an author 'sees' a work they evaluate it according to both kinds of forms, i.e., the compositional and architectonic. The author brings to the work a unity of evaluation in which both form and content are assessed according to aesthetically significant values, and Bakhtin describes this evaluation as 'determined axiologically'.[67] In other words, the author brings to the work a mix of interacting and overlapping values and expresses a valuation according to their assessment of its worth. Of course, the author is not unrelated or indifferent to the work for the very reason that they brought it into being. Indeed, in taking responsibility for the work and 'signing' it as their own, the author has a particular relationship to the work because it embodies their creative activity: 'The creator finds himself in it and feels intensely his own creative activity in it.'[68] Thus, for Bakhtin, 'seeing' involves both these aspects of the relationship.

Moreover, both the evaluative and the answering aspects of 'seeing' are ethically constituted. For Bakhtin, this is true at the level of the author's 'seeing' of the work as a whole, and at the level of their relationship with the hero(es). Of course, the author's vision and consciousness encircles and contains that of the hero, but, given this constraint, how the two relate is an ethical matter: 'When the hero and the author coincide or when they find themselves standing either next to one another in the face of a value they share, or against one another as antagonists, the aesthetic

---

66. Bakhtin, 'Supplement: The Problem of Content', pp. 257–267.

67. 'The artist assumes an essential *position outside* the event as a contemplator who is disinterested but who *understands the axiological sense of what is coming to pass*'. Bakhtin, 'Supplement: The Problem of Content', p. 282.

68. Bakhtin, 'Supplement: The Problem of Content', p. 316.

event ends and an *ethical* event begins . . .'[69] Bakhtin asserts time
and again that the aesthetic activity of both author and hero has
ethical content and that the quality of their relationship is a
significant factor in the creative act. Discussion of every aspect of
the novel, e.g., the spatial form of the hero in the novel, is linked
to discussion about ethical value.[70] Aesthetic appreciation of the
work quickly spills into ethical consideration and is integral to
the creative and productive relationship between author and
hero.[71] Ethical value is viewed not as a given but as a task still to
be accomplished in all aspects of the work, not least in the verbal
art of the hero, the hero's relationship to the horizon of their
world and to their immediate environment.[72] The author's 'seeing'
of a work includes all these aspects and is the basis of ongoing
relationship with the hero.

Critical and interpretive issues when reading Genesis 1:1 – 2:4a

With this in mind, let's consider the affirmation 'God saw' which
is repeated like an echo throughout Gen. 1:1 – 2:4a (1:4, 10, 12, 18,
21, 25, 31). What kinds of relationship occur between God/the
author and creation/the hero? How are these relationships structured? How does the God/the author react to creation/the hero
and what do we learn about the ethical constitution of their
relationship? Some critical issues should inform our consideration.
Scholars of the historical-critical paradigm, notably Gerhard von
Rad but also G. Ernest Wright, Claus Westermann and others,
insist that the creation accounts cannot be isolated from different
traditions of Old Testament faith and witness to God's saving acts
in history. According to this way of thinking, Gen. 1:1 – 2:4a is,
most likely, a liturgical narrative which dates from during or after

---

69. Bakhtin, *Art and Answerability*, p. 22.
70. Bakhtin, *Art and Answerability*, pp. 96–97.
71. Bakhtin, *Art and Answerability*, pp. 47–59.
72. Bakhtin, *Art and Answerability*, pp. 97–99.

the Israelite exile in Babylon.[73] Those who counterbalance this emphasis on history with an emphasis on canon urge us to take seriously the place of the creation accounts within the canon of scripture. Those who attend to the rhetoric of the lyrical statements in Gen. 1:1 – 2:4a impress upon us that the mood of the

---

73. Gerhard von Rad urged that we interpret Gen. 1:1 – 2:4a as bearing manifold witness to interaction between God and creation. For him, the relatively late composition of Priestly origin conveyed the authority of God/the author, not as an abstract formula or standard of knowledge, but as the product of historical experience. The affirmation 'God saw' is an expression of faith regarding the status of creation in the eyes of the creator, as understood by the people of Israel. Indeed, Israel only discovered the theological relationship between creation and salvation upon learning to see creation as connected theologically with 'saving history'. Israel's oldest formulations of faith had been of special historical experiences of Jahweh, in which Israel had an immediate relationship of faith to its saviour and guide, though von Rad is convinced that a developed understanding of God as creator emerged from Israel's confession of God as redeemer and lord of history, and argues that confessions of the authority of God as creator succeeded, rather than preceded, confession of the saving acts of Jahweh in history. 'The theological derivation of Jahweh's power over history from his authority as Creator is . . . a comparatively late idea (Jer. 27:4ff; Is. 45:12f).' Gerhard von Rad, *Old Testament Theology*, Vol. 1 (Edinburgh and London: Oliver & Boyd 1962; German edition 1957), p. 138. Von Rad pays particular attention to Deutero-Isaiah wherein it is plain that witness to Jahweh as creator is secondary to soteriological statements about Jahweh's redeeming power in history. He argues that allusions to creation strengthen confidence in Jahweh because creation is viewed as a saving event (Is. 44:24, 54:5). This was supported in the first edition of the International Critical Commentary on Genesis: 'during a long development within the sphere of Hebrew religion it [biblical cosmogony] was gradually stripped of its cruder mythological elements, and transformed into a vehicle for the spiritual ideas which were the peculiar heritage of Israel'. John Skinner, *A Critical and Exegetical Commentary on Genesis* (Edinburgh: T. & T. Clark, 1910/1930), p. 6. See also Emil Brunner, *The Christian Doctrine of Creation and Redemption*, trans. Olive Wyon (London: Lutterworth Press, 1952); Stephen Lee, *Creation and Redemption in Isaiah 40–55* (Hong Kong: Alliance Bible Seminary, 1955); G. Daly, *Creation and Redemption: A Study in Pauline Theology*, Supplements to Novum Testamentum, Vol. XXVII (Leiden: Brill, 1971).

passage is one in which God is lauded as supreme creator whose name is worthy of blessing and praise. Walter Brueggemann writes: 'The world given in these liturgical utterances is a "contrast-world", compared to the world of exile that holds threat, anxiety, and insecurity.'[74] There are many issues here regarding critical method. We can assume, however, that whether or not confessions of God as lord of history preceded confessions of God as creator, Israel's testimony to God as creator is part of a larger testimony in which confession of the authority of God as creator was closely related to experience of God as saviour and shaped by faith.[75]

Such critical and interpretive issues bear upon our main purpose of trying to hear from the text about the significance of God's 'seeing', and the kind of relationship with Israel that God's

---

74. Brueggemann, *Theology of the Old Testament*, p. 153.

75. This is supported by Brevard S. Childs who, after reviewing critical readings of von Rad's thesis, concludes: 'Israel's faith developed historically from its initial encounter with God as redeemer from Egypt, and only secondarily from this centre was a theology of creation incorporated into its faith.' Brevard S. Childs, *Biblical Theology of the Old and New Testaments* (London: SCM Press, 1992), p. 110. See also Brueggemann, *Theology of the Old Testament*, pp. 154–156, for comments about 'Creation Faith in Israel's Larger Testimony'. This is reflected textually in Deutero-Isaiah which provides some of the clearest acclamations of God as creator in the Old Testament. For example, after recalling the Lord's dealings with Judah following the delivery of Jerusalem from the Assyrians, Deutero-Isaiah urges the people: 'Lift up your eyes to the heavens; consider who created these, led out their host one by one, and summoned each by name' (Is. 40:26 *REB*). 'It is I who help you, declares the LORD; your redeemer is the Holy One of Israel . . . I shall open rivers on the arid heights, and wells in the valleys' (Is. 41:14, 18 *REB*). 'These are the words of the LORD who is God, who created the heavens and stretched them out, who fashioned the earth and everything that grows in it, giving breath to its people and life to those who walk on it' (Is. 42:5 *REB*). Allusions to God as creator strengthen affirmations of God as historical redeemer. Redemption and creation are interlinked, especially in Is. 51:9–10 in which allusions to God as creator (the Lord who dried up the seas of the abyss) are intermingled with allusion to redemption (the Lord who made a path for the people through the waters of Egypt).

'seeing' involves. Having noted that historical considerations convince us that the text of Gen. 1:1 – 2:4a arose from a complex of faith that developed variously among the people of Israel, we can consider the canonical position that Gen. 1:1 – 2:4a occupies in the Old Testament. As presented to us in the opening pages of the Old Testament, the text teaches us that the whole world was created by God. This indicates that we may legitimately approach the text with theological and ethical questions, and, arguably, that confession of God as creator is a fitting starting point for theological reflection and practice. The liturgical mode of presentation is significant because, as liturgy, the text invites readers/speakers to join in its song of praise by acknowledging that creation happened because of God's creative being and will, according to God's will, and that God's creative being and will is the source of its meaning and purpose. The recurring patterns in the text have a rhetorical effect which reinforce the theological affirmation that God's Word is effective. The slightly varied but repeated affirmations, 'God said . . .', 'so God created . . .', 'and God saw that it was good', affirm that creation was no careless accident or secondary result but the creative work of God which is valued positively by God for itself.[76]

---

76. For the Christian ethicist, this presupposes that, ultimately, it is in Christ that we know God is 'for us' and it is in Christ that we learn what ethical purity is. Arguably, Bakhtin also acknowledged this. Consider the following passage: 'Hence, in all of Christ's norms the *I* and the *other* are contraposed: for myself – absolute sacrifice, for the other – loving mercy. But *I-for-myself* is the *other* for God. God is no longer defined essentially as the voice of my conscience, as purity of my relationship to myself (purity of my penitent self-denial of anything *given* within myself), as the one into whose hands it is a fearful thing to fall and to see whom means to die (immanent self-condemnation). God is now the heavenly father who is *over me* and can be merciful to me and justify me where I, from within myself, cannot be merciful to myself and cannot justify myself in principle, as long as I remain pure before myself. What I must be for the other, God is for me. What the other surmounts and repudiates within himself as an unworthy given, I accept in him and that with loving mercy as the other's cherished flesh.' Bakhtin, *Art and Answerability*, p. 56.

These theological affirmations allow us to approach the text with Bakhtin's questions in mind concerning how God/the author reacts to the work produced and how this reaction shapes the relationship between author and hero, creator and created: Is it legitimate to envisage creation as an aesthetic event? If so, in what ways does God/the author accept responsibility for the worth of a product? Does God react to creation in a way that establishes a basis for ongoing relationship? Many treatments of Gen. 1:1 – 2:4a which take account of God as artist are satisfied with testimony to God's great power and skill in forming dry land and the waters, the birds and fish, etc., or focus on Yahweh the potter who forms the clay according to a divinely conceived plan.[77] Bakhtin provokes us, however, into new ways of interpreting and giving expression to the meaning of the text. His questions about how God/the author reacts to the work produced invite us to look again at the recurrence of the statement 'God saw' with a view to its significance in the creative process. This is mainly the task of the next sections. For the moment, note that the recurrence of 'God saw' throughout the creative process indicates Israel's conviction that great care and attention were taken at every stage. Note how it points to creation being treated as a unity by God and to the theological fact that all creatures stand before God in the same way. Note how a major affirmation of the text is the relationship of creator and created, and how 'God's seeing' is the context for all subsequent ongoing relationship.

Note also how the canonical position of the text sets up a tension between 'God's seeing' the initial goodness of creation and also foreseeing the difference that sin will make. There is no indication in Gen. 1:1 – 2:4a that creation will become anything less than 'very good'. However, by drawing on wider Old Testament canonical resources, we observe that God's seeing is a primary way of depicting a relationship between God, creation and the

---

77. A similar point is made by Brueggemann, *Theology of the Old Testament*, pp. 250–251.

people of Israel. In Gen. 6:12, God saw that the earth was corrupt because it was filled with violence. Ex. 2:25 speaks of God looking upon the Israelites and taking notice of them because they groaned under their slavery and cried out: 'The cry of the Israelites has now come to me; I have also seen how the Egyptians oppress them' (Exod. 3:9). According to Deut. 9:13, the Lord has seen that this people is a stubborn people: 'Let me alone that I may destroy them and blot out their name from under heaven.' The emotional-volitional relationship expressed in these verses is too active in character to be understood in a formal or materialist sense by treating creation/the work as simply a material thing.[78] Rather, the relationship is replete with divine intention and spills quickly into ethically related matters. God sees the people when they suffer and responds to their needs (1 Sam. 9:16; Ps. 31:7); God sees their tears and heals them (2 Kgs 20:5; Is. 38:4–6, 57:18). God searches the heart (1 Chron. 29:17), sees the spiritual struggles of those who hated without cause and wronged their neighbours (Ps. 35:22; Lam. 3:59), and also the abominations of wickedness (Jer. 14:7, 23:14). God also sees repentance (Jon. 3:10). Biblical witness is that God, who is the framer of all things, sees to the core of their being in a manner that gives the power for total control yet without using this power to dominate. By virtue of being creator, God/the author has an 'excess of seeing' which goes beyond and encompasses the vision of the creation/the hero and which has ongoing ethical content.[79]

Bakhtin is not the first to hint at 'God's seeing' as an interpretive focus through which to perceive something of Israel's witness to divine creativity. Athanasius wrote of God's seeing that there is no creature 'that is not manifest in His sight; but all things are naked and opened unto the eyes of Him with whom we have to

---

78. I draw here on Bakhtin, *Art and Answerability*, p. 264.

79. '[T]he composition of this excess tends towards a certain stable constancy.' Bakhtin, *Art and Answerability*, p. 24.

do' (quoting Heb. 4:12–13).[80] For Athanasius, the biblical language of creation does not refer only to the origin of a thing but also to its intended status and/or way of being: to be created is to exist within the full and inescapable sight of God. Yet because of the graciousness of God, this divine excess of vision does not petrify but calls the creature into their future:

> the single word 'He created' does not simply denote the essence and mode of generation, David shews in the Psalm, 'This shall be written for another generation, and the people that is created shall praise the Lord' (Ps 102:18 LXX) . . . For neither David spoke of any people created in essence, nor prayed to have another heart than that he had, but meant renovation according to God and renewal.[81]

For Athanasius, as for Bakhtin, the aesthetic relationship between author and hero is not a relationship in which the author/artist treats the work observed as a material object but a living work with which personal and ethical relationship is possible.[82] The reaction of the author to their work is significant because it forms the basis of the ongoing, productive and constructive relationship.[83]

'And it was very good'[84]

But what kind of relationship is set in motion between God/the author and creation/the hero? Bakhtin provokes us to ask why and how the author's reaction to their work shapes the relationship

---

80. Athanasius, *Against the Arians*, Discourse II, ch. XVIII, *NPNF* Second Series, Vol. IV, p. 367.

81. Athanasius, *Against the Arians*, Discourse II, ch. XIX, *NPNF* Second Series, Vol. IV, p. 373.

82. He talks about emotional-volitional relationships which are too active in character to be understood in a formal or materialist sense by treating creation/the product simply as a thing. See Bakhtin, *Art and Answerability*, p. 264.

83. Bakhtin, *Art and Answerability*, p. 5.

84. From Gen. 1:31.

between author and hero, creator and created. Let's consider, therefore, the recurring (although slightly varying) phrase 'and God saw that it was good', and also the culminatory declaration in Gen. 1:31: 'God saw everything that he had made, and indeed, it was very good.' The declaration 'it was very good' is not found elsewhere in the Old Testament, but 'good' (*tov*) is used either of creation, or of God in connection with creation (Ps. 104:28, Ps. 136:1; Amos 9:4–6). As it stands, the declaration in Gen. 1:31 is a theological treatise in miniature which contains the essence of Israelite doctrine of creation: a compact and precise statement of Israelite belief that its relationship with God begins with God's creation of the world.[85] Much has been written about how the verses contrast with those found in other ancient texts. Gerhard von Rad states:

> The world and its fullness do not find their unity and inner coherence in a cosmological first principle, such as the Ionian natural philosophers tried to discover, but in the completely personal will of Jahweh their creator. Nor, as in so many myths of the creation, is the world traced back to a creative struggle between two mythical first principles regarded as persons.[86]

Indeed, one searches in vain within the Babylonian inscription *Enûma elish*, or related Babylonian creation stories, for a similar culminatory declaration.[87] In the Genesis account, creation exists on a completely different plane of being from that of the creator: 'if the world is the product of the creative word, it is therefore, for one thing, sharply separated in its nature from God himself –

---

85. For a simple statement of this, see Gerhard von Rad, 'The Biblical Story of Creation' in *God at Work in Israel*, trans. John H. Marks (Nashville, TN: Abingdon, 1980).

86. Von Rad, *Old Testament Theology*, Vol. I, p. 141.

87. At least, that is, in those translated by Alexander Heidel, *The Babylonian Genesis* (Chicago: UCP, 1942).

it is neither an emanation nor a mythically understood manifestation of the divine nature and its power.'[88]

Yet the culminatory declaration 'and it was very good' is more than a statement about the otherness and outsideness of God vis-à-vis creation. It is a theological statement about God's reaction to creation; it is an aesthetic – or consummatory – reaction of the author to the whole of a work of art. Gerhard von Rad comments: 'This "very good" could be translated better as "fully complete". That is to say, everything had come into being exactly as God had planned it. So far as that is concerned, no incompleteness attaches to the creation.'[89] Indeed, the text indicates that everything was as God had willed it because God's creative Word had been effective. Chaos had been replaced with order; waters and dry land; day and night; birds, animals, fish, reptiles, etc., of every kind; and male and female human beings. Life filled every part of it: the earth was to put forth vegetation (Gen. 1:1); birds and monsters in the seas were to 'be fruitful and multiply' (Gen. 1:22); so also were the human beings, who also had God-given authority over all other living creatures (Gen. 1:28). God had graciously applied Godself to the process of creation, and the consummatory declaration, 'it was very good', is a culminatory statement of God's goodwill towards it, of God's conferring of well-being upon it, and an indication that God is supremely happy with it. The declaration has all the characteristics of blessing, and reinforces the blessing (barak) given to the creatures of the air and sea (Gen. 1:22), to humankind (Gen. 1:28), and to the seventh day on which God rested (Gen. 2:3). The canonical context of the passage reminds us that the passage is positioned within the Hebrew scriptures as the beginning of the history of Israel in relationship with God. So also does its concluding sentence: 'These are the generations of the heavens and the earth when they were created'

---

88. Von Rad, *Old Testament Theology,* Vol. I, p. 142.
89. Von Rad, *God at Work in Israel,* p. 104.

(Gen. 2:4). Gen. 1:31 represents a culminatory moment which forms the basis for ongoing relationship.

But what characterises this relationship? Why does God/the author's positive reaction to creation/the product make a difference to it? Interestingly, Augustine answers this question in aesthetic terms in at least three ways. Consider the following passage in which he comments on Gen. 1:31 and refers to (i) the *beauty* of the ordered union of the completed, whole creation; (ii) the beauty of the *ordered* union of the completed, whole creation; (iii) the beauty of the ordered *union* of the completed, whole creation:

> And Thou, O God, sawest everything that Thou hadst made, and behold it was very good. We also see the same, and behold all are very good. In each particular kind of Thy works, when Thou hadst said, 'Let them be made', and they were made, Thou sawest that it was good. Seven times have I counted it written that Thou sawest that which Thou madest was 'good'; and this is the eighth, that Thou sawest all things that Thou hadst made, and behold they are not only good, but also 'very good', as being now taken together. For individually they were only good, but all taken together they were both good and very good. All beautiful bodies express this; for a body which consists of members, all of which are beautiful, is by far more beautiful than the several members individually are by whose well-ordered union the whole is completed, though these members also be severally beautiful.[90]

The beauty, order, and wholeness of creation are integral to its goodness. Like Bakhtin, Augustine works with assumptions about 'necessary principle', i.e., that time began with creation, not creation from time, and that God created the world by the power of his Word. This is reinforced by his contrasting of God's experi-

---

90. Augustine, *Confessions*, Bk XIII, ch. XXVIII, §43, *NPNF* First Series, Vol. I, p. 204.

ence of time to that of humanity, the implication being that this
relationship is productive and constructive because of the way in
which God responds to creation.[91] Of particular interest is the
difference that God's declaration, 'and it was very good', makes to
subsequent relationship between God/the author and creation/the
hero. We cannot know what would have happened if, for some
reason, God was not pleased with creation. Such a question would
take us into pointless speculation. We can, however, ask about the
significance of the declaration as regards a theology of divine
authority. Building on the biblical witness that creation was, in
God's eyes, 'very good', we can enquire into the kind of two-way
interaction this positive reaction initiates between God/the author
and creation/the hero.

For Augustine, it is of note that God took pleasure in creation
because the declaration 'it was very good' provides the basis for
an interactive relationship in which human souls can delight in
God:

> But as for those who through Thy Spirit see these things,
> Thou seest in them. When, therefore, they see that these

---

91. 'And I looked attentively to find whether seven or eight times Thou sawest
that Thy works were good, when they were pleasing unto Thee; but in Thy
seeing I found no times, by which I might understand that thou sawest so often
what Thou madest. And I said, "O Lord, is not this Thy Scripture true, since
Thou art true, and being Truth hast set it forth? Why, then, dost Thou say unto
me that in Thy seeing there are no times, while this Thy Scripture telleth me
that what Thou madest each day, Thou sawest to be good; and when I counted
them I found how often?" Unto these things Thou repliest unto me, for Thou
art my God, and with strong voice tellest unto Thy servant in his inner ear,
bursting through my deafness, and crying, "O man, that which My Scripture
saith, I say; and yet doth that speak in time; but time has no reference to My
Word, because my Word existeth in equal eternity with Myself. Thus those things
which ye see through My Spirit, I see, just as those things which ye speak through
My Spirit, I speak. And so when ye see those things in time, I see them not in
time; as when ye speak them in time, I speak them not in time.' Augustine,
Confessions, Bk XIII, ch. XXIX, §44, *NPNF* First Series, Vol. I, p. 205.

> things are good, Thou seest that they are good; and whatso-
> ever things for Thy sake are pleasing, Thou art pleased in
> them; and those things which through Thy Spirit are pleasing
> unto us, are pleasing unto Thee in us.[92]

Creatures can delight in God because God has first taken pleasure
in creation. God's positive response to creation is not a net balance
of pleasure over pain, because the world contains nothing that is
not good. Rather, implies Augustine, it is the basis of ongoing
relationship between God and creation in at least two regards.
First, the Spirit of God which has been breathed into humankind
(Gen. 2:7; Matt. 10:20; 1 Cor. 2:12) enables humanity to recognise
that creation is good. 'How, then, do we . . . know "what things
are given us by God"?' he asks. How do we know what is good?
Because of the witness of the Spirit: 'so whatever they see by the
Spirit of God that it is good, it is not they, but God who "sees
that it is good".'[93] This great privilege is God's gift and anticipates
both God's pentecostal gift of the Holy Spirit to the church (Rom.
5:5) and the final eschatological rest of eternal life.[94] Second, the
rest that God enjoys on the seventh day of creation is a gift of
God to creation. Its peace is an image of that which will be
enjoyed in eternity with God. Until that time, its rest is a gift to
creation which God has blessed and sanctified.[95] God grants the
human soul (and creation) the kind of rest which restores and
sanctifies. As the day of rest was a gift to all creation, a blessing
to the people of Israel, and an anticipation of eternal life, so the
Lord's day (i.e., Sunday) is a time when the soul can rest and be
renewed:

---

92. Augustine, *Confessions*, Bk XIII, ch. XXXI, §46, *NPNF* First Series, Vol. I, p. 205.

93. Augustine, *Confessions*, Bk XIII, ch. XXXI, §46, *NPNF* First Series, Vol. I, p. 205.

94. Augustine, *Confessions*, Bk XIII, ch. XXXVI, §51, *NPNF* First Series, Vol. I, p. 207.

95. Augustine, *Letter LV*, ch. X, §§18–19, *NPNF* First Series, Vol. I, pp. 308–309.

Because, therefore, 'the love of God is shed abroad in our hearts by the Holy Spirit which is given to us', sanctification was associated with the seventh day, the day in which rest was enjoined. But inasmuch as we neither are able to do any good work, except as helped by the gift of God, as the apostle says, 'For it is God that worketh in you both to will and to do of His good pleasure', nor will we be able to rest, after all the good works which engage us in this life, except as sanctified and perfected by the same gift to eternity; for this reason it is said of God Himself, that when He had made all things 'very good', He rested 'on the seventh day from all His works which He had made'. For He, in so doing, presented a type of that future rest which He purposed to bestow on us men after our good works are done. For as in our good works He is said to work in us, by whose gift we are enabled to work what is good, so in our rest He is said to rest by whose gift we rest.[96]

Rest and renewal are integral to humanity's delighting in creation and in God. They are part of how, for Augustine, God's good pleasure in creation brings to birth the possibility of relationship between God/the author and creation/the hero. Rest and renewal are part of the environment in which finite creatures enjoy relationship with the infinite, and in which the relationship may blossom into delight as the Holy Spirit sheds the love of God abroad in the human soul. In this environment, it is as if the boundary between finite and infinite becomes permeable as the Spirit of God engages the human soul in the life divine. What then becomes of the human soul? It rests. Like the sleep that follows love, God restores and renews the soul that delights in him.

According to Augustine, the kind of delight we are talking about is not that of taking pleasure in oneself, because that is subject to

---

96. Augustine, *Letter LV*, ch. X, §19, *NPNF* First Series, Vol. I, p. 309.

capriciousness and will always be a lesser experience than delighting in God who does not change: 'When the soul finds pleasure from itself, it is not yet seeking delight in that which is unchangeable; and therefore it is still proud, because it is giving to itself the highest place, whereas God is higher.'[97] Rather, it is about the soul's delighting in God because 'the love of God is shed abroad in our hearts', and how, when this happens, love mingles with delight in an experience of pure joy. Augustine's treatment of this subject is effusive and evocative as he draws on a plethora of biblical passages to express the strength of love's effects. When delighting in God, the human soul becomes more than it was before. In being seized without reserve, the soul is freed from dependence on itself and granted the joy of a starry awakening in which God grants it the desires of its heart (Ps. 37:4). Never is the human soul appropriated to the desires of God; never is life sucked out of the human soul to satisfy the desires of the absolute Other. Rather, divine authority and a relationship of delight between creator and created imply one another. Delight and authority are not often words that are used together. However, when divine authority is cast in terms of God's authoring, we begin to see their connection.

Delighting in God

Traditional Christian confession is that this creaturely experience of delighting in God has infinite possibility. As author of creation, God gives of Godself to it. As created being, the creature's enjoyment has the potential to be as infinite as that of the power of the creator. Gregory of Nyssa states:

> the First Good is in its nature infinite, and so it follows of necessity that the participation in the enjoyment of it will be infinite also, for more will be always being grasped, and yet something beyond that which has been grasped will always

---

97. Augustine, *Letter LV,* ch. X, §18, *NPNF* First Series, Vol. I, p. 309.

be discovered, and this search will never overtake its Object, because its fund is as inexhaustible as the growth of that which participates in it is ceaseless.[98]

Humanity has the potential for experience of infinite delight because God's goodness is without end. Creation is good because God is good. God's goodness is the reason which gave it existence: 'The fountain, the origin, the supply of every good is regarded as being in the world that is uncreate, and the whole creation inclines to that, and touches and shares the Highest Existence only by virtue of its part in the First Good.'[99] There is no limit to the delight that created beings can enjoy because there is no limit to God's goodness.[100] It is difficult for the human mind to express any thoughts that are worthy of this kind of encounter between God/the author and creation/the hero. Yet the argument in this chapter is that God's authoring of creation is the motive and ground of our whole discussion of Christian ethics. And, if this is correct, we do well like Hilary of Poitiers to press along profitable roads that lead to true knowledge of God.[101] If, as Bakhtin argues, human authoring at its best entails an encounter between author and hero in which there is a positive and 'delightful' relationship, then how much more might this be the case with the divine authoring of creation?

It is worth noting at this point that, for Bakhtin, aesthetic activity proper is much more than the author's response to the inner state expressed by a work. (This view of expressive aesthetics is, he thinks, 'unsound at its very foundations' because this kind

---

98. Gregory of Nyssa, *Against Eunomius*, Bk I, *NPNF* Second Series, Vol. V, p. 62.
99. Gregory of Nyssa, *Against Eunomius*, Bk I, *NPNF* Second Series, Vol. V, p. 60.
100. For human experiences of delight in God and of God's delighting in humanity, see Deut. 10:15; 2 Sam. 22:20; 1 Kgs 10:9; Pss. 1:2, 16:3, 18:19, 22:8, 36:2–7, 44:3, 112:1, 119:14, 147:10; Prov. 11:20, 12:22, 15:8; Is. 11:3, 42:1, 58:14, 62:4, 65:18; Jer. 9:24; Mal. 3:1; Rom. 7:22.
101. I draw on Hilary of Poitiers, *On the Trinity*, Bk 1, §§1 and 4, *NPNF* Second Series, Vol. IX, pp. 40–41.

of co-experiencing prohibits aesthetic reaction which encounters the work as a whole.[102]) Rather, aesthetic activity proper is about active encounter between author and hero (and, arguably, also contemplator), which expresses the quality of their relationship. As illustration he considers aesthetic experience of Raphael's *Sistine Madonna* and the question of how one fully appreciates the relationship between the artist and his work. His argument is that an aesthetic relationship proper is about appreciation of the creative will of the artist and how the work/the hero(es) participate in it. It's not enough to look at Raphael's *Sistine Madonna* for what it expresses of the main character, because it also expresses something of Raphael-as-man in relationship to the Madonna. The form of a work cannot be separated from the content, though content is expressed in form. Aesthetic activity is not located in the main character's expression of an inner state, or in the self-identification of artist with this inner state, but with relationship between artist and character. So, what happens, asks Bakhtin, in the moment at which the artist regards the whole work of art? Does the artist co-experience the inner state expressed by the work of art? Is the aesthetic experience an act of co-encountering that inner state?[103] Does the artist (or any contemplator) find their identity in the contemplated object by 'abiding within it' and sharing with it a single plane of consciousness? Most definitely not, he thinks, because that would make the object's outward expression of its state the medium through which the author encounters it. In such a scenario, the author would react to the work through its subjective value in their own experience, and this would prevent rather than enable the author's reaction to the work as a whole. It would reduce the value of the work to that of utility rather than something created for its own sake by the artist.

Bakhtin makes the same point with regard to aesthetic appreciation of Leonardo da Vinci's painting *The Last Supper*. Can I, he

---

102. Bakhtin, *Art and Answerability*, p. 64.
103. Bakhtin, *Art and Answerability*, pp. 61–64.

asks, experience the inner state of Christ, or of each of the disciples, by empathising myself into their experience? Only at the expense of experiencing the work as a whole. Why? Because aesthetic experience is not about empathising with figure(s)/hero(es) within the work, but is about contemplation of their place within the work as a whole. If, for example, I co-empathise with the self-expression of stubbornness or pride in a figure or character, I cannot contemplate that experience properly without seeing the whole of the work. Aesthetic reaction is less about co-experiencing with figures within the work, than about the creative will of God/the author, and how creatures/heroes participate in it. The life within each goes beyond its own bounds, and, in ceasing to be in-itself-and-for-itself, becomes something new in relation. The expression of each emerges and grows in relationship with the other. Consider, for example, his notion of 'transgredience'. Transgredience is the movement between author and hero which presupposes the outsideness of the author vis-à-vis the text and also the movement between the consciousness of the hero and that which is beyond. He describes transgredient moments as follows:

> What constitutes these transgredient moments, i.e., moments that exceed self-consciousness and consummate it, are the outer *boundaries* of inner life – the point where inner life is turned *outward* and ceases to be active out of itself. These boundaries are first and foremost *temporal* boundaries: the beginning and the end of a life ... [T]he other ... God.[104]

Transgredience is about movement between hero(es), and between and beyond the hero and their own self-consciousness, and also about the author's activity above and beyond the hero.[105] It

---

104. Bakhtin, *Art and Answerability*, pp. 103–111.

105. 'All determinations that possess aesthetic validity are transgredient to lived life itself and to the world's givenness as experienced from within lived life, and it is only this transgrediency that produces their power and validity; without transgrediency, they would be spurious and empty. The necessary condition ▷

presupposes the outsideness of God/the author vis-à-vis the text and hero but yet expresses a two-way movement between both parties.

It is arguable that Bakhtin drew some of his ideas about the two-way movement that occurs between author and hero from Russian Orthodox spirituality. There are few if any direct references but plenty of strong similarities in thought patterns and allusions to divine grace, not least the relationship of trust which God/the author opens through grace, and the language of 'warmth' and 'value-related atmosphere' which conveys this aspect of the creative authoring process.[106] The following prayer of St Simeon the New Divine (which forms part of an Orthodox office of preparation for holy communion) is about the grace of God which allows humanity to partake of the life divine:

> My God and Master, every word of thine is true: when I partake of thy divine and deifying graces, then am I not alone, but am with thee, my Christ, light of the threefold sun which lighteneth the world. Suffer me not to dwell alone apart from thee, Giver of Life, who art my breath, my life, my joy, the world's salvation: it is for this cause that, as thou seest, I draw nigh to thee with tears and with a contrite soul: I beseech thee that I may receive the absolution of all my

---

for giving an aesthestic form to present-on-hand being is the author's self-activity as an activity *above* present-on-hand being. I must be active, in order that being may be trustfully passive . . .' Bakhtin, *Art and Answerability*, pp. 134–135.

106. It is interesting to note that the Orthodox liturgy includes a prayer for the blessing of the warm water added to the chalice of wine. The deacon, taking the warm water, says to the priest: 'Pray, Father, bless the warmth', following which he pours crosswise into the chalice, saying: 'The fervour of faith, full of the Holy Ghost'. See *The Orthodox Liturgy being the Divine Liturgy of S. John Chrysostom and S. Basil the Great according to the use of the Church of Russia* (London: SPCK, for the Fellowship of SS. Alban and Sergius, 1939), p. 87. The origin of this ceremony is obscure. Hugh Wybrew suggests that it was connected with the belief that the body of Christ never lost its warmth between the cross and the resurrection. See his 'The Byzantine Liturgy' in Cheslyn Jones et al. (eds), *The Study of Liturgy* (London: SPCK, 1978), p. 213.

transgressions, and uncondemned partake of thy life-giving spotless mysteries.[107]

This passage contains many central themes of Orthodox spirituality. God communicates with humanity through his Word. For humans to respond is to partake of God's grace, to enjoy the light which shines from God, to know the presence of the breath of life, to live in joy, to experience salvation as union with God, to delight in divine mystery. There is a movement between God and humanity which depends upon the initiative of God, yet draws humanity into its life. The person praying this prayer knows the reality of sin and weakness: 'I have sinned more than the harlot ... Thou knowest all the multitude of mine ills, thou knowest my scars and dost behold my sores ...' Yet the prayer is for perfect union with God as human will is joined with the will of God. Salvation is linked closely to participation in the life divine which is granted through the gift of the Holy Spirit: 'I who am grass partake of fire, and lo, a mighty wonder! I am bedewed and not consumed thereby ...'[108] This experience of blessing, like transgredience, is a movement between God/the author and creation/the hero which is beyond imagining.

In Orthodox liturgy, this blessing is known most fully at the eucharist where God is spoken of as 'lover of humankind'. The deacon articulates the prayer of the people: 'I will greatly rejoice in the Lord, my soul shall be joyful in my God; for he hath covered me with the garments of salvation; he hath covered me with the robe of righteousness, as a bridegroom decketh himself with ornaments, and as a bride adorneth herself with her jewels' (Is. 61:10). The robe of righteousness is given by God who alone has mercy upon and cleanses the sinner. Nothing detracts from the 'necessary principle' that God/the author is radically other than creation; the sexual imagery does not imply equality although

---

107. *The Orthodox Liturgy*, pp. 12–13.
108. *The Orthodox Liturgy*, p. 13.

it does imply happiness, delectation, ecstasy, enjoyment, rapture, joy and transport. The deacon's delight in God is as sweet as that of a bridegroom and bride in one another. The liturgy also speaks of God's opening the door of the temple to sinful persons, opening the gate of paradise to the robber on the cross, opening the 'bowels of thy loving-kindness'.[109] There is no place within such an understanding of authority for a paradigm of domination or control. To use Bakhtin's words, the aesthetic relationship is inherently ethical in its constitution because it has to do with the character and quality of an I–Other relationship.[110] Authoring is an interactive relationship which can be expressed as both grace and transgredience, as the life of God/the author exceeds its own bounds and creates a relationship with creation/the text. Significant for our purposes is that God's authoring-authority establishes relationship with creation and invites creatures to become 'partakers in . . . incorruptible good things'.[111]

God Blessed and Said to Them . . .

These connections between divine authority and our being created in the image of God invite further reflection on the relationship established between God/the author and creation/the hero. Because human beings are created in the image and likeness of God, divine authority is not alien to them or overbearing. To the contrary, divine authority is the basis for a dialogic relationship of trust. Divine authority is not manifest as some externally imposed set of laws and regulations but rather in the establishing of a relationship that has the capacity for communion and dialogic

---

109. *The Orthodox Liturgy*, p. 15.

110. For Bakhtin, the ethical content of any interaction is developed, in part, in terms of human need for the unmerited gift of forgiveness and redemption, confessional self-accounting, petitionary prayer, and absolution. See esp. Bakhtin, *Art and Answerability*, pp. 143–149.

111. *The Orthodox Liturgy*, p. 9.

interaction. Thus, God gave to Adam and Eve wide-ranging responsibilities for reproduction and care of the earth (Gen. 1:28–30). Augustine writes of this blessing that God gave to humankind a soul, mind, reason and understanding, so they were capable of knowledge and of receiving instructions. They were 'fit to understand what is true and to love what is good'.[112] They were capable of growing in virtue and had the capacity for communion with God:

> It is by this capacity the soul drinks in wisdom, and becomes endowed with those virtues by which, in prudence, fortitude, temperance, and righteousness, it makes war upon error and the other inborn vices, and conquers them by fixing its desires upon no other object than the supreme and unchangeable Good.[113]

This again implies that, by its very nature, the authority of God is never dominating or controlling but relational and trusting. Divine authority is not forceful or resentful but enabling of human creativity and invention:

> For over and above those arts which are called virtues ... has not the genius of man invented and applied countless astonishing arts, partly the result of necessity, partly the result of exuberant invention, so that this vigour of mind, which is so active in the discovery not merely of superfluous but even of dangerous and destructive things, betokens an inexhaustible wealth in the nature which can invent, learn, or employ such arts? What wonderful – one might say stupefying – advances has human industry made in the arts of weaving and building, of agriculture and navigation! With what

---

112. Augustine, *City of God*, Bk XXII, ch. 24, *NPNF* First Series, Vol. II, pp. 502–503.
113. Augustine, *City of God*, Bk XXII, ch. 24, *NPNF* First Series, Vol. II, pp. 502–503.

endless variety are designs in pottery, painting, and sculpture produced, and with what skill executed! . . .[114]

Significant for Christian ethics is how being created in the image of God is inextricably bound to growth in the divine image, growth in virtue, and to the potential for realising good in manifold ways.

The Beginning of Evil and Sin

We must reckon, however, with the beginning of evil and sin. According to Christian teaching, God is not the author of evil. Athanasius teaches that evil has no positive existence even though its effects are very real: 'what is evil is not, but what is good is.'[115] According to Basil, it is blasphemous to suggest that evil has its origin from God because nothing can proceed from its opposite:

> Life does not engender death; darkness is not the origin of light; sickness is not the maker of health. In the changes of conditions there are transitions from one condition to the contrary; but in genesis each being proceeds from its like, and not from its contrary. If then evil is neither uncreate nor created by God, from whence comes its nature? Certainly that evil exists, no one living in the world will deny. What shall we say then? Evil is not a living animated essence; it is the condition of the soul opposed to virtue, developed in the careless on account of their falling away from good.[116]

God is the origin of good and not evil, life and not death. So from where does evil and death come? The traditional answer that evil had its source in the devil, a fallen angel who rebelled against God and tempted humanity to imitate his defiance of God, is rarely convincing today. Moreover, the meaning of 'the fall' is a

---

114. Augustine, *City of God*, Bk XXII, ch. 24, *NPNF* First Series, Vol. II, p. 503.
115. Athanasius, *On the Incarnation*, §4, *NPNF* Second Series, Vol. IV, p. 38.
116. Basil, *The Hexameron*, Homily II, §4, *NPNF* Second Series, Vol. VIII, p. 61.

matter of much dispute. The association of the concept, and that of original sin, with the quasi-hereditary transmission of the sin and guilt of Adam and Eve to each successive generation, has done untold harm to Christian people in their endeavours to understand the corrupting powers of sin and death. This is because the western tradition has, broadly speaking, followed Augustine's translation and interpretation of Rom. 5:12 to read: 'as sin came into the world through one man, and death came through sin, and so death spread to all *in whom* all have sinned'. (The phrase *eph' ho pantes hemarton* was interpreted by Augustine as 'in whom all sinned', the implication being that all are subject to death because all sinned in Adam, rather than 'because all sinned', the implication here being that all are subject to death because all sinned and were responsible personally for their own sin.) Augustine's teaching was framed in the context of polemic dispute with Pelagius' heretical views about moral responsibility and the idea that humans sin only by example. Augustine objected to Pelagius' teaching that disease and death are not the consequences of the sin of Adam and Eve but were characteristic of human nature from the beginning. He rightly warned against the dangerous dismissal of the concept of sin and its effects as inherited from the first parents, and protected the church from unrealistically high estimations of human ability outside the economy of salvation. Augustine spoke of humans begotten from the 'seminal nature' which existed in Adam, so that each brings with them at their birth the beginning of their death.[117] We are all 'in Adam' in the sense that we share his human nature which had become corrupted at the root: 'For we were all in that one man, seeing that we all *were* that one man who fell into sin through the woman who was made from him before the first sin.'[118] Consequently, one must be cleansed of this sin at baptism in order to enter the church. However, his teaching leads to the easy confusion of original sin

117. Augustine, *City of God* (London: Penguin, 1972), Book XIII, ch. 15, §§13–14.
118. Augustine, *City of God* (London: Penguin, 1972), Book XIII, ch. 15, §14.

and original guilt. Why, critics ask, should God hold you, or a new-born baby, responsible for the sin of previous generations? It's immoral! Augustine's position was never as crude as this, but resulted in an obscuring of the divine potential in human persons for communion with God. Consequently, we need more nuanced terms in which to discuss the effects of sin and the abuse of freedom by both ourselves and our ancestors.

Eastern Orthodox theologians tend to make a clearer distinction than their western counterparts between Adam and Eve's personal guilt and the effects of the fall. At the risk of over-generalisation we can say that, according to Orthodox teaching, Adam and Eve sinned, and we are their descendants, but their sin and guilt is not transmitted to us seminally. They were in some sense the gateway for sin: 'sin came into the world through one man . . .' (Rom. 5:12a). There is a link between the (mythic) account of the entry of sin into the world with the sin of Adam and Eve; sin entered the world at the point at which they chose self-sufficiency rather than communion with God. Paul is not, however, inter- preted as making nonsensical assumptions about our sharing their guilt as if we were present ourselves in the garden and could have urged them not to eat.[119] Rather, Adam and Eve's sin resulted in death and that death 'spread to all'. For this reason Orthodox teaching takes seriously the link between the first sin and the sinful condition in which we all live today, but uses the term 'ancestral sin' (Greek *progoniki hamartia*) in preference to that of 'original sin' (Latin *peccatum originale*). We are all 'in Adam' in the sense that Adam and Eve have transmitted to us the inheritance of mortality, but they have not transmitted to us their 'original guilt' that is commonly associated with the concept of 'original sin'. We are born into a sinful world, and the proof of this is death

---

119. See Cyril of Alexandria, 'Scholia on the Incarnation of the Only Begotten' in John A. McGuctin, *St. Cyril of Alexandria The Christological Controversy: Its History, Theology, and Texts*, Supplements to Vigiliae Christianae (Leiden: E.J. Brill, 1994), pp. 294–295.

and corruption. However, we need not despair, because sin and evil are not part of our originally created nature. Evil is not a substantial part of or integral to human nature but results from the failure of moral purpose. Adam and Eve chose autonomy rather than communion with God and the result was their own self-requested separation from God. They separated themselves from the source of life, and the result was death and the corruption of death.[120] God had not created death, but it resulted from Adam and Eve's failure to live up to their divine calling. Thus we do not inherit the guilt of their personal sin. There is no quasi-genetic transmission of guilt. But we do inherit the sickness of death because we share their humanity; we are co-essential or co-substantial (*homoousiotitos*) with their humanity.[121] Sin is the peculiar privilege of each person alone, but we have received mortality from our ancestors' sin and are heirs to the corruption of death.[122]

---

120. Athanasius, *Incarnation of the Word*, §3, *NPNF* Second Series, Vol. IV, p. 38.

121. John Chrysostom, *Homilies on the Epistle to the Romans*, Homily X on Rom. 5:12, NPNF First Series, Vol. XI, pp. 401–403.

122. This links to Basil's comment that there is no need to look beyond oneself when seeking for the origin of evil. Speculation about the original nature of wickedness is pointless. Rather, '[e]ach of us, let us acknowledge it, is the first author of his own vice.' Basil, *The Hexameron*, Homily II, §5, *NPNF* Second Series, Vol. VIII, pp. 61–62. Evil has no origin other than our own disposition and choice, even though we are born into a world in which poverty, sickness and death are now regarded as natural, and need to be understood theologically in ontological as well as voluntary terms. Such conditions are not in any way essential to our humanity and were not part of God's creation. They are, however, now inseparable from the human condition. Natural evil (e.g. destructive viruses and cancers, hurricanes, floods) and ethical evil (e.g. murder, envy and malice) clearly exist. But remember, urges Basil, that the very same ability possessed by the first human beings to reject evil and choose the good is available to humans today: 'evil . . . has no other origin than our voluntary falls.' Human choice is responsible for all ethical, and some natural, evil. God permits this evil because, unless this kind of self-determination were possible, human life would be ▷

Feeling the need to hide from God

We need to inquire further, however, into the effects of sin and the corruption of death. What are the effects of sin and of the abuse of freedom both ancestrally and today? Let's look first at the effects of sin in the lives of Adam and Eve. The first effect recounted in Gen. 3:7 is that 'the eyes of both were opened, and they knew that they were naked; and they sewed fig leaves together and made loincloths for themselves.' Adam and Eve experienced an alienation from their bodies and became subject to a self-consciousness that separated them one from the other. They became subject to necessities not previously known. The second effect recounted in Gen. 3:8–10 is an attempt to deceive Yahweh.

> They heard the sound of the LORD God walking in the garden at the time of the evening breeze, and the man and his wife hid themselves from the presence of the LORD God among the trees of the garden. But the LORD God called to the man, and said to him, 'Where are you?' He said, 'I heard the sound of you in the garden, and I was afraid, because I was naked; and I hid myself.'

Adam and Eve tried to hide themselves from God's sight, 'wishing to be hidden when called by God with that voice which wounded the soul of him who was hiding'.[123] They were burdened by a guilty conscience and judged themselves before hearing God's word; they sought cover in the flimsy illusion that their deeds were not bare before God. The first effect recounted in Gen. 3:12–13 is that they implicated each other rather than taking personal responsibility for their own actions: 'The man said, "The woman

---

determined in all respects by God and humanity/the hero would have no ability to choose or change for the good, to worship and pray to God, to write novels or school essays.

123. Ambrose, *On Repentance*, Bk II, ch. I, §103, *NPNF* Second Series, Vol. X, p. 358.

whom you gave to be with me, she gave me fruit from the tree, and I ate." Then the LORD God said to the woman, "What is this that you have done?" The woman said, "The serpent tricked me, and I ate." ' They spoke against one another, experiencing division and separation between them (cf. Mt. 12:25). Their voices no longer spoke in harmony as they accused one another of disregarding God's command. To use the language we shall develop in Chapter 3, 'polyphony' had become 'heteroglossia'.

Personal existence at constant risk of individualism

Thus sin results in creaturely difference sinking into craven division and opposition.[124] However, in light of the above, we need ontological as well as relational categories to describe its results. Note how Adam and Eve become subject to a variety of natural instincts and impulses that limit their existence (Gen. 3:16–21). Pain in childbirth, the woman's subjection to the mastery of her husband, an accursed earth, and scant reward for one's labour, were to become determinative of human existence. Adam and Eve's personal existence in free communion with God would become existence subject to biological and socio-economic constraints. An alienation had been introduced between their personhood and their nature or substance as human beings. They were still free persons, but their personhood was no longer in harmony with their nature or substance. They were to live in daily awareness of their recently acquired mortality: 'you are dust, and to dust you shall return' (Gen. 3:19); and were liable to the vicissitudes and passions of biological existence. They had become tragic figures destined to die, and would struggle to live fully personal lives under the constraints of what had become their natural necessity. Their very being had changed as their minds were drawn towards physical needs rather than enjoyment of God. Moreover, each person was subject individually to the needs of their biological existence. Each was subject to natural instincts, to isolation, and

---

124. Athanasius, *Letter X*, §4, *NPNF* Second Series, Vol. IV, p. 529.

to death. John Zizioulas makes the point: 'Death is the "natural" development of the biological hypostasis, the cession of "space" and "time" to other individual hypostases, the sealing of hypostasis as individuality.'[125] Neither the human body nor the endeavours of individuals had become inherently sinful. Thus Athanasius can write: 'He is blessed who, being freely yoked in his youth, naturally begets children.'[126] However, in turning away from God, they had turned away from life and their sin had become laden with death. All forms of necessity, including the biological necessities of food, reproduction and death, are the results of the fall. Personal exist- ence was at risk of individualism: the kind of existence that is determined by the needs of natural survival rather than self-giving love. Autonomous individuality, experienced as fear in the face of extinction and the threat of death, now separated one person from another. Sin, said the Lord to Cain, 'is a demon crouching at the door' (Gen. 4:7 *REB*) and, as the Genesis story tells us, he mur- dered his brother Abel in a futile attempt to improve his own lot, trusting in his own individuality while rejecting brotherly relations with his sibling. The perpetuation of Adam and Eve's fall from personal relations into individualism, from polyphony into hetero- glossia, is evident throughout the early books of the bible as the God-given freedom of personhood is renounced time and again in favour of individual autonomy. Consider the stories, not only of Cain and Abel, but also of the flood and the tower of Babel, Abram's disregard for Sarai, Jacob's deceiving of Esau and Isaac, and the brothers' betrayal of Joseph. The 'fall' is an ongoing process.

We also note that, despite the order, beauty and splendour of creation, and despite their God-established relationship of delight with one another and with God, Adam and Eve no longer felt convinced in their hearts that God was not only 'over them' but

---

125. John D. Zizioulas, *Being as Communion* (Crestwood, NY: St Vladimir's Seminary Press, 1985), p. 51.
126. Athanasius, *Letter XLVIII*, *NPNF* Second Series, Vol. IV, p. 557.

'for them'. They needed more than their natural faculties to learn
the truth of God. Even for them – and how much more for us
today? – empirical evidence for the graciousness of God was not
overwhelming. They did not yet have the gospel of Christ in which
to learn that God was not only 'over them' but 'for them' in loving
mercy and restoration.[127] Nor did they have Christ's revelation of
the unqualified nature of God's being for humanity.[128] Adam and
Eve's pre-fall image of God was now distorted and opaque. Separation between God and humanity, and between human persons,
now characterise the fallen condition. Adam and Eve had become
mortal and could not undo this effect of sin (Gen. 3:19b), nor the
biological constraints (notably the need to eat and reproduce)
with which they were now obliged to live (Gen. 3:16–19a). They
could not forgive their own sin and effect restoration but only

---

127. In believing the gospel of Christ, writes Hilary of Poitiers, 'the soul makes
an advance beyond the attainment of its natural capacities, is taught more than
it had dreamed concerning God'. Here we know not only that creation speaks
of God's goodness, but that God is 'for us' to the extent that Christ died for us:
'From his fullness we have all received, grace upon grace' (Jn 1:16). Hilary of
Poitiers, *On the Trinity*, Bk 1, §10, *NPNF* Second Series, Vol. IX, p. 43.

128. Bakhtin expresses something of this sense of the burden of sin and the need
to hide from God by taking refuge in solipsism, in the following passage from a
section in 'Author and Hero in Aesthetic Activity' entitled 'The Value of the
Human Body in History': 'In Christ we find a synthesis of unique depth,
the synthesis of unique depth, the synthesis of *ethical solipsism* (man's severity
towards himself, i.e., an immaculately pure relationship to oneself) with *ethical–
aesthetic kindness* towards the other. For the first time, there appeared an infinitely
deepened *I-for-myself* – not a cold *I-for-myself*, but one of boundless kindness
towards the other . . .' (Bakhtin, *Art and Answerability*, p. 56). The passage is not
written very plainly but the nub of the matter is that 'God for me' in Christ
surmounts the human need to be saved from the burden of sin and justifies
what I cannot put right or purify myself. Outside of Christ, the implication is
that a burden of unworthiness and fear drives humans into the mistaken and
solipsistic belief that their own self is the only existent thing in which there is
any comfort. Coldness characterises the typical 'for me' relationship of one
human being to themselves and to others. By contrast, Christ's being 'for me' is
realistic and mercifully warm.

repent, confess and be penitent. Yet the biological constraints that now determine fallen human nature are not the end of the story. The canonical position of this story in Genesis suggests it is the start of a much larger story of God's dealings with humankind. God/the author does not leave humanity bereft of help, even before the advent of the Word. To the contrary, God/the author has built into creation/the text certain structural conditions that continue to allow genuine freedom and the potential for fulfilling relationship, and it is to these that we shall turn at the start of the next chapter. In the meantime, let's summarise our reflections on why the genesis of ethics is found in the authority of God.

Christian Ethics and the Authority of God

Thus, our point of departure has been the biblically and tradition-ally affirmed truth that God authors each person into relationship with Godself and with other human persons and that, therefore, human life is an existential adventure in personhood and enjoy-ment of God. We have argued that God's authoring-authority establishes and maintains humanity in a relationship of trust which provides for creator and created to delight in each other. The authoring-authority of God provides the value-and-meaning structure of creation/the work as a whole.[129] God/the author's reaction 'it was very good' imbued creation with an internal unity of meaning that is life-affirming. God/the author's creative act provided a context of trust in which creation/the hero is answer-able for their own creativity.[130] In our fallen human condition, just looking at the current state of the created order probably leaves us ambivalent as to whether God is 'for creation' or indifferent to it. It is only in Jesus Christ that we know God to be truly for us; the Word of God's assumption of human flesh is the hermeneutic axiom whereby we interpret God's activity in creation. Hence the

---

129. Bakhtin, *Art and Answerability*, p. 194.
130. Bakhtin, *Art and Answerability*, p. 206.

need to move quickly in the next chapter to consider God's Word in dialogue and to enlarge our theological understanding of that to which Jn 1:14 bears witness. However, far from being repressive, disabling and incompatible with human well-being, the authority of God/the author is affirming of human freedom, enabling and conducive to human well-being. It is the foundation upon which to speak about the worth with which all creation is imbued, and about the essential and inalienable human dignity given to all persons created in the divine image. The creative energy of God/the author bestows on humanity gifts of freedom, self-determination and the power to choose the good. Consequently, Christian ethics has to do with personal response in freedom to existence as given by God, a person's existential answer to God's invitation to live in the Spirit. A Christian understanding of ethics is integral to confession of the divine power to initiate, establish and nurture life, and, therefore, its task will involve the identification of values and patterns of relationship that reflect the authoring-authority of God.

Chapter Two

God's Word
in Dialogue

Christian Ethics and Dialogue

Dialogue and ethics are concepts that often belong together. Dialogue and authority are not. Authority is often thought to override dialogue and render it unnecessary. Etymologically defined, dialogue is a word or conversation between two people (Greek *dia* and *logos*). To put something into dialogic form is to present it as an exchange of views, with the likely intention of reaching agreement. Thus Bertram's question in *All's Well that Ends Well*, 'But shall we have this dialogue between the fool and the soldier?'[1] In a pluralist society, in which old ideologies have broken up and few hope for certainty or foundations in philosophy, there is no escape from dialogue, because ethics requires that we nurture understanding between participants in discourse communities. We should aim, writes Richard J. Bernstein, at a kind of dialogic ethos and necessary pragmatism, 'an engaged fallibilistic pluralism' in which each person is responsible for taking their own fallibility seriously, and for being willing to listen to and learn from others.[2] Unless humanity can nurture dialogue communities which share insights and experiences, then barbarism threatens.[3] But what place does dialogue have in Christian ethics? Is the genesis of Christian ethics found in dialogue between Christian persons, denominations and traditions? Is it found in dialogue with God, and/or with other

---

1. William Shakespeare, *All's Well that Ends Well*, Act 4, Sc. 3. See also *Love's Labour's Lost*, Act 5, Sc. 2, *Much Ado About Nothing*, Act 1, Sc. 3, *Timon of Athens*, Act 2, Sc. 2.
2. Richard J. Bernstein, *The New Constellation* (Oxford: Blackwell, 1991), p. 336.
3. Bernstein, *New Constellation*, pp. 338–339.

disciplines? Arguably, even at an interpersonal level, dialogue is something more than an exchange of views; it is a constitutive aspect of human being and a way of relating from which none are exempt. This chapter argues that dialogue is implied within a Christian understanding of divine authority, although the kind of dialogue implied is not simply a phenomenological description of communication between persons, despite the significance of this constitutive part of human existence. Nor is what is implied simply a pragmatic appeal for improved interpersonal skills in the churches or, necessarily, for more democratically accountable decision-making processes. Rather, it is dialogue understood primarily at the ontological levels of structural conditions built into creation, and of salvation in Christ and renewed vocation to union and communion with God.

Dialogue is not a biblical term and, of itself, has more ready association with Socratic and Platonic philosophy than with a Christian theology of the authority of God. What is biblical, however, is repeated witness to a God who speaks. God possesses Logos, writes Gregory of Nyssa in *The Great Catechism*.[4] God is not without Word. Moreover, says Gregory, the utterance of humans is expressed by the same term; humans also speak and 'possess logos'. God's word is different to ours. God's word is creative and became incarnate in Jesus Christ. Our words often vanish with little effect. However, to be created in the image of God includes our capacity to speak and communicate. This is part of the image in which we have been created and, despite the effects of the fall, human persons are still able to dialogue with one another and with God. More than this, says Gregory, humans have the capacity to hear Wisdom speak. When discussing what of divine goodness is present in human nature, Gregory writes: 'This truth is, I think, taught in the Gospel, when our Lord says, to those who can hear what Wisdom speaks beneath a mystery, that "the Kingdom of

---

4. Gregory of Nyssa, *The Great Catechism*, ch. I, *NPNF* Second Series, Vol. V, p. 475.

God is within you" '.[5] Humans can hear God's communication to them, but can also shut their ears to God and refuse to hear God's wisdom.[6] No one is forced to speak with God. God authors the whole of life, but offers to human persons a dialogical relationship. The challenge in this chapter is to consider why and how this is significant for Christian ethics.

God's Word in Dialogue

In what sense, therefore, can there be dialogue between creator and created? As I shall argue below, the kind of dialogue in question does not depend in a human sense upon the conditions of speech that pertain between participants, and is not oriented towards the consensus that they may or may not reach, but is the kind of a relationship that both Athanasius and Bakhtin describe as characterised by 'grace'. In any relationship between creator and created, it is always God who takes the initiative and all we can do is respond. The conditions in which humans enjoy freedom and self-determination are dependent upon the free act of God's will; God is the one who 'calls into existence the things that do not exist' (Rom. 4:17). God is the creator and sustainer of all that is.[7] God gives to humanity the vocation to union and communion with him, and restores this vocation in Christ. To speak of dia-

---

5. Gregory of Nyssa, *On Virginity*, ch. XII, *NPNF* Second Series, Vol. V, p. 358.

6. This is a paraphrase of Gregory's image of shutting one's eyes to sun. *On Virginity*, ch. XII, *NPNF* Second Series, Vol. 5, p. 357.

7. Gregory Nazianzen writes: 'Now our very eyes and the Law of Nature teach us that God exists and that He is the Efficient and Maintaining Cause of all things . . . [including] natural Law because through these things and their order, it reasons back to their Author. For how could this Universe have come into being or been put together, unless God had called it into existence, and held it together.' *Oratio* XXVIII, §VI, *NPNF* Second Series, Vol. VII, p. 290. Augustine writes of God being the author of time and of all genius. See *On Christian Doctrine*, Bk II, ch. 28, §44 and Bk IV, ch. 7, §21, *NPNF* First Series, Vol. II, pp. 549 and 581.

logue, however, implies an experience of communication which is incomplete without human response. God alone is the author of our life and salvation; we have no claim upon God but are invited into relationship with God. Simultaneously, however, the invitation to relationship with God requires a response which involves free will and different kinds of emotional, intellectual and physical effort. God enables this response by virtue of the structural conditions built into creation and the operation of the Holy Spirit in enlivening our many faculties and applying the work of Christ to us personally. We can speak of dialogue between creator and created only because God's grace makes such communication possible. Yet God's Word is not adrift in the cosmos without intention or design, but is directed towards intended hearers in anticipation of response; God's Word is answerable. In so far as this response or answering occurs within the ethical dimensions of life, then it is the concern of Christian ethics.

Biblical and traditional witness to the human vocation to communion with God

Let's start by noting traditional witness to humanity's vocation to communion with God. This takes different forms, but the dialogic authority of God is evident when we consider that the human power of speech is linked to rational nature. Humans partake of reason and their lives are ordered by mind. What's especially important about this is that, as Gregory says, reason was not, strictly speaking, given by God, but imparted. It became part of human nature; it was something to be used and developed. There was a certain open-endedness and lack of finality about the gift. God gave humans the imprint of his image, and reason was the means by which the divine image was realised in them. The illustration that he uses is of a skilled musician who needs instruments with which to make music. Humans are created in the image of God with the rational ability to 'make music' and realise their gift. In giving the gift of music however, God did not provide only one set of scored notes. The gift of reason was open and not closed or limited. There is an openness and lack of finality about God's gift, which tells us again that his authority is of an enabling and dialogic kind. God's dialogical authority is also evident to believers in their lives of prayer. In the *Great Catechism*, Gregory of Nyssa explains that God has promised to be present always with those that believe: 'He remains among them collectively and has special intercourse with each one.'[8]

Nor is this special intercourse a New Testament development. Consider, for example, how Old Testament wisdom literature suggests that human experience of interaction with divine Wisdom is dialogic in so far as the structural conditions for dialogic relationship between God/the author and creation/the hero are given by the Spirit of God, who is both eternal and present within time-limited creation. There is some disagreement among biblical scholars as to the relationship between creation and wisdom.[9] As Leo G. Perdue outlines, wisdom has been interpreted within a paradigm of history (G. Ernest Wright, Gerhard von Rad), within dialectic of history and creation (Claus Westermann), in canonical perspective (Brevard Childs), and in rhetorical and feminist terms (Phyllis Trible, and, we might add, C. A. Newsom, Claudia V. Camp, Elisabeth Schüssler Fiorenza and Elizabeth Johnson). Some of these differences can be explained by the ambiguity of language in biblical passages that speak of wisdom at length. For example, the following passage speaks of wisdom both as a defining structural feature of the world, and as a companion present with God from eternity:

> The Lord created me at the beginning of his work,
>   the first of his acts of long ago.
> Ages ago I was set up,
>   at the first, before the beginning of the earth.

---

8. Gregory of Nyssa, *The Great Catechism*, ch. XXXIV, *NPNF* Second Series, Vol. V, p. 501.

9. For a useful summary of recent developments, see Leo G. Perdue, *Wisdom and Creation* (Nashville, TN: Abingdon Press, 1994).

When there were no depths I was brought forth,
   when there were no springs abounding with water.
Before the mountains had been shaped,
   before the hills, I was brought forth –
when he had not yet made earth and fields,
   or the world's first bits of soil.
When he established the heavens, I was there,
   when he drew a circle on the face of the deep,
When he made firm the skies above,
   when he established the fountains of the deep,
when he assigned to the sea its limit,
   so that the waters might not transgress his command,
when he marked out the foundations of the earth,
   then I was beside him, like a master worker;
and I was daily his delight,
   rejoicing before him always,
rejoicing in his inhabited world
   and delighting in the human race.

                    (Prov. 8:22–31)

The meaning of the phrase, translated in the *NRSV* as 'the Lord created me', is at the centre of this dispute because the Hebrew *qanah* can be rendered 'possessed' (*AV*), or 'brought forth' (alternative reading in *NIV*). Carole R. Fontaine notes that the Targum, and also Greek and Syriac versions, understood *qanah* as 'begot me', and that the ambiguity of the phrase has given rise to widely variant understandings of wisdom as 'a sexually conceived child of God or a pre-existent entity whom Yahweh acquires in order to begin creation'.[10] Thus Gerhard von Rad can write of this passage: '[T]here is nothing directly divine and nothing mytho-logical about wisdom. It is certainly not a divine attribute which

---

10. Carole R. Fontaine, 'Proverbs' in Carol A. Newsom and Sharon H. Ringe, *Women's Bible Commentary Expanded Edition* (Louisville, KY: Westminster John Knox Press, 1998), p. 156. See also Athalya Brenner (ed.), *A Feminist Companion to Wisdom Literature* (Sheffield: Sheffield Academic Press, 1996).

has become independent. Nor has one any grounds for speaking of a personification.'[11] By contrast, Elisabeth Schüssler Fiorenza argues strongly that 'Wisdom' is divine: 'Wisdom' is the divine power of liberation: 'Divine Wisdom-Sophia, as G*d the Creator and Liberator ... is at work among all peoples, cultures, and religions ... Divine Wisdom encompasses and sustains everything and everyone.'[12]

For present purposes, we can accept Michael Welker's conclusion that these passages witness to early experiences of the Spirit of God's power, and that Christian tradition later interprets them in explicitly trinitarian terms.[13] Of interest to us, however, are the links between wisdom's role in creation and the knowledge of creation that it imparts to humankind, and the kind of relationship it establishes between creator and created. Consider how, in Proverbs 1–9, the wisdom given to those who fear the Lord (Prov. 2:5) is also the wisdom used by God in ordering of the world, and in establishing the structural conditions of the cosmos. Wisdom calls to persons of every age and is 'a tree of life to those who lay hold of her' (Prov. 3:18). But wisdom is also depicted as divine skill or knowledge by which God planned the universe:

> THE LORD by wisdom founded the earth;
>   by understanding he established the heavens;
> by his knowledge the deeps broke open,
>   and the clouds drop down the dew.
>
> (Prov. 3:19–20)

Wisdom is metaphorically presented as a teacher calling to human-

---

11. Gerhard von Rad, *Wisdom in Creation* (London: SCM, 1972), p. 148.

12. Elisabeth Schüssler Fiorenza, *Sharing Her Word* (Edinburgh: T. & T. Clark, 1998), p. 180.

13. Michael Welker, *God the Spirit* (Minneapolis: Fortress Press, 1994, German edition 1992), ch. 2, esp. pp. 105–107. He notes, for example, that Wisd. of Sol. 9:17 treats receiving wisdom and receiving the Spirit as one thing, or at least as parallel to each other: 'Who has learned of your counsel, unless you have given wisdom and sent your holy Spirit from on high?'

kind, in whose presence knowledge, beauty, insight, fertility (of body and mind), prudence and justice cohere:

> 'To you, O people, I call,
>   and my cry is to all that live.
> O simple ones, learn prudence;
>   acquire intelligence, you who lack it.
> Hear, for I will speak noble things,
>   and from my lips will come what is right;
> for my mouth will utter truth;
>   wickedness is an abomination to my lips.'
>
> (Prov. 8:4–7)

Wisdom is of inestimable worth to human persons and can be sought by them (Prov. 8:18–21). But it is also presented metaphorically as a divine attribute or companion who delighted in the human race from the beginning, and was brought forth by God before the origins of the earth (Prov. 8:22–31).

The New Testament distinguishes more clearly between the person of the Holy Spirit and the gifts which she bestows on persons (1 Cor. 12). In the Old Testament, however, distinctions are less clearly drawn between the wisdom by which God created and the calling to humanity to participate in the divine perfections. What is important to our argument, however, is that it is the same Spirit of God by which the universe was created, by which the universe continues to be sustained in being, and by which humankind is endowed with gifts of freedom, self-determination, and the power to choose the good. Gregory of Nyssa hints at this when speaking of God's ordering of the universe so that the intellectual and sensible aspects of human experience are in harmony with one another because both are pervaded by the presence of the Spirit:

> The world of thought is bodiless, impalpable, and figureless; but the sensible is, by its very name, bounded by those perceptions which come through the organs of sense. But as

in the sensible world itself, though there is a considerable mutual opposition of its various elements, yet a certain harmony maintained in those opposites has been devised by the wisdom that rules the Universe, and thus there is produced a concord of the whole creation with itself, and the natural contrariety does not break the chain of agreement; in like manner, owing to the Divine wisdom, there is an admixture and interpenetration of the sensible with the intellectual department, in order that all things may equally have a share in the beautiful, and no single one of existing things be without its share in that superior world.[14]

According to God's ordering of human nature, the intellectual and sensible have a harmonious unity because both are held in being by the Wisdom of God. This Wisdom is the power by which God realised the divine creative will in creation/the product: 'an essential power, regarded as self-centred in its own proper person, yet equally incapable of being separated from God in whom it is, or from the Word of God whom it accompanies, as from melting into nothingness'.[15] The Old Testament evidences ambiguity regarding Wisdom as a name for one of the three persons of the Trinity, a divine attribute, a divine energy, or the source of all human wisdom. In Christian tradition, however, it is established that the name 'Wisdom' communicates to us all of the above, and also that creation is bound to the creative will of God within the economy of the Holy Spirit.

There is little doubt in orthodox Christian tradition that contemplation of the divine mystery transcends human knowledge and relies on grace rather than reason.[16] Human thought breaks

---

14. Gregory of Nyssa, *The Great Catechism*, ch. IV, *NPNF* Second Series, Vol. V, p. 480.

15. Gregory of Nyssa, *The Great Catechism*, ch. II, *NPNF* Second Series, Vol. V, p. 477.

16. Vladimir Lossky, *The Mystical Theology of the Eastern Church* (London: James Clarke & Co., 1957), ch. 1.

down before the glory of God. This said, there is place for reasoned reflection on the mystery of God, as revealed in the grace of revelation; the theological task is, in part, to present the coherence and reasonableness of Christian truth. Silence and discourse mutually imply one another. Thus, in the wisdom literature, readers are urged to live in fear of the Lord (Prov. 2:5), to allow wisdom into their hearts (Prov. 2:10), to learn from wisdom's prompting (Prov. 3:1), not to forsake her but to love her (Prov. 4:6), and to say to her ' "You are my sister" ' (Prov. 7:4). Each of these encouragements is an invitation to reasoned reflection in communication with a living person. Thus, wisdom invites her followers to 'Come, eat of my bread and drink of the wine I have mixed' (Prov. 9:5), and is 'at home in the mind of one who has understanding' (Prov. 14:33). In Job, wisdom is about discovering the deep things of God (Job 11:7), and learning that '[w]ith God are wisdom and strength; he has counsel and understanding' (Job 12:13). Job associates wisdom with silence in the face of God. Yet he regards God as a dialogue partner: 'Hear, and I will speak; I will question you, and you declare to me' (Job 10:1–3ff, 13:3, 42:4). And God answered Job and spoke with him (Job 38:1, 40:1). Wisdom is the possibility of communion with God that, within human experience, is dialogic in character.

Dialogue as manifest in different types of discourse

Thus, it is arguable that biblical witness to the Spirit of Wisdom gives sufficient warrant to investigate the possibility that the kenotic authority of God/the author has dialogic character. Let us pursue the matter by employing the same kind of discourse analysis used by Bakhtin in his investigation of Dostoevsky's novels. According to Bakhtin, Dostoevsky is unlike his predecessors in allowing his authorial voice to be hidden or disguised. His authority was exercised in kenotic and dialogic fashion, and Bakhtin argues that we see this most clearly in the various types of discourse found commonly in novels. If we look carefully at the types of dialogue mentioned by Bakhtin, it becomes evident that the authority of authorship need not be restricted to an agent of control and discourager of self-expression. To the contrary, discourse in a novel by Dostoevsky can be genuinely interactive, open-ended, and enabling of human self-expression.

In what follows, I take Bakhtin's perception of the four main types of discourse found commonly within novels, including those of Dostoevsky, and apply his findings to various biblical witnesses to divine authority. What emerges is that the bible contains examples of witnesses to all four types of discourse and the kind of authority that they represent. Of particular interest to us is the fact that the bible, and also Christian tradition, witness to the authority of God as dialogic. Bakhtin lists four main types of discourse: (1) Direct, unmediated discourse directed exclusively towards its referential object as an expression of the speaker's ultimate semantic authority; (2) objectified discourse (discourse through a representative person); (3) discourse with an orientation towards someone else's discourse (double-voiced discourse); (4) discourse that is hidden and indirect.[17] He is not unconcerned with categories (1) and (2), remarking, for instance, that the element of address is essential to every discourse in Dostoevsky.[18] However, his interest is mainly with categories (3) and (4), the former because it is in the interchange between voices that dialogue lives, and the latter because it is here that his 'theology' of authoring is most explicitly informed by Christology. Just as the Word of God took human flesh in Christ, so the words of the author become embodied and active in literary forms. If we apply these types of discourse to a Christian understanding of the authority of God, we get some surprising results. Types (1) and (2) are familiar to us. Type (3) is less familiar but, if we widen our consideration of God's authority to include type (3), we find several instances of it in both bible and tradition.

---

17. M. M. Bakhtin, *Problems of Dostoevsky's Poetics*, ed. and trans. Caryl Emerson (Minnesota: UMP, 1984), p. 199.
18. Bakhtin, *Problems of Dostoevsky's Poetics*, p. 237.

Type 1: Direct and unmediated discourse

For example, if we opt primarily for etymological and lexical studies in our consideration of God's authority, we uncover a picture of God's authority which is indirectly analogous to Bakhtin's discourse type (1). Using etymological and lexical studies only, it is easy to conclude that God's authority in the Old Testament has to do solely with this kind of authority because it associates God's authority with concepts of being master of, or having dominion over, subjects who need to be governed. Hebrew has no word for the abstract concept described by the English 'authority', though the Septuagint used *exousia* to translate a number of Hebrew words, an example being *shalat* which was used of the seizure or exercise of political power (Esth. 9:1; Eccl. 5:19, 6:2). When applied to God, the implication is that God's authority is that of an absolute monarch (Eccl. 8:4), king or judge (Ecclus 9:13). This is the kind of authority in which much more emphasis is placed on the objective than on subjective moments of communication. These texts, however, are of relatively late authorship within the canon and do not supply the sole material with which to construct a biblically informed theology of authority, and do not exhaust a reading of the Old Testament on our subject.

Type 2: Discourse through a representative person

There are also many occasions at which the Old Testament recounts for us how God used intermediaries to convey his message. God becomes a 'represented person', to use Bakhtin's phrase, whose word is spoken or reported by another (i.e., type (2) discourse). Moses, for example, is portrayed by each of the Yahwist, Elohist and Priestly sources of the Hexateuch to be a spokesperson of God. In what is (probably) the Yahwist source, God speaks directly to Moses as the representative of the people of Israel and Moses, in turn, conveys the word of God to the people (Exod. 3:7–15). Moses is an inspired shepherd whom Jahweh used to make his will known.[19] The Elohist source stresses the priestly and miraculous character of Moses' representative role (Ex. 3:10–22, 4:16, 9:23), and the Priestly document indicates that Moses' representative role was assigned to Aaron (Ex. 7:9, 19; 8:5, 16), although Moses' primary function remains that of passing the word of God on to Israel. As Gerhard von Rad notes, the most impressive corroboration of Moses' mediatory role is the fact that the corpus of Deuteronomy is put into the form of his words.[20] Another major mediatory figure is Elisha, who brought the word of the Lord that Jehu and the house of Israel should march against Jehoram and the house of Ahab (2 Kgs 9 – 10). And there are many others (Num. 24:14; 1 Sam. 9:27; Jer. 5:14; Ezek. 3:27).

Type 3: 'Double-Voiced' Discourse

Thus there is plenty of evidence in the Old Testament to suggest that God's authority is direct and unmediated, and that his will is conveyed through the mouths of appointed representatives. Are there any instances in which the bible speaks of God's authority in ways corresponding to Bakhtin's discourse type (3), i.e., in dialogical terms, in which authority becomes known in more discursive fashion? Astonishingly, there are. Examples abound not only in the wisdom literature where they might be expected, but also in prophecy, various forms of historical narrative and myth. In the wisdom literature, Job says that he would speak with the Almighty and is ready to argue with God (Job 13:3). He experienced times when God did not answer his pleading (Job 30:20), yet he invites the Almighty to state his case against him (Job 31:35). Having put questions to God and listened to God's answers, Job realises that no human has the right to argue with God (Job 40:2, 42:4–6). There has, however, been a real struggle between

---

19. This point is made by Gerhard von Rad, *Old Testament Theology* (Edinburgh and London: Oliveer & Boyd, 1962; German edition 1957), Vol. 1, p. 293. I am indebted to his work in this section.
20. Von Rad, *Old Testament Theology*, Vol. 1, p. 294.

the two parties, and the closing verses do not represent the elimination of Job's voice but his gaining of wisdom. Deutero-Isaiah pleads with the people to open their ears to the words of the Lord and respond when he calls them by name (Is. 42:20, 43:1). The Lord calls for witnesses to pass judgement on his dealings with Israel (Is. 43:8–12) and invites the people to consult with him (Is. 45:21). God is not deaf to the people's cries and even argues and disagrees with them (Is. 65:24; Ezek. 14:4). There is, of course, always what Bakhtin might call a 'surplus' of divine authority in the sense that the relationship between God and the people is never a relationship of equals. Israel's covenant relationship with God reinforces that point. There are, however, many examples of 'double-voiced discourse' in which there is an interchange of meaning between two parties, one of which is God. This is also true of narrative literature. Consider how Abraham bartered with the Lord over the number of innocent people that would warrant the sparing of Sodom and Gomorrah (Gen. 18:23–33), or how Moses was (according to all traditions) frequently permitted to speak directly with God (Ex. 19:19, 33:11, 34:35; Deut. 18:20) and how he successfully beseeched God to heal the skin disease with which Miriam had been smitten (Num. 12:13–15). David consulted the Lord concerning the cause of a three-year famine and received a clear reply (2 Sam. 21:1). He called to the Lord regarding the site of the temple and the Lord answered with fire from heaven (1 Chron. 21:26, 28). Elijah's communication with God at Horeb was not so dramatic: 'the Lord was not in the fire', but spoke in a faint murmuring sound (1 Kgs 19:12 *REB*) to ask Elijah why he was there. In mythic literature also, God is portrayed as walking and talking with humanity (Gen. 3:3–13).

These examples come from a range of sources which reflect different periods within, and perspectives on, the history of Israel. They represent what Bakhtin might call examples of micro-dialogue, i.e., small components of a larger dialogue ongoing over a longer period of time, and include many instances in which the voices of humans meet, and sometimes collide, with the voice of

God. In each example, we can observe a twofold direction to the discourse so that rejoinders are taken into account, responded to and anticipated. In none of the examples cited is discourse dealt with as if only one of the parties was a genuine participant; discourse is not treated 'within the limits of a *single monologic context*'.[21] The macro-dialogue within which they are included is God's covenant relationship with all Israel, which belongs to the concrete context of the history of salvation. Philosophers of religion might describe Israel's covenant relationship with God as a form of theological determinism because, given God's lordship and foreknowledge of history, there is an inevitability or necessity in events or human actions. This was not, however, how Israel experienced it. There was never a time when Israel stood in a neutral relationship to God; its existence and history never occurred outside of God's providence, and biblical texts indicate that Israel's freedom to choose whether or not to obey God's command was real (Deut. 30:19; Josh. 24:15; Is. 7:15, 16). Thus Gerhard von Rad can devote one chapter in his *Old Testament Theology* to God's covenant with David, and give the following chapter the subtitle: 'Israel's Answer'.[22]

There is a twofold direction to discourse between Israel and God at both macro-and micro-levels. God's relationship with Israel as creator, redeemer and faithful covenant partner is characterised by dialogue in which the speech of each party is oriented towards that of the other. To borrow Bakhtin's words: 'dialogic relationship can permeate inside the utterance'.[23] God's utterances, which are intended to bless and save his people, are dialogic in character. Dialogue happens in Israel's relationship with God, and in the relationships of named persons with God. There are instances of dialogue which can be described as Bakhtin's types (1) and (2). However, God speaks to the people not only with the kind of

---

21. Bakhtin, *Problems of Dostoevsky's Poetics*, p. 185.
22. Von Rad, *Old Testament Theology*, Vol. 1, chs C and D.
23. Bakhtin, *Problems of Dostoevsky's Poetics*, p. 184.

authority that tolerates no opposition, or in ways that are mediated through representative persons, but also in ways that engage named persons intimately in affairs of the heart. If we turn our attention to the New Testament, we find that the kind of dialogue which Bakhtin names type (3), i.e., double-voiced or interactive in a twofold direction, is even more typical of God's relationship with the people, in that the Word of God is embodied in Jesus Christ (Jn 1:14; Phil. 2:6–8). God actually enters into the dialogue-world of a particular time and place, and interacts with a polyphony of voices, some of which were openly hostile. Jesus' teaching ministry, and especially his teaching in parables, could be analysed in terms of the kind of dialogic interactions they evoke. For the moment, let us note biblical witness to the fact that the kind of authority exercised by God, the author of all creation, does take into account the words of others in dialogical relations of a two-way direction.

Type 4: Hidden and indirect discourse

It is also arguable that God's authority as author is real in hidden and indirect ways. Bakhtin describes a type of dialogic practice in which one party is hidden and direct communication is either omitted or suspended, which is, again, suggestive of a divine activity. Once again, his consideration of various ways of authoring provokes fresh consideration of our topic. 'Imagine', he urges,

> a dialogue of two persons in which the statements of the second speaker are omitted, but in such a way that the general sense is not at all violated. The second speaker is present invisibly, his words are not there, but deep traces left by these words have a determining influence on all the present and visible words of the first speaker. We sense that this is a conversation, although only one person is speaking, and it is a conversation of the most intense kind, for each present, uttered word responds and reacts with its fibre to the invisible

speaker, points to something outside itself, beyond its own limits, to the unspoken words of another person.[24]

Again, there is no direct analogy to the creative authorship of God because of the category difference between the authoring of creation and the authoring of a novel. However, his suggestion invites consideration of whether God's authority of authorship is also in some sense indirect, and, if so, whether this tells us more about the character of God's authority and human experience of it.

Despite working within a Wellhausen-inspired school of thought, Gerhard von Rad warns us against an over-simplistic assumption that Israel did not venerate God as creator in some way before the sixth or seventh centuries, on grounds that it is hard to imagine that, with knowledge of Canaanite, Babylonian and other creation myths, Israel would not have made some connection between Jahweh and the existence of the earth, stars, sea, plants etc. This is confirmed by mention of creation in a small number of old passages (Gen. 14:19, 22; 24:3; 1 Kgs 8:12; Ps. 19:1ff). He is convinced that a developed understanding of God as creator emerged from Israel's confession of God as redeemer and lord of history.[25] With these provisos, it would still appear that confessions of the authority of God as creator are closely related to confession of the saving acts of Yahweh in history. This is reflected in Deutero-Isaiah which provides some of the clearest acclamations of God as creator in the Old Testament. For example, after recalling the Lord's dealings with Judah following the delivery of Jerusalem from the Assyrians, Deutero-Isaiah urges the people: 'Lift up your eyes to the heavens; consider who created these, led out their host one by one, and summoned each by name' (Is. 40:26 *REB*). 'It is I who help you, declares the LORD; your redeemer is the Holy One of Israel . . . I shall open rivers on the arid heights,

---

24. Bakhtin, *Problems of Dostoevsky's Poetics*, p. 197.
25. 'The theological derivation of Jahweh's power over history from his authority as Creator is . . . a comparatively late idea (Jer. 27:4ff; Is. 45:12f).' Von Rad, *Old Testament Theology*, Vol. 1, p. 138.

and wells in the valleys' (Is. 41:14, 18 *REB*)'. 'These are the words of the LORD who is God, who created the heavens and stretched them out, who fashioned the earth and everything that grows in it, giving breath to its people and life to those who walk in it' (Is. 42:5 *REB*). Allusions to God as creator strengthen affirmations of God as historical redeemer. Redemption and creation are interlinked, especially in Is. 51:9–10, in which allusions to God as creator (the Lord who dried up the seas of the abyss) are intermingled with allusions to redemption (the Lord who made a path for the people through the waters [of Egypt]).[26] Israelite confession of the authority of God as creator develops as a dialogical kind of interaction between persons that allows for interchange between Israel and God/self and other, and is open to growing conceptions of truth.

The Incarnation as Dialogue

Thus, there are many different ways in which the Old Testament witnesses to dialogue between creator and created. God does not reduce hearers to passive partners but engages them in genuine relationship as 'other' to his 'I'. Dialogic interaction happens throughout the Old Testament as God's Spirit of Wisdom bestows on creatures the power of creaturely wisdom. It is the incarnation, however, which provides the paradigm from which to rethink the very nature and structure of dialogue.[27] Christian confession is that truth itself is embodied in Christ the incarnate Word of God. As Athanasius states:

---

26. On this, see Von Rad, *Old Testament Theology*, Vol. 1, pp. 137–138.

27. For Bakhtin, this is true also and is linked to the fact that authoring has to do with the incarnation of meaning, and meaning has dialogue at its heart. For example, he talks in 'Author and Hero in Aesthetic Activity' about authoring as involving 'an incarnation of meaning in existence' as distinct from 'a validation and demonstration of the truth of an idea'. M. M. Bakhtin, *Art and Answerability*, (Austin, TX: University of Texas, 1990), p. 10.

> What then was God to do? or what was to be done save the
> renewing of that which was in God's image, so that by it
> men might once more be able to know Him? But how could
> this have come to pass save by the presence of the very Image
> of God, our Lord Jesus Christ? For by men's means it was
> impossible, since they are but made after an image . . .
> Whence the Word of God came in His own person, that, as
> He was the Image of the Father, He might be able to create
> afresh the man after the image.[28]

Humanity was predestined to communion with God but was
hindered by the effects of sin. The incarnation restored the human
vocation to grow in the likeness of God, and it is with this growth
in godliness that Christian ethics is concerned. Such theological
affirmations might appear to be related to the practicalities of
moral decision-making only superficially. The contrary is true,
however, because the truths affirmed here affect profoundly the
purpose and potential of human life and, therefore, provide direction and criteria for the processes of moral reasoning. To use
Irenaeus's words, 'the Word of God, our Lord Jesus Christ . . . did,
through His transcendent love, become what we are, that He
might bring us to be even what He is Himself.'[29] The second
person of the holy Trinity assumed human nature in order that
we might share in the divine nature (2 Pet. 1:4). Christian ethics
(*ethos*) is shaped and coloured by what the incarnation makes
possible: restoration of the life lost through sin, sanctification of
the body (Rom. 12:1), acquiring of the mind of Christ (1 Cor.
2:16), and the fulfilling of God-given potential to attain maturity
in the faith which is to have the stature of Christ (Eph. 4:13).
These are fundamental theological affirmations, made possible
only in Christ who united humanity and divinity in his person.
They do not of themselves provide detailed prescriptions about

---

28. Athanasius, *Incarnation of the Word*, §13, *NPNF* Second Series, Vol. IV, p. 43.
29. Irenaeus, *Against Heresies*, *ANF*, Vol. I Bk V, Preface, p. 526.

particular forms of action, but they do provide appropriate goals and ideals to be realised in Christian freedom.

Typically, ancient eastern theologians talk about the mystery of the incarnation and salvation by affirming that the Word of God became truly human in order that humans might share in the divine life. The words of Irenaeus cited above are echoed by Athanasius, Gregory of Nazianzen, Gregory of Nyssa, and others, each of whom urges that the true content of salvation is union with God, and that the Word of God became human in order to make this possible. Athanasius writes: 'For He was made man that we might be made God.'[30] Similarly, Gregory of Nazianzen affirms: 'What is not assumed cannot be healed and what was united to God is saved.'[31] The kind of dialogue entailed can be understood primarily at the ontological level of salvation in Christ and renewed vocation to union and communion with God. The incarnation of the Word and the salvation effected by the life, death, resurrection and ascension of Jesus Christ are closely linked to participation in divine goodness and the restoration of human destiny to be united with God.

According to Athanasius, it was not fitting that any part of God's good gifts of creation should go to rack and ruin. It was not worthy of God's goodness that the things God had created should waste away because of 'the deceit practised on men by the devil'.[32] All things in God's good creation had been originally moved and quickened by the Word of God. Therefore, at the incarnation, all things were once more filled by the presence of the Word: 'For this purpose, then, the incorporeal and incorruptible and immaterial Word of God comes to our realm . . . He has filled all things everywhere, remaining present with His own Father.'[33] No part of creation had been left void of the Word at

---

30. Athanasius, *Incarnation of the Word*, §54, *NPNF* Second Series, Vol. IV, p. 65.
31. Gregory Nazianzen, *Letter CI*, to Cledonius, *PG* 37 col. 181, c.184a.
32. Athanasius, *Incarnation of the Word*, §6, *NPNF* Second Series, Vol. IV, p. 39.
33. Athanasius, *Incarnation of the Word*, §6, *NPNF* Second Series, Vol. IV, p. 40.

creation. Therefore, no part was excluded when the Word assumed humanity and shared our human life:

> He 'delivered' to Him [the Son] man, that the Word Himself might be made Flesh, and by taking the Flesh, restore it wholly. For to Him, as to a physician, man 'was delivered' to heal the bite of the serpent; as to life, to raise what was dead; as to light, to illumine the darkness; and, because He was Word, to renew the rational nature.[34]

Because of what God has done in Christ, the natural movement of all creation is towards God. This is not a denial of the difference of creation to God, but affirmation of the human vocation in Christ and of the fact that the Word of God became truly human and 'henceforth the whole conspiracy of the enemy against mankind [sic] is checked'.[35] It was not proper that God's good creation which had been made for incorruption should die because of the wiles of the devil, and, therefore, so Athanasius argues, the Word of God did what was required for creation to be saved from the penalty of death: 'For by the sacrifice of His own body, He . . . made a new beginning of life for us, by the hope of resurrection which He has given us.'[36] The Word of God, who had filled all things at creation, was 'alone of natural fitness' to recreate all things, including the human destiny to become one with God. The remainder of this chapter is concerned with how we interpret the implications of this destiny in the ethical spheres of life. There will be implications for, *inter alia*, our understanding of Christ's claim to be the truth (Jn 14:6), the scope of Christian ethics, the status of human moral capacities, the difference between a Christian understanding of person and secular concepts of the

---

34. Athanasius, *On Luke X. 22 (Matt. XI. 27)*, NPNF Second Series, Vol. IV, p. 87.
35. Athanasius, *Incarnation of the Word*, §6, NPNF Second Series, Vol. IV, p. 41.
36. Athanasius, *Incarnation of the Word*, §10, NPNF Second Series, Vol. IV, p. 41.

individual, the existential unity of soul and body, ethical relations with other persons in Christ, and with one's body.[37]

Developing a Chalcedonian Way of Thinking

In the post-Enlightenment era, a Chalcedonian way of thinking has been subjected to criticism from many points of view. F. C. Baur maintained that Paul's orthodoxy outweighed everyone else's.[38] Early in the twentieth century, William Temple argued that Chalcedon marked the bankruptcy of Greek patristic theology and the start of the breakdown of Christian theology in general, because the agreed definition merely stated the problem and did not attempt a solution.[39] In our own day, similar questions are asked about the 'myth of orthodoxy' in which clerical and politically established Christianity supposedly won out over the original form of the Jesus movement. Rosemary Radford Ruether argues that Paul began an insidious process of obscuring the quality of Jesus' humanness, so that his own opinions became the touchstone of the Christian church and its ministry, thus imposing his authority on the diverse and syncretistic Christian movement, with the result that Chalcedon became associated with the gender-

---

37. Not all of these implications can be considered in this chapter, but we shall pick up questions about the scope of Christian ethics and the status of human moral capacities, and others will be developed in later chapters. Central to each, however, are questions about what the incarnation reveals about the truth of human existence, and what difference an understanding of Christ's personhood makes to perceptions of our own personhood, embodiment, relationality and God-given potential.

38. F. C. Baur, *Paul the Apostle of Jesus Christ: His Life and Works, His Epistles and Teachings*, trans. A. Menzies, 2nd edn (London: Williams & Norgate, 1873, 1875), *passim*.

39. See William Temple's essay in B. H. Streeter (ed.), *Foundations: A Statement of Christian Belief in Terms of Modern Thought by Seven Oxford Men* (London: Macmillan, 1913), Essay V, p. 230.

and generational-hierarchy of patriarchy in the Christian church.[40] For different reasons, Jürgen Moltmann thinks that a Chalcedonian approach risks leading us to 'speculate in heavenly riddles' in ways that detract from the totality of either the person of Christ or the task of ecclesiology.[41] He seeks an ecclesiology based on a reconstructed Messianic Christology which rethinks the traditional Chalcedonian statement of faith, starting with 'the church in history' rather than the church as the body of Christ, and is wary of a two-nature Christology and an ecclesiology that deals in negative and oppositional definitions and arrives continually at impasse.[42] The question for Christian ethics is whether a Chalcedonian way of thinking, which looks to Christ for the perfect synergy (Greek *syn*, meaning 'with' and *ergon*, meaning 'work') of divine and human wills and for the possibility of human union and communion with God, is subject to similar kinds of problems. Can a Chalcedonian way of thinking, according to which the

---

40. Orthodoxy, as embodied in the ecumenical creeds, became complicit with state power; thus Augustine is the 'father of the inquisition, applying his views of original sin to rationalise coercive use of state power to force dissenting Christians to submit to church authority'. Rosemary Radford Ruether, *Women and Redemption: A Theological History* (London: SCM, 1998), pp. 75 and 126.

41. Jürgen Moltmann, *The Crucified God* (London: SCM, 1974), pp. 200–207, esp. p. 207.

42. For a useful account of J. Moltmann's ecclesiology, see Richard Bauckham, *The Theology of Jürgen Moltmann* (Edinburgh: T. & T. Clark, 1995), ch. 6. In some similarity, Wolfhart Pannenberg argues that when 'the contradiction between God and the creature is the starting point for thought', i.e., when we start from the two natures, it is not possible to proceed to understanding of their unity: 'Jesus now appears as a being bearing and uniting two opposed substances in himself. From this conception all the insoluble problems of the doctrine of the two natures result.' He thinks that the definition was an unsatisfactory compromise between Alexandrian and Antiochene theology, leading to an unsatisfactory way of doing Christology which begins with the duality of divinity and humanity and results in the insoluble problems of the doctrine of the two natures. Wolfhart Pannenberg, *Jesus – God and Man*, trans. Lewis L. Wilkins and Duane A. Priebe (London: SCM, 1968, German edn 1964), p. 284.

incarnation is related directly to the truth and goal of what it is to be human, give direction and shape to Christian ethics?

It is clearly to swim against a strong tide to maintain that a Chalcedonian way of thinking can and should be employed in contemporary discourse about divine authority and Christian ethics. In what follows, however, I argue that there is more to be gained from ancient credal ways of thinking than this kind of criticism allows. A Chalcedonian way of thinking need not end up with a 'Christology without Jesus', or an ethic that speculates in heavenly riddles, and yet can remain faithful to Christian confession that the living Word became truly human in order that 'the entire humanity fallen through sin might be created anew'.[43] At issue are epistemological questions concerning the source of truth about Christian living, soteriological questions about the effects of sin upon humanity's creation in the image of God, anthropological questions about human nature as coexistence of body and soul, and eschatological questions about the hope of union with God. More specifically, there are ethical questions about the hope and goal(s) of Christian living, humanity's liability to sin, the restored human capacity to receive the *theoria* or vision of God, and the possibilities in both this life and the next of human participation in the life divine. All these were issues that concerned the church in the fourth and fifth centuries AD – not least in debates between Athanasius and Apollinarius concerning the question of the human soul of Jesus Christ, and between Nestorius and Cyril concerning the unity of Godhead and humanity – and the church dealt with them by finding ways to hold together and distinguish two things: the truth of God in Christ and the reality of the human condition. Chalcedon has been criticised as both resulting from and leading to dichotomous ways of thinking.[44] It has been

---

43. Gregory Nazianzen, *Letter CI*, to Cledonius, *NPNF* Second Series, Vol. VII, pp. 439–443.
44. Pannenberg, *Jesus – God and Man*, pp. 287–307, 183–187. For Pannenberg, Jesus' unity with the Father is found in its general immediacy, i.e., in the ▷

condemned as a compromise providing no definition or explanation, and as not achieving any resolution for the two opposing solutions of Antioch and Alexandria; it was, indeed, the result of concerns in a particular historical context. These difficulties acknowledged, a Chalcedonian way of thinking allows us to affirm both that the truth of humanity is revealed to us from another realm of existence and is not generated by ourselves, and also that Christian ethics concerns daily response in personal freedom to the truth revealed in Christ (Jn 1:17, 8:32, 17:17; Rom. 9:1, 15:8; Gal. 5:7; Eph. 5:9; 1 Tim. 2:4).

This said, it is important to observe that the declaration is apophatic in character: 'the union of the two natures is expressed by four negative definitions.'[45] The authority of the Word of God, as the union of divinity and humanity in Christ, remains for us a mystery. So also does the synergy of divine grace and human will. Humanity can never become *theioi* or sons (*sic*) of God as Christ is: 'He is the Father's Power and Wisdom and Word, not being so by participation'.[46] It is also important to set the statement within the theological context of the second and third centuries AD. Otherwise we risk turning it into an abstract formula to be applied indiscriminately to disparate theological problems. There is nothing mystical or mathematical about the declaration itself;

---

concept of intention. Jesus' self-consciousness consists in 'perfection in dedication'; sonship is 'taking his relationship to the Father as the point of departure'. Ontology features little, and he does not claim that Jesus' work points at every step to ontological and epistemological implications. He denies that Jesus was only 'a man like Socrates', and affirms that ontological certainties are noetically confirmed only through the unity of Jesus' intent with the will of the Father, and later through the vindication of the resurrection. Messianic titles, especially, e.g., Jn 10:30 ('I and the Father are one'), are judged to be problematic.

45. I.e., Christ is unconfusedly, immutably, indivisibly, inseparably two natures in one person. This point is made by Lossky, *Mystical Theology of the Eastern Church*, p. 143.

46. Athanasius, *Against the Heathen*, III, §46, *NPNF* Second Series, Vol. IV, pp. 28–29.

it is simply an ecumenically agreed statement in which fundamental tenets of Christian doctrine are confessed in conformity
with the Niceno-Constantinopolitan Creed. These fundamental
tenets concern the full humanity and divinity of Christ and the
consequent renewal of the human vocation – which is at the heart
of Christian ethics – to union and communion with God. It is
also important to observe that the declaration is cataphatic in
character; it affirms unambiguously that the Word of God did not
assume human nature as a single lump but, rather, full human
personhood. Ancient Christian arguments that the incarnation
annihilated the principle of corruption, and that humanity is freed
from alienation from God, should not be taken to mean that personal distinctiveness is somehow lost in a vast ocean of humanity.
In assuming humanity, the Word did not assume a homogeneous
mass but became a human person united to God through conscious
apprehension and free will.[47] Similarly, humans are not portions
of humanity, or of Christ, but persons, each one of whom is absolutely original and unique. Persons, not humanity per se, make
decisions for good or ill, and are responsible for their actions.[48]

---

47. It was Apollinarius, not Athanasius, for whom divinity and humanity could
not be coexistent in one person because, as human, Jesus Christ would have
been liable to sin; as divine, the Logos was immutable (*atreptos*) and impassible
(*apathes*). For Apollinarius, human nature once tainted could not be cleansed;
at the fall, the human soul became utterly irrational and without life so that
there was no human nature free from sin for Christ to assume. To some extent
similarly, Athanasius holds that sin was the turning of understanding away from
God; disobedience and idolatry resulted in the image of God, which was rational
and vital, becoming irrational and mortal. For Athanasius, however, sin was not
the essence of humanity. The image of God was never completely lost; there
could be renewal and recreation. The authority of the Word was not limited by
the fallen human condition. Athanasius, *Against the Heathen*, Part II, §34, *NPNF*
Second Series, Vol. IV, p. 22.
48. Some qualification of this statement is needed with respect to the very
seriously mentally ill and, arguably, those enduring exceptionally intolerable
circumstances. There are also issues here relating to various kinds of determinism: genetic, psychological and social. I maintain, however, that Christian ▷

In what sense, therefore, is a Chalcedonian way of thinking dialogic? Is the incarnation directed towards dialogue and incomplete without an answer? What ethical implications follow? An adequate answer to these questions will, I suggest, have two dimensions. First is the recognition that Christian ethics is a response to divine initiative; as creatures we can make no claim upon God or presume to be engaged in dialogue with God. This means that Christian ethics is not first and foremost about choosing one course of action in preference to another, or weighing the relative value of rights and/or duties – even though these matters may be integral to the task. Rather, it is a response to divine initiative which entails ethical obligation. In assuming humanity, the Word of God healed its brokenness, thus restoring the human vocation to perfection (Matt. 5:48). Thus Christian ethics is a way of being that is sustained by God's mercy and directed by God's love. In this sense, it is not different in kind from prayer and worship and is informed by the norm of God's gracious relationship to us. Grace may be defined as God's being for us in ways that are truly affirmative of us. Following contemplation of Jn 1:1–14, Hilary of Poitiers writes that his trembling soul had learned there of the grace of God, and that this informed his understanding of the nature of liberty and power:

> Herein [i.e. in confession that the Word became flesh and dwelt among us] my soul, trembling and distressed, found a hope wider than it had imagined. First came its introduction to the knowledge of God the Father. Then it learnt that the eternity and infinity and beauty which, by the light of natural reason, it had attributed to its Creator belonged also to God the Only-begotten. . . . This lesson in the Divine mysteries

---

theologians will want to keep a clear distinction between such predispositions and human responsibility for sin which is located in the will. We may have much more to learn about, e.g., genetic predisposition or determinism, but it will never be the same as human free will. The truth about human beings is much greater than their genetic, psychological or social make-up.

was gladly welcomed by my soul, now drawing near through the flesh to God, called to new birth through faith, entrusted with liberty and power to win the heavenly regeneration, conscious of the love of its Father and Creator, sure that He would not annihilate a creature whom He had summoned out of nothing into life.[49]

Similarly for Augustine: 'Now here the grace of God is displayed with the greatest power and clearness.'[50] Christ is a clear manifestation of divine grace. So also for John Chrysostom, in his homily on Colossians 1:9–10: 'For he that hath not known the Son, knoweth not the Father either.'[51] Unless Jesus Christ assumed full humanity, then, we have no ontological basis for unity with him and there is neither ground for hope in God nor ethical obligations that arise from that hope.

Second is the recognition that Christian ethics is a response to divine initiative which involves working out what it means to respond or 'answer' to God's Word in ways that signify the truth revealed. To emphasise the unmerited grace of God does not mean that human response to divine grace is downplayed. To the contrary, the dialogic nature of God's utterance invites a response, calling all persons to re-evaluate the truth of their own lives. As Bakhtin points out, a living word may or may not be a question but it always provokes an answer, anticipates an answer, and structures itself in the direction of an answer.[52] Dialogue is not rhetoric, because it seeks not only to persuade the addressee but to be genuinely open to their answer. The Liturgy of St Basil the Great speaks of God the Father being shown forth by the 'Living Word . . . the Wisdom before the ages, the Life, Sanctification, Power, the true Light. . . '. It contains several prayers that

49. Hilary of Poitiers, *On the Trinity*, Bk 1, §11, *NPNF* Second Series, Vol. IX, p. 43.

50. Augustine, *Enchiridion*, ch. 36, *NPNF* First Series, Vol. III, pp. 249–250.

51. John Chrysostom, *Homily II on Colossians*, *NPNF* First Series, Vol. XIII, p. 265.

52. Bakhtin, 'Discourse in the Novel', in *Problems of Dostoevsky's Poetics*, p. 280.

believers be instructed in 'the Word of truth', and 'partake' of the 'Wisdom and Word of God and Power . . . in the day without evening of thy kingdom'. The focal point of the liturgy is what God does for creation, but much attention is also given to the response of the people of God to divine grace. A prayer of Simeon the New Divine designated for use during holy communion includes the earnest request:

> receive this prayer, my Christ, and despise not my words . . .
> Suffer me to speak boldly that which I desire . . . O Word:
> but suffer me to embrace and kiss thy feet . . . O Word: forgive
> me my transgression and grant me pardon . . . My God and
> Master, every word of thine is true: when I partake of thy
> divine and deifying graces, then I am not alone, but with
> thee, my Christ . . . who art my breath, my life, my joy, the
> world's salvation . . .'[53]

Christ the living Word receives and hears the words of his hearers. He speaks words of truth and forgiveness, inviting addressees to partake of divine grace. He assumes the uniqueness of personal encounter and speaks directly to the heart. Thus Simeon the New Divine can say with confidence: 'No single tear-drop lieth hid from thee, my God, my Maker, my Deliverer, no, nor any part thereof. Thine eyes behold things in me that as yet are not . . .'[54] These eastern fathers emphasise the God-given role of human freedom in the Christian life, in the belief that God does not destroy our liberty but desires that we commune with the Godhead voluntarily (2 Cor. 6:1–2) and in ways that have ethical implications.[55] Ethically, this means that we are not passive recipients

---

53. *The Orthodox Liturgy, being the Divine liturgy of S. John Chrysostom and S. Basil the Great according to the Use of the Church of Russia* (London: SPCK, for the Fellowship of SS. Alban and Sergius, 1939), pp. 11–12.

54. Simeon the New Divine, cited in *The Orthodox Liturgy*, p. 12.

55. On this, see Anon., *Orthodox Spirituality*, published for The Fellowship of SS. Alban and Sergius (London: SPCK, 1957), p. 24.

of God's action, but called to responsive or answering action in the process of realising our full human potential. At issue is the character and quality of response to God's Word as enabled by the Holy Spirit.

In the remainder of this chapter, I argue that a more developed understanding of the God's Word in dialogue, especially God's Word as answerable, is essential to Christian ethics. The working assumption is that the authority of God's Word is not that of *auctoritas* (the power to enforce obedience) but grace, and that this prevents Christian ethics proper from ever being legalistic or rule-based, because the truth of God revealed in Christ is personal and dialogical. God created humans in the divine image rather than as automatons, and so it is fitting that the Word of God calls for an answer rather than smothers human response. According to ancient orthodoxy this dialogic relationship has eternal, ontological significance in so far as the Word of God assumes humanity and restores the human vocation to become like God (*theosis*) and to share in God's glory, love and peace (Is. 65:17–18; 1 Cor. 15:50–57; Eph. 4:13; Col. 2:10; 2 Pet. 1:4). It also has daily, practical significance in so far as the incarnation is the primary source of truth about Christian living. As Athanasius teaches, living the faith is to be related closely to the truth of salvation; God's Word is Word not only in name or notion but in reality, and that reality became incarnate that humanity might once more be able to know God.[56] To this end, I draw upon Bakhtin's work in thinking about dialogue as involving moments of utterance, event and answerability.

---

56. Athanasius, *Four Discourses Against the Arians*, Discourse IV, ch. XXV, §12, *NPNF* Second Series, Vol. IV, p. 437. Athanasius, *Incarnation of the Word*, §§11–13, *NPNF* Second Series, Vol. IV, pp. 42–43.

God's Word uttered

In a post-Barthian theological context, we are familiar with thinking about God's Word as utterance.[57] For Karl Barth, dogmatic reflection involves first hearing the Word of God which is uttered, and then speaking it faithfully. Christian ethics consists in the truth of the good revealed and given as the command of God.[58] Despite being delivered at a relatively early point in his career, Barth's 1928 and 1929 lectures on ethics centre around the utterance of God as the command of life. Obedience to God's utterance or command is an act of grace made possible in Christ. God alone is our witness and God alone is our judge.[59] The content of God's command is our reconciliation to God which takes place for Christ's sake and not because of human merit. As Barth makes plain, the Word of God is spoken as an answer to human need:

> God's revelation, which is the basis of Christian preaching, is the answer to our question how we can overcome the contradiction in our existence, which we have to view not as our destiny but as our responsible act, and which we know that we cannot overcome. But we know ourselves in this regard only as God makes himself known to us. We would not ask about God had not God already answered us. Because of this, we can neither evade the question about God nor settle it in any sense.[60]

This statement, which functions as a fundamental premise of *The Göttingen Dogmatics*, asserts that to stand before God means to

---

57. See Karl Barth, *The Göttingen Dogmatics: Instruction in the Christian Religion* (Grand Rapids, MI: Eerdmans, 1991), §1.
58. Karl Barth, *Ethics*, trans. G. W. Bromiley (Edinburgh: T. & T. Clark, date of publication not given), p. 73.
59. Barth, *Ethics*, p. 350.
60. Barth, *Göttingen Dogmatics*, §4.

set oneself under the question which God's Word addresses to humanity.[61] The miracle of faith is that one can recognise and accept God's authority though this encounter or address has the character of a question. It is clear in Barth's writings that God's Word as utterance and command does not force or coerce obedience, because human beings created in the image of God are created free. Truth is not synonymous with happiness, sincerity or well-meaning, but with the revelation of God in Jesus Christ. The world is sinful and weakened in its capacity to receive the utterance of divine love but, in Christ, the grace of God – which includes God's authority over humankind, the authority to judge, to reveal the truth about sinful humankind to itself and to effect judgement – is revealed.[62]

In some sense similar to Barth, Bakhtin regards utterance as having a fundamental role in the communication of a word/the Word as dialogic. Like Barth, Bakhtin (arguably) owes much to Augustine. Indeed, some interpreters see Bakhtin's work as a 'theology' of the Word which provides a quasi-Augustinian ontological framework within which to consider the dialogic nature of human existence. Alexandar Mihailovic writes:

---

61. Barth, *Göttingen Dogmatics*, §7.

62. For Barth, a Chalcedonian way of thinking is the most theologically adequate approach to both Christology and ecclesiology: '[T]here can be no question of abandoning the *vere Deus vere homo*. If it is a matter of the reconciliation of man with God in Jesus Christ, i.e., the reconciliation of man with God and by God, then obviously we have to do truly and wholly with God and truly and wholly with man. And the more exact determination of the relationship between God and man in the famous Chalcedonian definition, which has become normative for all subsequent development in this dogma and dogmatics, is one which in our understanding has shown itself to be factually right and necessary.' Karl Barth, *Church Dogmatics* IV.1, §58 (Edinburgh: T. & T. Clark, 1956), pp. 128–138. Barth, writes Hunsinger, has a 'deeply imbued Chalcedonian imagination', implying that the character of Christian truth, as expressed in the Chalcedonian definition, shapes his every thought-form. See George Hunsinger, *How to Read Karl Barth: The Shape of His Theology* (Oxford: OUP, 1991), p. 85.

What Bakhtin and members of his circle took from the theology of the Word was not just a specific structural paradigm (i.e., the relation of discourse to human or social reality) but also the very *idea* of structure, hypostasizing it into an architectonic metaphor. The Word thus becomes both edifice and event, a blend of time as well as space.[63]

He links Bakhtin's theology explicitly to the linguistic ontology of Augustine, suggesting that it is appropriate to make tentative connections between human perceptions of utterance, dialogue, existence in time and space, and Christ the living Word. Arguably more than Barth, however, Bakhtin regards every utterance as potentially dialogic: 'Every word is directed towards an *answer*

---

63. Alexandar Mihailovic, *Corporeal Words: Mikhail Bakhtin's Theology of Discourse* (Evanston, Illinois: Northwestern University Press, 1997), p. 44. Many readers of Bakhtin refuse to accept that a theology of the Word of God informs every aspect of his literary theory. I maintain, however, that Bakhtin's work is thoroughly informed by the Logos motif of Jn 1:14, and that this is sufficient reason to spur us on in our considerations. Michael Holquist wrote in 1982 that, in the 1920s, the incarnation was the epicentre of Bakhtin's work as he struggled to make connections between Christian confession that the Word became flesh, modern linguistics, and Soviet politics. (Michael Holquist, 'The Politics of Representation' in Stephen J. Greenblatt (ed.), *Allegory and Representation* (Baltimore, MD: Johns Hopkins Univ. Press, 1982), pp. 163–183.) He explained how the creative process of embodying ideas and lives in literary form has its correlate in the incarnational act of God in Jesus Christ. The incarnation in Christ was the paradigm according to which the incarnation of meaning in a text was understood. Eight years later, Caryl Emerson broadly agreed with Holquist but set Bakhtin's theological influences much more explicitly within the context of Russian Orthodoxy. Christ, writes Emerson, 'becomes the carrier' of Bakhtin's world-view. With reference to Chapter 3 of *Problems of Dostoevsky's Poetics* he writes: 'But can such a dialogically interdependent world acknowledge any genuine authority? Bakhtin says yes, and submits as his (and Dostoevsky's) ideal the image of Christ. Christ's truth is real, but its authority cannot always be known as dogmatic or as proposition.' (Caryl Emerson, 'Russian Orthodoxy and the Early Bakhtin', *Religion and Literature*, Vol. 22, Nos 2–3 (Summer-Autumn 1990), p. 113.)

and cannot escape the profound influence of the answering word that it anticipates.'[64] His open orientation towards the addressee means that the speaker does not cease to be active once a word/ the Word has been spoken, because the process of understanding reception and response remains under way. This process will vary according to the context into which a word/the Word is spoken, intonation, the addressee's state of consciousness, and many other variables.

Both Barth and Bakhtin share a sense that in the event of communication, every act of understanding is active and involves both speaker and addressee. For Barth, the Holy Spirit bears witness to Godself and enables a person to hear the Word: 'As the miracle of faith and obedience, this knowledge [i.e., of the Word of God] and action are both effected by the Holy Spirit, whom no one and nothing can replace as the subjective possibility of revelation.'[65] For Bakhtin, the utterance aspect of any event of communication comes to fruition in the response which the spoken word anticipated: 'Understanding and response are dialectically merged and mutually condition each other; one is impossible without the other.'[66] For each, a word/the Word is uttered at the boundary between its own context and that of the addressee and the dialogic aspect of the utterance calls for an answer. As Bakhtin writes, every utterance is 'pregnant with responses and objections'.[67] A word/the Word uttered becomes an event as its me,ning unfolds among persons and within situations that are unic,ue. The sense/content of a word, even when linked grammatically to other words, does not drop into one's head as 'a meteor from another world' but is 'woven into the unitary fabric of my emotional-volitional, my living and effective, thinking–

---

64. Bakhtin, 'Discourse in the Novel', p. 280.
65. Barth, *Göttingen Dogmatics*, §7.
66. Bakhtin, 'Discourse in the Novel', p. 282.
67. Bakhtin, 'Discourse in the Novel', p. 281.

experiencing' capacity.[68] Every word spoken enters into verbal exchanges already under way: 'The word is born in a dialogue as a living rejoinder within it; the word is shaped in dialogic interaction with an alien word that is already in the object. A word forms a concept of its own object in a dialogic way.'[69] Words that communicate cannot be abstracted from the 'babel' of multiple speech worlds. If speaker and addressee are to communicate, they require an openness to one another, and an appreciation of the dialogic activity of understanding they are engaged in.[70]

The significance for Christian ethics lies in the character and quality of response to God's utterance. There are no pre-made answers because, as Bakhtin expresses clearly, the context into which a word/the Word is spoken, and in which we live, is like the mixing of languages at the Tower of Babel: 'the socially heteroglot multiplicity of ... names, definitions and value judgements.'[71] There is a multitude of possible meanings, routes and paths, laid down by layers of social-consciousness. No word, except the mythical first word of Adam, can avoid being caught up in among the many-tongued voices amidst which it is spoken: 'Only the mythical Adam, who approached a virginal and as yet verbally unqualified world with the first word, could really have escaped from start to finish this dialogic inter-orientation with the alien word that occurs in the object.'[72] Any subsequent word cannot be

---

68. M. M. Bakhtin, *Toward a Philosophy of the Act*, trans. and notes by Vadim Liapunov, ed. Vadim Liapunov and Michael Holquist (Austin, TX: University of Texas Press, 1993), p. 33.

69. Bakhtin, 'Discourse in the Novel', p. 279.

70. In his early work, Bakhtin makes clear that this requires sensitivity on the part of the addressee to the speaker's intonation because tone expresses attitude, and, simultaneously, sensitivity on the part of the speaker to ways in which the hearer is responsive to intonation. See Bakhtin, *Toward a Philosophy of the Act*, pp. 32–33.

71. Bakhtin, 'Discourse in the Novel', p. 278.

72. Bakhtin, 'Discourse in the Novel', p. 279.

considered apart from its intonation and value in the historical particularity into which it is spoken.[73] The incarnate Word is the new Adam (Rom. 5:12–20) whose truth and answerability is not conditioned by time or relative to certain historical conditions; divine truth has an autonomy and purity which is independent of human vicissitudes. To our ears, the Word of truth may be distorted or unclear. Hence the need to be alert to every aspect of the 'event-ness' of an utterance, including the process of its becoming actual in the experience of its hearers: 'The act is truly real . . . only *in its entirety.*'[74] God's utterance is eternally true, and Christian ethics is nothing unless it holds fast to this affirmation. Yet a word/the Word is uttered at the boundary between its own context and that of the addressee. Consider, urges Bakhtin, how the 'content/sense moment' and the 'individual-historical moment' of an event of communication are indivisible in any evaluation of an answerable act or deed.[75] This provokes us into thinking further about how the Word of God is uttered in a way that is directed towards relationship with its hearers, and how a more developed sense of the utterance and answerability of God's Word gives Christian ethics both direction and shape.

God's Word as event

That the answerability of God's Word gives Christian ethics direction and shape becomes more evident when we consider God's Word as event, by which I mean an event of communication which anticipates a response. The bible leads us to think about God's Word as an event which has effects of various kinds. The

---

73. Several years after Bakhtin, George Steiner stressed that each tongue can construe worlds of meaning from just a few words; words contain within themselves the boundless potential for humans to uncover new meanings, interpret dreams, conjecture about metaphysics, and discourse at law. George Steiner, *After Babel*, 2nd edn (Oxford: OUP, 1992), esp. p. xiv.

74. Bakhtin, *Toward a Philosophy of the Act*, p. 2.

75. Bakhtin, *Toward a Philosophy of the Act*, p. 3.

Lord says to Jeremiah, 'I am watching over my word to perform it' (Jer. 1:12); and to Ezekiel, 'But I the Lord will speak the word that I speak, and it will be fulfilled' (Ezek. 12:25). The Hebrew verb *asah*, meaning to do, is used in both instances. There are frequent references to God performing (Heb. *qum*) his word in the sense of bringing it to actuality (e.g., 1 Sam. 3:12; 2 Chron. 6:10). God kills with the words of his mouth (Hos. 6:5; Amos 8:11), speaks words that are like fire (Jer. 23:29), and tests (Ps. 105:19). God's word also nourishes (Deut. 8:3) and comforts (Ps 119:50; Is. 40:1). It comes to be and does not return to the Lord empty (Is. 55:11). We are interested in particular, however, in God's Word as an event of communication in which the addressee is drawn into relationship. For example, in the New Testament, to hear the word of God is to be cleansed (Jn 15:3) and called to obedience (Acts 6:7). God's Word is said to be at work in believers (Col. 3:16; 1 Thess. 2:13, 5:13; 1 Tim. 4:5; Heb. 4:12; 1 Tim. 4:5) calling them to prayer and holy action, and enabling their life of abiding in Christ. In these many different ways, God's Word is an event which makes dialogical claims upon the hearer, breaks into meaning variously, and anticipates differing responses.

This said, the character and quality of human response to God's utterance depends both upon recognition of its truth, and upon our not reducing its truth to an artificial or preconditioned status which can be abstracted from the dialogic situation into which it is spoken. Let us think about the truth of God's Word by considering its utterance both as an event which enlightens, and as an event of personal intensity because it calls all those who encounter it to re-evaluate the truth of their own lives.

An event which enlightens

In eloquent witness to the eternal existence of the Word of God, the writer of the fourth gospel affirms: ' . . . in him was life, and the life was the light of all people. The light shines in the darkness, and the darkness did not overcome it' (Jn 1:4–5). The incarnation is an event which enlightens because the Word incarnate is 'full of grace and truth' (Jn. 1:14). In the Liturgy of John Chrysostom, the priest prays that the light of divine knowledge may 'open the eyes of our mind to the comprehension of the preaching of thy Gospel'. All the people confess that the Son of God is Light of Light, true God of true God, and the choir sings: 'We have seen the true Light. We have received the heavenly Spirit. We have found the true Faith, worshipping the undivided Trinity, for He hath saved us.'[76] The implication is that the Christian ethic involves persons ontologically. 'For once you were in darkness, but now in the Lord you are light. Live as children of light – for the fruit of light is found in all that is good and right and true' (Eph. 5:8–9). Salvation involves changes in a person's being, and Christian ethics is about the development of this new being by becoming imitators of God and trying to find out what is pleasing to God. Here again we need to keep in tension the two dimensions of new life in Christ: God's work of salvation and the human, ethical work of imitating what we know of God in Christ. Ethically speaking, these two dimensions of new life in Christ interact throughout a person's whole mode of being, not least with respect to their character, growth in the virtues, and refinement of conscience. As Stanley Harakas writes:

> The communion of the believer with Christ in faith and sacrament presupposes the ethical imitation of Christ by the

---

76. Alexandar Mihailovic addresses directly the question: 'In what sense was Bakhtin "Orthodox"?' See Mihailovic, *Corporeal Words*, p. 1. He concludes that there is some ambiguity as regards Bakhtin's relationship with Russian institutional Orthodoxy, and that, at times, his writings display 'joyous irreverence' towards Orthodoxy in a denominational sense. He is, however, convinced that Bakhtin uses theological concepts and paradigms mediated through institutional Orthodoxy, especially Johannine logology, incarnation, *kenosis, perichoresis*, and revelation. Comments in this chapter about what Bakhtin may or may not derive from Russian Orthodox liturgy presuppose Mihailovic's conclusions. Much work on the influence of Russian Orthodoxy on Bakhtin was also done by Katerina Clark and Michael Holquist in their biography, *Mikhail Bakhtin* (Harvard: HUP, 1986).

believer. That ethical imitation of Christ therefore is more than certain discrete acts. Rather, it is a mood, a certain life-style, and ethos which permeates our motives, intentions and choices.[77]

An illustrative point is made by Bakhtin in an allusive passage which speaks of Christ's life and death, or 'Being-as-Event', as a great symbol of an encounter in which an answerable act/deed called the world into relationship to it: 'The world from which Christ has departed will no longer be the world in which he had never existed; it is, in its very principle, a different world.'[78] In a later work, Bakhtin uses the image of a ray scattering light to convey his intended sense. When a word/the Word is uttered, it becomes a complex play of light and shadow as it comes into contact with objects. His use of the image is worth citing in full because it bears remarkable similarity to images used by ancient eastern theologians to speak of the Trinity. A word/the Word is, says Bakhtin, like a ray that scatters light, or breaks into meaning, as it encounters an object:

> If we imagine the *intention of* such a word, that is, its *direc-tionality towards the object*, in the form of a ray of light, then the living and unrepeatable play of colors and light on the facets of the image that it constructs can be explained as the spectral dispersion of the ray-word, not within the object itself . . . but rather as its spectral dispersion in an atmosphere filled with alien words, value judgements and accents through which the ray passes on its way towards the object; the social atmosphere of the word, the atmosphere that surrounds the object, makes the facets of the image sparkle.[79]

When a ray of light encounters an object, or passes through a

---

77. Stanley S. Harakas, *Toward Transfigured Life* (Minneapolis: Light and Life, 1983), p. 203.
78. Bakhtin, *Toward a Philosophy of the Act*, p. 16.
79. Bakhtin, 'Discourse in the Novel', p. 277.

different atmosphere, light is exhibited and its colours change. So, when an utterance is spoken, meaning is conveyed and interacts with the context into which it is spoken. Unless it is to go unnoticed, it cannot fail to be in active engagement with hearers and the socio-verbal environment into which it enters.[80] By analogy, God's Word is an event which has ontological effect in the lives of believers, with implications for their setting of priorities, formation of conscience, decision-making processes, and lifestyle.

Of course, according to ancient orthodoxy, the illuminating effect of the incarnation is not limited to believers only but has wider cosmic and eschatological significance. Creation cannot be viewed pessimistically as in pitch darkness or as cut off utterly by nature from God. As Athanasius puts it, in Christ, all humanity – who, at creation had been given 'a portion even of the power of His own Word' – was restored to become once more partakers of God's image.[81] Grace is no longer extrinsic to nature, because the natural state of true humanity is, once again, conformation

---

80. The image of the ray-word occurs frequently in patristic writings, one of the clearest examples being Athanasius' employment of the image to counter Arian heresy: 'Having then such notions, they speak falsely; whereas the Son and the Father are one in such wise as has been said, and in such wise is the Son like the Father himself and from Him, as we may see and understand Son to be towards Father, and as we may see the radiance towards the sun . . . [F]or in the Image is contemplated the Father, and in the Radiance is the Light . . . For one and the same grace is from the Father in the Son, as the light of the sun and of the radiance is one, and as the sun's illumination is effected through the radiance' (Athanasius, *Four Discourses Against the Arians*, Discourse III, ch. XXV, §11, *NPNF* Second Series, Vol. IV, p. 400). Here, the Word is the ray of light which has its source in the Father, shares the essence of the Father, and shows the oneness of the Father and the Son. It cannot be established incontrovertibly that an allusion to patristic use of the image was intended by Bakhtin, though the imagery of the Father as light and the Son as light from light is found frequently in the liturgies of St Basil and St Chrysostom that were probably familiar to him.

81. Athanasius, *Incarnation of the Word*, §6, *NPNF* Second Series, Vol. IV, p. 39.

with the Word of God.[82] The work begun in Christ is not yet complete. This dialogue is, to use Bakhtin's phrase, 'oriented towards a future answer-word'.[83] Yet the truth remains that, in assuming human nature, Jesus Christ healed all that belonged to it and united it to God. The cross of Christ is still God's condemnation of fallen creation, but the final realisation of God's saving work is yet to come in the economy of the Spirit. We live in the existential gap between what has been accomplished in Christ and its realisation in the new creation. The illuminating truth of Christian ethics is identical to the truth of God in Christ and is oriented towards the future.

An event which is personal

As an event of communication, the utterance of God's Word has two dimensions: divine initiative and human responsibility in response. To use Bakhtin's language, these are dimensions of the event of God's communication in its entirety, and he encourages us to contemplate this event as including both the activity of its being spoken and of its being received in an ongoing process. Critics of Christianity often perceive its approach to ethics as limited to the external; to laws, regulations, and 'thou shalt nots'. Thus Richard Holloway opposes a Christian ethic of command to a non-religious ethic of consent.[84] He illustrates the ease with which one can allow discussion in this area to fall into false opposites: divine truth versus human freedom; obedience versus self-determination; command versus consent. A more adequate understanding of God's Word as an event of communication will,

---

82. This emphasis corrects those aspects of western theology which place a divide between nature and grace, natural and the supernatural, secular and sacred. As Vladimir Lossky reminds us: 'Eastern tradition . . . recognises no distinction, or rather division, save that between the created and the uncreated.' See Lossky, *Mystical Theology of the Eastern Church*, p. 88.
83. Bakhtin, 'Discourse in the Novel', p. 280.
84. Richard Holloway, *Godless Morality: Keeping Religion out of Ethics* (Edinburgh: Canongate, 1999), p. 159.

I suggest, avoid false polarities and seek instead a consideration of the work of the Holy Spirit in the ethical sphere of Christian life. Such a task will also require an adequate Pneumatology with which to explore how God's event of communication is fully personal yet does not compromise biblical affirmations that in Jesus Christ, the incarnate Word, God's glory was manifest in 'grace and truth' (Jn 1:14, 14:6), and that he is 'the true light, which enlightens everyone' (Jn 1:9a) who gives power to all who believe to become 'children of God' (Jn 1:12b). The matter hinges on biblical affirmation that truth and freedom are interrelated: 'If you continue in my word, you are truly my disciples; and you will know the truth, and the truth will make you free' (Jn 8:31–32). Faith affirms that this truth is perceptible to, but not accessible to, human reason: 'The Son was proclaimed as God's Wisdom and Word.'[85] This does not mean that human response to the divine initiative in communication will be simply recognition of an external authority that never attains to genuine internal persuasiveness. Yet Christian people cannot refuse to compromise in their affirmation that Jesus Christ is the way, and the truth, and the life (Jn 14:6) without also compromising their own, personal integrity.

Arguably, Bakhtin helps us again in his explorations of the relationship between external and internal authority in dialogic relationships. He speaks in 'Discourse in the Novel' about different kinds of authority: external and internal. External authority is of the sort that might be learned and recited, or transmitted to us from long ago. This kind of authority is determined by such things as the distance in time between ourselves and the text or tenets in question, the fact that a given tradition has had a largely positive attitude towards it, and has revered, interpreted and applied it in various ways, and that its associated concepts and language have

---

85. Athanasius, *Four Discourses Against the Arians*, Discourse IV, ch. XXV, §1, *NPNF* Second Series, Vol. IV, p. 433.

become familiar through use.[86] He describes externally authoritative words or discourses as follows:

> The authoritative word demands that we acknowledge it, that we make it our own; it binds us, quite independent of any power it might have to persuade us internally; we encounter it with its authority already infused to it. The authoritative word is located in a distanced zone, organically connected with a past that is felt to be hierarchically higher.[87]

Examples of such an externally authoritative word in Christian tradition might include anything from the decalogue to the moral prohibitions of, e.g., the Council in Trullo, AD 692, which stated that the clergy should not witness any plays in the theatre and forbade homosexual sex.[88] Few Christian ethicists today uphold the prohibition against theatre attendance; considerable controversy surrounds the practice of homosexual sex; whereas most regard the decalogue as still identifying essential rules of conduct for the continued existence of any social group. These particular examples of authoritative words vary in status and recognition owed to them, for reasons related to the socio-historical context of the day. There is no reason, however, to reduce the whole of Christian morality to such examples of externally authoritative words. If the substance of a prohibition becomes fixed and inert, like a thing in itself that bears no necessary relation to anything or anyone, as in the case of prohibition against theatre attendance, then its external authority will be either oppressive or meaningless in practice. In less obvious matters, e.g., homosexual sex, we witness a gap opening up between authoritative discourse that is 'prior', i.e., given from a time long ago, and that which is contemporary, and this variation illustrates the difference between authority that

---

86. Bakhtin, 'Discourse in the Novel', pp. 342–345.
87. Bakhtin, 'Discourse in the Novel', p. 342.
88. E.g., *The Canons of St Basil*, Canons VII and LXII in *The Seven Ecumenical Councils*, NPNF Second Series, Vol. XIV, pp. 604 and 608.

remains external and that which is internally persuasive. The point, however, is that we need to appreciate the interplay between external and internal authority if Christian ethics is neither to become irrelevant and redundant, nor to lose touch with the ground that nourishes it.

We shall consider in subsequent chapters how the personal dimension of Christian ethics becomes fully realised in the church. For the moment, let us note the integrality of a Spirit-enabled, subjective, personal and internally persuasive dimension to the event of divine communication. This is not to suggest that God's Word is in any sense dependent upon human response for its truth, rather that, as an event of communication, it remains incomplete and unproductive unless the addressee is persuaded of its truth. We must, of course, reckon with the reality of sin and with the effects of sin upon the human capacity to perceive and respond to the things of God.[89] No claims can be made for human infallibility with respect to hearing and interpreting the Word of God. Yet sensitivity is needed to the personal nature of human response to God's Word, not least the dialogic interaction between external and internal authority. As Bakhtin recognises, the authority of a word/the Word, text, or declaration is dialogic when its external nature and internal persuasiveness are united. To be internally persuaded of the truth of a word/the Word, is to share in its capacity to convey meaning and to be open rather than closed to its future: 'The semantic structure of an internally persuasive discourse is *not finite*, it is *open*; in each of the new contexts that dialogise it, this discourse is able to reveal ever newer *ways to mean*.'[90] As an addressee, he affirms: 'I occupy a place in once-occurrent Being that is unique and never repeatable, a place that cannot be taken by anyone else and is impenetrable for anyone

---

89. See Martin Luther, *Commentary on Genesis* 1:26: 'Let us make a man according to our image and likeness', *Luther's Works*, Vol. 1, ed. J. Pelikan (St Louis, MO: Concordia, 1958), pp. 55ff.

90. Bakhtin, 'Discourse in the Novel', p. 346.

else.'[91] No one else can take my place because my personhood is irreplaceable. No one else can answer the living word/Word as given to me in a unique and unrepeatable moment in time. No one else is established as an answerable and responsible person with respect to that word/Word because its answerability entails a responsibility which cannot be abdicated without lessening personhood. It requires honesty with oneself, unless one is to turn into an impostor or pretender.

For an event of communication to be fully personal, it must, argues Bakhtin, involve an element of internal persuasion and dialogic involvement; only this kind of relationship will be productive of meaning in people's lives. Paul seems to be saying something similar in Rom. 4:21 where he speaks about being 'fully convinced' or persuaded (*plerophoreo*) that God is able to do what he has promised. Later, in Rom. 14:5, when discussing the specific issue of the observance of one day of the week, he urges every person to be persuaded – or to carry the matter through fully – in their own mind. He is talking about a matter of order and observance in the Christian community and not the authority of the Word of God per se, yet the point is made that each person must be convinced of the appropriateness of their action, or the action will be in vain. The salvific unity of persons with Christ (their *ousia* as given in Christ) has to be lived out in terms of what is personal, through the lives of the many people of God in which the Church subsists (its *tropos* lived in the power of the Holy Spirit). This is the work of the Holy Spirit in leading the children of God in their new life which is free from legalism (Rom. 7:6, 8:14), does not entail blind or passive obedience to a command which instantiates itself as a law or philosophical formulation, but invites persons to deeper knowledge of the truth and dignity of God from whom this new life is derived.[92] In John's

---

91. Bakhtin, *Toward a Philosophy of the Act*, p. 40.
92. On this, consider Gregory Nazianzen's welcoming of the way in which the Holy Spirit supplied 'a clearer demonstration' of the nature of God to ▷

gospel and the ancient fathers, the Word of God (like God) is not a 'thing' or object for study, which has physical quantity or proper-ties that can be measured or manipulated at will.[93] Rather, it comes to us as an invitation to a two-way interaction in which neither human freedom nor divine truth are compromised.[94] Christ is the measure of all things, not least knowledge of God, because: 'He [the Lord, i.e., Jesus Christ] has therefore, in His work of recapitulation, summed up all things . . .'[95] However, to respond to the Word ethically is not to sink into mental atrophy, or make the self the source of truth, or to will one's person into non-existence, but, rather, is to make one's whole life – including its intellectual aspects – a Spirit-enabled dialogue with the Word of God.

A similar emphasis on the particularities of personal response to God's Word is found in many of the ancient fathers. In assuming humanity, writes Athanasius, the Word of God walked and talked with people, engaged their senses, and called them back to God again:

> For seeing that men, having rejected the contemplation of God, and with their eyes downward, as though sunk in the deep, were seeking about for God in nature and in the world of sense, feigning gods for themselves of mortal men and demons; to this end the loving and general Saviour of all, the Word of God, takes to Himself a body, and as Man walks

---

Christian believers, making perfect their powers of understanding. Gregory Nazi-anzen, *On the Holy Spirit*, Fifth Theological Oration, §XXVI, *NPNF* Second Series, Vol. VII, p. 326.

93. The so-called Athanasian Creed states: 'The Father is made of none, neither created, nor begotten . . .' The first of the Thirty-Nine Articles of the Church of England (1562), affirms: 'There is but one living and true God, everlasting, without body, parts, or passions . . .'

94. Vladimir Lossky makes this point in *Orthodox Theology: An Introduction*, trans. Ian and Ihita Kesarcodi-Watson (New York: St Vladimir's Seminary Press, 1978), p. 13.

95. Irenaeus, *Against Heresies*, *ANF*, Vol. I, Book V, Preface, p. 548.

among men and meets the senses of all men half-way, to the
end, I say, that they who think that God is corporeal may
from what the Lord effects by His body perceive the truth,
and through Him recognise the Father.[96]

Athanasius is convinced that Jesus Christ embodied true humanity
and is committed to convincing others that there are good reasons
for believing this also. There is, however, an existential realism
about this passage which recalls the physicality of the incarnation
and reminds us that each person makes up their own mind to
seek or reject God and good. Fear of the Lord, writes John Chrysostom, does not petrify but evokes personal response to that
goodness which reconciled God and humanity in Christ: 'For if
through Him we live who were dead; to Him we ought to live
through Whom we live.'[97] The implication is not that the Word
of God is in any sense dependent upon humanity for its truth or
existence but, rather, that as an event of communication it comes
to fruition in the response of unique and unrepeatable persons,
each of whom is created with a rational soul in the image of God.
Ethical decision-making should allow no escape into an abstract
notion of universal humanity but require me, in my unique place
in existence, to answer to God's Word.

God's Word as answerable

So far, we have been considering two major dimensions in
Christian ethics: divine initiative and human responsibility in
response. We have considered how, as creatures, we can make no
claim upon God or presume to be engaged in dialogue with God.
Yet we have also considered how the living Word of God engages
us personally in dialogic relationship, and how the Holy Spirit
enables the synergy or working together of divine grace and

---

96. Athanasius, *Incarnation of the Word*, §15, *NPNF* Second Series, Vol. IV, p. 44.
97. John Chrysostom, *Homilies on Second Corinthians*, Homily XI, *NPNF* First
Series, Vol. XII, p. 332.

human will. In this section, we shall consider further the relation-ship of the work of Christ and of the Spirit in the life of a believer. Made in the image of God, humanity is capable of responding to God and of working together with God in order to become more like God. This working together (*synergy*) involves a reciprocity which is the response of persons to the invitation of the Spirit. It is exemplified in Jesus' answer to God: 'not my will but yours be done' (Lk. 22:42), and in Mary's response to the angel: 'Here am I, the servant of the Lord; let it be with me according to your word' (Lk. 1:38). God's *fiat* (command or act of will) cannot forcibly impose the divine will upon Jesus because that would turn it into evil. Nor can God answer for Mary because, as a unique person, she must answer for herself: 'To the *fiat* of the Creator corresponds the *fiat* of the creature.'[98]

Mary's answer to the angel

Why and how does the answering of Mary the Mother of God inform the task of Christian ethics? Feminist theologians, especially Protestants, often hesitate before speaking about Mary because of the impossible ideal of virgin-mother that she is thought to represent for women, and because this impossible ideal is mapped with reference to Eve's (woman's) supposed responsi-bility for the entry of sin into the world.[99] There is also the problem of Mary contributing symbolically to the construction of

---

98. Paul Evdokimov, *Woman and the Salvation of the World* (New York: St Vladimir's Seminary Press, 1994), p. 193.

99. '[T]he knot of Eve's disobedience was loosed by the obedience of Mary. For what the virgin Eve had bound fast through unbelief, this did the virgin Mary set free through faith.' Irenaeus, *Against Heresies*, Bk III, ch. XXII, §3, *ANF*, Vol. I. For feminist treatments of this subject, see Marina Warner, *Alone of All Her Sex* (London: Picador, 1990); Elaine Pagels, 'The Politics of Paradise: Augustine's Exegesis of Genesis 1–3 versus that of John Chrysostom', *Harvard Theological Review*, Vol. 78, Nos 1–2 (1985), pp. 67–99; Rosemary Radford Ruether, 'Dualism and the Nature of Evil in Feminist Theology', *Studies in Christian Ethics*, Vol. 5, No. 1(1992).

female difference in Christian tradition, along the lines of passivity and obedience rather than activity and self-determination. In this section, however, I am not interested in Mary as an ideal for women but as representative of all humanity, who exemplifies synergy or co-operation between humanity and God. Nicholas Cabasilas, the noted fourteenth-century commentator on the Orthodox Divine Liturgy, wrote:

> The Incarnation was not only the work of the Father, of His Power and His Spirit . . . but it was also the work of the will and faith of the Virgin . . . Just as God became incarnate voluntarily, so He wished that His Mother should bear Him freely and with her full consent.[100]

God does not force the divine will on Mary but waits for her free response, following which the Holy Spirit enabled her to become the mother of God. No other human being has ever since had this exact same calling; there is only one Mary who gave birth to the Christ-child. She does, however, personify humanity and the church in communion with God, which is the *telos* of Christian ethics.

The fact that a human person could bear God within her was disputed in the early church, not least by Nestorius – a pupil of Theodore of Mopsuestia and extreme representative of the *Logos-anthropos* school which stressed the genuine and complete humanity of Christ – and Cyril of Alexandria who was accused of Monophysitism, i.e., the heresy associated with Eutyches, also from Alexandria, who maintained that Christ had a single divine nature. The issues centred around how the incarnation is understood in relation to the Virgin Mary and use of terms *Christotokos* (Christ-bearer) and *Theotokos* (God-bearer). For Nestorius, use

---

100. P. Nellas (ed.), *The Mother of God: Three Homilies by Nicholas Cabasilas on the Mother of God* [in Greek] (Athens, 1974). Cited by Christopher Veniamin, 'The Sinlessness of the Mother of God according to Saint Nicholas Cabasilas', *Alive in Christ*, No. 3 (1995).

of the latter admitted of change and suffering in God and was tantamount to blasphemy. Nicaea did not, he argued, teach anything contrary to scripture, notably Heb. 7:3, which states that Christ is without mother. Better, therefore, to refer to Mary as *Theotochos* (God-receiver) or *Christotokos* (bearer of the Word as human). Christ was the only begotten Son of the Father. For the Godhead there could be no second birth from woman. Nestorius, though, was not successful, and the Council of Ephesus (AD 431) approved *Theotokos*. For Cyril, *Theotokos* did not mean compromise. The Logos was unchangeable but, as the first anathema states, 'If anyone does not acknowledge that Emmanuel is in truth God, and that the Holy Virgin is in consequence *Theotokos* ... let him be anathema.'[101] It was insufficient for the human nature of Jesus to be regarded as only a garment for the Logos. Unless the Word of God was united hypostatically to human flesh our salvation is in jeopardy. The second anathema states, 'If anyone does not acknowledge that the Word united with the flesh ... one and the same, God and man together ... let him be anathema.' In his second letter to Nestorius, Cyril writes, the 'Word was not ... changed or transformed ... but having united to himself in his own hypostasis in an ineffable and inconceivable manner, flesh animated with a rational soul, became man.'[102] Specifically against Nestorius' concept of *prosopon* he writes, 'For scripture has not declared that the Word united to himself a man's person but that he became flesh.' This means that for Cyril the incarnation is not the Antiochene conjunction, but the Word 'abased himself by submitting ... to the limitations of the human condition', and was born of the woman Mary.

Of interest to us ethically is the importance attached in biblical and traditional witness to Mary's answer to God. This is because,

---

101. Anathema 1, Council of Ephesus 431, in *The Decrees and Canons of the Seven Ecumenical Councils*, NPNF Second Series, Vol. XIV, p. 206.
102. For Cyril's *Second Epistle to Nestorius*, see http://www.newadvent.org/fathers/3811.htm.

arguably, it sheds light on how we understand the nature and task of Christian ethics as daily response in personal freedom to the Spirit's revelation of truth in Christ (Jn 1:17, 8:32, 17:17; Rom. 9:1, 15:8; Gal. 5:7; Eph. 5:9; 1 Tim. 2:4). Without her answer, she would not have borne the Christ-child or played a part in the divine mystery. By contemplating her answer to the angel, we realise that the grace of God cannot be mixed with human will in some quasi-mechanical way, because that would deny the meaning of created humanity which consists in freedom to respond to divine love. Rather, God's Word is genuinely dialogical. Response to it has to be an act of freedom and co-operation. As Bakhtin implies, a word/the Word spoken is a word born in dialogue because it anticipates an answer: '[E]very word is directed towards an *answer* and cannot escape the profound influence of the answering word that it anticipates.'[103] Her answer never attracts attention away from Jesus. The fact that Orthodox iconography, and also artistic representations of Mary in the West, never portray Mary alone but always with the Christ-child indicates that her place in Christian tradition is significant only because she is the servant of God (Lk. 1:48); her significance lies only in drawing others to worship Christ. This said, the incarnation could not have happened in the way it did without her 'yes' which allowed the event of divine communication to reach its intended completion. The 'event-ness' of a word/the Word involves both utterance and answer because '[t]he act is truly real . . . only *in its entirety*'.[104] Moreover, in this responsibility of response she stands in essential solidarity with all humanity. Hers was an exceptional calling, but not different in kind from that to which every human person is called, i.e., to

---

103. Bakhtin, 'Discourse in the Novel', p. 280. 'Like the Johannine divine Word, Bakhtin's *slovo* denotes communality of those interacting with it and not any particular word or utterance: at the same time, in its capacity as a reified and embodied phenomenon, the Bakhtinian use of the term can also, in some instances, represent the individual utterance.' Mihailovic, *Corporeal Words*, p. 18.
104. Bakhtin, *Toward a Philosophy of the Act*, p. 2.

an integrity of nature and personhood oriented towards God in complete self-dedication.[105]

This raises the question of the acclaimed virginity of Mary which sets her apart from the rest of humanity. What sense are we to make of the credal affirmation that Jesus Christ 'was conceived by the Holy Ghost, born of the Virgin Mary'? How can a virgin mother be representative of all humanity and exemplify human answering of God's Word? There is, of course, no way of knowing conclusively if Mary had sexual relations with a man before the birth of Jesus. The Hebrew word *almah* refers simply to a young woman (Is. 7:14), and the Greek *parthenos* does not necessarily imply that the woman in question would conceive while remaining a virgin (Matt. 1:23; Lk. 1:27).[106] On the other hand, there are reasons to doubt that the earliest church would simply have invented the notion.[107] In my judgement, these reasons are sufficient to warrant affirmation of the Niceno-Constantinopolitan creed in its entirety without intellectual compromise, though they might not be sufficient for everyone. This said, attestation of the literal meaning of the virgin birth is of little use without reflection upon its theological significance, not least the integrity of Mary's human nature and personhood as infused by the Holy Spirit. Whether or not we can assent intellectually to the probability that Mary's hymen had not been broken by Joseph's penis is of less significance than the truth entailed in her experience of

---

105. On this, see Georges Florovsky, 'The Ever-Virgin Mother of God' in *Creation and Redemption* (Massachusetts: Norland Publishing Co., 1976), p. 184.

106. On this, and other matters relating to New Testament attestation of the virgin birth, see C. E. B. Cranfield, 'Some Reflection on the Subject of the Virgin Birth', *Scottish Journal of Theology*, Vol. 41 (1988), pp. 177–189.

107. C. E. B. Cranfield notes the following as significant: (i) 'that the earliest Church was firmly convinced that Jesus was the Messiah; (ii) that there was no pre-Christian expectation that the Messiah would be virgin-born; (iii) that there was a very strong – if not quite universal – expectation that the Messiah would be a descendant of David; (iv) that the Davidic descent of Joseph was affirmed'. 'Some Reflection', p. 186.

the Spirit: 'The angel said to her, "The Holy Spirit will come upon you, and the power of the Most High will overshadow you" ' (Lk. 1:35a). For Gregory of Nyssa, virginity is found in all whose instinct and will are constituted by virtue and beautified with purity.[108] Mary's answer is part of her communion or reciprocal relationship with God, and makes the event of divine communication complete; hers is an experiential truth which entails communion with God. She witnesses to the fact that the Holy Spirit brings to each person the presence of Christ, inviting believers to question and answer it for themselves; 'so that the intellect guiding its [the soul's] path by it, may be able to comprehend it, in so far as it is accessible to human nature to learn concerning the Word of God'.[109]

Mary's answer and the ethics of icons

That Mary's answer was enabled by the Spirit of God is attested in scripture (Matt. 1:18; Lk. 1:35) and witnessed to by many ancient writers.[110] Iconic representations of her answer depict this spiritual reality by means of particular artistic devices. For example, the deliberate flatness of form emphasises the spiritual rather than literal significance of that being depicted. What matters is not verisimilitude but evocation of the experience that Mary had of the Spirit of God. The icon is a transparent window through which to see how she, and other saints, responded to God's Word and lived in ways enabled by the Spirit. Icons generally play a negligible role in the spiritual lives of western Christians. Yet arguably, they recall us to something important concerning relationships between the material, form and content of the ethical life. An untrained eye sees simply a slightly odd form imposed on

---

108. This links with Gregory of Nyssa's exposition of the virginity, i.e., the passion-less existence and incorruptible purity, of the Godhead: *On Virginity*, ch. 2, *NPNF* Second Series, Vol. V, p. 344.

109. Athanasius, *Incarnation of the Word*, §57, *NPNF* Second Series, Vol. IV, p. 67.

110. Irenaeus, *Against Heresies*, Bk III, ch. XXI, §3, *ANF*, Vol. I, p. 452.

the raw material of paint and canvas. A Christian committed to icons sees something which conveys spiritual meaning and an experience of godliness; the truth of the icon lies in the experience of the Spirit it conveys. John Zizioulas writes of icons and the relationship between truth and aesthetics as follows:

> This tradition [the Greek patristic tradition in its under-standing of icons] presents truth not as a product of the mind, but as a 'visit' and a 'dwelling' (cf. Jn 1:14) of an eschatological reality entering history to open it up in a communion-event. This creates a *vision* of truth not as Platonic or mystical contemplation understands it but as pic-turing a new set of relationships, a new 'world' adopted by the community as its final destiny.[111]

He does not link the discussion directly to Christian ethics, but the point is made that neither truth nor beauty are adequately represented as facts but can only properly be grasped relationally, through experience and embodiment. An icon is the material representation of truths which are not only conceptual but ex-periential and spiritual, and which await embodiment in practice. The famous *Virgin of Vladimir* icon, which depicts Mary cradling the Christ-child with tenderness and love, has odd spatial relations between the characters but conveys a beauty and spiritual nobility that can only result from sublime harmony between Mary and the child.

Christian ethics and iconography are clearly not the same, but there is something about both which becomes united in the matter of response to the Word of God. In contemplating the icon, the believer knows instinctively that no intellectual concepts are adequate for the actualisation of tenderness and love, and that their value can only be actualised in the living of human life. Bakhtin expresses something similar when he writes of the

---

111. John D. Zizioulas, *Being as Communion* (Crestwood, NY: St Vladimir's Seminary Press, 1985), p. 100.

relationship between aesthetics and moral action: 'a moral action actualises (at its highest level) a value which can only be accomplished and cannot be expressed and cognized in an adequate concept.'[112] There are no concepts adequate to relate beauty and truth because they require moral action to be realised; goodness, truth and beauty are united only in the embodiment or reality of love. Iconography invites a way of seeing which appreciates this unity or integration and grasps the witness of icons to an experience or event of communion in which they are one. Christian ethics describes a way of being (*ethos*) which imitates Christ and also the saints whose lives were flooded by the Spirit. Such imitation is not external or of the kind that requires legalistic conformity to certain practices; it would, in any case, be pointless for finite humans to imitate God who is infinite. An internal imitation occurs as the believer partakes of Christ through the Spirit, and manifests itself externally as the Spirit continues the divine work of sanctification. Athanasius writes:

> [T]aking patterns for man from divine subjects, the Saviour says; 'Be ye merciful, as your Father which is in heaven is merciful'; and, 'Be perfect, as your heavenly Father is perfect.' And He said this too, not that we might become such as the Father; for to become as the Father, is impossible for us creatures, who have been brought to be out of nothing; but as He charged us, 'Be ye not like to horse', . . . that we should not imitate their want of reason, so, not that we might become as God, did He say, 'Be ye merciful as your Father', but that looking at His beneficent acts, what we do well, we might do, not for men's sake, but for His sake, so that from Him and not from men we may have the reward. For as, although there be one Son by nature, True and Only-

---

112. M. M. Bakhtin, 'The Problem of Content, Material, and Form in Verbal Art' in *Art and Answerability* (Austin, TX: University of Texas Press, 1990), p. 266.

begotten, we too become sons, not as He is in nature and truth, but according to the grace of Him that calleth . . .[113]

Like things, says Athanasius, are naturally one with like. Those who share the life divine, through partaking of the Spirit, are drawn to be like the divine in every disposition. Christ is the pattern for all that is good, true, just and merciful, and, in so far as icons direct one's attention towards his perfection, they can be spiritually beneficial. In so far as icons of Mary and the saints represent something of what it means to model oneself on what is best, and convey an inkling of what it means to answer 'yes' to the Word of God with one's heart, soul and mind, then contemplation of them will be conducive to spiritual and ethical growth. They can be 'image(s) and example(s) of the matter in hand' which invite the viewer to co-experience of the transforming grace of God in which goodness, truth and beauty cohere.[114]

Christian ethics and iconography thus share similar tasks and problems. Both must express what cannot be expressed by human means. The iconographer endeavours to give outward expression to the likeness of God in humanity.[115] The Christian ethicist – and every believer in the ethical aspects of their discipleship – endeavours to think about how the church might reflect the kingdom of God on earth. Iconic images of Mary and the saints are images of humanity suffused with divine beauty. This was recognised by the Seventh Ecumenical Council which formally saluted iconic images of Christ and the saints, including 'the all-holy Mother of God, from whom he [Christ] was pleased to take flesh', and prayed that persons might be led back to reflection upon

---

113. Athanasius, *Four Discourses against the Arians*, Discourse III, ch. XXV, §19, *NPNF* Second Series, Vol. IV, p. 404.

114. Athanasius, *Four Discourses against the Arians*, Discourse III, ch. XXV, §19, *NPNF* Second Series, Vol. IV, p. 405.

115. See L. Ouspensky, *The Meaning of Icons* (New York: St Vladimir's Seminary Press, 1978), p. 49.

the Word and to gain a share in holiness.[116] Ethical envisioning of relationship with God is an envisioning of what the Christian ethos looks like in practice. To the eyes of faith, the icon shares the same nature with the person represented. The challenge for the church is to become, like the icon, the image of Christ or of true humanity in response to God, a representation of the unrepresentable. Again, Mary's answer to the angel is helpful to us, not least because Mary is sometimes thought to be a type of the church and to foreshadow its conceiving and bringing forth of the Word of God. Ambrose writes:

> Rightly is she [i.e., Mary] betrothed, yet a virgin, because she is the type of the Church, which is immaculate yet married. The virgin [Church] has conceived us by the Spirit, the Virgin brings us forth without pain. And therefore perhaps is the holy Mary married to one [Joseph], but filled with another [the Holy Spirit], because the individual Churches, too, are filled by the Spirit and his grace, but are externally joined to a mortal priest.[117]

The Word becomes incarnate by just one mother, though every believer brings forth Christ by faith. Mary's body was temple of God in a unique way, but every believer and the church as a whole can receive the Word of God in integrity and image its truth.[118]

---

116. The Second Council of Nicaea, AD 787, *The Seven Ecumenical Councils*, *NPNF* Second Series, Vol. XIV, p. 541.

117. Ambrose, *Commentary on Luke's Gospel*, cited by Hilda Graef, *Mary: A History of Doctrine and Devotion* (London: Sheed & Ward, 1985/1963, 1965), pp. 84–85.

118. Ambrose, *Of the Holy Spirit*, Bk III, *NPNF* Second Series, Vol. X, p. 146. Ambrose is careful to make plain that God alone is to be worshipped and not a human person; Mary was the temple of God, not God of the temple. See also Augustine, *On the Psalms* No. XLV, §3, *NPNF* First Series, Vol. VIII, p. 146.

Imitative incarnations of divine love

Christian ethics will always entail more than external imitation of Christ's actions. This said, the incarnation offers something of a model which invites us to imitation. To participate in the life of Christ includes an imitative dimension. 'We are', urges the writer to the Ephesians, 'what he has made us, created in Christ Jesus for good works, which God prepared beforehand to be our way of life' (Eph. 2:10). There is a 'way of life' that God has prepared for and requires of Christian people, which is exemplified in Christ. It has a particular character and practical content, how it exists, its *tropos*, *hyparxis*, or *hypostasis*, which we learn from contemplation of the life of Christ. Gregory Nazianzen links his interpretation of Eph. 2:8–10 with Eph. 5:1, which speaks of being 'imitators of God'. Similarly Cyril of Jerusalem writes: 'So then, the Creator being good, created for good works.'[119] This has nothing to do with the old bogey 'salvation through works', but with the way of union with God to which the Church is called. The Greek phrase used in Eph. 2:10, literally 'in order that we might walk', or the 'way of life' which God has prepared beforehand, is from the verb *peripateo* meaning to walk, or, in a metaphorical sense, to pass one's life or conduct oneself. Used to translate the Septuagint *halak*, meaning 'to walk, to follow, or to go on habitually', it describes Noah's blameless life before God: 'Noah walked with God' (Gen. 6:9); and also God's journeying with the people of God: 'And I will walk among you, and will be your God, and you shall be my people' (Lev. 26:12).

The ontological basis for the Christian life (what it is in terms of its principle, or *logos*) implies a mode of being (how it exists, or *tropos*). The *tropos* of Christian life will be directed and shaped by its *logos*, entailing many imitative dimensions of divine life. But what does imitation of the divine life entail? Jesus' answer to

---

119. Gregory Nazianzen, *Oration on the Holy Lights*, NPNF Second Series, Vol. VII, p. 354; Cyril of Jerusalem, Lecture II, *NPNF* Second Series, Vol. IV, p. 87.

the lawyer's question is important in this regard: 'You shall love the
Lord your God with all your heart, and with all your soul, and
with all your strength, and with all your mind; and your neighbour
as yourself' (Lk. 10:27). Christian ethics is about the supremacy
of love in every aspect of human life. We must be careful not to
turn love into an abstract idea or nostalgic feeling which verges on
sentimentality. Like Bakhtin in his complaint against the literary
theorists of his day, we need to guard against interpreting a word-
as-event/the incarnation as either an empty formula whose semantic structure is static, dead, and cut off from the ecclesial context
in which Christology lives today, or as an ill-founded philosophy
or truth-claim which pays little attention to the realities of human
existence.[120] Like Bakhtin in his struggle with the philosophy of
Kant, we need to guard against assuming that truth is either
abstract and impersonal or relative and conditioned.[121] Word-as-
event, he argues, need neither deny the autonomy of truth nor
collapse into relativism because, as an actually occurring event
which calls persons into answerability, it is an event in which we
are participants.[122] The lawyer's question 'who is my neighbour?'
(Lk. 10:29b) warns against contemplation of love as abstract idea
or mystical void.[123] The parable of the good Samaritan allows no

---

120. I use a phrase from Bakhtin, 'Discourse in the Novel', p. 343.

121. Bakhtin, *Toward a Philosophy of the Act*, pp. 9–10.

122. Bakhtin, *Toward a Philosophy of the Act*, p. 17. Against the abstractness of
Kant's ethical philosophy according to which one makes judgements 'as if' they
would affect each neighbour rather than 'as if' they would have universal,
theoretical validity, Bakhtin asserts personal responsibility for every act or deed
as the basis for good judgement, because this presupposes the truth of the event
which is each person's participation and 'ought' in relationship to the other
person: 'Man-in-general does not exist; *I* exist and a particular concrete
other exists – my intimate, my contemporary (social mankind), the past and
future of actual human beings (of actual historical mankind).' Bakhtin, *Toward
a Philosophy of the Act*, p. 47.

123. For Bakhtin, Dostoevsky's novels provide something of an answer because
in them the 'idea' (or ideas) of the novel become embodied in the lives of
characters. An idea placed into the mouth of a character is no fixed state- ▷

escape into an abstract notion of universal humanity but requires me, in my unique place in existence, to answer to the other person's need as a fellow being. Ethics is not an isolated part of the Christian life but the practical expression of divine–human reciprocity.

Christian Ethics and God's Word in Dialogue

When cast within a theology of divine grace, the authority of God can be spoken of properly in kenotic and dialogic terms. God's authority is that of an author who brings new life into being; God/the author speaks creation into existence in freedom and love and delights in relationship with it. But God's grace is seen pre-eminently in the incarnation and, in this chapter, we have considered God's Word as an event of communication – not as a demand for blind or passive obedience but as an event which requires each person, in their unique place in existence, to answer God's address. God's incarnate Word is a word/the Word in dialogue, who does not reduce hearers to passive partners but engages them in genuine relationship as 'other' to his 'I'. We have considered how such an event of communication becomes a synergy between divine grace and human will, as enabled by the Holy Spirit, and how God's Word as dialogic is open to new meaning and realisation in the lives of different persons without falling into a kind of relativism in which truth is invented by each. The answerability of God's Word extends throughout all time and space, and also to the particularities of personal experience. All humanity is included within the structure of divine address. However, God does not force salvation upon humanity, but requires a response such that persons become deified in a double

---

ment with a meaning that is final, but is part of that character's existence and is inseparable from every aspect of their personhood and dialogic interaction with others. Bakhtin, *Problems of Dostoevsky's Poetics* ed. and trans. Caryl Emerson (Minnesota: UMP, 1984), pp. 27, 23; ch. 3 *passim*.

movement or exchange of attributes in which creator and created commune without separation or confusion. Christian ethics is located in the interplay between divinity and humanity as persons respond to God's Word and as human capacities are utilised for healthy development. The divine initiative creates a space in which growth in the divine likeness may happen, and Christian ethics is located in this interplay between divine and human wills.

Several implications can be noted. First, Christian ethics will be characterised by a movement of love in the direction of the other. Second, Christian ethics knows nothing of extreme relativism – by which I mean a conception of morality based on de facto relations between humans, and often between cultures, in which basic moral commitments are thought to vary or to be inconsistent – because Christ manifested a true humanity. As the God-human, he revealed deification to be the norm of humanity. Third, Christian ethics may be understood as a movement or growth towards God-likeness. God's address to humanity creates a space for response in which persons are invited to move intentionally and morally. The human vocation to communication and communion with God includes the responsibilities of moral decision-making.

Chapter Three

Polyphony and the Spirit of Freedom and Truth

So far we have reflected upon authority as of the essence of the Godhead. God is the 'author' of creation who calls all things into being and sets limits to the kind of existence enjoyed by creation. We have also considered divine authority as dialogic: Jesus Christ is the Word of God incarnate who embodies God's call to humanity to live in answer to divine truth. By becoming human, dying on the cross and rising again, the Word of God made possible our renewed participation in divine life. By the power of the Spirit, the Word of God restores our most basic vocation and reason for living. But how are we to live? Each day brings choices to be made in 'the existential adventure of our freedom'.[1] How are we to make decisions about what is good and right in a given situation? If God's authority is not is of a controlling or dis-empowering kind, and if – like the author who writes a genuinely polyphonic novel – God builds the freedom of the creature into the design and form of creation, what is the process by which we arrive at good moral judgements? Such questions have exercised great minds throughout the centuries, though that does not excuse anyone from attending to such matters for themselves. Jesus said to the crowds:

> 'When you see a cloud rising in the west, you immediately say, "It is going to rain"; and so it happens. And when you

---

1. Christos Yannaras, *The Freedom of Morality* (Crestwood, NY: St Vladimir's Seminary Press, 1984), p. 24.

> see the south wind blowing, you say, "There will be scorching heat"; and it happens. You hypocrites! You know how to interpret the appearance of earth and sky, but why do you not know how to interpret the present time? And why do you not judge for yourselves what is right? (Lk. 12:54–57).

Each person is responsible for their own decision-making while interpreting the signs of the time. Each must judge for themselves; there can be no alibi. In the approaching time of trial, says Jesus, each is to trust the Holy Spirit for instruction as to what to say (Lk. 12:12). Like the rich man with many barns, each is responsible for the way they live (Lk. 12:16–21). The ethical aspects of the life of faith cannot be arranged vicariously.

Such affirmations raise many questions. How are we to make decisions that are fitting for a follower of Jesus? What happens when one Christian person's decision conflicts with that of another? To what extent is there space within Christian faith for differing and conflicting voices? To illustrate the problem, one need only recall newspaper articles about clashes in the Church of England over sexual orientation at the 1998 Lambeth Conference. Bishop Richard Holloway was cited as saying: 'In northern Atlantic countries we live in a post-traditionalist society in which you can't simply apply anything by authority. You have to offer reasons.'[2] The church, he argues, cannot retreat behind a drawbridge and go back to a particular paradigm, the implication being that, at the very least, the teaching ministry of the church needs to be re-thought in the light of personal experience and choice. The quotation from Archbishop George Carey in the same newspaper read: 'I stand wholeheartedly with traditional Anglican orthodoxy. I see no room in scripture or Christian tradition for any sexual activity outside matrimony of husband and wife.' The statement finally released by the Church of England at the Lambeth Conference included a clause rejecting homosexual practice as incompatible

---

2. 'Clash on Gays like Islam, Bishop Says', *The Independent*, 7 August 1998.

with scripture, and replacing the working party's recommendation of chastity outside of marriage with abstinence for those not called to marriage.[3] What the churches should teach about sexuality, and what Christians should and should not do regarding sexual expression, is more contentious than most topics. However, it is one among many areas of life in which tension arises between conformity to the moral and doctrinal teaching of the church and personal choice.

This tension leaves in some people's lives a divide between a Christian understanding of authority (found in the economy of the triune God) and public perceptions of the church as institution. Personal freedom is set over against the corporate life of the church. The teaching authority of the church conflicts with personal responsibility in moral decision-making; the two appear to be mutually exclusive. In this chapter I argue that such a divide or dilemma is false. There is no reason to oppose moral freedom in the Spirit to the teaching authority of the church. This is not to downplay issues such as that illustrated above. Nor is it to deny the continuing importance of the teaching authority of the church. What the church teaches does not take precedence over the reality of salvation in a person's life: 'For Christ is the end of the law so that there may be righteousness for everyone who believes' (Rom. 10:4). Compliance is not set above liberty. But neither is the church a democratic society in which truth is vested in the people and exercised by them without reference to God. Nor is it a pluralistic society of the kind in which all boundaries are abolished and values jostle for place. The church guards and hands on a priceless deposit of faith, but this does not equate to the clergy guarding an object-like treasure or to their effective rule over the laity. We should not feel forced to choose between personal responsibility and the traditions of the church. Why? Because both personal freedom in the Spirit and the authority of the church to teach have roots in the Holy Spirit's work of sanctification. The 'genesis

---

3. ACNS LC093: Text of Lambeth Conference resolution on sexuality, §a.

of ethics' is found also in the work of the Holy Spirit. Hence the need in Christian ethics for an adequate Pneumatology.

In developing this theme, I draw on the help of Mikhail Bakhtin to talk about freedom in the Spirit in terms of 'polyphony', and to contrast 'polyphony in the Spirit' with problems associated with 'monologism' and 'heteroglossia'. For Bakhtin, the concept of polyphony is a way of talking about the personal distinctiveness associated with a particular kind of authoring in which the author surrenders monologic control in favour of allowing the heroes to live independently. In the novel, polyphony is a mode of living characterised by many voices, which incarnates the personal freedom given by the author to each human being. In this chapter, I develop the concept in relationship to personal freedom in the Spirit and the many-voicedness that characterises Christian testimony to the truth revealed in Christ. The intention is to link Christian ethics clearly to the work of the Holy Spirit in enabling believers 'to have the mind of Christ' (1 Cor. 2:16). Ancient writers confess that such subject matter will always require contemplation of the mystery of the holy Trinity: 'For, not as if in need, but as a Father in His own Wisdom hath God founded the earth, and made all things in the Word which is from Him, and in the Son confirms the Holy Laver' [i.e. baptism].[4] God the Father is the primordial cause of creation. God the Son is the operating cause. God the Spirit is the perfecting cause.[5] The three persons are one in nature and essence, and cannot be divided one from the other. As Vladimir Lossky writes: 'In relation to itself it [creation] amounts to nothing.'[6] In relation to the holy Trinity, creation is

---

4. Athanasius, *Against the Arians*, Discourse II, ch. XVIII, *NPNF* Second Series, Vol. IV, p. 370.

5. Vladimir Lossky, *The Mystical Theology of the Eastern Church* (London: James Clarke, 1957), p. 100. See Basil, *On the Spirit*, ch. XVI, *NPNF* Second Series, Vol. VIII, p. 23.

6. Vladimir Lossky, *Orthodox Theology: An Introduction* (Crestwood, NY: St Vladimir's Seminary Press, 1978), p. 54.

free to be itself: 'another freedom' in relation to that of God. It is the nature of human 'freedom' – especially moral freedom – in relation to God that is our subject for consideration.

Defining Polyphony

The word 'polyphony' means a variety of tones or speech (Greek *polloi* meaning many and *phone* meaning a voice or sound). It is readily associated with styles of musical composition in which the parts move in apparent independence and freedom through fitting together harmonically. For Bakhtin, polyphony is a particular way of authoring a novel. The polyphonic authorial point of view is not single, fixed or monologic, but multiple and dynamic, almost creating chaos and lack of direction because many different voices coexist and interact.[7] Polyphony is never defined closely by Bakhtin but has to do with how the freedom of heroes is built into the design and form of the novel; how the novel is about the heroes' ideas and discourse and not those of the author. An author's authority is dialogic when the conditions for polyphony are built into the structural features of a novel. Thus he writes of Dostoevsky's novels:

> A plurality of independent and unmerged voices and consciousnesses, a genuine polyphony of fully valid voices is in fact the chief characteristic of Dostoevsky's novels. What unfolds in his works is not a multitude of characters and fates in a single objective world, illuminated by a single authorial consciousness; rather a plurality of consciousnesses, with equal rights and each with its own world, combine but are not merged in the unity of the event.[8]

The author creates a novel in which the authoring process involves

---

7. M. M. Bakhtin, *Problems of Dostoevsky's Poetics*, ed. and trans. Caryl Emerson (Minnesota; UMP, 1984), esp. pp. 5–9.
8. Bakhtin, *Problems of Dostoevsky's Poetics*, p. 6.

listening to the voices of the heroes. Each hero and novel has a self-developing character in which the author writes in relation to the independent consciousness of the heroes. In the dialogic novel, many voices enter into dialogue within the novel, and the author also enters into dialogue with each hero/interlocutor. The question is whether Bakhtin helps us with his ideas about polyphony to express the many-voiced nature of witness to God in the bible and Christian tradition, and to link that many-voicedness to questions about ethics and the teaching authority of the church.

Drawing on the work of Bakhtin, I suggest in broad terms that the problem of polyphony in Christian ethics and moral theology is the problem of differing and conflicting responses to the good news of Christ. The possibility of polyphony is found in the glorious liberty of Christian people liberated from the law of sin and death, and from the slavery of sin (Rom. 6:18, 8:2). The actual word 'polyphony' is not particularly significant, but what is important is the multiple witness to God that it can be used to describe. Consider, for example, how Walter Brueggemann, in his *Theology of the Old Testament*, regards witness or testimony to Yahweh as constitutive of Israel's faith. Utterance, he argues, is more central to Israel's embrace and explication of Yahweh than are the claims of history and ontology.[9] A central thesis of his book is that the metaphor of testimony, alongside recognition of the pervasiveness of counter-testimony and dispute, is likely to be helpful in Old Testament theology today. This thesis rests not only on the observation that such an approach accords with the lived reality of which the Old Testament texts speak, but that utterance is generative of social reality; when a word/the Word is spoken, its invitation and its summons call new relationship into being. For Brueggemann, theology is not simply analysis of the practice of speech but an engagement with speech practices, in order to adjudicate what is and what is not 'true speech' or 'speech about

---

9. Walter Brueggemann, *Theology of the Old Testament: Testimony, Dispute, Advocacy* (Minneapolis: Fortress Press, 1997), p. 721.

the truth'. Arguably, Bakhtin helps us to think more about self-expression though utterance and testimony in ways that hold on to questions about truth and have application to Christian ethics.

Is the concept of polyphony embedded in the bible?

But what, if anything, of polyphony is embedded in the bible? In answer to this, consider how Brueggemann's account of the Old Testament's plural witness to Yahweh is congruent with many emphases in Mikhail Bakhtin's work regarding polyphony and embodied truth. Brueggemann's assumptions regarding the (i) the central importance of speech as the mode of divine and human actuality; (ii) the disputatious quality of truth; and (iii) the lived, bodied form of testimonial – or discursive – communities, are shared with Bakhtin.[10] Both create space within their respective disciplines for adequate recognition of pluralism in any interpretative context. Both envisage God/the author's relationship to the world as that of grace-filled and interactive communication. Both refuse to reduce truth to propositional statements but cast it in relational terms. Note, for example, how Brueggemann emphasises the intimate connection between the claims of Yahweh and Israel's multifold witness to 'the true God'.[11] He notes how faith in Yahweh is sometimes harsh and demanding (Josh. 24:19–20); Israel's act of testimony frequently requires the re-ordering of all other allegiances. The lives of the people become the ground of dispute as they stake their existence upon their testimony that God alone is the Lord:

> I, I am the LORD,
>   and besides me there is no saviour.
> I declared and saved and proclaimed,
>   when there was no strange god among you;
>   and you are my witnesses, says the LORD.

---

10. Brueggemann, *Theology of the Old Testament*, p. 716.
11. Brueggemann, *Theology of the Old Testament*, pp. 748–749.

> I am God, and also henceforth I am He;
>   there is no one who can deliver from my hand;
>   I work and who can hinder it?
>   (Is. 43:11–13)

The lives of the people are expressed in their many voices. Israel's many voices – which have many times contested the ordering of community life – risk everything in confessing God in the face of the powers of Babylon. Brueggemann is well aware of tension between Israel's testimony to God as true and sovereign, and its counter-testimony to its experience of God's absence, hiddenness, ambiguity and negativity. Israel's witness is multifold; the sovereign elusiveness of God, as well the covenantal faithfulness of God, escapes single definition; in the end, 'no ideological statement of Yahweh is permitted finally to prevail'.[12] Thus, for Brueggemann, there is an openness and an unfinalisability about Old Testament theology because the people's witness to God is diverse and polyphonic.

In the New Testament, the theme of polyphony is linked closely to the enabling power of the Holy Spirit. On the day of Pentecost the Holy Spirit endowed the disciples with the ability to speak in other tongues (Acts 2:4). The phenomenon of glossolalia was interpreted as a manifestation of the Holy Spirit. Peter, filled with the Holy Spirit, spoke with power (*dynamis*) before the Jewish rulers and elders (Acts 4:7); Stephen was chosen as deacon because he was 'a man full of faith and the Holy Spirit' (Acts 6:5). At Caesarea, when the Holy Spirit fell on the gentiles who had listened to Peter's message, they spoke in tongues of ecstasy and extolled the greatness of God (Acts 10:46). Paul could begin his work among the gentiles only because he was filled with the Holy Spirit (Acts 13:9). He could continue it only because of the sanctifying power of the Holy Spirit (Rom. 15:16), the love inspired by the Spirit (Rom. 15:30), and because of the power of interpretation

---

12. Brueggemann, *Theology of the Old Testament*, p. 724.

and words taught by the Spirit (1 Cor. 2:13). Nor is this enabling power confined to the leaders of the early church. The Holy Spirit floods the hearts of all believers with the love of God (Rom. 5:5). The body of every believer is a temple of the Holy Spirit (1 Cor. 6:19); each person is graced by the presence of the Spirit and enabled with gifts for some useful purpose (1 Cor. 12:7).

The New Testament witness is that many voices proclaim the glory of God. The polyphony of faith follows from the distributive and personal work of the Holy Spirit. As Lossky writes: 'The work of Christ concerns human nature which He recapitulates in His hypostasis. The work of the Holy Spirit, on the other hand, concerns persons, being applied to each one singly.'[13] The work of Christ unifies and that of the Holy Spirit divides, as the Holy Spirit brings to each person the presence of Christ. As, according to Chalcedonian logic, there is a distinction of persons in the unity of one divine nature, so also in the church; a multiplicity of persons is united to God through the person of Jesus Christ. The unifying effect of the incarnation is complemented by the multiplying effects of Pentecost. Thus Paul writes to the Galatians about the freedom of faith given to those who are adult offspring of God and not slaves under the law. 'Did you receive the Spirit', he asks, 'by doing the works of the law or by believing what you heard?' (Gal. 3:2). Christ bought freedom from the law in order that Jew and Gentile alike might receive the Spirit through faith. It is the Spirit of Christ who enables the children of God to cry: 'Abba! Father!' because they enjoy the freedom of children and heirs, and not the yoke of slavery which is the law. But the freedom of faith given to each believer is no licence for unspiritual behaviour. Paul writes: 'For you were called to freedom, brothers and sisters; only do not use your freedom as an opportunity for self-indulgence, but through love become slaves to one another. For the whole law is summed up in a single commandment, "You shall love your neighbour as yourself" ' (Gal. 5:14). The Christian

---

13. Lossky, *Mystical Theology of the Eastern Church*, p. 166.

does not live in abjection as one who is submissive and under domination, like one who has lost the power of free thought or resistance. The Christian does not follow their God servilely or conform to that which is demanded. Neither, however, does the Christian deny the obligatoriness of the moral life. Faith is not the opposite of obligation to keep the moral law but brings with it responsibilities to live in the form of Christ (Gal. 4:19). As those under the influence of the Holy Spirit (1 Cor. 12:3) – or as sharers in the life of the Spirit (Heb. 6:4) – each is called to testify as a woman or man of God. The writer to the Ephesians prays: '[L]et the Holy Spirit fill you: speak to one another in psalms, hymns, and songs; sing and make music from your heart to the Lord' (Eph. 5:19 *REB*). The polyphony of the people of God is the condition for harmonious praise and worship.

Reasons for Thinking about Polyphony and the Spirit of Freedom and Truth

Thus it appears that the concept of polyphony is embedded in the bible. But what are our more specific reasons for thinking about the matter? I suggest that there are both negative and positive reasons for talking about polyphony in our contemporary situation. One reason is the need to refute some misplaced accusations. A charge levelled frequently against Christianity – even if not stated in the exact same words – is that it does not allow for polyphony and hinders individual human expression. Nietzsche charged Christianity with the kind of 'hostility against life' which shows itself in the condition called faith. Faith, he jibes, is 'closing one's eyes to oneself once and for all, lest one suffer the sight of incurable falsehood'.[14] Christianity breeds such weak and mindless human beings that, he argues, they cannot live with themselves. Christians who acknowledge the authority of God and the church

---

14. Friedrich Nietzsche, *The Antichrist*, §§8–9 in *The Portable Nietzsche*, trans. and ed. Walter Kaufmann (New York and London: Penguin, 1976), pp. 574–575.

are burdened with guilt, have directed their natural instincts away from what is healthy, and are full of vengeance against those who are happy and powerful. They pander to some metaphysical notion of truth when, in fact, truth is 'a mobile army of metaphors'.[15] It's just a way of producing an effect on one's addressee.[16] Truth is made, not revealed. Buddhism has the advantage, he argues, of making egoism 'the one thing needful' rather than belief in fictitious notions about originary causes (God), imaginary effects (sin, redemption, grace), and intercourse between imaginary beings (God, spirits, souls).[17] Buddhism struggles against suffering rather than sin and, because of this, offers more scope for individual freedom than life according to Christian confessions of truth. He wants humans to despise Christianity, and sees no particular need to replace its superstition with another religion, although the advantage of Buddhism is its supposed amenability to the well-being of the person.

Nor are charges of lack of self-expression and moral inadequacy levelled only by dead white European males. Many feminist writers accuse Christianity of stifling human expression, creativity and polyphony, especially as far as the spiritual life is concerned. In her survey of the feminist spiritual movement, Rita Gross observes that, rather than seeking conformity with orthodox doctrine, spiritually minded individuals are 'to experiment to find what works for them'.[18] Each is responsible to and for themselves, and the criterion used is 'was it good for you?' Each woman and man is endowed with spiritual capacity and spiritual significance is conferred by choice. Authenticity is tested by love of feminist principle. The more voices the better, because truth is plural and

---

15. Friedrich Nietzsche, 'Twilight of the Idols' in *The Portable Nietzsche*, pp. 46–47.
16. This is Richard Rorty's interpretation of Nietzsche's sense. See *Contingency, Irony and Solidarity* (Cambridge: CUP, 1989), pp. 17–18.
17. Nietzsche, *The Antichrist*, §§15–20 in *The Portable Nietzsche*, pp. 581–588.
18. Rita Gross, *Feminism and Religion* (Boston, MA: Beacon Press, 1996), p. 228.

should not be reduced to just one kind or class. The truth that matters is contingent upon selfhood; there is no need any longer to worship anything as divine, only to respect human selfhood, language, conscience and relationality. There may or may not be an horizon of significance beyond individual choice. The concept of God may or may not be required to 'perform a transcendental function', in order to define how to respect each person's project of self-realisation.[19] It is the self that is centre-stage because it is a source of truth and what is important is that persons are true to themselves in their quasi-spiritual lives.[20] The accusation is that Christianity is more about monologism than polyphony, and is the kind of faith in which God/the author communicates divine revelation to a pyramidal hierarchy which then transmits it to the rest of the church. There is little space for self-expression and moral choice, with the result that many feel the need to move 'beyond God the Father'.[21] Such accusations are common but misplaced. Thus, one reason for talking about polyphony in the Spirit is to demonstrate why they are wrong.

Another reason is the need to express the distinctiveness of Christian testimony regarding moral freedom. If Nietzsche and radical anti-Christian feminists get it wrong, then we need to explain why they are wrong and to lay out an alternative and more convincing understanding of Christian theology and ethics. In so doing, we need to be aware that over-easy appeals to bible and tradition are not likely to be well received. Increasingly, theologians recognise (and welcome) that the time for hegemonic interpretations of the bible and authoritarian teaching practices is past:

What goes under the general term of *postmodern* signifies the

---

19. For an argument in favour of retaining the notion of God to refer to a dimension of all that is, see Daphne Hampson, *After Christianity* (London: SCM, 1996), p. 244.
20. Hampson, *After Christianity*, p. 283.
21. Mary Daly, *Beyond God the Father* (Boston, MA: Beacon Press, 1973), *passim.*

break-up of any broad consensus about what we know or how we know what we know. This means, in my judgement, that no interpretive institution, ecclesial or academic, can any longer sustain a hegemonic mode of interpretation, so that our capacity for a magisterial or even a broadly based consensus about a pattern of interpretation will be hard to come by. In fact, interpretation is no longer safely held in the hands of certified, authorized interpreters, but we are faced with a remarkable pluralism.[22]

As Brueggemann is aware, we live in an age when the authority of personal choice carries more weight for the majority than the pronouncements by leaders or the synodical gatherings of mainstream denominations. This does not mean that we should fall into a new 'situation ethic' in which the criteria for judgement are derived solely from the requirements of love in the given situation; conformity in the face of moral absolutes and the arbitrariness of unrestrained relativism are false opposites. Rather, we need to be able to articulate the distinctiveness of Christian ethics and polyphony within a pluralistic interpretive context.

All this raises questions about the teaching authority of the church. At a time when established centres of authority – especially religious authority – are being dislodged and decentred, what kind of teaching ministry can or should the church still exercise? We can no longer assume that the church either has or should have an effective teaching ministry, especially as far as ethics and moral reasoning is concerned. Zygmunt Bauman touches a nerve when he writes: 'The insecurity of speakers is the true subject matter of the discourse whose ostensible topic is the security of tradition.'[23] The church cannot assume that its authority will go unquestioned

---

22. Brueggemann, *Theology of the Old Testament*, pp. 709–710.
23. Zygmunt Bauman, 'Morality in the Age of Contingency', in Paul Heelas et al. (eds), *Detraditionalization* (Oxford: Blackwell, 1996), p. 50.

because many now hold that concepts like tradition, divinity and metaphysical truth are dispensable and should be abandoned without delay. Few Christian theorists accept either Bauman's presuppositions or his conclusions, but postmodern sensibilities leave some Christian, as well as non-Christian, people suffering from powerlessness, closure and 'blankness'.[24] At the risk of over-generalisation, postmodern sensibilities urge people to leave behind the redundant and false certainties of the modern era (including the Christian metanarrative), but promise nothing more than a plurality of world-views which slides easily towards fragmentation and confusion.[25] The postmodern a/theologian Mark C. Taylor writes of wandering aimlessly without any map or compass with which to find a way ahead. In an essay, entitled 'Reframing Postmodernisms', he speaks of religion being in the desert or place of absence. In the desert or wilderness the only appropriate actions are those of waiting, wandering and removing from our theologies all inessential baggage.[26] He plays on the two meanings of 'desert' to suggest that contemporary theological

24. These descriptive terms are used by Michael Welker in *God the Spirit* (Minneapolis: Fortress Press, 1994, German edition 1992), pp. 28–40.

25. Postmodernism is a name given to cultural tendencies that are characterised by change and the need to leave behind redundant and false certainties of the modern era. Broadly speaking, the certainties of rational truth, enlightenment and progress can no longer be relied upon. The modern assertion, 'everything real is rational, everything rational is real', was refuted once and for all in the gas chambers of Auschwitz. Communist beliefs in proletarian democracy were dashed as workers rose up against the Party, e.g., in Czechoslovakia, 1968. Established theories of economic liberalism fell apart in the crises of 1911 and 1929. Enlightenment values of instrumental or goal-directed reason and progress have resulted in a culture less marked by freedom than by the 'iron cage' of bureaucracy that Weber foretold. (This account draws upon that of Jean-François Lyotard, *The Differend: Phrases in Dispute*, trans. George van den Abbeele (Minneapolis: UMP, 1988).)

26. Mark C. Taylor, 'Reframing postmodernisms' in Philippa Berry and Andrew Wernick (eds), *Shadow of Spirit: Postmodernism and Religion* (London and New York: Routledge, 1992), *passim*.

experiences of barrenness are deserved because of theological complicity with false gods of modernity.

In this kind of climate, it is difficult to talk about the teaching authority of the church without falling into the falsely polarised alternatives of conformity versus arbitrary personal choice. Tensions between conformity to pre-established dogma and exaggerated reliance on one's own insight, monologism and unrestrained relativism, are especially evident in Christian ethics and moral theology. According to Bakhtin, this is the Hobson's choice of typically modern thought: '[E]ither there is a system or there is nothing; either there are comprehensive closed structures or there is chaos; either there is in principle an all-encompassing explanatory system or there is total relativism (or perhaps: either God exists, or all is permitted).'[27] We should not allow the assumption that there are only these two alternatives to blind us to other possibilities. Beware, warns Bakhtin, of approaching our subject with trammelled ways of thinking which offer us either an ethic of absolutes (composed of rules and moral norms) or an ethic or relativity (in which we are indifferent to truth). Beware of identifying authority with monologism and polyphony with relativism. It was an unfortunate tendency of the modern era to try to squash God into humanly constructed systems and theories; systematised thinking of the worst sort falsely reduced – and continues to reduce – God to a factor within a human schema. To fall victim to this kind of thinking is likely to render us blinkered and insensitive to the proper concerns of ethics and moral theology.

Moral Freedom, Polyphony and Divine Grace

With these reasons in mind, let us proceed to a consideration of freedom and responsibility in the life of faith. Our determining question is the extent to which there is space in Christian ethics for differing and conflicting voices. I assume that Christianity is

---

27. I use a phrase and draw from G. S. Morson and C. Emerson, *Mikhail* ▷

not a monologic faith in which each person's utterance must be measured and controlled like that of voiceless slaves. But is Christianity a polyphonic faith whose truth invites many voices for its expression? If so, how easily does this sit with traditional understandings of the teaching ministry of the church?[28] Paul

---

Bakhtin: Creation of a Prosaics (Stanford, CA: SUP, 1990), p. 233.

28. In this chapter I do not develop a denominationally specific answer but, rather, develop ways of thinking about how Christian ethics and moral theology need to be linked to Pneumatology. This said, we need to be aware that the ministry of teaching takes different forms in different traditions and denominations. This is not the place for detailed consideration of these differences, but it is worth noting a few major emphases. In the Orthodox Church, bishops receive their staff of office at the words: 'Receive thou the pastoral staff, that thou mayest feed the flock of Christ entrusted unto thee: and be thou a staff and support unto those who are obedient. But lead thou the disobedient and the wayward unto correction, unto gentleness, and unto obedience; and they shall continue in due submission' (*Service Book of the Holy Orthodox-Catholic Apostolic Church*, trans. Isabel Hapgood (New York: Syrian Antiochene Orthodox Archdiocese, 1922)). Bishops are expected to teach the people what is in accordance with Orthodox Catholic Christian faith and to preserve the peace of the church. The highest authority of the Orthodox Church is the synod of bishops and, while it functions by normal human fashion and not directly as an instrument of the Holy Spirit, it is the body by which is expressed the infallibility with which the church is endowed. Its authority extends to moral as well as doctrinal matters. In the Roman Catholic Church, the bishops 'have the obligation of fostering and safeguarding the unity of the faith and of upholding the discipline which is common to the whole Church' (*Lumen Gentium* (21 November 1964), ch. III, 'The Church is Hierarchical' in *Vatican Council II, The Conciliar and Post Conciliar Documents*, ed. Austin Flannery OP (Dublin: Dominican Publications, 1992)). Bishops are the official teachers of the church responsible for, among other things, safeguarding the moral teaching of the church from distortion and error. They are empowered to teach that which is, in some sense at least, normative for the faith life of believers. (This is a summary arrived at by Richard R. Gaillardetz in his detailed and careful study, *Teaching with Authority: A Theology of the Magisterium in the Church* (Collegeville, MN: Michael Glazier, 1997, p. 31).) In the Anglican Church, the episcopate symbolises and secures in an abiding form the apostolic mission and authority within the church. (This is a paraphrase of the classic statement of the nature of episcopacy, as accepted in the Church of England, and found in the Report of the Archbishops' Commis- ▷

speaks of the Holy Spirit as distributing gifts to each person individually: 'All these [gifts] are activated by one and the same Spirit, who allots to each one individually just as the Spirit chooses' (1 Cor. 12:11). But he also speaks about the need for unity of mind and thought among the believers (1 Cor. 1:10). He wants the saints in Corinth to be 'united in the same mind and the same purpose', welcoming what we are calling polyphony in the Spirit while warning against divergences and quarrelling. Is Paul overexcitedly naïve at this point, or do his writings betray a thinly veiled authoritarianism? Can we speak today about freedom in the Spirit without implying patterns of relation marked by eclecticism and arbitrary choice? Can we speak about the teaching authority of the church without implying subjection and the worst aspects of moral puritanism? What prevents a Christian understanding of

---

sion on Christian Doctrine, *Doctrine in the Church of England*, 1938, pp. 122–23.) Social factors have influenced and continue to influence how episcopal ministry in the Anglican Church is understood and exercised at a given place and time, but it remains a function of the episcopate to guard the church against erroneous teaching. Lutheran churches regard the role of persons in episcopal ministries as that of, *inter alia*, 'advising and supporting the congregations in their life of worship, witness and service ... assuring that the teaching of the church is in harmony with the gospel as interpreted in the confessions of the church and to warn against false teaching and help people in their struggle against it' (*Lutheran World Federation Studies: Ministry, Women, Bishops*, Report of an International Consultation, Cartigny, Switzerland, 1992 (Geneva: The Lutheran World Federation, 1993)). Ministers ordained to the episcopal office of leadership and spiritual supervision (*episkope*) are elected, and their fundamental task is to proclaim the gospel in its purity and administer the sacraments according to the gospel. The Baptist Union of Great Britain maintains that the whole church is called to be 'apostolic' in witnessing to the good news of Christ and the forgiveness of sins as the Apostles did, but some are called to be guardians of the apostolic tradition. There are spiritual leaders in whom *episkope* is focused and who have primary (though not exclusive) responsibility for the ministry of the word in the community (*Forms of Ministry among Baptists: Towards an Understanding of Spiritual Leadership*, by The Faith and Unity Executive Committee Doctrine and Worship Committee, 1994, §10).

moral freedom from falling into arbitrariness, self-illusion, and/ or antinomianism?

Drawing on the Thought of Mikhail Bakhtin

In addressing these questions, I draw once more upon the writings of Mikhail Bakhtin. Bakhtin writes about polyphony and ethics most explicitly in *Problems of Dostoevsky's Poetics* (1929). However, his treatment of the subject of ethics is more widespread and began earlier in his career, notably with his first major work, *Toward the Philosophy of the Act* (1919–1921). He writes about the relationship between ethics and aesthetics most explicitly in 'Author and Hero in Aesthetic Activity' (1920–1923). In what follows, we shall give brief consideration to each of the above, paying particular attention to where his ideas about moral freedom and polyphony appear to be influenced by Christianity, and to how he negotiates a path between unlimited freedom and despotism.[29] I do not assume that Bakhtin always has something to teach us. However, I am sufficiently convinced of the congruity between his work and major themes in biblical and ecumenical-traditional teaching to allow him to provoke us into fresh consideration of the polyphony inspired by the Holy Spirit.

Before proceeding, we should note that polyphony is most definitely not identical to heteroglossia. For Bakhtin, polyphony concerns the relation of an author to a text and heteroglossia (*raznorcie*) is used to describe the multiplicity of voices and the wide variety of links and interrelationships between them in a novel: 'The novel orchestrates all its themes, the totality of the world of objects and ideas depicted and expressed in it, by means of the social diversity of speech types (*raznorcie*) and by the

---

29. One of Dostoevsky's characters in *Possessed* observed: 'Starting from unlimited freedom, I arrive at unlimited despotism' (Pt 2, ch. 7, sec. 2), cited in Morson and Emerson, *Mikhail Bakhtin*, p. 470.

differing individual voices that flourish under such conditions.'[30] Heteroglossia is used to convey speech diversity, and is often employed when he speaks of the tension in language between centripetal and centrifugal forces. In any language, he says, there are historico-social forces at work which pull variously toward: (i) centralisation, a unified or 'correct' language in which linguistic norms tend to overcome diversity, and sameness of verbal and ideological life; and (ii) decentralisation, disunification, and the kind of speech diversity that is contradiction-ridden and tension-filled.[31] Heteroglossia has to do with the decentralising tendencies in the life of any language. According to Michael Holquist, it is 'the base condition governing the operation of meaning in any utterance'. It is the state in which words have meaning. Its randomness ensures the primacy of context over text and more or less guarantees that a word uttered in one place and time will have a different meaning than the same work uttered at another place and time.[32] Heteroglossia is hostile to any attempt at linguistic domination and nurtures subversion. Polyphony allows for heteroglossia but the two are not synonymous.

By extension, it is important to emphasise that polyphony in Christian ethics is not identical to relativism or pluralism. Polyphony – as understood in the remainder of this chapter – is about the many-voiced nature of witness to God that the Spirit of God inspires. By contrast, relativism is the view that (moral) knowledge is relative to the limited nature of the human mind and the conditions of its knowing. Nor is polyphony identical to pluralism, if by pluralism is meant a world-view which recognises more than one principle of being, or more than one set of equally valid moral principles. Plural witness to God is not the same as pluralism in

---

30. Bakhtin, 'Discourse in the Novel', p. 263.

31. Bakhtin, 'Discourse in the Novel', p. 272.

32. See 'Glossary' in Michael Holquist (ed.), *The Dialogic Imagination: Four Essays by M. M. Bakhtin*, trans. Caryl Emerson and Michael Holquist (Austin, TX: University of Texas Press, 1981), p. 428.

this sense. We must be careful here not to trip ourselves up by failing to identify where definitions of words vary slightly from one author to another. For instance, Michael Welker speaks approvingly of the 'pluralism of the Spirit', but what he means by pluralism is not the assertion of difference for its own sake, or the false appearance of the endless to and fro of discourse. This 'bad' kind of pluralism masks illusion and individualism. Rather, he means the unity of the Spirit in creaturely difference; a unity which equates neither to homogeneity (homophonia) nor to unrighteous difference.[33] I use the word 'polyphony' rather than 'pluralism' precisely because of difficulties involved in distancing a Christian understanding of pluralism from a secular understanding, and because of the etymological sense of 'many voices' which, in turn, implies utterance, speech and communication.

The theme of polyphony overlaps in Bakhtin's work with the themes of authoring and dialogism. Thus, in the following passage from Bakhtin's 1961 'Toward a Reworking of the Dostoevsky Book' we see explicit connections between polyphony and dialogic authoring. In the passage immediately prior, Bakhtin has defined monologism as 'a denial of the equal rights of consciousnesses vis-à-vis truth (understood abstractly and systematically)'.[34] Monologism is summed up as follows: 'God can get along without man, but man cannot get along without Him.' Authority is monologic when God/the author controls and uses the power to make a hero express a truth. According to monologic understandings of authority, it is ultimately only God/the author's voice that matters and truth is measured against what they hold to be correct. By contrast, the polyphonic author creates space for the development of the hero's personality, enables the hero to grow and develop through varied experiences, and establishes conditions in which their voices are fully valid. Of particular interest to us is how Bakhtin makes direct reference to the Christian confession that

33. Welker, *God the Spirit*, pp. 25–26.
34. Bakhtin, *Problems of Dostoevsky's Poetics*, p. 285.

God created morally free people and that this is the kind of moral freedom in which the author neither passively reproduces the views of others nor disregards their personhood:

> Our point of view in no way assumes a passivity on the part of the author, who would then merely assemble others' points of view, others' truths, completely denying his own point of view, his own truth. This is not the case at all; the case is rather a completely new and special interrelationship between the author's and the other's truth. The author is profoundly *active*, but his activity is of a special *dialogic* sort. It is one thing to be active in relation to a dead thing, to voiceless material that can be moulded and formed as one wishes, and another thing to be active *in relation to someone else's living, autonomous consciousness*. This is a questioning, provoking, answering, agreeing, objecting activity; that is, it is dialogic activity no less active than the activity that finalizes, materializes, explains, and kills causally, that drowns out the other's voice with nonsemantic arguments. Dostoevsky frequently interrupts, but he never drowns out the other's voice, never finishes it off 'from himself', that is, out of his own and alien consciousness. That is, so to speak, the activity of God in His relation to man, a relation allowing man to reveal himself utterly (in his immanent development), to judge himself, to refute himself. This is activity of a higher quality. It surmounts not the resistance of dead material, but the resistance of another's consciousness, another's truth.[35]

To Bakhtin's mind, the activity of God/the author creates a world of existential freedom in which persons are called to be fully themselves. Each person/hero is called to knowledge of themselves and others. This is because, as Bakhtin wrote of Dostoevsky's insight, the very being of humanity is found in communion. *To be* means to exist in communion and to communicate, in different

---

35. Bakhtin, *Problems of Dostoevsky's Poetics*, pp. 285–286.

ways and at different levels, with God and others. To be means to be for another and through the other and, only thereby, for oneself. Absolute death (non-being) is the state of being unheard, unrecognised, unremembered and unloved.

Polyphony and the gift of freedom

When Bakhtin writes about polyphony, he is interested primarily in the relationship of an author to characters in a text. More specifically, he is interested in the structural features of a novel whereby an author allows for the character's discourse to be independent of the single authorial consciousness in such a way that the characters are capable of standing alongside their creator, of not agreeing with them, and even of rebelling against them.[36] Bakhtin's discussions of the nature of ethics are closely related to the dynamics of this creative process. The freedom that the characters enjoy is wholly dependent upon the will of the author; their freedom is derivative and cannot be improved upon. Yet the astonishing freedom of Dostoevsky's characters is due, he argues, to specific artistic means; to 'the very structure of the novel, vis-à-vis the author – or, more accurately, their freedom vis-à-vis the usual externalising and finalising authorial definitions'.[37] Each character is, as it were, predestined to freedom. It is the author's intention that holds the novelistic world together, but in a way that does not compromise the autonomous voice of each character. Thus he writes:

> It seems that each person who enters the labyrinth of the polyphonic novel somehow loses his way in it and fails to hear the whole behind the individual voices. It often happens that even the dim outlines of the whole are not grasped; the artistic principles governing the combination of voices cannot be detected by the ear. . . . The unity of the polyphonic

---

36. Bakhtin, *Problems of Dostoevsky's Poetics*, p. 6.
37. Bakhtin, *Problems of Dostoevsky's Poetics*, p. 13.

novel – a unity standing above the word, above the voice, above the accent – has yet to be discovered.[38]

The polyphonic novel has unity but it is a unity bestowed by the artist whose being is supremely outside the work. The novel has a wholeness, but only of the sort that can be perceived by the author.

This encourages us to think about the kind of freedom enjoyed by human persons. Is it the kind of freedom that allows us to be responsible for our actions? Are we capable of standing (metaphorically) alongside our creator, of not agreeing with God and even of rebelling against God? What, if any, are the limits of this freedom? How does it shape our moral lives? For Bakhtin, the freedom enjoyed by the characters in a novel is best understood as relative to that of the author before it is relative to that of one another. Significantly, the characters in Dostoevsky's novels enjoy freedom of a personal kind because their freedom is, in this derivative sense, of the same kind as that of the author. Dostoevsky is free to write characters into existence within the creative world of the novel. But his characters are also free. Each has the right and the power to determine how they will act. Each has their own field of vision, and limited opportunity for the exercise of intellectual and corporeal faculties. The existence enjoyed by each entails a freedom that is relative to the freedom of the author to create before it is relative to that of other characters to make choices and determine their actions. Dostoevsky, he says, has a clear sense of his authorial task and creative freedom: 'Only in the light of Dostoevsky's fundamental artistic task . . . can one begin to understand the profound organic cohesion, consistency and wholeness of Dostoevsky's poetics.'[39]

By analogy, it is only in the light of God's authorial task and creative freedom that we can begin to understand the divine gift

---

38. Bakhtin, *Problems of Dostoevsky's Poetics*, p. 43.
39. Bakhtin, *Problems of Dostoevsky's Poetics*, p. 8.

of freedom to us. This is fundamental to Christian ethics. Like the freedom of Dostoevsky's characters, human freedom is wholly derivative and without it human life is meaningless and absurd. Gregory of Nyssa writes of free will as integral to humanity's being made in the image of God:

> Being the image and the likeness . . . of the Power which rules all things, man kept also in the matter of a Free-Will this likeness to Him whose Will is over all. He was enslaved to no outward necessity whatever; his feeling towards that which pleased him depended only on his own private judgement; he was free to choose whatever he liked; and so he was a free agent, though circumvented with cunning, when he drew upon himself that disaster which now overwhelms humanity.[40]

God's will is outside of what can be contemplated by rational faith; the creature cannot make sense of 'how' questions regarding creation. Indeed, it would be absurd to postulate that the creature can know anything about the workings of the divine will, though they do know about the reality of the freedom that they enjoy. As Gregory indicates, there is a difference in the quality of freedom enjoyed by the human creature before and after the fall. Sin resulted (and continues to result) in alienation from God which means that each person must continually make choices about how to live their lives.[41] Each person's free decision to rebel against God results in their having to decide continually either for or against God. Having once closed one's eyes to the good, one knows the difference between light and dark and is forced to choose between them.[42] There is, however, nothing which can take

---

40. Gregory of Nyssa, *On Virginity*, ch. XII, *NPNF* Second Series, Vol. V, p. 357.

41. Gregory of Nyssa, *Against Eunomius*, Bk II, §13, *NPNF* Second Series, Vol. V, p. 127.

42. Gregory of Nyssa, *The Great Catechism*, ch. VI, *NPNF* Second Series, Vol. V, p. 481.

away this ability to choose. For the ancient, eastern fathers, sin and death have tremendous capacity to corrupt and destroy but they cannot ultimately deprive the human person of the freedom of choice, because the Word of God has saved humanity from this fate: 'For Him only Who at the first had given the life was it possible, or fitting, to recover it when lost.'[43] God's gift of freedom has been restored in Christ; repentance is possible even for the worst of sinners.[44]

Many ancient eastern fathers emphasised the God-given role of human freedom within the divine work of salvation, in the belief that God does not destroy our liberty but desires that we commune with the Godhead voluntarily (2 Cor. 6:1–2). This said, we learn most about the divine gift of freedom by consulting biblical texts. In what follows, I shall cite three texts from Genesis. In each, the surprising thing is the extent to which God's freedom is, within the limits of the narrative, the same as that of the people involved. To a limited extent, God and the people in the accounts are equally free. Neither can force the other to do anything: God will not destroy the freedom already given to human people; they have no right to tell God what to do. In the text that recounts God's institution of a covenantal relationship with Abram (Gen. 15), God and Abram bind themselves to each other in a treaty-like relationship in which mutual rights and responsibilities are out-lined. In the text that recounts God's testing of Abraham (Gen.

---

43. Gregory of Nyssa, *The Great Catechism*, ch. VIII, *NPNF* Second Series, Vol. V, p. 485.

44. John Breck draws helpfully on St Maximus the Confessor's distinction between 'gnomic' and 'natural' will, and his conclusion that the former possesses an inviolable capacity for freedom of choice: 'Understood as a function of the human *person* rather than of being – a hypostatic rather than a natural property – the gnomic will *can* respond to God's will with faith, love and obedience . . . This is because sin originates with the personal rather than with the natural dimension of human existence.' John Breck, *The Sacred Gift of Life: Orthodox Christianity and Bioethics* (Crestwood, NY: St Vladimir's Seminary Press, 1998), p. 31.

22), Abraham exercised his freedom on rational grounds afforded by the moral conduct of God previously. In the text that recounts Jacob's wrestling with God (Gen. 32:22–32), God was impotent in regard to Jacob and could not compel his surrender. The seemingly scandalous reference to divine impotence is justified by the text for reasons which will become clear. Each of these texts makes astonishing claims for the equality of the freedom of God and the human persons involved, if by freedom we mean the power to determine one's actions. Each also indicates links between faith in God and certainty regarding the moral excellence of God's character.

God and Abram: equally but differently free

Genesis 15 tells of Yahweh's covenant with Abram and of Israel's covenantal obligation to Yahweh.[45] It also tells of Abram's freedom to reason whether or not to base his life on the seemingly irrational promise of God. The passage is surprising in the extent to which it suggests that the covenantal relationship between God and Abram was one of respect on both sides. Abram is free to commune with God voluntarily and God does not violate this freedom. Scholarly opinion concerning the date and provenance of the text is varied, as are interpretations given to Israel's relationship with Yahweh. A frequently drawn distinction is that between the covenant as either conditional or unconditional, i.e. between whether it was established unilaterally by Yahweh or agreed to bilaterally by both Yahweh and Israel. Walter Brueggemann's opinion is that the distinction between conditional and unconditional is misleading, because the covenant is at the same time utterly giving and utterly demanding of both parties. Grace and law are twin aspects of covenant.[46] Working on this assumption,

---

45. For a useful summary of scholarship surrounding this passage, see Ernest W. Nicholson, *God and his People: Covenant and Theology in the Old Testament* (Oxford: Clarendon Press, 1986).

46. Brueggemann, *Theology of the Old Testament*, pp. 419–421.

let us consider what the text tells us about why Abram's faith regarding God's promise of descendants was reckoned to him as righteousness (Gen. 15:6). Abram, we are told, put his faith in Yahweh following Yahweh's promise to make his descendants as numerous as the stars in the sky. Having previously left his country and kin at Yahweh's command (Gen. 12:1–3), Abram judged Yahweh's word to be true despite all the odds and was justified in the eyes of God as a result of his faith. Why was he justified? Paul answers this question by reminding us that Abram's decision of faith was not a whim of the moment but a certitude based on theologico-rational grounds: 'No distrust made him waver concerning the promise of God . . . being fully convinced that God was able to do what he had promised' (Rom. 4:20–22). Faith is the larger working category than reasoned conviction and/or decision in this encounter between Yahweh and Abram, though Abram's faith included the free exercise of reason and was expressed in his decision based upon reasoned moral grounds. For Abram not to have trusted Yahweh would have been tantamount to declaring that God does not keep his promises and is not morally upright. It would have been to conclude that God either does not know what he is talking about or deceives people deliberately. Abram decided that to conclude as much would be more contrary to reason than to conclude that a post-menopausal woman could give birth. Thus he glorified God with his powers of reason and free will, and his faith was counted as righteousness.

The interplay in these passages between faith, love and duty is delicate, and not suited for close definition. Abram was obliged to obey God because God is God, and also because God had promised him and Sarai a future. God was obliged to respect Abram's decision because Abram had been created free and God would not destroy this gift of grace. The covenant signified the relationship of respect between them: 'On that day the LORD made a covenant with Abram, saying, "To your descendants I give this land . . ." ' (Gen. 15:18–20). God's duties to Abram were to provide for his happiness and that of his descendants: 'I shall make you exceedingly fruitful; I shall make nations out of you, and kings shall spring from you' (Gen. 17:6), and Isaac was born to Sarai shortly afterwards. Abram's duty to God was to trust in divine goodness, faithfulness and power. The exercise of this duty, with the help of God's Spirit, constituted his ongoing life of faith (Gal. 3:5–6). It included circumcision. 'God said to Abraham, "For your part, you must keep my covenant . . . This is how you are to keep this covenant" ' (Gen. 17:9–11 REB). Circumcision was a sign of blessing: an outward mark of a God-given grace.

Why, then, did Abraham unhesitatingly obey Yahweh's command to sacrifice Isaac? The writer to the Hebrews thought Abraham reckoned that God had the power to raise Isaac from the dead and so to give him back to him again (Heb. 11:19). Genesis 22 gives us no indication of this, though we told of Abraham's faith that 'God will provide' (Gen. 22:8). The suggestion in the text is that Abraham was free to exercise his free will, and did so in faith. He had no humanly rational ground on which to suppose that the act he was to perform – the sacrifice of Isaac – was good in itself. Rather, God could not have ordered him to do anything wrong or evil and, therefore, he should do as God commanded. Here we see Abraham's exercise of freedom in a most remarkable way. He was free to choose for God, even though every instinct in him impelled him to disobey. Presupposing the covenant between him and God, Abraham had an exact knowledge of their mutual expectations and obligations. Moreover, given the accounts in Gen. 20, it seems reasonable to suppose that he had an unshakeable confidence in God's – though not his own – possession of moral excellence. Abraham's morality was of the sort that trusted in God's morality rather than his own worthiness. His rationality was of the sort acquired through experience and faith. His only way to keep the covenant was to act in the dutiful certainty that God was true. Abraham kept the covenant and fulfilled his obligations to Yahweh. Thanks to his rational exercise of free will, Abram fulfilled the expectations of his relationship with God as was right, good, reasonable and fit. Yahweh also kept the covenant and fulfilled the divine obligation to Abraham. In this sense, the treaty between them was made and kept between persons equally, though differently, free.

Human freedom and divine impotence[47]

Perhaps the most difficult aspect of the Gen. 22 account is the assertion at its outset that God put Abraham to the test. It is the sort of action that we should probably decry if our chosen life-partners were to do the same to us. 'It's beneath you!' we might exclaim. Yet the text makes plain that God tested Abraham and he emerged unsullied and victorious from the ordeal. We don't know why God tested Abraham in this way, though we are told that Abraham's faithfulness gave cause for divine rejoicing and evoked abundant generosity (Gen. 22:16–17). Yet it is clear that Abraham proved a match for God's testing; his will was equal to God's will despite the effects of sin in his life. Divine omnipotence could not prevail against the will of a man in possession of the divine gift of freedom, because, in giving the gift of freedom, God had assumed a kenotic impotence. God could not have tested Abraham in this way if Abraham's freedom were illusory. Indeed, the contrary seems to have been true. Abraham's freedom was real and the God who tested was impotent in the face of Abraham's free decision of faith.

Something similar is true of God's wrestling with Jacob in Gen. 32. While preparing to meet his brother Esau, many years after stealing his lawful birthright, Jacob was unexpectedly wrestled by a man till daybreak. The man could not get the better of Jacob and so struck him in the thigh to dislocate the bone. At daybreak the man surrendered and attempted to withdraw, but Jacob refused to allow this until the man had given him a blessing. Then the man said, 'You shall no longer be called Jacob, but Israel, for you

---

47. In this section, I draw on some ideas in Apostolos Makrakis, *The Foundations of Philosophy*, trans. D. E. Cummings (Chicago: Orthodox Christian Educational Society, 1955).

have striven with God and with humans, and have prevailed'
(Gen. 32:28). Upon asking the man's name and receiving his
blessing, Jacob named the place Peniel, saying, 'For I have seen
God face to face, and yet my life is preserved' (Gen. 32:30). At
first glance, there seems to be no obvious meaning to God's
wrestling with Jacob. Upon closer examination, the text speaks
about the power of Jacob's freedom within the domain given
to him by God. Remember Yahweh's promise to Jacob in Gen.
28:13–15:

> 'I am the LORD, the God of Abraham your father and the
> God of Isaac; the land on which you lie I will give to you
> and to your offspring; and your offspring shall be like the
> dust of the earth, and you shall spread abroad to the west
> and to the east and to the north and to the south; and all
> the families of the earth shall be blessed in you and in your
> offspring. Know that I am with you and will keep you
> wherever you go, and will bring you back to this land; for I
> will not leave you until I have done what I have promised you.'

Recall also Jacob's response to this divine commitment in Gen.
28: 20–22. Jacob vowed:

> 'If God will be with me, and will keep me in this way that I
> go, and will give me bread to eat and clothing to wear, so
> that I come again to my father's house in peace, then the
> LORD shall be my God, and this stone, which I have set up
> for a pillar, shall be God's house; and of all that you give me
> I will surely give one tenth to you.'

Yahweh and Jacob are committed mutually one to the other.
Twenty years later, Jacob returns to the land of his family and
sends word to Esau of his reappearance. Jacob is in great fear of
Esau because of the wrong he had done him and prays to Yahweh
with great remorse:

> 'O God of my father Abraham and God of my father Isaac, O

Lord who said to me, "Return to your country and to your kindred, and I will do you good", I am not worthy of the least of all the steadfast love and all the faithfulness that you have shown to your servant, for with only my staff I crossed this Jordan; and now I have become two companies. Deliver me, please, from the hand of my brother, from the hand of Esau, for I am afraid of him; he may come and kill us all, the mothers with the children. Yet you have said, "I will surely do you good, and make your offspring as the sand of the sea, which cannot be counted because of their number." '

(Gen. 32: 9–12)

Jacob places himself at Yahweh's mercy while also reminding Yahweh of the agreement between them. As we have learned from Jacob's dealing with Laban, he is a shrewd man who is accustomed to striking a deal. Here the sub-text of his prayer seems to be: 'O God, I have done as you commanded me; I have been dutifully faithful to our agreement. Now it's your turn to honour our agreement by rescuing me from the coming danger.' God's reply to Jacob comes in the form of the nocturnal wrestle – in which God is impotent as compared to Jacob's strength – and the reassuring message: ' . . . you have striven with God and with humans, and have prevailed.'

In the wrestle with Jacob, Yahweh is not potent but lacking in power, strength and vigour. Yahweh appears to be defeated and unable to retreat. Why? The answers lie in the history of their quasi-covenantal agreement whereby Yahweh is under obligation to Jacob to bless him and his offspring and Jacob was entitled to receive this blessing. Yahweh became omnipotently impotent because of the relationship of mutual commitment into which he and Jacob had freely entered; Jacob's rights were to be respected. In the struggle, Jacob wrested his blessing from Yahweh as Yahweh allowed himself to be prevailed over. Why? Because Jacob's free entry into quasi-covenantal agreement was worthy of acknowledgement; the wrestle was Yahweh's way of fulfilling the divine obligation, by assuring Jacob that he could gain in strength vis-à-vis Esau who was less of a match than Godself. Yahweh was under obligation to Jacob because Jacob had chosen freely to observe his side of the agreement.[48] Because of the nature of divine love, God's freedom was constrained by human freedom and subject to its conditions.

The Abuse of Freedom and Its Results

These biblical passages remind us of God's amazing gift of freedom to human persons. Each person with whom God relates is unique and unrepeatable. Each speaks with their own voice and is free to make their own decisions in response to God. However, as we are all too aware, the gift of freedom can be abused. The free person may depart from contemplation of what is good and cease to occupy themselves with the things of God. A free person may choose what is of lesser worth in preference to that of greater worth, or may choose what is possible rather than what is expedient and edifying.[49] A free person may slander and insult rather than encourage and correct, devise evil and become obsessed with pleasure rather than incline towards the good, speak falsehoods rather than the truth. A free person may seek to become 'like God' (Gen. 3:5) by following after the dream of self-sufficiency and autonomy within the limits of human nature, and by rejecting personal relationship with God. Adam and Eve, as the first creatures to be called human, made just such a choice. Called into existence by God from a state of non-existence, they lacked the

---

48. Apostolos Makrakis writes: 'We are mistaken, therefore, in thinking that only God is omnipotent: He is in an equal measure wholly impotent . . . I worship the impotent God – the God who cannot withstand reason, who was defeated by Abraham, Isaac, and Jacob; the God who was defeated by the syllogism of a Greek woman' [see Mk 7:26]. Makrakis, *Foundations of Philosophy*, p. 26. I am indebted to his work in this section.

49. I draw in this paragraph on Athanasius, *Against the Heathen*, §§3–9, *NPNF* Second Series, Vol. IV, pp. 5–9.

wisdom to choose the true good and chose instead the possibility to determine their own nature. Athanasius writes: 'For God has not only made us out of nothing; but He gave us freely, by the Grace of the Word, a life in correspondence with God. But men, having rejected things eternal, and, by counsel of the devil, turned to the things of corruption . . .'[50] These 'things of corruption' were lawless and unseemly and stemmed from Adam and Eve's preference for autonomy over loving communion with their creator. The result was not that human beings lost the personal mode of their existence; the biblical accounts of Abraham and Jacob's struggles of faith witness to that. Rather, something about the personal mode of their existence changed; perfect communion with God and with one another became broken and divisive.

When polyphony becomes heteroglossia

The question of the effects of sin is an important one. Few would dispute that sin breaks and spoils relationships. But what other changes, if any, does it bring about? Do we need ontological as well as relational categories with which to describe its results? The stories recounted in Genesis tell us that the effect of sin was not to obliterate personhood. Adam and Eve and their descendants remained capable of personal relationships and had responsibility for the quality of those relationships; they made decisions either to reject or accept communion with God. The bible gives us repeated and uncompromising affirmations that God does not compel human action. Abraham and Jacob, like all other human persons, had free wills and responsibilities as persons created in the image of God. The entry of sin into the world did not result in the loss of personhood. To the contrary, personhood remained the very condition that presupposed human ability to choose either for or against God. So what did result from the first and successive abuses of human freedom? What kind of freedom is

---

50. Athanasius, *Incarnation of the Word*, §§4–5, *NPNF* Second Series, Vol. IV, pp. 38–39.

left to us? Does the concept and language of 'the fall' remain of use to us? These are weighty questions in any consideration of Christian ethics because they concern the possibility of our participating in the loving communion with God, the human need for salvation, and the truth and meaning of salvation offered in Christ.

With this in mind, and given our particular interest in polyphony and heteroglossia, let us turn briefly to the story of the tower of Babel and consider what it tells us about how the whole family of humanity sought the same autonomy and self-sufficiency which had tempted Adam and Eve (Gen. 11:4). Genesis 3:32 informs us that the separate nations on the earth were the descendants of the families of the sons of Noah and were included in the covenant made between God and Noah. Yet the nations rejected the God-given, life-affirming covenant with Noah in favour of their making a name for themselves and seeking the (false) security of pretension and the symbols of power. The story is linked to God's gift to humanity of the power of speech and their rightful use of that gift. As John Chrysostom states, God's gift of speech was part of his loving kindness to humanity but, when 'they did not use the gift rightly . . . they lapsed to utter folly' and he took away that which he had given.[51] Like Adam and Eve, the nations sought to become like God; they 'desired to lay hold on the height of heaven itself'. To speak of things was not to use their gift of speech rightly. They had abused the freedom of polyphony and God responded by confusing their language so that they would not understand what each was saying to the other. Polyphony – in the particular sense of different voices speaking a single language and using the same words – became heteroglossia: 'God . . . rightly divided them by difference of speech.'[52] According to John Chrysostom, God's

---

51. John Chrysostom, *Homilies Concerning the Power of Demons*, Homily I, §4, *NPNF* First Series, Vol. IX, pp. 181–182.
52. John Chrysostom, *Homilies Concerning the Power of Demons*, Homily I, §4, *NPNF* First Series, Vol. IX, pp. 181–182.

action was one of mercy because it set limits to their capabilities for self-destruction: 'If they do not pay the penalty now, and be restrained from the very root of their sins, they will never cease from wickedness.' If their wickedness and self-destruction had been allowed to continue, it would have taken hold as a fire takes hold of a pile of dry wood: 'He inflicted difference of speech upon them, in order that they might not fall into greater wickedness.'[53] God had done the nations no evil, though heteroglossia – in the sense of confused and babble-like language which tended to separate rather than unite its speakers – was an indication of fallenness. It was a result of the human demand for autonomy, and meant that the blessed state of the unity of voices was irretrievably lost.

Polyphony and the problem of conflicting voices

There is a big difference between the ethics of polyphony and the ethics of heteroglossia. The former is related to the truth of the person and the personal distinctiveness that each enjoys through self-expression, utterance and testimony, and the latter to individualism which – more often than not – is related to the greatest possible amount of sensuous enjoyment, and/or the need for self-admiration and self-sufficiency. In what follows, we need to keep this distinction in mind and to be clear that Christian ethics is concerned with the former. Christian ethics has not always presented itself as concerned with polyphony and the truth of the person. Thus J. S. Mill associated Christianity (Calvinism in particular) with a narrow theory of life in which individuals had no choice: 'Thus you must do, and no otherwise; "whatever is not a duty is a sin".'[54] Mill's charicature of Calvinism is filled with

---

53. This argument holds even if one rejects John Chrysostom's extension of it to God's sending of famines and pestilences, drought and immoderate rains, upon the earth.

54. John Stuart Mill, 'On Individuality, as One of the Elements of Wellbeing' in *On Liberty* (London: Oxford University Press, 1912), ch. III, p. 76.

inaccuracies and misrepresentations. Nevertheless, it poses again for us the challenge to orient our ethics with reference to God's call to full personhood, and to avoid confusion between confidence in the Spirit of God with control and/or human assumptions about authority, ideology, ideal, or economic might. Christian ethics is not monologic, because it has God-given freedom at its heart and concerns the response of personal freedom to the Word of God. However, the problem of conflicting voices in Christian ethics is real. Christian people disagree frequently about whether or not a decision or action is wrong. They disagree about whether or not premarital sex is sinful, whether homosexual men and women should be abstinent, whether masturbation is morally reprobate, whether embryo or 'pre-embryo' research of any kind should be sanctioned, what, if any, experiments on animals should be permitted, whether animals should be bred for xenotransplantation, whether the genetic modification of plants is always wrong, what kinds of financial investments count as 'ethical', etc. The list could go on. . . . Therefore, we must ask: At what point does polyphony descend into heteroglossia and relativism? What room should be allowed for personal judgement in the sorting of essentials from non-essentials in matters of faith and morals?

Bakhtin's challenge, which resonates with evidence in the Old and New Testaments regarding polyphonic witness to the grace of God, is that a polyphonic ethic, like a polyphonic novel, must take shape in a special way, or it will inevitably become either monologic or heteroglossic. It must allow for genuine, ongoing, personal and dialogic activity on the part of both author and hero, and be regarded as an open process that can be surprised at every step of the way, if its human participants are to grow in and through its dialogic processes.[55] According to Bakhtin, the unity of a polyphonic novel transcends the unity of monologic auth-

---

55. In phrasing this sentence I have drawn on wording in Morson and Emerson, *Mikhail Bakhtin*, pp. 245–247.

oring of either plot or single idea.[56] The unity of a novel does not depend upon monologic control and is compatible with polyphony. It is a unity more complex and profound than the monologic novel because it allows for personal difference; it is a qualitatively different unity to that imposed by a controlling author because its personal character demands a certain open-endedness. For Bakhtin, the unity of a polyphonic novel is preserved by the author's position outside the text, by the author's surplus of vision, and by the fact that the author does not use their surplus vision to bring about 'finalisation', i.e. the premature closing-off of the development of a character's life:

> This surplus is never used as an ambush, as a chance to sneak up and attack from behind. This is an open and honest surplus, dialogically revealed to the other person, as surplus expressed by the addressed and not by the secondhand word. Everything essential is dissolved in dialogue, positioned face to face.[57]

There are higher and lower forms of unity. The unity of a monologic novel is lower and inferior to that of a polyphonic novel, which does not have a single controlling voice but allows scope for lots of voices to express themselves freely: 'Unity not as an innate one-and-only, but as a dialogic *concordance* of unmerged twos or multiples'.[58] Following this prompt from Bakhtin, our question is what kind of unity characterises a Christian ethic of polyphony and how it relates to the teaching authority of the church.

---

56. Bakhtin, 'Toward a Reworking of the Dostoevsky Book' in *Problems of Dostoevsky's Poetics*, p. 298.
57. Bakhtin, 'Toward a Reworking of the Dostoevsky Book', p. 299.
58. Bakhtin, 'Toward a Reworking of the Dostoevsky Book', p. 289.

Polyphony and the Teaching Authority of the Church

Despite our casting of this problem in terms of 'polyphony', 'heteroglossia' and 'monologism', the problem itself is not new. It was an issue known by Paul (or the writer of the letters to Timothy) who urged Timothy 'to ... instruct certain people not to teach any different doctrine, and not to occupy themselves with myths and endless genealogies that promote speculations rather than the divine training that is known by faith' (1 Tim. 1:4). There was a need, probably in the face of Gnosticism, to guard what had been entrusted to the faithful and to avoid 'the profane chatter and contradictions of what is falsely called knowledge' (1 Tim. 6:20–21). Yet adherence to 'sound teaching' was not a matter of blind subservience but of maturity in the faith, moral uprightness and godliness: 'the aim of such instruction is love that comes from a pure heart, a good conscience, and sincere faith' (1 Tim. 1:5). These early Christians knew the tensions associated with the freedom of salvation and legalistic interpretations of it, the renewal and distinctiveness of personal existence as given in Christ and human failure to overcome the desire for autonomy and self-sufficiency. The writer to Timothy reminds us of the difference between human life as given by God and renewed in Christ, and as subject to the power of sin: 'If we have died with him, we will also live with him; if we endure, we will also reign with him; if we deny him, he will also deny us; if we are faithless, he remains faithful – for he cannot deny himself' (2 Tim. 2:11–13). Those who have died with Christ shall live with him eternally. Witness to this fact is more important than mere 'wrangling over words' which only ruins those who are listening (2 Tim. 2:14). Timothy is urged to defend this truth which has been entrusted to him for safe keeping: 'Timothy, guard what has been entrusted to you' (1 Tim. 6:20). Similarly: 'Guard the good treasure entrusted to you, with the help of the Holy Spirit living in us' (2 Tim. 1:14). The letter suggests that the aim of the church's teaching ministry is to witness to, and provide possibility for, moral freedom; its teaching is true when its goal is love (1 Tim. 1:5) and growth in faith and person-hood. However, to do this realistically, in full knowledge of the effects of sin, it must hold to standards of sound teaching.

How, then, does a Christian ethic of polyphony relate to the teaching authority of the church? There seems to be no dilemma in these passages between moral freedom in the Spirit and the need for the church to exercise a teaching ministry which holds fast to standards of doctrine and behaviour. Yet the challenge to the church is to exercise its teaching ministry so as not to undermine the ethos of polyphony that characterises new life in Christ. Each believer is responsible for their own answer to God and for their own moral judgements. Yet the church has a responsibility to guard the truth of its proclamation in matters of both doctrine and morals. The teaching of the church is apostolic in so far as it is guided by the apostles and their successors as they were, and continue to be, moved by the Spirit of God, and in so far as it continues to proclaim the same simple message of faith in Jesus Christ that enlivened the first believers. Christian truth is living and not something to be preserved and passed on as if it were dead. However, the kind of symbols often used with respect to the teaching authority of the church give the contrary impression, e.g., the 'deposit of faith', 'treasure', 'guardianship', and the process of 'handing on'. Each symbol can give rise to problematically monologistic ways of thinking that sometimes need to be broken apart by the many-voicedness that the Spirit engenders. The true ethos of the church is polyphony in the Spirit, but the problems associated with both heteroglossia and monologism are never far away. In the remainder of this chapter I address this issue with reference to some commonly used symbols of the teaching authority of the church, especially that of 'deposit of faith'. Paul Ricoeur remarked that language and, in particular, metaphorical symbols, is often closer to the heart of the matter than systematic theological and/or philosophical inquiry.[59] Whether or not this is correct, symbols have great power to influence the way we think. They suggest constellations of meaning at various levels of reflection and within changing cultural horizons.[60] The symbol 'deposit of faith' is particularly problematic because it appears to imply monologism in the teaching authority of the church.

I press the issue with reference to the 'deposit of faith' because the symbol of 'deposit' is frequently abused and reduced to an inert entity or formula. However, far from being part of the problem, I suggest that a rethinking of the symbol (or abbreviation) can help us see how the unity of personal moral freedom and the teaching of the church is found in the life of the Holy Spirit within the church. The argument is that because the symbol is applied by ancient Christian writers to all that constitutes an expression of divine truth, including the person of Jesus Christ, the bible and tradition, this implies that it is inherently dynamic and not static. For the same reason, and especially because it refers to the person of Christ, the guarantee of truth 'contained' in the deposit overflows that which is legal or formal. Its liberty comes from the life of the Spirit (2 Cor. 3:17) and is in itself a communication of divine grace. The argument is also that the symbol's association in the early church with the themes of 'guarding' and 'handing on' is open to diverse interpretation. The 'deposit of faith' can be interpreted as a quasi-physical entity which is passed along a horizontal line of transmission in a quasi-automatic process. Alternatively, it can be interpreted with much more explicit reference to the life of the church as a whole. Arguably, it can be interpreted as the capacity, or conscience, of

---

59. Don Ihde makes this observation. See editor's Introduction, Paul Ricoeur, *The Conflict of Interpretations*, ed. Don Ihde (Evanston, IL: Northwestern University Press, 1974), p. xix.

60. Ricoeur uses this word to describe the clustering together of images and/or themes, *Conflict of Interpretations*, p. 291.

the church to discern the truth in matters of morals as well as faith.

Deposit of faith: a study in meaning

Let us start by saying a few words about the history of the use of the symbol. The idea of a deposit, meaning something that has been entrusted for safe keeping, was familiar to the fathers of the ancient church. Latin translations of 1 Tim. 6:20 and 2 Tim. 1:12, 14 render *paratheke* (sometimes translated as 'what has been entrusted' or 'treasure') as *depositum custodi*. Irenaeus of Lyons refers in *Against Heresies* to the preaching of the church as a well-grounded system which tends to salvation 'as if it were some precious deposit (*depositum*) in an excellent vessel'.[61] He speaks of the message of the church in every time and place and at each moment as consistent and unchanging. Its teaching encompasses the entirety of God's plan for the world and is a precious deposit kept in a lovely and secure place:

> Since therefore we have such proofs, it is not necessary to seek the truth among others which it is easy to obtain from the Church; since the apostles, like a rich man [depositing his money] in a bank, lodged in her hands most copiously all things pertaining to the truth: so that every man, whosoever will, can draw from her the water of life.[62]

Irenaeus refers to the treasure which the apostles brought to the church and identifies it with the tradition of truth which has been entrusted to the church for the nourishment and life of its members. The blessed apostles passed on this rule of truth and Irenaeus lists a line of succession from Peter and Paul to Linus, Anacletus, Clement of Rome, Evaristus et al., commenting that, '[i]n this order, and by this succession, the ecclesiastical tradition from the apostles, and the preaching of the truth, have come

---

61. Irenaeus, Against *Heresies*, Bk III, ch. 24, §I, *ANF*, Vol. I, p. 458.
62. Irenaeus, Against *Heresies*, Bk III, ch. 4, §I, *ANF*, Vol. I, pp. 416–417.

down to us.'[63] The apostles have, he believes, brought to the church the whole of the truth so that anyone at all who wishes can come and take from it the elixir of life. Shortly afterwards, however, he identifies this deposit with Christ himself. *Against Heresies*, Bk IV, ch. 26 is especially interesting in this regard: 'For Christ is the treasure which was hid in the field, that is, in this world (for "the field is this world"); but the treasure hid in the Scriptures is Christ . . .'[64] This treasure was hidden in the scriptures and symbolised by figures and parables and must have seemed full of enigmas and ambiguities to their hearers who lacked their explanation, i.e. the coming of the Son of God in human flesh. A few lines later, he identifies the treasure with the text of scripture read by Christians. In the space of a few hundred words, he uses many images, including those of a deposit, rock and sand, filthy water, broken cisterns, harvesting and gathering of fruit. This is, perhaps, an example of what Ricoeur calls the language of avowal. There is an ambiguity in the meaning of the symbol, but there is a sense in which this very ambiguity constitutes its theological profundity; the treasure is both Christ himself and truth about him.

Equivocation is, suggests Ricoeur, revealing of the dynamics of symbol in general. Where equivocation is lost there results an impoverishment of 'symbolic richness'.[65] Indeed, we see something of such a loss of symbolic richness in some of the writings of Tertullian of Carthage. Occasionally, he treats the theme of guardianship of the deposit more like a comparison or analogy than a symbol, that is, he looks at the 'outside' of the meaning rather than the 'inside', restricting the theme of guardianship to that of keeping watch or escorting in a way that is more strictly analogical than symbolic. Ricoeur describes analogical thinking as proceeding: A is to B as C is to D. This applies to Tertullian in so far

---

63. Irenaeus, Against *Heresies*, Bk III, ch. 3, §3, *ANF*, Vol. I, p. 416.

64. Irenaeus, Against *Heresies*, Bk IV, ch. 26, §I, *ANF*, Vol. I, pp. 496–497. The biblical references here are to Matt. 13:38 and 13:44.

65. Ricoeur, *Conflict of Interpretations*, p. 291.

as bishops are to apostolic teaching what guards are to treasure not their own. In so far as there is no movement of meaning beyond this pattern of reasoning, his readers are assimilated to the symbolised meaning less effectively than in a more dynamic ordering. Note how Tertullian warns his readers to shun heresy that leads to self-condemnation, even going so far as to urge them to resist the kinds of questioning that would challenge the rule of faith.[66] If questioning leads to 'sophistication' of the rule of faith, he argues, then one is better to remain in ignorance. The treasure is to be guarded against questioning; unduly curious people are not to be admitted to discussion of the scriptures in the first place.[67] Note his interpretations of Paul's words to Timothy: 'Paul said to Timothy: "O Timothy, guard that which is entrusted to thee"; and again: "That good thing which was committed unto thee keep".'[68] The apostolic faith is to be guarded against change. Stasis is preferable to innovation, and unity is superior to diversity. The truth of the law of faith is original, and anything which comes after that original is suspect.[69] It is to be guarded as a soldier protects his charge. In his struggle to preserve the integrity of the faith against the Gnostics, Tertullian links the symbol of the deposit of faith more closely to 1 Tim. 6:20 than to Matt. 13:44. He emphasises the public rather than secret nature of the content of the apostles' preaching and teaching. He is also keen to knock

---

66. Tertullian, *On Prescription against Heretics*, Bk I, chs XXV and XXVI, *ANF,* Vol. III, p. 255.

67. Tertullian, *On Prescription Against Heretics*, Bk I, ch. XVI, *ANF,* Vol. III, p. 251.

68. Tertullian, *On Prescription Against Heretics*, Bk I, ch. XXV, *ANF,* Vol. III, pp. 254–255.

69. One of the tests of apostolicity which Tertullian applies to new churches is that their teaching does not vary from that of the apostles (see Bk I, ch. XXXII, *ANF,* Vol. III, pp. 258–259). Diversity of teaching is to be attributed to falsification of the scriptures: 'Where diversity of doctrine is found, *there,* then, must the corruption both of Scriptures and the expositions thereof be regarded as existing' (see Bk I, ch. XXXVIII, p. 261).

down the philosophical objection that the deposit refers to the whole of human knowledge. His central point is that the rule of faith was that by which all Christians believed. It has been taught by the apostles and was everywhere the same, namely, there is but one God who is none other than the creator of the universe and Jesus Christ is his son. This deposit was given by Christ to the apostles, to be preserved by them and their successors.[70]

Compare this analogical usage of the image of guardianship to the more dynamically ordered symbolic usage in some writings of Hippolytus of Rome (c. 170–c. 236). Hippolytus does not allow us to follow an 'A is to B as C is to D' pattern of thought that looks at the subject from the outside, as it were. This is because his use of the image hints at a latent meaning and draws the reader more fully into the richness of his topic. In *The Refutation of all Heresies* he refers to the successors of the apostles as 'guard-

---

70. See also Tertullian, *Against Marcion*, Bk IV, ch. V, *ANF*, Vol. III, p. 350. Thus Irenaeus of Lyon and Tertullian of Carthage interpret the symbol of the deposit of faith differently. Irenaeus understands it as an image of the person of Christ himself and Tertullian understands it as an image for the rule of faith. Each has his own rational apparatus by which he arrives at an understanding, and each believes himself to be reflecting upon a legitimate meaning of the symbol. In the case of Tertullian, it is probable that the threat of Gnosticism was the impulse that drove him towards a propositional rather than personal interpretation. It is perhaps noteworthy that Clement of Alexandria, who has frequently been dubbed 'the Christian Gnostic', also interprets the symbol as meaning true knowledge of truth (Clement of Alexandria, *The Stromata*, Bk II, ch. XI, *ANF*, Vol. II, p. 359). Clement draws a distinction between the wisdom or Gnosis in which Christ instructed the apostles and the supposed wisdom of the Gnostic heretics. The former was secret and hidden only in the sense that it had been given to the few apostles, and should not be cast like pearls before swine. It was not secret or hidden in the sense that it should not be proclaimed aloud and shouted from the rooftops (Matt. 10.27) (Clement of Alexandria, *The Stromata*, Bk VI, ch. XV, *ANF*, Vol. II, p. 506). Like Tertullian, he interprets the symbol of the deposit to mean the teaching of the Lord as received from the apostles, referring explicitly to apostolic teaching both in unwritten form and as transmitted and explained in the scriptures, according to the rule of truth.

ians of the Church' who do not grow weary of working with all their strength to give meritorious service in return for God's good gifts.[71] He regards the successors of the apostles as guardians of the apostolic tradition which has been taught down the generations and has lasted to the present day.[72] At no point, however, is guardianship only the protection of a charge. It is always more than this because the church itself is guarded by the Holy Spirit; the church is where the Holy Spirit confers fullness of grace that enables correct belief:

> But none will refute these [heresies], save the Holy Spirit bequeathed unto the Church, which the Apostles, having in the first instance received, have transmitted to those who have rightly believed. But we, as being their successors, and as participators in this grace, high-priesthood, and office of teaching, as well as being reputed guardians of the Church, must not be found deficient in vigilance.[73]

This audacious theological statement blows apart any literal meaning of the analogy of guardianship because the church could never literally guard its guard; it cannot guard the Holy Spirit, the Lord and Giver of life. The symbolic charge of this statement is explosive in the sense that it destroys its own meaning. The church is to keep the tradition of the apostles. To do this is simultaneously to receive the grace of the Holy Spirit because God the Father has put this grace at the service of human beings. The symbol of guardianship is thus surpassed by its own content, and has a tendency towards iconoclasm. If not, it would 'solidify into an

---

71. Hippolytus, *The Refutation of All Heresies*, Bk 1, 'The Prœmium', *ANF*, Vol. V, p. 10.
72. Hippolytus, *Appendix to the Works of Hippolytus: Hippolytus on the Twelve Apostles*, *ANF*, Vol. V, pp. 254–255.
73. Hippolytus, *The Refutation of All Heresies*, Bk 1, 'The Prœmium', *ANF*, Vol. V, p. 10.

idolatry'.[74] Where Tertullian's use of the symbol tends towards the literal, Hippolytus' use blows apart old meanings and creates new ones.[75]

The symbol 'deposit of faith' was closely associated with the theme of 'handing on'. 'Handing on' is a frequently occurring theme or motif which is usually associated with episcopal office and the authority to teach. Thus Irenaeus states:

> It is incumbent to obey the presbyters who are in the Church, – those who, as I have shown, possess the succession from the apostles; those who, together with the succession of the episcopate, have received the certain gift of truth, according to the good pleasure of the Father.[76]

Similarly, Tertullian associates authority with dimensions of apostolicity. In *On the Flesh of Christ*, he asks by what authority Marcion preaches as he does, asserting that the apostles preached openly and in public; the successors of the apostles agree with their teaching; ordinary believers believe what has been handed down. If Marcion is none of these, then 'cease to live'.[77] Tertullian

---

74. Ricoeur, *Conflict of Interpretations*, p. 293.

75. It is worth noting here that Ricoeur defines symbol as 'any structure of signification in which a direct, primary, literal meaning designates, in addition, another meaning which is indirect, secondary, and figurative and which can be apprehended only through the first' (Ricoeur, *Conflict of Interpretations*, pp. 12–13). He draws attention to the fact that symbols are expressions with a double meaning, and suggests that this field of equivocation is where interpretation is often required. Interpretation is 'the work of thought which consists in deciphering the hidden meaning in the apparent meaning, in unfolding the levels of meaning implied in the literal meaning' (Ricoeur, *Conflict of Interpretations*, p. 13). A symbol rarely, if ever, conveys an absolute meaning that exists in and of itself without necessary relation to other qualifiers. Therefore, the task of interpretation involves investigation of how the symbol is used which, for our purposes, has implications for how the symbol of the deposit of faith both refers to and is derived from an understanding of the teaching authority of the church.

76. Irenaeus, *Against Heresies*, Bk IV, ch. 26, §I, *ANF*, Vol. I, p. 497.

77. Tertullian, *On the Flesh of Christ*, ch. II, *ANF*, Vol. III, p. 522.

wants to undermine Marcion's authority to teach, and, in so doing, creates the impression of a process of handing on which is similar to a physical process in which an object is passed from one to another.

Having used Tertullian above to exemplify how symbol is reduced to analogy, let us consider whether he allows less restrictive usage of the image of 'handing on'. Careful reading of other passages in *Prescription against the Heretics* reveals that he does at times relinquish analogical control of the image by associating it with other symbolic expressions. Interestingly, this happens most often in connection with apostolic churches when the symbol of 'handing on' is submerged in the experience of the church-corporate. Here it is as if Tertullian is driven to take up new symbolic images because the symbol itself breaks out of the intellectual control of analogy. For example, when dealing with questions about authoritative teaching in the context of the threat of Gnosticism, he does not tie the concept of apostolicity exclusively to the succession of bishops in the church. For him, this would be of no use because it would provide no test as to the genuineness of apostolicity; the test is given by the apostolic churches which stand in the unique tradition of the same mystery. Jesus himself taught plainly and openly. So also did the apostles. They preached first in Judea and then much wider afield, taking the same teaching of the same faith to all nations:

> Then they in like manner founded churches in every city, from which all the other churches, one after another, derived the tradition of the faith (*traducem fidei*) and the seeds of doctrine, and are every day deriving them, that they may become churches ... In this way all are primitive, and all are apostolic, while they are all proved to be one, in (unbroken) unity ...[78]

Interestingly, Tertullian draws on themes and motifs – many of

---

78. Tertullian, *On Prescription against Heretics*, ch. XX, *ANF*, Vol. III, p. 252.

which are biblical – to express a new category of apostolicity which includes public verifiability and openness. In so doing, it seems to become less easy to dominate the symbol intellectually by reducing it to analogy. 'Handing on' is no longer analogically controlled as a physical process of handing an object down the line but is refracted in multiple images which signify the living faith of new churches in the diaspora. The unity of teaching is essential, but here Tertullian also emphasises the importance of the testimony of local churches in the ascertaining of authority to teach. Local, apostolic churches are 'primordial wombs of faith', and their witness to the rule of faith is vital in ascertaining what does and does not count as truth.[79] It is the church as a whole, and not an educated élite, which has the capacity for knowing the truth.

The practice in the early church of choosing presbyters and bishops in the presence of the people reinforces this emphasis on the apostolic work of the whole church. Cyprian of Carthage (Bishop of Carthage AD *c.* 248–258) approves the custom in a letter to Christians in Spain: '[T]he priest should be chosen in the presence of the people under the eyes of all, and should be approved worthy and suitable by public judgement and testimony.'[80] The authority of the bishop to teach is thus tested by the people, at least to the extent that they judge his worthiness to hold a teaching office. Basil of Caesarea (d. 379) makes an even stronger case concerning the apostolic undertakings of local churches which together comprise the church catholic, in his arguments in favour of the full divinity of the Holy Spirit. His opponents maintained that the doctrine was not stated in the bible, to which Basil responded that not all the mysteries of the church were written down, and that many were preserved

---

79. I draw here on Robert B. Eno's translation of ch. XXI of Tertullian's *Prescription against the Heretics* in *Teaching Authority in the Early Church*, Message of the Fathers of the Church 14 (Delaware: Michael Glazier, Inc., 1984), p. 20.
80. Cyprian, Epistle LXVII, *ANF* Vol. V, p. 369.

in the memory of the church.[81] Instead of written evidence, Basil offered to produce 'a large number of witnesses' who had held on to non-written traditions.[82] This unwritten holding on and 'handing on' is, according to Basil, appropriately deemed apostolic because it pertains to traditions of the church which had become rooted in the church through long usage. He cites 1 Cor. 11:2 and 2 Thess. 2:15 in support of his case, illustrating how the image of 'handing on' accrues meaning in a multiplicity of usages. Restrictive analogical usage is again inappropriate; it is in interpretation of multiple meanings that understanding is gained.[83]

These different nuances in use of the symbol can be explored further with reference to the Roman Catholic tradition in which the symbol of the deposit of faith remained familiar but was not developed extensively as a quasi-technical term until Vatican Council I. At Vatican Council I, it was linked to the developing practice of the issuing of official teaching by the pope and bishops, in encyclicals, dogmas and decrees. The Dogmatic Constitution *Pastor Aeternus*, ch. IV, speaks of synods and other means by which the saving doctrine of Christ could be propagated among all peoples of the earth. Roman pontiffs were required to preserve this doctrine as pure and sincere as when they received it: 'For the Holy Spirit promised to the successors of Peter, not that they

---

81. Basil, *On the Holy Spirit* ch. XXX, §79, *NPNF* Second Series, Vol. VIII, p. 50.
82. Basil, *On the Holy Spirit*, ch. XXIX, §71, *NPNF* Second Series, Vol. VIII, p. 45.
83. Origen (*c.* 185–*c.* 253) also mentions the orderliness of the succession wherein the church's preaching has been handed down (*De Principiis*, Preface §I, *ANF*, Vol. IV, p. 239). Athanasius (*c.* 296–373), in his defence of the Nicene Definition against the Arians prior to the councils of Arminium and Seleucia in 359, uses the image of 'handing on' in his attributing of authority to the council (*Defence of the Nicene Definition*, ch. VI, *NPNF* Second Series, Vol. IV, p. 166). However, the symbolism rarely takes shape simply around the image of an object being passed down a line in a physical process. At times, it can seem as if the process can be observed from the outside; the analogical relationship can be objectivised. More often than not, these symbols have overlapping and related, but also distinguishable, layers of meaning.

would unfold new doctrine which He revealed to them, but that, with His assistance, they would piously guard and faithfully expound the revelation or deposit of faith handed on through the Apostles.' The symbol of the deposit of faith is here given a solemnity linked to papal jurisdiction and infallibility. Under certain conditions the pope has jurisdictional and doctrinal primacy, and this is expressed in terms of his responsibility to guard the deposit of faith. Interestingly, *The Catholic Encyclopaedic Dictionary* expresses the significance of this development in the observation that the symbol was 'consecrated' at the first Vatican Council, quoting Session iii. cap. 4 in support: 'And the doctrine of faith which God revealed is proposed, not as a mere philosophical discovery to be elaborated by human minds, but as the divine deposit delivered by Christ to his spouse, to be by her faithfully guarded and infallibly declared.'[84] It is arguable that the hostile philosophical context of Vatican Council I had either the direct or indirect effect of making the Council over-defensive in the face of idealist notions of the progression of historical consciousness. Of interest for our purposes is that the symbol has now acquired a quasi-technical sense related to the infallibility of the Roman pontiff and the sacred magisterium.

At Vatican II we find that the force of the symbol is again slightly different because its interpretation is guided by an emphasis on the shared work of ordained and lay persons. In the Dogmatic Constitution on Divine Revelation, *Dei Verbum*, promulgated on 18 November 1965, ch. II, §10, the symbol is used as follows:

> Sacred tradition and Sacred Scripture form one sacred deposit of the word of God, committed to the Church. Holding fast to this deposit the entire holy people united with their shepherds remain always steadfast in the teaching of the Apostles, in the common life, in the breaking of bread and

---

84. Donald Attwater (ed.), *The Catholic Encyclopaedic Dictionary*, 2nd edn (London: Cassell and Co., 1949).

in prayers (see Acts 2:42, Greek text), so that holding to, practising and professing the heritage of the faith, it becomes on the part of the bishops and faithful a single common effort.

The importance of the teaching authority of the church is explained as contributing effectively to the salvation of souls, it having been stated previously that God had made provision in his mercy so that his revelation for the salvation of all nations 'would abide perpetually in its full integrity' (ch. II, §7). This provision was that divine revelation should be handed on to all generations in sacred scripture and also the tradition which comes from the apostles and develops in the church. *Dei Verbum* places great importance on apostolic preaching in which the gospel is kept alive within the church, but it also places importance on the faith of the people of God so that 'the Church, in her teaching, life and worship, perpetuates and hands on to all generations all that she herself is, all that she believes' (ch. II, §8). Believers are called to study and to 'treasure these things in their hearts' (ch. II, §8); they are to be active recipients of 'the sure gift of truth'.[85] The task of interpreting the word of God authentically has been entrusted to the teaching office of the church, and, to reinforce the point, the Constitution makes reference to the First Vatican Council, *Dogmatic Constitution on the Catholic Faith*, ch. 2, 'On Revelation'. In this respect, the bishops have particular responsibility to ensure the active support of all who seek 'excellent knowledge of Jesus Christ' (ch. VI, §25). It is clear, however, that the teaching office of the church should be exercised in service of the whole church (ch. II, §10), and that the whole church hands on and preserves the sacred deposit of the word of God, as it moves towards the fullness of divine truth; the treasure of revelation is 'entrusted to the Church' (ch. VI, §26). *Lumen Gentium* also expressly states

---

85. The biblical reference here is to Luke 2:19, 51.

that bishops draw on the treasury of revelation but that it is not the property of the magisterium.[86]

The symbol of the 'deposit of faith' does not occur in this exact form in the text of *Lumen Gentium*, but reference is made to 'the deposit of revelation, which must be religiously guarded and loyally and courageously expounded' (ch. III, §25 para. 3) and its signification is woven into the Constitution as a whole. In this text, therefore, it should be regarded – to use Ricoeur's words – as a second- rather than a first-degree symbol because its usage is neither frequent nor varied.[87] How, then, do the symbol 'deposit' and the image of 'handing on' function symbolically in relation one to the other? In its opening paragraph, *Lumen Gentium* refers to the church as being 'in the nature of sacrament – a sign and instrument, that is, of communion with God and of unity among all men' (ch. I, §1). Before any elaboration of symbolic signification of the ministries of the church, the Constitution makes the church itself the primary symbol to which all its ministries should be referred. The economy within which the symbol functions is given by reference to Christ, in whom the church exists, and the symbol functions in the opening words of the Constitution to provide a focus of unity for all that is to be stated about the nature and

---

86. Vatican II, *Lumen Gentium*, ch. 25. Kevin McNamara comments on the extent of the Church's infallibility in *Lumen Gentium*, especially the section entitled *divinae revelationis depositum, sancte custodiendum et fideliter exponendum*, as follows: 'The English translation could be misleading here since it may not convey the full meaning of the Latin which sees the "guarding of the deposit" and its "faithful exposition" as all falling within the scope of the magisterium's infallibility. The Council wishes to include within the range of infallibility any truths which are necessary for preserving the deposit of divine revelation, even if such truths have not been themselves revealed.' Kevin McNamara, *Vatican II: The Constitution on the Church: A Theological and Pastoral Commentary* (London: Geoffrey Chapman, 1968), p. 209.

87. The symbol 'deposit' is used in sections dealing with the duties and privileges of bishops; bishops are 'endowed with the authority of Christ' (III, §25 para. 1) and are to inform and direct the thinking of people assigned to them.

purpose of the church. The church does not signify only one thing, but all that it does signify should be understood in relation to the dispensation of Christ because Christ communes fully with both God and men (*sic*). At the semantic level, therefore, we are seeking meaning in the field of movement between symbols, as the symbol of the church as 'sign and instrument' is ordered in the light of Christ, and as symbols of the teaching authority of the church are ordered in relation to the symbol of the church. The economy of the whole document is thus framed so that the reader is alert to signification between symbols; 'each symbol signifies potentially all the others'.[88] The guiding theme for inter-pretation of this movement between symbols is given in I, §4 para. 4: 'Hence the universal Church is seen to be "a people brought into unity from the unity of the Father, the Son and the Holy Spirit".'

This unity is understood primarily in terms of the symbol of Christ's body (I, §7), and, as we might expect, its meaning is unfolded in terms of another symbol – the eucharistic bread. Our particular interest, however, is with authority in the church and how perceptions of authority to teach signify much about how the being of the church is understood. Let us, therefore, focus attention on the movement between symbols that have direct application to this topic: deposit and body. What, if anything, will the movement between these symbols signify of their relationship one to the other, and to the church which is both sign and instrument of communion with God? In the first two chapters, the symbol 'body' is used in the Constitution of several objects: pastors, bishops, all the faithful, and of the church catholic which comprises the members of the body of Christ. It occurs in connec-tion with the teaching office of the church in II, §12, concerning the church as the people of God sharing in Christ's prophetic office:

---

88. Ricoeur, *Conflict of Interpretations*, p. 59.

> The holy People of God shares [also] in Christ's prophetic
> office . . . The whole body of the faithful who have an anoin-
> ting that comes from the holy one (cf. 1 Jn 2:20 and 27)
> cannot err in matters of belief. This characteristic is shown
> in the supernatural appreciation of the faith (*sensus fidei*) of
> the whole people, when, 'from the bishops to the last of the
> faithful' [footnote: Cf. S. Augustine, *De Praed. Sanct.* 14, 27]
> they manifest a universal consent in matters of faith and
> morals. By this appreciation of the faith, aroused and sus-
> tained by the Spirit of truth, the people of God, guided by
> the sacred teaching authority (*magisterium*), and obeying it,
> receives not the mere word of men, but truly the word of
> God (cf. 1 Thess. 2:13), the faith once for all delivered to the
> saints (cf. Jude 3).

The chapter is headed 'The People of God' and is about, among
other things, how the whole people of God shares in the priestly
and prophetic offices of Christ. With reference to the teaching
aspect of the prophetic office of Christ, the passage cited above
indicates that the people as a whole are led and enriched by the
Holy Spirit. Each has an anointing from the Holy Spirit by
the strength of which they spread abroad a living witness to God,
through a life of faith and love.[89]

The symbol of the 'deposit' occurs in connection with the
teaching office of the church in III, §25, which concerns the infallibility with which the church is endowed in defining doctrine
pertaining to faith and morals:

---

89. McNamara sums up the first two chapters of *Lumen Gentium* as presenting
a biblical vision of the church, and interprets relevant paragraphs referring to
teaching authority in ch. II as follows: 'When he teaches the faithful or directs
and guides his Church, a bishop should not lightly presume that he acts under
the immediate influence of the Holy Spirit, but should be courageous and honest
enough to seek approval for his teaching and directions by giving reasons for
them.' McNamara, *Vatican II*, p. 205.

This infallibility... is co-extensive with the deposit of revelation, which must be religiously guarded and loyally and courageously expounded. The Roman Pontiff, head of the college of bishops, enjoys this infallibility in virtue of his office, when, as supreme pastor and teacher of all the faithful – who confirms his brethren in the faith (cf. Lk. 22:23) – he proclaims in an absolute decision a doctrine pertaining to faith or morals. [footnote: Conc. Vat. I, Const. dogm. *Pastor Aeternus*] For that reason his definitions are rightly said to be irreformable by their very nature and not by reason of the assent of the Church, in as much as they were made with the assistance of the Holy Spirit promised to him in the person of blessed Peter himself; and as a consequence they are in no way in need of the approval of others, and do not admit of appeal to any other tribunal.

This chapter is headed: 'The Church is Hierarchical' and is about, among other things, the authenticity of teaching authority in the church. With reference to the teaching authority of the Roman pontiff and college of bishops, the passage cited above indicates in what sense infallibility is present in the body of bishops, and why the assent of the body of the faithful is not required for this teaching authority to be genuine. Of interest for our purposes is the analogical pattern of thought that is set up in the sentence: 'This infallibility . . . is co-extensive with the deposit of revelation, which must be religiously guarded and loyally and courageously expounded.' The word 'co-extensive' means 'extends equally', and in this context it set up a clearly analogical relationship between the 'deposit of revelation' and the infallibility of the teaching authority of the Roman pontiff and college of bishops. As deposit is to teaching authority, so revelation is to infallibility. The symbol is reduced to analogy as the image of the 'deposit' is confined within limits that are fixed.

More recently, Pope John Paul II ordered the publication of the

Catechism of the Catholic Church by the Apostolic Constitution, *Fidei Depositum*, on 11 October 1992, in which he said:

> The *Catechism of the Catholic Church* . . . whose publication I command today in virtue of the apostolic authority, is a presentation of the Church's faith and of Catholic doctrine witnessed to or clarified by sacred Scripture, the apostolic tradition and the Church's magisterium. I acknowledge it as a valuable and authorized instrument at the service of the ecclesial communion and as a sure and certain standard for the teaching of the faith.

Similarly, in *Ad Tuendam Fidem* we read that the deposit of faith has been entrusted to the church which is under the leadership of the sacred magisterium. The apostolic letter is issued in order to protect the faith of the Catholic Church against errors arising among the faithful, in particular among those who dedicate themselves to the discipline of theology. The introductory paragraph speaks of the duty of the church to preserve the truths of the Catholic faith and to confirm the brethren [*sic*] in that faith. To this end, the letter proposes to institute a canonical sanction concerning the preservation and explanation of the truths of the Catholic faith. Several legal expressions of the universal legislation of the church are cited in the form of the Codes of Canon Law and the Codes of Canons of the Eastern Churches, as gaps in the universal law as regards the authority of the magisterium to be filled with new regulations. The quasi-legal setting restricts interpretation by identifying the symbol 'deposit of faith' with truths that are written or handed down by tradition and which are proposed as definitive truths by the magisterium of the Church. The setting prevents the symbol from saying more than it says – which is the essence of symbolic function – thereby transposing it from the field of interpretation to that of tightly controlled definition. To use Ricoeur's words, the danger is that '[i]t is transformed into heritage and into sediment at the same time that it is rationalised'.[90]

Semantic analysis of the symbols 'deposit of faith' and the process of 'handing on' has shown that multiple meanings are 'shown-yet-concealed' within their fields of signification.[91] We have also begun to appreciate how the task of interpretation involves investigation of the systems of meaning within which the symbol is employed, i.e. how it refers to and is derived from an understanding of the being of the church. We have begun to see something of what Ricoeur calls 'the revealing power of symbol': how the symbol gives rise to multivocal meanings and, in so doing, opens up avenues for further thought.[92] We have seen how analogical interpretations tend to be restrictive because they limit the interpretive process to an 'A is to B as C is to D' pattern of thought, and we have seen that part of the revealing power of symbol lies in the equivocity that gives rise to multiple meanings. We have observed that the way in which a symbol is used and interpreted is usually determined by the framework of understanding within which it is placed. To use Ricoeur's words, hermeneutics involves the task of 'criteriology', which seeks to show how and why a given symbol is employed variously in different texts by different authors in different contexts. Consider Ricoeur's observation about the kinds of intentionality that are implied in every symbol: 'Symbol conceals in its intention a double intentionality. There is, first, the primary or literal intentionality . . . But upon this first intentionality is built a second intentionality . . . which points to a certain situation of man in the Sacred.'[93] By this he means that the literal meaning designated

---

90. Ricoeur, *Conflict of Interpretations*, p. 29.

91. Ricoeur uses the phrase 'shown-yet-concealed' in *Conflict of Interpretations*, p. 12.

92. Ricoeur, *Conflict of Interpretations*, p. 287.

93. Ricoeur, *Conflict of Interpretations*, pp. 289–290.

by the symbol gives rise to secondary, indirect and figurative meanings. Thus, the literal meaning of 'deposit' does not resemble the theological matter under discussion, i.e. the teaching authority of the church, but gives rise to certain meanings that can be arrived at through interpretation of the literal and obvious meaning. We have seen that symbol should not be reduced to analogy. This, says Ricoeur, is essential to the nature of symbol, because the interpreter is drawn beyond the primary meaning to seek for something more. As far as the aforementioned dilemma between moral freedom in the Spirit and the church's authority to teach is concerned, the argument is that there is no necessary dilemma. A dilemma occurs only when the teaching ministry of the church is interpreted as a quasi-mechanical and impersonal process.

The conscience of the church

In the Roman Catholic Church, 'deposit of faith' is an important symbol which signifies a body of teaching containing truths to be believed, and which the Roman pontiff, as successor to the apostles, is authorised to declare to the faithful. In this tradition, and among the several writers consulted, the symbol is rich in meaning. As a result, it is not easy to substitute the words 'deposit of faith' with other words, because one needs to embrace many ideas at a time. A symbol of this nature does not lend itself to precision analysis because the fullness of its meaning overflows most limits put upon it. This is necessarily the case because it is applied to expressions of divine truth. However, with reference to our topic, the symbol is often problematic because of its alleged association with monologism rather than polyphony. The symbol becomes an expression of single-voicedness in the church, understood as God communicating divine revelation to a pyramidal-type hierarchy which then transmits it to the rest of the church; there is little space for self-expression and moral choice, with the result that many ordinary members feel compelled to conform, to rebel, or move outside the church. Failing that, they get depressed. We have seen, however, that for some writers in Christian tradition there is no need to oppose this symbol of the teaching authority of the church with polyphonic freedom in the Spirit. Many thought about the deposit of faith in terms of an ecclesial receiving and transmitting of expressions of divine truth. Remember Tertullian's emphasis on the importance of the testimony of local churches in the ascertaining of authority to teach, and on local, apostolic churches as 'wombs of faith'. Faced with this richness of the symbol, and its reference to its process and mode of transmission, I suggest that there is scope for thinking about it as a faculty of judgement: the deposit of faith as a principle of Christian knowledge or the conscience of the church.

Thus, we have argued that the deposit of faith comprises expression(s) of divine truth, notably, the Word of God incarnate, the Word of God in scripture and orthodox tradition. Guarding of the deposit has to do with living in the light of the Word of God and being kept by the Spirit of truth. Even when not referring directly to the person of Christ, the bible or tradition, the symbol functions as an abbreviation for a grace of the Holy Spirit within the life of the church. Consequently, guarding the deposit of faith is a responsibility which belongs to the church as a body comprising many members; it requires a faculty or capacity for knowing how to do the truth and relies utterly upon the grace of the Spirit. There is nothing automatic about the growth in knowledge of God entailed. Indeed, we know in part (1 Cor. 13:12). Partiality and provisionality are constant features of Christian response to contemporary moral issues. This process of seeking correct judgement is, however, an ecclesial and polyphonic rather than a monologic or heteroglossic affair which presupposes community living (*orthokoinia*) and reference to active membership of a local church or body of Christians.[94] It also presupposes participation in the life of the church catholic. To guard the

---

94. Harakas coins the term *orthokoinia* in Stanley S. Harakas, *Contemporary Moral Issues Facing the Orthodox Christian* (Minneapolis, MN: Light and Life Publishing Co., 1982), p. 16.

deposit of faith does not mean to live by a list of moral formulae but to acquire critical judgement and live by the light of the Spirit. To transmit the deposit of faith is to live in a way that communicates the grace of God in accordance with the conscience of the church.

The conscience is a human moral capacity (1 Cor. 8:7; 1 Tim. 4:2; Heb. 10:22). It is part of what it is to be a living human person and is subject to both formation and deformation during the course of a lifetime. It is an inward fountain which exhorts people to seek God and to order their minds better;[95] a particular kind of life-disposition which shapes character in search of the truth;[96] a guide to action wherein persons weigh everything that they do according to a reasonable judgement of the mind.[97] As Stanley Harakas writes: 'The conscience, thus, is the chief locus for the moral life ... a process or ability to discern, to distinguish, to evaluate and to judge moral realities.'[98] It is the place where the truths of salvation and revelation meet a person's psychological and moral functioning. But conscience is not often thought about in a corporate sense. Hauerwas makes some moves in this direction by talking about the kind of community the church is and should be. The church, he argues, is a 'truthful polity' whose social significance is peculiar to itself and whose virtue, social ethics and politics are distinctive.[99] The task for the church is to be the kind of community that embodies the truth of Jesus. But does this mean that we can talk about the church as having a

---

95. Augustine, *On the Profit of Believing*, §33, *NPNF* First Series, Vol. III, p. 363.

96. John Chrysostom, *Homilies on Timothy*, Homily XII on 1 Tim. 4:1–3, and Homily I on 2 Tim. 1:1–2, *NPNF* First Series, Vol. XIII, pp. 446 and 476.

97. John Cassian, *The First Conference of Abbot Theonas*, ch. XXII, *NPNF* Second Series, Vol. XI, p. 511.

98. Stanley S. Harakas, *Toward Transfigured Life* (Minneapolis, MN: Light and Life, 1983), p. 35.

99. Stanley Hauerwas, *A Community of Character* (Notre Dame, IN: University of Notre Dame Press, 1981), pp. 1–4.

moral conscience? In what sense can a conscience be corporate? How can a corporate conscience discern, distinguish, evaluate and judge moral realities?

To answer these questions we need to think carefully about the being of the church. John Chrysostom reminds us that the body of Christ is one before it is many parts. Paul, he wrote, 'said not, "being many, are of one body", but "the one body itself is many" and those many members are this one thing'.[100] The church is not an undifferentiated mass but a gathering of persons called to be saints who, having been saved through faith (Eph. 2:8), is called to declare its mysteries. Membership comprises being grafted into the life of the 'true vine' (Jn 15:1ff), remaining united with Christ and bearing the fruit of his life. Members are participants in the body of Christ who eat his flesh and drink his blood (Jn 6:53–54). As John Chrysostom writes: 'For the church is nothing else than a house built of the souls of us men.'[101] Each person is called to live a life worthy of membership of Christ's body, and to build others up in the faith. The church is one body, and has one spirit and one hope. It is bound together as one by the one Spirit of God, by love for God and for one another: 'as great and as perfect a union as though it were between limb and limb'.[102] The church is the body of Christ formed in the Spirit (1 Cor. 12; 2 Cor. 13), existing as a eucharistic community and maintained by the love of God in anticipation of eternal life (2 Cor. 4:18). The church as a whole is called to have the eyes of its heart enlightened and to be strengthened in its inner being (Eph. 3:16–19). Its unity is never homogeneous; personal distinctiveness is not diminished

---

100. John Chrysostom, *Homilies on First Corinthians*, Homily XXX, *NPNF* First Series, Vol. XII, p. 175.

101. John Chrysostom, *Homilies on Ephesians*, Homily X, *NPNF* First Series, Vol. XIII, p. 101.

102. John Chrysostom, *Homilies on Ephesians*, Homily XI, *NPNF* First Series, Vol. XIII, p. 102.

but enhanced. The church needs virtue.[103] However, this virtue of the whole is realised in the lives of the members.[104]

By analogy, the conscience of the church is its critical faculty for judging in the light of the Holy Spirit's guidance. It belongs to the church as a whole and is realised in the lives of its members. If so, then we must be careful not to reduce its function to the purely cognitive. If the 'deposit of faith' refers to expressions of divine truth, including the person of Jesus Christ, the bible and tradition, then we must not reduce its nature to propositions, laws or formulae. If divine truth is as much (if not more) a matter of moral practice as systematic theory, then part of the task of Christian ethics is to perceive and articulate the interweaving of the cognitive and the practical. To do so requires the church to perceive connections between divine truth and moral goodness in everyday life. It requires the church to look for points of convergence between everyday decision-making and divine truth, to seek for wisdom in everyday life, and to express divine truth in responsible discipleship. But how should such a task proceed? How is the conscience of the church to be exercised? No answer which engages with practicalities – the reality of poverty, the latest technologies, the complexities of national and international politics – will be easy or quick. The moral life of the church is not a mechanism which will infallibly make known the truth in the face of new technologies, risks and horrors. What is needed, however, is a corporate responsibility shared by all Christian

---

103. John Chrysostom, *Homilies on Ephesians*, Homily IV, *NPNF* First Series, Vol. XIII, p. 68.

104. In a marvellous passage on this subject Clement of Alexandria writes: 'Christian conduct is the operation of the rational soul in accordance with a correct judgement and aspiration after truth, which attains its destined end through the body, the soul's consort and ally. Virtue is a will in conformity to God and Christ in life, rightly adjusted to life everlasting. For the life of Christians, in which we are now trained, is a system of reasonable actions – that is, of those things taught by the Word – an unfailing energy which we have called faith.' *The Instructor*, Bk I, ch. XII, *ANF*, Vol. II, p. 235.

people to cultivate the conscience of the church. The exercise of this responsibility is polyphonic and multi-dimensional in nature; the knowledge, experience and judgement of many people is required.

Christian Ethics and the Polyphony of the Christian Ethos

This chapter has been about personal moral freedom in the Spirit and whether it (necessarily) conflicts with the authority of the church to teach. I have argued that we introduce a false divide in Christian ethics if we force a choice between the two. There is no need to choose between the spiritual and moral growth of the person and the teaching of the church, between radical and institutional Christianity. The church's teaching ministry accords with the gospel when it summons each person to reflect divine love and live in the freedom of the Spirit; the church is a community of persons called by God to the freedom of holiness (Lev. 11:44, 19:2; Deut. 7:6; 14:2, 21; 26:19; Is. 62:12). Those led by the Spirit of God do not inhabit a life of fear but rather the glorious liberty of the children of God (Rom. 8:14, 21). Yet we live at a time when, for many, old definitions of faith and moral strictures seem dry, dusty and unable to offer the spiritual refreshment needed. The personal adventure of freedom seems reduced to the instantiation of rules or to compliance with laws and norms. In response, I have focused the question on how polyphony in the Spirit relates to the teaching authority exercised by the church, and argued that polyphony is constantly at risk of falling into either monologism or heteroglossia, and suggested that the authority of both is illusory. I have also suggested that we rethink some of the most commonly used symbols for the teaching authority of the church, notably, 'deposit of faith', 'handing on' and 'guarding'. Drawing on resources from the patristic period, we have thought about the 'deposit of faith' as expression(s) of divine truth, and about the corporate task of 'handing on' and 'guarding', in terms of the ceaseless renewing of the conscience of the church. The importance of the conscience of the church lies in its being able to distinguish between good and evil, right and wrong, what is fitting or unfitting for a disciple of Christ. However, these are not judgements imposed by the few on the many; the conscience of the church is a faculty given to the church which comprises many members.

Chapter Four

Authority and the Church as Body of Christ

Approaching the Problem(s) of Authority and the Church

In times like these, who needs the church? It has often been 'weighed in the balance' of secular – or other kinds of – morality and been found wanting. Many dismiss its moral influence as alternatively socially irrelevant or socially harmful. Others charge it with poking its spiritual nose into political or secular affairs. Even Christian people sometimes find it difficult to take seriously the moral teaching of their church when it does not represent what they think and believe to be right, or when it differs from that of another denomination. The time is clearly past when Christian leaders can repeat well-worn arguments about the moral authority of the church in trite and over-easy fashion. Many Christians feel uneasy at claiming that they know an action to be right or wrong because of the arrogance implied in their judgement of others. Many are ashamed of the bloodstained history of conflicts in the name of religion, and are convinced that truth can easily be mistaken for sincerely held bigotry. Some have personal experience of fixed principles being used as blunt tools by the religious authorities to whom they went for help with a delicate moral dilemma, not least in matters of human sexuality. Many meet and share with people of other faiths, humanists, atheists and others, and meaningful dialogue in these contexts leads them to doubt that there are fixed and universal standards against which an action should be measured. Some think that behavioural rules within a given society derive mainly from primal drives that promote the well-being of the species.[1] What, then, are we to make of authority as exercised in the Christian church? Why investigate doctrinal links between moral theology and ecclesiology and why keep asking about the church and moral authority?

Answers to these questions do not lie – at least primarily – in what can be seen of the church today. To look at the church in the present might not tell us much about what it actually is because, in one sense, it is a gathering of sinners who fail to live up to their high calling. Viewed humanly, the church is nothing more than a gathering of those who have responded in faith to the call of Jesus Christ. It often seems old-fashioned, out of touch with contemporary culture, boring and negatively judgemental, especially as regards sensual pleasure. Nor can we look solely to the history of the church to discover its true nature. Church historians trace the story of church life as a narrative community with varied traditions, memories and expectations, but their discipline cannot reflect explicitly on the being of the church in Christ and the Holy Spirit. Yet there can hardly be a church member who has not been confronted with accusations from atheist or agnostic friends about the hypocrisy of the church, atrocities committed during the Crusades, witch burnings, the Inquisition, and many other sins of both omission and commission. The authority of the church has frequently been marred by elements of violence. Hannah Arendt describes times when political motives produced unholy alliances between throne and altar,

> when kings, frightened at the prospect of revolution, believed that 'the people must not be permitted to lose its religion' because, in Heine's words, *Wer sich von seinem Gotte reisst,/ wird endlich auch abtrünnig werden/ von seinen irdischen*

1. Richard Dawkins, *The Selfish Gene* (Oxford: Oxford Paperbacks, 1989), *passim*.

Behörden ('who tears himself away from his God will end by deserting his earthly authorities as well').[2]

Authority can be variously defined and exercised, but this implied accusation of sleazy political compromise and manipulative power-games suggests that popular memory of the Christian church has been sullied by examples of worst rather than best practice. Alternatively, however, if theological reflection on the being of the church neglects to take account of either its history or its present reality, then we end up with a distorted and idealised presentation of the church as a 'sublime other'.[3]

This is the perennial problem of the divide between the essential nature of the church (found in the economy of the Son and the economy of the Spirit), and public perceptions of the church as institution. As the body of Christ, the material and social reality of the church reflects and refracts another, divine reality. Bonhoeffer comments on Matt. 5:13ff: 'It is not for the disciples to decide whether they will be the salt of the earth, for they are so whether they like it or not, they have been made salt by the call they have received.'[4] The church is what it is because of what God has done in Christ, through the Holy Spirit. However, experience confronts us (often in discussions with atheist or agnostic friends) with the many failings of the church, and a gap continually emerges between theological truth – that as the body of Christ the church does not equal itself but signifies something more – and the reality of church life which we experience and which historians record.

---

2. Arendt, 'What is Authority?' in Hannah Arendt, *Between Past and Future* (London: Penguin, 1961/1993), p. 134.
3. This phrase is used by Gillian Rose, *Mourning Becomes the Law* (Cambridge: CUP, 1997), p. 26.
4. Dietrich Bonhoeffer, *The Cost of Discipleship* (London: SCM, 1948/1959), p. 105.

Developing a Chalcedonian Way of Thinking

Difficult times are not a new phenomenon for the church. Basil of Cæsarea knew of the human difficulties involved in being the church when he wrote:

> We live in days when the overthrow of the churches seems imminent . . . There is no edification of the church; no correction or error; no sympathy for the weak . . . no remedy is found either to heal the disease which has already seized us, or as a preventive against that which we expect. Altogether the state of the church (if I may use a plain figure through it may seem too humble an one) is like an old coat, which is always being torn and can never be restored to its original strength.[5]

Basil's way of seeking wisdom was to encourage his fellow presbyters and Christians of Tarsus to expend 'great effort and diligence' in the pursuit of unity and to join themselves to the Nicene Creed.[6] In similarly difficult times, John Chrysostom wrote of his belief that the church of God can be strengthened with might through knowledge of the love of God: 'Be it our care, therefore, beloved, to understand the love of God.'[7] Nothing could be so beneficial or so deeply affecting than to avail themselves of this kind of knowledge. For both, commitment to the theological truth of what the church is, rather than digging more deeply into ourselves and our predicaments, is the right way to proceed in questions concerning the church and moral authority, because

---

5. Basil, Letter CXIII, *NPNF* Second Series, Vol. VIII, p. 189. Basil was concerned, in particular, with the lack of unity within the church, and urged communion among all who joined themselves to the Nicene Creed.

6. On contemplation, see Basil, Letter VIII, *NPNF* Second Series, Vol. VIII, pp. 189–190.

7. John Chrysostom, *Homilies on Ephesians*, Homily VII, *NPNF* First Series, Vol. XIII, p. 82.

what best strengthens faith and builds up the community is knowledge of God. Like Basil and John Chrysostom, this chapter seeks
links between what the church is and how it should live (its ethic
or *ethos*), in the belief that moral theology is grounded in the
mysteries of salvation and the triune God.

To develop a Chalcedonian way of thinking is to confess that
there is something unutterably mysterious at the heart of the
church's being because it exists in Christ and through the
enlivening of the Holy Spirit. The church is the church of
the triune God and has mystery at its heart. Its truth and vitality
are found in God, but in a way which does not swallow or diminish
its humanness and historicity, and herein lies the problem of
authority. The Holy Spirit continuously forms and renews the
church as the body of Christ in the world. Yet the church never
ceases to be fully human and to experience human problems,
especially regarding the exercise of authority. This accounts for
the gap that continually emerges between the being of the church
in Christ and its historical reality. With this in mind, I argue that
a Chalcedonian way of thinking offers a way of understanding the
two natures of the church 'without confusion or change' and
'without separation or division'. The divine and human dimensions of the church's life are conceptually distinct and should not
be confused, yet they cannot be separated or divided without
rendering New Testament teaching meaningless. As Chalcedon
spoke of the incarnate Word as embracing both humanity and
divinity, so a Chalcedonian way of thinking provides a way of
talking about the human and divine dimensions of the life of the
church.[8] To use Barth's words: 'The life of the children of God,
and therefore the Church, the subjective reality of revelation, is
divine and human, eternal and temporal, and therefore visible
and invisible. It is also human, also temporal, also visible. Always

---

8. The phrase 'Chalcedonian pattern' is used by Deborah van Deusen Hunsinger,
Theology and Pastoral Counseling: A New Interdisciplinary Approach (Grand
Rapids, MI: Eerdmans, 1995), ch. 3 *passim*.

in its entire hiddenness in God it is also an historical reality.'[9] The
ordering of the divine and human aspects of church life is not
symmetrical.[10] As Karl Barth was convinced, the two natures are
'not conceived as ordered according to a scale whereby they would
differ only in degree'.[11] They are conceived asymmetrically because
they share no common measure or standard of measurement.[12]
Yet the two natures share an indissoluble unity.

The church: 'An organism with two natures'

A Chalcedonian way of thinking thus has to do with the mystery
at the heart of the incarnation. But there are some warnings that
we should bear in mind. For many of the early fathers, the mystical
and mysterious union of humanity with divinity in Jesus Christ
was the primary insight into the nature and being of the church.
As M. J. Congar remarked in *Divided Christendom*, the ancient
Greek fathers rarely made the church, as such, a topic of study.
Theirs was, he says, a relatively feeble ecclesiology, the fact being
that their emphasis was on Christology, and still more on Pneumatology, rather than the being of the church of itself.[13] Vladimir
Lossky makes the similar point that early eastern theologians never
thought of the church apart from Christ and from the Holy Spirit;
study of the church should not reduce it to its 'earthly aspect'
and 'human implications' because of the risk of 'abandoning its
true nature which distinguishes it from every other human

---

9. Karl Barth, *Church Dogmatics*, I.2, §16, 4 (Edinburgh: T. & T. Clark, 1956), p.
219.
10. See also Hunsinger, *Theology and Pastoral Counseling*, ch. 3, for a helpful
discussion of the term 'symmetrical' within a Chalcedonian way of thinking.
11. Barth, *Church Dogmatics*, III.3, p. 104.
12. I am indebted for the clarity of this observation and its expression to George
Hunsinger, *How to Read Karl Barth: The Shape of his Theology* (Oxford: OUP,
1991), pp. 286–287.
13. M. J. Congar, *Divided Christendom* (London, 1939), p. 12. Noted by Vladimir
Lossky, *The Mystical Theology of the Eastern Church* (London: James Clarke,
1957), p. 175.

society'.[14] To heed Lossky's word of caution is to attend to the mystery of christological and pneumatological aspects of the church, as expressed at Chalcedon, and to be clear that theological reflection on the nature and experience of the church cannot be separated from the work of Christ and the Holy Spirit. Both ecclesiology and Christian ethics are grounded in the work of Christ and the Holy Spirit; study of the church is study of the divine realities (to use Lossky's words) of the economy of the Son and the economy of the Spirit. Both are chapters of Christology and, as Chalcedon spoke of the incarnate Word as embracing both humanity and divinity, so a Chalcedonian way of thinking about Christian ethics provides an approach whereby to talk about the human and divine aspects of the church.[15]

Too often, Chalcedonian Christology and ecclesiology has been associated with male-dominated and politically compromised

---

14. Lossky, *Mystical Theology of the Eastern Church*, p. 175.

15. We must clearly be careful not to fall into, or repeat, old heresies. On the one hand, we are likely to be susceptible to a quasi-Nestorian form of heresy which stresses too much the duality of the human and divine aspects of the church. The Nestorians saw clearly the human reality of Jesus Christ, but failed to appreciate that, in Jesus Christ, the divine and human were brought together and united in his person. If we divide the church into its human and divine aspects, and fail to express the deep Christian conviction that, as the body of Christ, two natures are united in one subsistence (*hypostasis*), then we risk perceiving only the external characteristics of the church, thus emptying its divine aspect of meaning. On the other hand, we are likely to be susceptible to a quasi-Monophysite heresy which stresses too much the divine and sacred being of the church. The Monophysites recognised the difficulty of finding a suitable expression of the two natures in the one person of Jesus Christ, but stressed his divine nature to the extent of negating the significance of the humanity. If we indulge in a falsely elevated or introverted ecclesiology, and fail to heed the cruciform calling of the church as part of God's purposes of salvation for the whole world, then we risk perceiving a partial truth, with concomitant consequences for an understanding of mission and ministry. It can be argued, however, that a Chalcedonian way of thinking, which affirms two natures (*physis*), united in one subsistence (*hypostasis*), is still a viable way to guard against both these tendencies.

frameworks of theological meaning. Elisabeth Schüssler-Fiorenza argues: 'The Chalcedonian promulgation of the doctrine of the Incarnation is a good example of how kyriocentrism and kyriarchy feed on and reinforce each other'; classical christologies are rooted in imperial kyriarchal theology which links the rule of God to the rule of the emperor/master/lord/father/husband.[16] As she points out, christological debates in the fourth and fifth centuries AD were speeded along by imperial desire for unity throughout the empire. Constantine called the Council of Nicaea in AD 325 and was conspicuous by his presence.[17] Arguably, the matter is not as scandalous as sometimes suggested, because imperial support soon waned for significant defenders of Nicene orthodoxy. Thus, when Athanasius refused the imperial request to restore Arius to his position in Alexandria for political purposes, he was banished to Gaul. Schüssler-Fiorenza is justifiably wary of co-operation between church and state politicians in securing a religious base for political stability.[18] However, it is not clear that Chalcedonian Christology is necessarily linked to 'kyriarchal' theo-political configurations. This chapter seeks to demonstrate the capacity of a Chalcedonian way of thinking to disrupt and overturn humanly constructed norms of authority and governance. If the church is the body of Christ, then Christ's way of being should pervade all the limbs and organs in imitation of the divine nature. As Gregory of Nyssa writes: 'The characteristics of the true Christian

---

16. Elisabeth Schüssler-Fiorenza, *Jesus: Miriam's Child, Sophia's Prophet* (London: SCM, 1995), p. 20.

17. See Friedrich Loofs's entry in *Realencyklopädie für Theologie und Kirche*, 2:14, 15 which demonstrates that Constantine was active in supporting changes to the Caesarean creed which secured agreement from opposing parties.

18. Useful studies include: Hans von Campenhausen, *Ecclesiastical Authority and Spiritual Power in the Church of the First Three Centuries* (London: Adam & Charles Black, 1969); Peter I. Kaufman, *Church, Book and Bishop: Conflict and Authority in Early Latin Christianity* (Colorado: Westview, 1996); Peter Brown, *Power and Persuasion in Late Antiquity: Towards a Christian Empire* (Madison, WI: University of Wisconsin Press, 1992).

are the same we apply to Christ. We imitate those qualities we can assume while we venerate and worship what our nature cannot imitate.'[19]

In response to these challenges, this chapter argues that the ethic appropriate to the church – i.e., the standards and norms which characterise its life – will be derived from a theological understanding of what it is to be the body of Christ in the world. The interpretative framework within which we work is Chalcedonian and confesses Christ as fully human and divine 'without confusion and separation'.[20] Questions about authority will feature strongly, and the answers at which we arrive indicate something of the interrelationship between ethical imitation and worship of Christ. Working with Paul Ricoeur's understanding of

---

19. Gregory of Nyssa, *On Perfection*, translated and published in *The Greek Orthodox Theological Review*, Vol. 29, No. 4 (Brookline, MA, 1984), pp. 349–379.
20. Barth addressed similar issues and argued that the doctrine of the two natures of Christ is the necessary presupposition of all ecclesiology. The mystery of the Christian community is given in its head, Jesus Christ: he was 'elected the Head of all humanity (as the last and true Adam, 1 Cor. 15:45f) . . . He was made the one Mediator between God and all men (1 Tim. 2:5) . . . He died for the sins of the whole world (1 Jn 2:2) . . . and rose again as the Revealer of the right and life of all men (1 Cor. 15:21f)' (*Church Dogmatics*, IV.1 §62, p. 667). He remarks that the language of 'body' is used in the New Testament only of the Christian community, and not of the whole human community, because it pertains to the fellowship of the body that breaks and eats one bread together (1 Cor. 10:17). Recognising that, at times, the language might seem 'esoteric', he insists that its reality is found in the concrete life of the community. If the community becomes a 'ghetto' defined by its own limits, then it ceases to exist as a 'promise of the emergence of the unity in which not only Christian but all men are already comprehended in Jesus Christ' (*Church Dogmatics*, IV.1 §62, p. 665). Nevertheless, the union of the Christian community with Christ – which is 'a real presence of his body' and the predestining purpose of God, in the fullness of time, 'to gather up all things in him' – is, says Barth, the 'Magna Carta of the being of the community in Him' (*Church Dogmatics*, IV.1 §62, p. 666). Far from ending up in abstractions and hopeless contradictions, Chalcedon acknowledges that Christ's two natures combine in some reciprocity in his person, and that this is also true of the church in so far as its being is grounded and hidden in Christ.

metaphor, and Mikhail Bakhtin's understanding of carnival, we are interested in interpretation of biblical references to 'the body of Christ' (e.g., Rom. 12:5; 1 Cor. 12:12–26; Eph. 4:15–17, 5:23, 30; Col. 1:18, 2:19). The word 'body' is a focus of attention and will be interpreted within the context of Bakhtin's treatment of embodiment in *Rabelais and His World*. This book is an examination of Rabelais's representation of the popular humour and folk culture of the Middle Ages and the Renaissance. It reviews Rabelais's place in the 'history of laughter', expounds his use of the 'language of the marketplace' and also of popular-festive forms. Particular attention is paid to banquet imagery and grotesque images of the body. At first glance, it may seem an odd place from which to interpret the metaphor of the church as body of Christ, and an even odder place from which to glean insight about the church and authority as informed by Chalcedonian ways of thinking. Arguably, however, Bakhtin shocks us into seeing afresh that a theandric logic of opposites is less a formal contradiction than a suspension of the kind of reasoning that confines a Christian understanding of authority within humanly constructed norms.

The significance for Christian ethics is given in the basic pre-supposition that Christian ethics is about identification with, and imitation of, the life and death of Jesus Christ. Ethical identification with, and imitation of Christ is more than performing certain actions (1 Cor. 11:1). Rather, it is a way of being, a lifestyle, and an ethos that pervades the whole of life. Discrete decisions and actions are, of course, of undeniable importance in the ethical life. But it is important to see how individually distinct decisions and actions fit appropriately within a life as a whole. Similarly, there are many ways in which different traditions and denominations of the church manifest and live out the Christian life. All of these, however, share in some sense the common ethic of Jesus Christ and seek to develop a general mode of existence appropriate to the Christian vocation of becoming more Christ-like. In this chapter, we are interested in how identification with, and imitation of Christ is facilitated less by individual moral choices than by a life-direction or spiritual orientation that is 'a way of relationship with the world, with other people, and with God'.[21] In particular, I argue that Bakhtin's ideas about carnival (derived from Rabelais) provoke us to think in fresh ways about the logic of opposites that characterises a Chalcedonian way of thinking, and that this has implications for many aspects of the church's ethos as a eucharistic community. We shall explore how the eucharist constitutes a fundamental aspect of the church's existence and its relationship to the wider society and world. Eating and feasting are the primary ways in which the community is bound together, and this is reflected in ethical terms in how the church lives and invites others to share its life in Christ.

Drawing on the thought of Mikhail Bakhtin

It is impossible to convey in a few paragraphs the multifaceted nature of both Rabelais's and Bakhtin's explorations: the corrective value of laughter; the truth that comes to light through parody; the sense of solidarity engendered by exaggerated and grotesque representations of the human body; and the perichoretic relationship between images of life and death in carnivalesque revelry. Broadly speaking, however, they offer a literary and quasi-philosophical treatment of the symbolic destruction of officialdom and hierarchical authority. The theological influence is not readily evident, but, upon careful attention, it can be perceived in several ways, not least the unmistakable juxtaposition of seeming opposites in ways that mutually inform one another, in the way that laughter – although not the reduced and cold laughter of sarcasm – liberates a regenerating power, and in the way that feasting is the primary locus of the social and creative life of the people. Bakhtin makes several explicit references to Christian traditions of Easter and Christmas laughter when Christians were

---

21. Cf. John D. Zizioulas, *Being as Communion* (Crestwood, NY: St Vladimir's Seminary Press, 1985), p. 15.

allowed to tell jokes and laugh in church as witness to the joyous regeneration of gospel truth.[22] He is thoroughly condemnatory of the prevalent solemn piety that generally characterised the church, remarking dismissively that laughter creates no doctrine and cannot become authoritarian.[23] What is important, however, is that laughter has the power to mock the pretensions of death, as also the pretensions of fanaticism, pedantry, naïveté and illusion. In laughter the world is seen anew, just as in popular culture the carnival fires of festivity burned up artistic representations of the fires of hell.[24] The banquet imagery of feasting and abundance implicitly juxtaposes the popular, market-place 'banquet for all the world' with eucharistic imagery. Bakhtin traces how the tradition of popular banquet imagery started with the famous *Coena Cypriani* or 'Cyprian's Supper', reputed by some to have been a parody of a sermon composed by Bishop Zeno, in which all biblical passages concerning food and drink were collected together and combined into one grandiose picture of a banquet.[25]

Alexandar Mihailovic lists many linguistic reasons for perceiving links throughout the book between carnival, embodiment, the Chalcedonian formula and the logos motif of John 1:14.[26] However, we need to be careful because, as Mihailovic is aware, the resonances in Bakhtin's work of Chalcedon may be more suggestive

---

22. Mikhail Bakhtin, *Rabelais and His World*, trans. Hélène Iswolsky (Bloomington, IN: Indiana University Press, 1984), pp. 78–82.
23. Bakhtin, *Rabelais*, p. 95.
24. Bakhtin, *Rabelais*, p. 119.
25. Bakhtin, *Rabelais*, pp. 286–288.
26. 'The idea and the varied terminology of restrictive borders or dividing lines opposed to it are reiterated time and again by Bakhtin: derivatives of the words *granitsa* (border, boundary), *rubezh* (border, verge, dividing line), *predel* (limit, or often other variants formed from the stem *del* such as *delenie* [division] and the Chalcedonian *razdel'no* [undivided]), and occasionally the terms *mezha* (boundary, boundary-strip) and *mezhdu* (between) reverberate throughout the book...' A. Mihailovic, *Corporeal Words: Mikhail Bakhtin's Theology of Discourse* (Evanston, IL: Northwestern University Press, 1997), p. 153.

than substantive.[27] Bakhtin is interested in the logic of opposites that Chalcedon enables, i.e., the way of thinking that allows diversity within unity, union that does not erase difference, and the dialogic penetration of one truth by another: 'Bakhtin uses the Chalcedonian formula to describe how mockery and exaltation are inextricably merged in carnival laughter . . . derision/abuse and triumph/praise taking the place of the twin human/divine sides of Christ's being.'[28] All of this, observes Mihailovic wisely, points to the unorthodoxy of an Orthodox believer.[29] Bakhtin's theology in this book should be 'handled with care'; it cannot be subsumed directly into a consideration of the church and moral authority. This said, he might shock us into noticing some of the more surprising aspects of the dynamism that arises from the theandric Chalcedonian logic of opposites. Bakhtin's book *Rabelais and His World* brings us close to what Kierkegaard/Climacus meant by paradox as involving 'believing against understanding', and to requiring distinction between 'nonsense' and 'the incomprehensible'.[30]

A sceptic might argue that none of these facts constitute conclusive evidence that Bakhtin alluded deliberately to Christian themes. This argument would have some force but would be similarly indecisive. On balance, I judge the evidence sufficient to believe that theological influences are detectable in the text, although this is not essential to what follows in this chapter regarding the church and moral authority. We should also bear in mind that many themes in *Rabelais and His World* fit ill with Christian theology, notably the linking of rebirth to exclusively biological and human

---

27. Mihailovic, *Corporeal Words*, p. 127.
28. Mihailovic, *Corporeal Words*, p. 145.
29. Mihailovic, *Corporeal Words*, p. 146.
30. Søren Kierkegaard, *Philosophical Fragments*, trans. D. F. Swenson (Princeton: PUP, 1936), ch. III. See also 'Entries from Kierkegaard's Journals and Papers' in *Concluding Unscientific Postscript to* Philosophical Fragments, trans. H. V. Hong and E. H. Hong, Vol. II (Princeton: PUP, 1992), p. 99.

relations. For Rabelais, at least, death is mocked as receding and dying give way in the natural world to rebirth and renewal. Any references to a Christian understanding of resurrection are ambivalent. This said, let us see what happens if we allow Bakhtin's logic of opposites and treatment of carnival to interact with a Chalcedonian-informed theology of the church. How does it affect our understanding of authority? What kind of authority survives the correction of Easter laughter and the abundance of the banquet that God prepares for all people?

Working with a residue of incomprehensibility

Of interest to Rabelais and Bakhtin are ways in which humans construct perceptions of religious, political and moral values. They explore what does and does not sanction existing patterns of norms and prohibitions, and how institutional powers and hierarchies are relativised when their seriousness is destroyed by parodying laughter. For example, according to Bakhtin, there is a philosophic dimension to Rabelais's laughter; his portrayal of the comic aspect of the world is entirely serious in the way that it exposes human claims to truth and power that rest shakily upon convention, inherited right, improperly acquired or exercised political power. Laughter is powerful because it can uncrown and degrade what seemed previously to be absolute. Laughter exposes falsehood and can initiate change for the better. Similarly, the language of the market-place can expose the language of officialdom, whether ecclesiastical or secular, as nonsensical and unproductive. It challenges any claim that a few should be guardians of truth for the many, and waits to see what survives without being burned up in the crucible of laughter. The popular-festive form of carnival suspends all humanly constructed hierarchy and makes the people a law unto themselves. Excessive feasting undermines all that is utilitarian, and banquet imagery sets joyful sociability against the cares of the world. Grotesque images of the body remind readers of the closeness in human experience of birth and death, clowning and wisdom. Both Rabelais and Bakhtin are prepared to suspend the familiar and attempt a logic of 'bottoms up' as they discover new representations and truths about the world.

Their work is pervaded by an ambivalent irreverence towards institutional Christianity. As Mihailovic explains: 'In this sweeping view, the church is a particularly egregious culprit in its attempts to nullify the demands of somatic existence; it plays a crucial role in promulgating and supporting the humorlessness of the hierarchical culture.'[31] The 'church' here refers to the institution in the Middle Ages and Renaissance alluded to by Rabelais and, arguably, to some extent, the Russian Orthodoxy with which Bakhtin was familiar. In what follows, I have no particular wish to reproduce this ambivalence towards the church as institution, being more concerned to further the work of the church by contemplating how the metaphor of 'body of Christ' unfolds with new meaning. Thus, any sense which emerges from the metaphor should be tested and interpreted with reference to biblical and Chalcedonian ways of thinking. This is the interpretive context within which the metaphor is intended to acquire sense.[32] Emphasis is less on the ability of the hearer or reader to create new worlds of meaning than on the world of meaning which the metaphor unfolds: 'The meaning is not something hidden but something disclosed ... Interpretation thus becomes the apprehension of the proposed worlds which are opened up by the non-ostensive references of the text.'[33] Meaning is not something to be created or uncovered but is disclosed; it lies not behind the words but in front of them.

---

31. Mihailovic, *Corporeal Words*, p. 183.

32. This is consistent with Paul Ricoeur's explanation of the function of metaphor as creating new meanings within new socio-historical contexts, but acquiring particular sense according to given frameworks of reference. See Paul Ricoeur, 'Metaphor and the Central Problem of Hermeneutics' in *Hermeneutics and the Human Sciences*, trans. John B. Thompson (Cambridge: CUP, 1981), ch. 6.

33. Ricoeur, *Hermeneutics and the Human Sciences*, p. 177.

As applied to the matter in hand, this means that we can expect the metaphor of the church as 'body of Christ' to give rise to meanings, and even to serve as a theological treatise in miniature.[34] But we should be cautious. When working with paradox and a Chalcedonian logic of opposites, it is appropriate to recall the principle held by many ancient eastern theologians that apophatic ways of doing theology are to be preferred to cataphatic ways, that is, one can proceed further towards knowledge of God by negative than by positive means. Maximus the Confessor writes that 'denial truly affirms the divine'.[35] To quote him again:

> If you theologize in an affirmative or cataphatic manner, starting from positive statements about God, you make the Word flesh (cf. John 1:14), for you have no other means of knowing God as cause except from what is visible and tangible. If you theologize in a negative or apophatic manner, stripped away of positive attributes, you make the Word spirit as being in the beginning God and with God (cf. John 1:1): starting from absolutely none of the things that can be known, you come in an admirable way to know Him who transcends unknowing.[36]

In this passage, Maximus' applies traditional apophatic and cataphatic ways of speaking about God to the incarnation. If we apply his method to the question in hand, then to affirm positive statements about the church is to study what it is from what is visible and tangible, and to make negative or apophatic statements is to acknowledge that we cannot grasp the spiritual realities of the church by conceptual and rational means. Just as God cannot be squashed into humanly constructed systems and theories,

---

34. This phrase is used by Ricoeur, *Hermeneutics and the Human Sciences*, p. 167.
35. Andrew Louth (ed. and trans.), *Maximus the Confessor* (London: Routledge, 1996), p. 131.
36. Maximus the Confessor, *Centuries on Theology and the Incarnate Dispensation of the Son of God*, II.39 in Louth, *Maximus the Confessor*, p. 53.

neither can the divine aspects of the church be exhausted by humanly constructed methods of study.

Following Maximus, to do theology in a cataphatic or affirmative manner is to 'make the Word flesh' in the sense that it is to speak of the Word of God in ways that are familiar to us, and that we understand; it is a way of doing theology that is analogous to the incarnation. The Word becomes flesh, the truth of God becomes comprehensible through embodiment in what we already know. Similarly, we talk about the mystery of church in language we can understand. The danger, of course, in speaking about the church from the things that can be known, is that we confuse our histories, current practices and customs with the true nature of the church as it is given in Christ. What is actual is not necessarily what is true, and what is true is not necessarily what is actual. We are susceptible to illusion; as someone once said, God's truth is beyond our understanding, but not beyond our misunderstanding. Yet to do theology in a cataphatic or affirmative manner is to acknowledge that no formal definition of the church, its mission and ministry, will be adequate. This is because statements about the church are, to a large extent, statements of an existential nature about experiences of God's saving power. Apophaticism, writes Lossky, 'is an existential attitude which involves the whole man: there is no theology apart from experience.'[37] It is an attitude of mind, and experience of existence as the body of Christ, which recognises that, in any study of the church, there will always be a residue of incomprehensibility. There is no point 'spinning abstractions' or over-stretching our imaginations, because the mysteries of God cannot be adapted to human thought.[38] Knowledge of God is a matter of experience, not speculation.[39] As Basil of Cæsarea writes (in convoluted fashion) in a note on John 15:1, which he links to observation about 1 Cor. 12:27:

---

37. Lossky, *Mystical Theology of the Eastern Church*, p. 39.
38. See Lossky, *Mystical Theology of the Eastern Church*, pp. 38–39.
39. Louth makes this point in his introduction to *Maximus the Confessor*, p. 33.

'If the head of the man is Christ, and the head of Christ is God', and man is not of one substance with Christ, Who is God (for man is not God), but Christ is of one substance with God (for He is God), therefore God is not the head of Christ in the same sense as Christ is the head of man. The natures of the creature and the creative Godhead do not exactly coincide.[40]

Christ is, by nature, of one divine substance with God, and humanity is not divine. It is not possible for human beings to cross the divide between created and uncreated being because we are confronted by what Lossky calls a 'divine darkness' of incomprehensible truth. Socrates thought that the first real step towards philosophical knowledge was a sense of one's own ignorance, but the way of negation urged by ancient eastern theologians is more radical. Rationally derived knowledge yields to experience of God and contemplation of the mystery of all humanity included in Christ. Apophasis is conscious awareness that God transcends all human conceptions, and that the only way to understand anything of God is to recognise the mind's failure to comprehend God. Apophaticism is not iconoclastic or anti-rationalistic; it neither smashes sacred art nor opposes the use of reason in theology. Rather it is the recognition that we cannot think of God in Godself. Apophatic method applied to the church will negate both that which the church is, and that which it is not: the church is not just a human society but neither is it the glorious reality that God wills it to be; the reality of the church is a mystery only ever grasped by faith.

40. Basil, On John XV.I, 'I Am the Vine', NPNF Second Series, Vol. VIII, pp. xxxix–xl.

'He was despised and rejected': the Body of Christ crucified and glorious

Thus, as Kierkegaard reminds us, a Chalcedonian way of thinking involves a non-formal sense of contradiction or paradox and requires a person to believe without – or even against – understanding, and to accept that matters of faith sometimes seem absurd. Its paradoxical nature lies in the qualitative difference between creator and created; the conjunction of temporality and eternity.[41] Finite human beings cannot comprehend infinity, yet, through the infinite assuming finitude, they participate in its perfection. This is the same paradox to which Athanasius witnesses in the first *Discourse against the Arians*:

> [T]he Word's becoming flesh, and undergoing death in flesh, has not happened against the glory of His Godhead, but 'to the glory of God the Father'. For it is the Father's glory that man, made and then lost, should be found again; and, when dead, that he should be made alive, and should become God's temple . . . For because of our relationship to His Body we too have become God's temple . . .[42]

In Christ, the likeness and unlikeness of temporality and eternity subsist together in such a way that 'if anyone is in Christ, there is

---

41. C. Stephen Evans expresses this nicely: 'Climacus says again and again that the heart of the paradox, both in itself and in relation to the believer, lies in the conjunction of the historical or temporal with the eternal. The paradox has a double aspect. There is first the event itself, the "God in time," which is "the absurdity that the Eternal is the historical". The second element in the paradox concerns the believer's relation to the absolute historical fact. Here the paradox again concerns eternity and history, for the contradiction lies in the believer's *becoming* eternal in time through a relation to something historical.' C. Stephen Evans, *Kierkegaard's* Fragments *and* Postscript (Atlantic Highlands, NJ: Humanities Press International, Inc., 1983), p. 226.

42. Athanasius, *Four Discourses against the Arians*, Discourse I, *NPNF* Second Series, Vol. IV, pp. 330–331.

a new creation . . . All this is from God, who reconciled us to himself through Christ, and has given us the ministry of reconciliation' (2 Cor. 5:17–18). As a paradoxical 'organism with two natures', the church has frequently fallen short of its calling. Many have accused it (both justifiably and unjustifiably) of exercising authority harmfully and perversely in the name of divine authority. Nietzsche accused the church of living a sick paradox in which it preached powerlessness and weakness because Christ was crucified, while nurturing a breed of priests who fed their egos through their role as confessors. On the one hand, he railed against the horrific paradox of the crucified God which, he thought, poisoned the human will to be strong.[43] On the other, he laughed at the church for breeding sickly male priests who grew bitter at the expectation that they were to be powerless, while thriving on power derived from hearing sins confessed:

> Psychologically considered, 'sins' become indispensable in any society organised by priests: they are the real handles of power. The priest *lives* on sins, it is essential for him that people 'sin'. Supreme principle: 'God forgives those who repent' – in plain language: those who submit to the priest.[44]

In some similarity, Mary Daly accuses the church both of sapping the strength of women to live fully their own lives, and of claiming divine approval for hierarchical and patriarchal systems of governance. This is how she describes the clues to her own philosophy contained in the frontispiece and cover of the new edition of *The Church and the Second Sex* which included a 'Feminist Post-Christian Introduction':

The frontispiece of the 1975 edition, designed by Emily, had

---

43. Friedrich Nietzsche, *On the Genealogy of Morals*, trans. Douglas Smith (Oxford: OUP, 1996), pp. 17–22.
44. Nietzsche, *On the Genealogy of Morals*, pp. 18–20 and *The Antichrist* in Walter Kaufmann (trans. and ed.), *The Portable Nietzsche* (New York and London: Penguin, 1976), p. 598.

several important elements. There was the head of a woman, with her hair streaking behind her, flying above and away from the church, represented by a church building with a steeple. Superimposed on the woman's head was the women's symbol, with a clenched fist extending into its circle. The church was inscribed by the masculinist symbol, with its arrow pointing upward, and the church steeple was erect within the arrow . . . It says directly that the Spirit/Spirits of women are departing from the church.[45]

She accuses the church of patriarchal authoritarianism and in-stitutionalised control, and urges sisters to envisage feminist community as something '*beyond* "church" '.[46] For her, the glorious paradox of the church's participation in Christ had become a corrupt excuse for domination of the less powerful by those in control.

These challenges should be taken seriously because at issue is the question of where exactly the absurdity of paradox lies. For Nietzsche, what is incredible is that people still believe the religious bunkum that priests are endowed with powers to act on behalf of God. For Daly, what is unreasonable is that the patriarchal church still claims to act as if it were God in the world. For both, the absurdity of the paradox is located elsewhere than in the conjunc-tion of temporality and eternity. Leaving aside for a moment questions about the culpability of the church in giving grounds for their criticism, the issue is the mislocation of the heart of the paradox in the 'two natures' of the church, rather than in the 'two natures' of God and humanity united at the incarnation. When the heart of the paradox ceases to be the incarnation of the Word of God but becomes the 'two natures' of the church, without explicit and direct reference to the incarnation, the way is open

---

45. Mary Daly, *Outercourse: The Bedazzling Voyage* (London: The Women's Press, 1992), p. 176.
46. Mary Daly, *Beyond God the Father* (London: The Women's Press, 1973), ch. 6.

for all sorts of distortion and abuse. Perhaps this is why Kierke-gaard was so strident in affirming that the Chalcedonian paradox is neither rational nor conceptual but practical and existential. His *Attack upon Christendom* was an attack upon Christians who claimed that the authority of the church was homogeneous with the authority of 'the world' and not characterised by the renunci-ation of power-control or by suffering:

> To want to have all worldly goods and advantages . . . and then at the same time to be a witness to the truth – one might Christianly say, 'The deuce of a witness this is! Such a witness to the truth is not merely a monster but an impossi-bility, like a bird which is at the same time a fish, or like an iron tool which has the remarkable peculiarity of being made of wood.'[47]

The paradoxes in these examples are risible, but no more risible than a church which claims authority in its own right, or exercises authority which does not accord with the renunciation and suf-fering of Jesus' ministry. In making his point, Kierkegaard employs paradox to fight against misplaced notions of the authority of the church. His seemingly silly examples of birds, fish and tools illuminate the ridiculousness of churchly claims to be the body of Christ on earth, when the life of the church was so unlike that of Jesus. In limited similarity to Nietzsche, Kierkegaard stretches the truth of his experience to excess and, in so doing, illuminates real or potential problems by carrying his thought through to exaggeration and grotesqueness. For each, the road of exaggeration leads to truth; truth is not in safety or in the middle but in pushing reality to its breaking point and experimenting with extremes.[48] What follows in the remainder of this chapter takes

---

47. Søren Kierkegaard, *Attack upon Christendom*, trans. Walter Lowrie (Princeton: PUP, 1968), p. 11.
48. I draw here on Norman O'Brown's meditations on 'Fraction' in *Love's Body* (Berkeley, CA: University of California Press, 1966), ch. XI.

inspiration from Kierkegaard in this regard in dealing with the central paradox of the Christian message, which is the glory of Jesus Christ crucified: 'the immense tension between the kenotic Christ of the Passion and the *Christus Victor* of Easter morning'.[49]

Paschal laughter and the body parodied

Rabelais and his World is different from Bakhtin's other books because dialogism is less evident and he writes about humour and irony. There is, however, considerable continuity as far his implicit Christology is concerned and, as we shall see, the subject matter of this book is not at odds with serious consideration of the loci and exercise of authority. Arguably, the best way of showing that the themes developed in *Rabelais and his World* are not nonsense when read theologically is to read them with theological questions in mind and with reference to the Chalcedonian Christology that informs Bakhtin's work. When read in this way, I suggest that his work can sharpen our critique of the exercise of authority, clarify where the locus of authority really lies and also the criteria employed when thinking about its exercise. In this chapter, I have chosen to discuss the themes of laughter, banquet imagery and perceptions of the body, as they bear connection to ancient traditions of paschal laughter, the eucharist and perceptions of the church. *Rabelais and his World* is not a book concerned directly with theology but my hope is that by engaging dialogically with it, we shall gain the ability to think more clearly and consistently about authority in the church.

In his discussion of Rabelais in the history of laughter, Bakhtin poses questions about the medieval culture of humour and how carnival applied the popular corrective of laughter to 'the narrow-minded seriousness of spiritual pretense'.[50] Bakhtin traces how most medieval church feasts had their comic folk counterparts in which the culture of folk humour parodied the church's cult.

---

49. Peter L. Berger, *Redeeming Laughter* (Berlin: Walter de Gruyter, 1997), p. 190.
50. Bakhtin, *Rabelais*, p. 22.

These parodies included language which mocked and insulted the deity, laughed at the grotesqueness of the human body, and which had the effect of relativising prevailing truths and authorities by parading 'alternative truths' in the market place:

> We find here a characteristic logic, the peculiar logic of the 'inside out' (à l'envers), of the 'turnabout', of a continual shifting from top to bottom, from front to rear, of numerous parodies and travesties, humiliations, profanations, comic crownings and uncrownings. A second life, a second world of folk culture is thus constructed; it is to a certain extent a parody of the extracarnival life, a 'world inside out'.[51]

There were lots of jokes against the church as ecclesiastical liturgy and teaching were parodied. For example, in the chapter on 'Rabelais in the History of Laughter', there are frequent condemnations of negative attitudes in early Christianity regarding laughter, and accounts of how carnivalesque events such as the 'feast of fools' and the 'feast of kings' mocked the seeming seriousness of the Christian world-view. The sacred is parodied and, through humour, the world is seen anew. The assumption, however, is that what really matters in life will survive the test of laugher: 'That which is important and essential cannot be comical.'[52] Laughter has therapeutic effect but, suggests Bakhtin, it is also a spiritual privilege linked to freedom of the human spirit and to speech. It breaks apart all that is petty and narrow and, in learning to 'clown wisely', the people expose pompousness and hypocrisy and herald more lasting truth. The clown has both social and religious meaning.

Bakhtin is familiar with the ambivalence in Christian tradition regarding laughter and mirth. For example, he mentions John Chrysostom's censure of laughter and excessive mirth because laughter is often linked to luxury, laxness, dissolution and

---

51. Bakhtin, *Rabelais*, p. 11.
52. Bakhtin, *Rabelais*, p. 67.

blasphemy and ill-befits a Christian who is sorrowful for sin.[53] Chrysostom said that he did not wish 'to suppress all laughter' but reminds his readers that Christ speaks much about mourning and blesses those who mourn. He recalls that Jesus Christ condemned the laughter of this world (Lk. 6:25) and contrasts this laughter with the joy of communion with God.[54] On the other hand, Bakhtin recalls the traditions of Easter laughter (*risus paschalis*) according to which amusing stories and laughter were permitted in church during the Easter season. Easter laughter was linked with German, especially Bavarian, preaching traditions in the fifteenth century, and was a way of embodying the triumph over death that Easter celebrates. Prohibited by Pope Clement X (1670–1676) – presumably because stories told about conflicts between Christ and the devil at the doors of hell gave opportunity for ribaldry and abuse of the word of God – the tradition fell slowly into disuse.[55] It was linked, however, with developing ideas about the Christian as the fool of God, and saintly folly in the name of the gospel. Easter laughter marked a reversal of social norms and was a reminder of how the Christian gospel often reverses social norms of status and decency, and reminded

---

53. Bakhtin, *Rabelais*, pp. 73–74. See John Chrysostom, *The Gospel of Matthew*, Homily VI, §9, *NPNF* Second Series, Vol. X, pp. 40–42. In *Concerning the Statues*, Homily XV, he writes: '[T]o laugh, to speak jocosely, does not seem an acknowledged sin, but it leads to acknowledged sin' (*NPNF* Second Series, Vol. IX, p. 442).

54. John Chrysostom, *Homilies on Philippians*, Homily XIV, *NPNF* Second Series, Vol. XIII, p. 246.

55. For information, see K.-J. Kuschel, *Laughter: A Theological Reflection*, trans. J. Bowden (London: SCM Press, 1994), pp. 84–87. See also Berger, *Redeeming Laughter*, p. 189. Both provide summaries of Christian sources which develop the idea that Christ was mocked and 'crowned as a king of folly' and how traditions of holy folly developed in which persons were fools in the eyes of the world for Christ's sake. Kuschel writes: 'The provocative joy, the kingdom of God theology which extends frontiers and breaks taboos, manifests itself in the way in which Jesus uses grotesque imagery . . . bold parables . . . disarming answers . . . radical paradoxes . . . perplexing beatitudes' (p. 77).

believers of the absurdity to human eyes of the self-humiliation, the *kenosis*, of God at the incarnation. It was a relatively localised phenomenon but was concurrent with the resumption of meat-eating, sexual intercourse and general gaiety that pervaded the church after the days of Lenten sadness.

It is this link between Easter laughter and kenotic authority that interests us here as Bakhtin challenges us to contemplate the entire reconstruction of our ecclesial and ideological perceptions of authority, the renunciation of many deeply rooted norms about the nature and exercise of authority, and the revision of many concepts and practices.[56] Let us pick up in particular on the themes of the church and carnival, banquet imagery, feasting and fooling, and perceptions of the body.

The Church as Carnival

The carnivals experienced these days by most western Europeans or Americans are mediocre and insipid in comparison to that about which Rabelais wrote. Carnival, for Rabelais, was not a spectacle to be viewed but something in which to participate with all the energy one could muster. We can, of course, view the concept of carnival in different lights. In one light it should be censured for derisive laughter and scandalous goings-on: 'what is truly unseemly, indecent even . . . the apparent eagerness of deans, chaired professors and presidents of learned societies to tumble from their offices into the streets, monstrous papier mâché phalluses fixed in place'.[57] In another light, it represents the extraordinariness of the Christian ethos, its reversal of worldly understandings of authority, and rejection of the ethics of individualism. It illustrates the 'bottoms up' logic or epistemological reversal of secular ways of thinking that the gospel entails. In what

---

56. I paraphrase Bakhtin, *Rabelais*, p. 3.
57. Terry Eagleton, 'Bakhtin, Schopenhauer, Kundera' in Ken Hirschop and David Shepherd (eds), *Bakhtin and Cultural Theory* (Manchester: MUP, 1989), p. 179.

follows, I assume the latter and understand carnival as a mode of existence which bears analogy with the eschatological age to come. This is because the ethos of carnival is that of gathering together, laughing, feasting and fooling. It is the ethos of excess, equality, participation and grotesque realism. When viewed in a certain light, the church as carnival serves as a prophetic contrast between the here-and-now and the yet-to-come.

Feasting and fooling

'Come, my beloved, the season calls us to keep the feast.' So wrote Athanasius in his Easter letter of AD 329. Easter was a time to celebrate God's work of salvation. It was a time to be glad, as at a wedding, and to blow the festal trumpets. The writer to Timothy had urged due proclamation and celebration of the Christian good news, not least because of its beneficial effects on the believer (2 Tim. 4:1–5). 'For our paschal lamb, Christ, has been sacrificed. Therefore, let us celebrate the festival, not with the old yeast, the yeast of malice and evil, but with the unleavened bread of sincerity and truth' (1 Cor. 5:7b-8). For Athanasius, not only Easter, but every Sunday also, was a holyday on which to be glad because Christ had delivered us from death and wickedness:

> For thus the saints all their lives long were like men rejoicing at a feast ... who have ceased from their course, and now keep the feast in heaven, and rejoice in what they formerly learnt through shadows, and from the types recognise the truth.[58]

It was appropriate for believers to be fools for Christ in order to expose the falsity of the conventional and the seemingly unreasonable and irrational truth of God in Christ:

> [L]et us glorify the Lord, let us become fools for Him who died for us, even as Paul said; 'For if we are foolish, it is to

---

58. Athanasius, Letter XIV, §1, *NPNF* Second Series, Vol. IV, p. 542.

God; or if we are sober-minded, it is to you; since because one died for all men, therefore all were dead to Him; and He died for all, that we who live should not henceforth live to ourselves, but to Him who died for us, and rose again.'[59]

Different kinds of (metaphorical) trumpet were to be sounded on holydays; some trumpets of warning that believers should 'hallow the fast', others trumpets of battle which called to war against sin. They were sounded, however, to help believers to celebrate and keep the feast, in order that they might be counted worthy of the joy which is in heaven.[60]

The reason for feasting in the church is thankfulness for what God has done in Christ (1 Thess. 5:18). The liturgy (Greek *leitourgia*, meaning public work, from work (*ergon*) and people (*laos*)) of the eucharist is corporate in character and is the heart of the church's life. It defines the church's ethos. As Yannaras writes: 'The morality of the Church is a liturgical morality, a liturgical ethos of unity and communion, a *personal* participation in the body of God the Word.'[61] Its ethos is anticipatory of the new ethos of the coming kingdom of heaven, and also egalitarian. Participants are equal before God; all are invited to the divine and incorruptible banquet where all will receive a crown.[62] The salvation it represents is offered to all.[63] Its ethos is friendly. Strangers are called friends as all share the same food and drink, and each holds frequent conversation with the host.[64] Its celebration is wholistic, in so far as it is an activity which touches not only a person's soul but also their bodily senses and emotions. Its ethos is that of excessive generosity: 'He gives them abundantly

59. Athanasius, Letter VI, §4, *NPNF* Second Series, Vol. IV, p. 520.

60. Athanasius, Letter II, §7, *NPNF* Second Series, Vol. IV, p. 512.

61. Christos Yannaras, *The Freedom of Morality* (Crestwood, NY: St Vladimir's Seminary Press, 1984), p. 82.

62. Athanasius, Festal Letter XXXVIII, *NPNF* Second Series, Vol. IV, p. 550.

63. Athanasius, Festal Letter XXII, *NPNF* Second Series, Vol. IV, p. 549.

64. Athanasius, Festal Letter XLV, *NPNF* Second Series, Vol. IV, pp. 553 and 547.

according to the multitude of his loving-kindness.'[65] Participants are urged to remember the poor.[66] Its ethos is that of freedom – the kind of freedom that has no legal bounds but only the bounds of virtue and the boldness of wisdom that enjoins activity in accord with the teaching of Jesus.[67] Its ethos is that of refreshment and delight, and also anticipation because God's promise is that one day all participants will be able to sit at table with the saints in heaven and 'to share in the one voice of gladness which is there'.[68] Feasting – with its ethos of joyful abandon in the Spirit and abundance – is characteristic of normal Christian living. John Chrysostom preached that Jesus 'considered everyone worthy of the same table'.[69] None were forgotten in Christ's invitation: 'For the sake of all alike was He broken, and became the body equally for the sake of all.'[70] The eucharist is the place where all humanity is invited to meet with God. None are forgotten or uninvited because, in Christ, none are unacceptable.

The reason for fooling in the church is inseparable from its reason for feasting. The church feasts in response to Jesus' invitation and in anticipation of God's coming reign (Matt. 9:15, 25:1; Mk 14:22–25; Jn 6:48–58). It fools in imitation of Christ's victory over the devil (Matt. 4:1–11). Fools in the church mock the powers and privileges of this world, gaining their strength from prayer and fasting. Their seemingly odd behaviour is a prophetic witness to the difference between God's coming reign and the reality of our fallen condition. Paul wrote that believers in Christ should become fools so that they might become wise (1 Cor.

65. Athanasius, Festal Letter XX, *NPNF* Second Series, Vol. IV, p. 549.
66. Athanasius, Festal Letter I, *NPNF* Second Series, Vol. IV, p. 510.
67. Athanasius, Festal Letter XX, *NPNF* Second Series, Vol. IV, p. 549.
68. Athanasius, Festal Letter XX, *NPNF* Second Series, Vol. IV, p. 549.
69. John Chrysostom, *Homilies on First Corinthians*, Homily XXVII, §3. Cited in Daniel J. Sheerin, *The Eucharist*, Messages of the Fathers of the Church 7 (Delaware: Michael Glazier, 1986), p. 212.
70. John Chrysostom, *Homilies on First Corinthians*, Homily XXVII, §3, cited in Sheerin, *The Eucharist*, p. 61.

3:18–19): 'the wisdom of this world is foolishness with God'. This was interpreted by some to mean the foolishness of ascesis. Consider the foolishness of St Isidora of Egypt (d. *c.* 369). Reputed to have fed herself with nothing but crumbs, to have covered her head with a rag and gone barefoot rather than wear cowl and sandals like other nuns, she was regarded by many as a mad woman.[71] Andrew of Constantinople (d. *c.* 475) is said to have taken the path of foolishness by struggling with the severest of bodily deprivations. Similarly Serapion the Syndonite (d. fifth century) who strove for the perfection of non-acquisitiveness by giving away everything he possessed, even his cloak. A biography cites him as striving to be free of the creditors of love of money, carnal desires and gluttony. His desire was to die to the things of this world, and to the constraints of mortality, because not the flesh but the spirit ascends to God.[72] The folly of ascesis makes little sense in our contemporary culture, and it is important to stress that this kind of folly is not about self-abasement for its own sake or seeking discomfort and suffering because they are good in themselves. Rather, it is about cutting connection with the devil and shunning the life of sin, because this is pleasing to God: 'It is no longer I who live, but Christ who lives in me' (Gal. 2:20). Much harm can been done through misinterpretations of such folly.

The ethical significance of carnival feasting and fooling is evident, not only in its replacement of official authority and introduction with egalitarianism, but also in its temporary suspension of the usual ethical standards and norms, especially those related to social utility. 'The feast has no utilitarian connotation (as has daily rest and relaxation after working hours). On the contrary, the feast means liberation from all that is utilitarian. It

---

71. See Anon., *God's Fools: The Lives of the Holy 'Fools for Christ'*, trans. Bishop Varlaam Novakshonoff, 3rd edn (Dewdney, Canada: Synaxis Press, 1997), pp. 2–3.
72. *God's Fools*, pp. 6–8.

is a temporary transfer to the utopian world.'[73] Carnival performs no intended social function.[74] It does not serve anyone's interests; the door of each house was left open for passers-by to enter and eat, as they had need. This lack of social utility was also represented in plays about utopian worlds of absolute equality of freedom, e.g., the wedding feast in Pantagruel, Book 4, ch. 13. Everyone was an equal participant at the feast and, moreover, there was no clear dividing line between the play and 'real life'. Carnival performances were noteworthy for their lack of footlights and thus the lack of separation between performers and spectators. There was no such separation because everyone participated: 'While the usual world order is suspended, the new utopian order which has come to replace it is sovereign and embraces all ... The utopian truth is enacted in life itself. For a short time this truth becomes to a certain extent a real existing force.'[75] In like manner, the eucharist has no intended or manipulable social utility, though its effect is sanctification of the faithful. As carnival could not be reduced to any particular content, aim or objective, neither can the eucharist. What matters is simply being with other members of the church, being the church, setting aside daily affairs, and being part of the celebration. Similarly, the eucharist knows no separation between 'performers' and 'spectators', clergy and laity. This is true in all churches, even those with hierarchical understandings of church polity and sacramental understandings of priesthood. Stanley Harakas cites Basil of Caesarea: 'Everything is equal between us [the clergy] and you [the laity] and we have the same measure of

73. Bakhtin, *Rabelais*, p. 276.
74. There is an argument which suggests that carnival did perform a social function, namely that of protecting the status quo by providing temporary relief from drudgery and oppression. It relieved social tension temporarily but made no lasting change. In response, I acknowledge this, and possibly other, reasons to be cautious of placing too much emphasis on any particular illustration or analogy. However, I emphasise that this is most definitely not the reason for talking about carnival here. Nor does it appear to have been Bakhtin's intention.
75. Bakhtin, *Rabelais*, p. 265.

goods for I do not receive more richly and you in a lesser measure from the Holy Table, but we equally draw from it.'[76] The church, not the priest, conducts the liturgy.

The equality of the eucharist was emphasised by Paul when writing to the Corinthians. 'I hear that there are divisions among you,' he wrote. 'For when the time comes to eat, each of you goes ahead with your own supper, and one goes hungry and another becomes drunk' (1 Cor. 11:18, 21). John Chrysostom commented on the passage by noting changes in practice that had occurred between the institution of the Lord's supper and its practice at Corinth. In the earliest days of the church, believers ate all things in common. Later, they feasted in common only when celebrating the Lord's supper. Now Paul notes that in Corinth this custom is threatened by individualistic and divisive practices. John Chrysostom writes:

> Since therefore this custom was broken through, a custom most excellent and most useful; (for it was a foundation of love, and a comfort to poverty, and a corrective of riches, and an occasion of the highest philosophy, and an instruction of humility) since however he saw so great advantages in a way to be destroyed, he naturally addresses them with severity . . .[77]

The true ethos of the eucharist makes love the basis upon which the church is built, the central tenet of its teaching, and that which makes it worthy of the name 'Christian'. It eases the grief and trouble of poverty by sharing things in common, thus giving strength and hope to those in need. It counteracts the temptations of riches by pointing out how poverty is a cause of harm and urging that a person's liberality should increase and become mani-

---

76. Stanley S. Harakas, *Living the Liturgy* (Minneapolis, MN: Light and Life Publishing Co., 1974), p. 48.
77. John Chrysostom, *Homilies on First Corinthians*, Homily XXVII on 1 Cor. II: 17, *NPNF* First Series, Vol. XII, p. 157.

fold, in proportion to their ability to give. The true ethos of the eucharist is that of wisdom and the lack of arrogance and pride which Chrysostom links to advancement in virtue and to not giving others cause to stumble in their path of faith (Matt. 18:7). Paul clearly expected an outflowing of communion from the practice of eating the Lord's supper and he 'seared with a hot iron' the consciences of those who broke with the customary, communal practices of eating together in favour of feasting in private:

> Perceivest thou how he intimates that they were disgracing themselves rather? For that which is the Lord's, they make a private matter: so that themselves are the first to suffer indignity, depriving their own table of its greatest prerogative. How and in what manner? Because the Lord's Supper, i.e. the Master's, ought to be common. For the property of the master belongs not to this servant without belonging to that, but is common to all. So that by 'the Lord's' Supper he expresses this, the 'community' of the feast.[78]

Individualistic practices went hand in hand with factions in the church. Paul had no desire in his teaching to destroy the liberty of those in his charge, or to place any necessity or compulsion in these matters on the people. To do so would have run counter to the liberty of the gospel. These were not matters that touched upon the necessary burdens prescribed in Acts 15:20, 28–29. Instead, he recounted some words of Jesus, allowing each person's own conscience to apply the meaning of his words.[79]

Thus, the Lord's supper or eucharist is not a private feast or individual indulgence. Rather, its ethos is that of the feast of a community; love for one another distinguishes its participants from those at any other feast. But its significance extends beyond

---

78. John Chrysostom, *Homilies on First Corinthians*, Homily XXVII on 1 Cor. II: 17, commenting on verse 21, *NPNF* First Series, Vol. XII, p. 159.

79. John Chrysostom, *Homilies on First Corinthians*, Homily XXVII on 1 Cor. II: 17, commenting on verse 19, *NPNF* First Series, Vol. XII, pp. 158–159.

the community of the church. In Jesus' parable of the wedding feast, the servant was told to go out into the streets and lanes of the town and bring in the poor, the crippled, the blind, and the lame (Lk. 14:21b). All were invited; it was a banquet for the world. Bakhtin writes of the banquet imagery of carnival:

> The popular-festive banquet has nothing in common with static private life and individual well-being. The popular images of food and drink are active and triumphant, for they conclude the process of labor and struggle of the social man against the world. They express the people as a whole because they are based on the inexhaustible, ever-growing abundance of the material principle . . . they are infused with gay time, moving towards a better future that changes and renews everything in its path.[80]

The 'material principle' of which he speaks is, in Rabelais, a naturalistic principle based on natural and biological life, the cyclical changes of nature and the body, sowing, conception, growth and death. This is not to be identified with the 'spiritual principle' or mystical life that pertains to the sacraments. He makes the point, however, that carnival broke out of private ways of life into corporate modes of existence. It liberated its participants from autonomous individualism and knew nothing, to use his words, of the bourgeois ego. Like carnival, the ethos of the eucharist is inclusive and welcoming. There is food and drink available for all.

Grotesque realism and the gaiety of death
One of the features of carnival that still upsets some spectators today is its grotesque realism: 'Not only parody in its narrow sense but all the other forms of grotesque realism degrade, bring down to earth, turn their subject into flesh. This is the peculiar trait of

---

80. Bakhtin, *Rabelais*, p. 302.

the genre . . .'[81] Rabelais wrote about 'the material bodily principle' in all-popular, festive form. In other words, he wrote about the human body, with its needs and desire for food, defecation, and sex. Flesh, the belly and genitalia, feature frequently in his work. So do images of bodily life, fertility and growth, in exaggerated and grandiose form. Grotesque realism in Rabelais's work is concerned with the lower stratum of the body, the womb and conception, the bowel and discharge of faeces. Yet it does so with a purpose in mind – namely, to reflect the phenomenon of transformation and the unfinished process of metamorphosis, death, birth, growth and becoming.[82] In *Rabelais and His World*, Bakhtin traces briefly the history of the grotesque in comic form. Of interest to us is his exposition of the complex themes of bodiliness and the regenerating power inherent in the grotesque, as bound up in the carnival relativisation of death and hope of new life. In order to be of interest to the Christian ethicist and moral theologian, Rabelais's grotesque realism must be read with a degree of licence for the sake of the insight gained. This acknowledged, it is not hard to make connections with the grotesque realism that confronts us in the crude physicality and grossness of the eucharist. Mark's gospel records Jesus' words: 'Take; this is my body.' 'This is my blood of the covenant, which is poured out for many' (Mk 14:22a, 24b). We don't know what effect his words first had on their hearers, but early Christian writers defended the church against charges of quasi-cannibalism. Justin Martyr distinguished Christian drinking of Christ's blood from pagan sacrificial rites: '[W]hen we drink our fill of blood, as it is said we do, we are [not] doing what you do before that idol you honour . . .'[83] In a less politically confrontational setting, Irenaeus emphasised the shockingness of eucharistic practice: 'For blood

---

81. Bakhtin, *Rabelais*, p. 20.
82. These are Bakhtin's words. See *Rabelais*, p. 24.
83. Justin Martyr, *The Second Apology of Justin for the Christians Addressed to the Roman Senate*, ch. 1, Introduction, *ANF*, Vol. I, p. 188.

can only come from veins and flesh, and whatsoever else makes up the substance of man, such as the Word of God was actually made.'[84] Remember, he urges, that we are redeemed by Christ's actual body and blood. Moreover: 'He has acknowledged the cup (which is a part of the creation) as His own blood, from which He bedews our blood; and the bread (also a part of the creation) He has established as His own body, from which He gives increase to our bodies.' 'Thou hast tasted the Blood of the Lord,' writes John Chrysostom, emphasising the physicality of the act.[85] With this in mind, let us consider whether Bakhtin provokes us into making important connections between the grotesque realism of the eucharist and the ethos of the Christian community.

According to Victor Hugo, the centre of Rabelais's artistic world is the belly. Bakhtin agrees, though he enlarges the image to include the open mouth as well as the belly swallowing.[86] Rabelais's characters are gluttonous and drunken; they are buffoons with little thought for anything other than immediate sensuous gratification or the joke being shared with a mate. Yet Bakhtin refuses to reduce Rabelais's work to the simply physiological and sees in it another dimension. Thus he writes of eating and defecation: 'In grotesque realism and in Rabelais's work the image of excrement, for instance, did not have the trivial, narrowly physiological connotation of today. Excrement was conceived as an essential element in the life of the body and of the earth in the struggle against death.'[87] Rabelais's work, he argues, has to be read against the thousand-year-old tradition which he represents. In emphasising the realism of the way in which the Christian church affirms its desire for and union with God, we too must not reduce the eating

84. Irenaeus, *Adversus Haereses*, Bk V, ch. 2, *ANF*, Vol. I, p. 528.
85. John Chrysostom, *Homilies on First Corinthians*, Homily XXVII on 1 Cor. II: 17, commenting on verse 27, *NPNF* First Series, Vol. XII, p. 162.
86. Bakhtin, *Rabelais*, p. 126.
87. Bakhtin, *Rabelais*, p. 224.

and drinking of the eucharistic elements to their physiological meaning. There is, however, some benefit in reflecting on this most concrete manner in which persons receive holy communion, if it stirs us up to contemplate what is being realised in our lives. Justin Martyr writes:

> And this food is called among us *Eukaristia* [the Eucharist] . . . For not as common bread and common drink do we receive these; but in like manner as Jesus Christ our Saviour, having been made flesh by the Word of God, had both flesh and blood for our salvation, so likewise have we been taught that the food which is blessed by the prayer of His word, and from which our blood and flesh by trans-mutation are nourished, is the flesh and blood of that Jesus who was made flesh.[88]

The flesh and blood of Christ are eaten by the believer for their spiritual nourishment and fortification, and in order that they can live in the world sacramentally. To live sacramentally is not possible unless the eucharistic elements are received frequently and on a regular basis. The spiritual food of the eucharist is as necessary to the soul as material food is to the body. In this sense, the open mouth and the belly are the centre of the Christian's world.

So what happens to the body and to food in the process of eating? Bakhtin answers as follows:

> [T]he body transgresses here its own limits: it swallows, devours, rends the world apart, is enriched and grows at the world's expense. The encounter of man with the world, which takes place inside the open, biting, rending, chewing mouth, is one of the most ancient, and most important objects of human thought and imagery. Here man tastes the world,

---

88. Justin Martyr, *The First Apology of Justin*, ch. LXVI, 'Of the Eucharist', *ANF* Vol. I, p. 185.

introduces it into his body, makes it part of himself. Man's encounter with the world in the act of eating is joyful, triumphant; he triumphs over the world, devours it without being devoured himself. The limits between man and the world are erased, to man's advantage.[89]

In the act of eating, the confines between the body and the world are blurred; the body eating and the body eaten have a living connection. The body is in the act of becoming. This is why banquets are frequently associated in classical literature, e.g., the *Iliad*, with nuptial celebrations. The banquet fulfils the function of an act of completion which contains the potential for new beginning and new life. Eating and the beginning of life are closely interwoven. Compare this sense of the fusion between the body eating and the body eaten in Bakhtin's representation of Rabelais with that in Paul's letter to the Galatians. Admittedly, the passage is not directly about the eucharist, but it is about the liberty enjoyed in the fellowship of Christ:

> I have been crucified with Christ; and it is no longer I who live, but it is Christ who lives in me. And the life I now live in the flesh I live by faith in the Son of God, who loved me and gave himself for me. (Gal. 2:19b–20)

As with Bakhtin, there is a sense in which the body eating transgresses its own limits and becomes something other than itself. It swallows and is enriched by the body and blood of Christ. An encounter takes place in the activity of eating which is of utmost importance in Christian life as well as in Christian thought and imagery. Here communicants taste the body and blood of Christ, introduce it into their own lives, and it becomes part of themselves. The encounter is joyful and triumphant, as one dies to sin and is

---

89. Bakhtin, *Rabelais*, p. 281.

raised to life with Christ, and as the limits between Christ and the believer are erased through absolute grace.[90]

Arguably, the western church has underplayed the grotesque realism of the eucharist. Several denominations use wafers, not fresh bread, and omit practices such as the Orthodox marking of the bread with symbols of Christ's passion, e.g., making an incision in the loaf to call to mind Christ's being slaughtered like a lamb (Is. 53:7). Bakhtin's account of carnival may, however, help us talk about how Christ's sacrifice, and the grotesque realism of the eucharist, signify the transformation of death into life and resurrection. Consider the intimate connection in carnival between birth and death. This connection was usually presented crudely and in jest. Thus it was not breath from the mouth that signified health, life and resurrection, but the fart. Babies were represented as sitting on coffins. In the third chapter of *Pantagruel*, when Gargantua's wife dies as their son is born, Gargantua does not know whether he should weep or rejoice. At first, we are told, he cries 'like a cow'. But then, thinking of his son, he exclaims:

> Ho, ho, ho, ho, how happy I am! Let us drink, ho! and put away our melancholy! Bring out the best wine, rinse the glasses, lay the table, drive out the dogs, poke up the fire, light the candles, close that door there, cut the bread in sippets for our pottage, send away these beggar folk but give them anything they ask for! You, there, hold my gown! I shall strip to my doublet to entertain the gossips better.

As he said this, he heard the priests chanting litanies and mementoes as they bore his wife off to burial.[91]

At face value, and without reference to the carnival spirit, this passage reads like the drunken response of an inveterately

---

90. On this also, see Gregory of Nyssa, *The Great Catechism*, NPNF Second Series, Vol. V, p. 480.
91. This passage is cited by Bakhtin, *Rabelais*, p. 407. The reference is to *Pantagruel*, Bk 2, ch. 3.

monstrous man with no inclination to mourn the loss of his wife. Yet suggests Bakhtin, when viewed alternatively, it represents the gayness of death. At one level, the gayness of death is explained biologically in the cyclical rejuvenation of one generation through its offspring. Even for Rabelais, however, this kind of renewal does not exhaust the significance of the event: 'Rabelais did not have in mind the biological renewal and rejuvenation of a man though his progeny. For him the biological element could not be separated from the social, historic, and cultural element.'[92] Rather, he offers a carnivalesque and travestied form of the eucharistic liturgy. Yes, of course the meal ordered by Gargantua is a debased, distorted and grossly inferior imitation of the eucharist proper. It is a parody of the eucharist, and more besides. Yet it speaks graphically of the ethos of eucharistic existence in which the death that leads to life is to be celebrated. In Rabelais's novel, writes Bakhtin, the image of death is devoid of all tragic or terrifying overtones: 'Death is the necessary link in the process of the people's growth and renewal. It is the "other side" of birth.'[93] Upon hearing about Gargantua's feasting, characters in *Pantagruel* and – more likely than not – participants at the carnival, fell about with laughter. They might even have died of laughing, laughter being one of the gay forms of death. Bakhtin tells us that Rabelais lists nine cases of death from joy, one of which was death from drowning in a barrel due to an excess of drinking. The very thought of such a spectacle might affront our well-brought-up sensibilities, but the point is that death is an ambivalent image for Rabelais, as it is at the eucharist where Christ's once-for-all death is celebrated. Better we die the gay death of laughter than suffocate from politically correct or religious niceties.

According to Bakhtin, the gay death of laughter was 'birth-giving death'.[94] Despite its grotesqueness, death was associated with

92. Bakhtin, *Rabelais*, p. 406.
93. Bakhtin, *Rabelais*, p. 407.
94. Bakhtin, *Rabelais*, p. 392.

birth, new life and gay transformation. This is why the image of the womb was linked frequently to carnivalesque representations of hell. The netherworld becomes the symbol of the defeat of death. Unlike the serious and official Christian view of hell, carnivalesque parody linked the tomb and the womb. The lowest becomes the best because it is life-giving. Normal, worldly patterns of power are overturned: 'The greatest treasures are hidden underground . . .'[95] Like the womb that was Jesus' tomb (Matt. 27:59–60; Lk. 23:53–54), there is a contradictory unity about the vital process of death becoming the means of life's rejuvenation. The more difficult question is whether this emphasis on the grotesque realism of Jesus Christ's death can help us to think more adequately about the ethos of the eucharist. Carnivalesque grotesque realism invites us to expect contradictory juxtapositions, inversions of the norm, and ambivalent symbols of life. Christian celebration of the eucharist offers us these exact same characteristics, but our understanding often gets stuck in a limited seriousness that has all the pretence of meaning but that becomes flat and monotonous. Feminist critics are correct to question whether the sacrifice in question is destructive rather than redemptive. Images of death are more readily associated with tragedy and meaninglessness than fertility and birth. What, they ask, distinguishes the symbol of death as renewal from that of death as malicious violence and pure negativity? As answer, consider the following passage by Nicholas Cabasilas, the fourteenth-century Byzantine theologian of the eucharist, who wrote graphically of the eucharistic sacrifice. At face value, the detailed recounting of the aggressive onslaught on Christ's body could seem like a spasm of indulgent sadism, made worse by the belief in Christ's eternal priesthood and eternal bearing of human nature, so that Christ eternally and continually offers the sacrifice for humanity, being priest and victim for ever:

---

95. Bakhtin, *Rabelais*, p. 403.

> When these words [the consecration of the offering, and the thanksgiving which precedes it] have been said, the whole sacred rite is accomplished, the offerings are consecrated, the sacrifice is complete; the splendid Victim, the Divine oblation, slain for the salvation of the world, lies upon the altar. For it is no longer the bread, which until now has represented the Lord's Body, nor is it a simple offering, bearing the likeness of the true offering, carrying as if engraved on it the symbols of the Saviour's Passion; it is the true Victim, the most holy Body of the Lord, which really suffered the outrages, insults and blows; which was crucified and slain . . . that Body which was mocked, scourged, spat upon, and which tasted gall. In like manner the wine has become the blood which flowed from that Body.[96]

Because of his unique status, nothing in Christ's death should become an excuse for inflicting physical or mental pain on others; he alone was the 'true offering'. It is easy to blunt the critical edge that radical feminists apply to Christian tradition. But it is also easy to protect ourselves from the grotesqueness of the crucifixion, and from the sacrificial aspects of the eucharistic celebration that have such provocative relevance for Christian ethics. Carnivalesque grotesque realism invites us to consider how the death of Christ brings a completely new order to things.

This new ordering of things is nicely expressed by a quasi-apocryphal Orthodox tradition, according to which Christ's blood from the cross fell upon Adam's (humanity's) bones, because Adam's tomb lay under the place of the cross on Golgotha. Adam's poisoned and poisonous blood was replaced with the life-giving blood of the God-human.[97] Christ's blood was life-giving, more like the prescription of a physician than the product of ritual

---

96. Nicholas Cabasilas, *A Commentary on the Divine Liturgy*, trans. J. M. Hussey and P. A. McNulty (London: SPCK, 1960), p. 70.

97. See http://www.goarch.org/access/Companion_to_Orthodox_Church/dogmatic_tradition.

slaughter. Indeed, it is common in Orthodox tradition to emphasise the healing rather than forensic or expiatory character of
redemption; relatively little use is made of theories about penal
substitution, vicarious atonement, and quasi-legal satisfaction.
Gregory of Nyssa speaks of the new birth of baptism in water and
the Spirit (Jn 3:3) as medicines assigned for healing: 'for his visible
body, water, the sensible element, – for his soul, which we cannot
see, the Spirit invisible, invoked by faith, present unspeakably'.[98]
A patient who needs to be healed must be touched. So also,
'humanity had to be touched by Christ. It was not in "heaven";
so only through the Incarnation could it be healed.'[99] Christ, writes
Athanasius, turned the corruptible to incorruption. He rendered
the mortal immortal, being Very Life itself.[100] Christ had to die so
that death, which had become so ingrained in human nature,
could be defeated:

> For this cause the Saviour reasonably put on Him a body, in
> order that the body, becoming wound closely to the Life,
> should no longer, as mortal, abide in death, but, as having
> put on immortality, should thenceforth rise again and remain
> immortal. For, once it had put on corruption, it could not
> have risen again unless it had put on life. And death likewise
> could not, from its very nature, appear, save in the body.
> Therefore He put on a body, that He might find death in the
> body, and blot it out.[101]

Sin had resulted in a loss of personal communion with God; a
fall into an inauthentic kind of existence, which was a kind of
spiritual death; and a loss of immortality, for 'the wages of sin is

---

98. Gregory of Nyssa, *On the Baptism of Christ*, NPNF Second Series, Vol. V, p.
519.
99. Gregory of Nyssa, *The Great Catechism*, ch. XXVII, NPNF Second Series,
Vol. V, pp. 496–497.
100. Athanasius, *Incarnation*, §20, NPNF Second Series, Vol. IV, p. 47.
101. Athanasius, *Incarnation*, §44, NPNF Second Series, Vol. IV, p. 60.

death' (Rom. 6:23). God's plan of salvation was to restore humanity to communion with God, but sin and death were obstacles to this restoration. Christ's death on the cross washed away the effects of our sin and redeemed us from the curse of death. Why and how? Because Christ died the death that resulted from sin and reunited us with God. Christ made his body an offering for our souls, thus winning back for us our lost immortality. The offering was sacrificial in so far as it was an offering unto death, but it was also a prescription for life because now God was able to create afresh the divine image of God.[102] This was the birth-giving death that happened on the cross.

To be emphasised here is that the term eucharist means thanksgiving. Thanksgiving defines the ethos of the Christian community; the liturgy is a big act of thanksgiving for Christ's birth-giving death. Biblical witness is that we can be thankful that the faithful participate in Christ's life: '[I]t is by God's will that we have been sanctified through the offering of the body of Jesus Christ once for all' (Heb. 10:10). Christ's sacrifice was once for all; he was offered once to bear the sins of humankind (Heb. 9:28). Christ alone is the sacrifice in this birth-giving death. Taking up one's cross (Matt. 10:38, Lk. 14:27) is not about subjecting oneself to an instrument of punishment but being identified with Christ's death of deaths, and separating oneself from all that still leads to death. This notion of sacrifice is often seen as problematic. Consider the feminist criticism of the notion that Christian people are called to imitation of Christ, victim and scapegoat. The radical feminist, Mary Daly, awaits an Antichrist which will liberate humankind from identification with Jesus who is humankind's most illustrious sacrifice, victim and scapegoat.[103] Others start back in horror at the acceptance of dependency on Christ and need as existential values, arguing that the result is a sacralisation

---

102. Athanasius, *Incarnation*, §13, *NPNF* Second Series, Vol. IV, p. 43.
103. Daly, *Beyond God the Father*, pp. 75–77.

of falsely created need and dependency.[104] For this reason, it is important to emphasise that becoming one with Christ has two interrelated aspects, one positive – the communion of love, union with God, growth in personhood, and freedom to choose the good, and one negative – the death of individualism, selfishness, pride, arrogance and all evil intent. The power of death still rules parasitically in creation, though God is on our side, so all will be well (Rom. 8:31–39). However, each day still brings its struggles with forces that lead to death. For the ancient fathers, this struggle was represented in the terms of demonology. Ignatius of Antioch had a particularly keen theological imagination in this regard, speaking frequently of the 'dreadful torments of the devil' and praying that 'no plant of the devil may be found' in his readers.[105] Christians today rarely use this kind of imagery, though most know all too well the impulses of 'natural', fallen existence: greed, lust, ignorance, sloth, malice, etc. Yet Cabasilas writes: 'There are two ways in which grace operates in the precious offerings; first, by grace they are sanctified, and secondly, by grace we are sanctified through them.'[106] The first working of divine grace – i.e., the consecration of the bread and wine – can be neither aided nor invalidated by human intent, since it is the work of the Holy Spirit. But the second working of divine grace in the life of the faithful – i.e., that of the remission of sins and sanctification – requires our co-operation, because God will not violate human freedom. No sacrifice of the faithful is required but yet we need to take seriously the fact that we are free either to refuse or accept the invitation to the feast, and also that, in coming to the feast and celebrating, something of our sinful self will die. Death does happen in any and every encounter of freedom between ourselves

---

104. Sallie McFague, *Models of God* (London: SCM, 1984), p. 134.
105. Ignatius of Antioch, *The Epistle to the Romans*, ch. V, *ANF*, Vol. I, p. 76; *The Epistle to the Ephesians*, ch. X, *ANF*, Vol. I, p. 54.
106. Cabasilas, *A Commentary*, p. 85.

and God, but the eucharist celebrates a gay death of death and of all that leads to corruption.

To be emphasised also is that the eucharistic community is fundamentally different to communities or social groupings based on the concept of the individual as a separate autonomous person. Here Bakhtin's ideas about the grotesque realism of the eating body prompt us to new perceptions of both the body of the person participating in the eucharist and the social body of the community which is constituted in the practice of eating. We must be careful not to allegorise Bakhtin's ideas in such a way that every aspect of his work is made theologically suggestive. Yet it is worth noting how his treatment of the grotesque realism of Rabelais's work – in which the open mouth and the belly are at the centre of carnival life – bears further analogy with the eucharistic community, in particular, in the way that eating in carnivalesque literature disturbs present-day cultural assumptions about relationships between the eater, what is eaten, and the world outside the self. The openness of the body blurs the distinction between its inside and outside, suggesting new ways of thinking about the body-boundary. The grotesque, eating (social) body functions as satirical comment upon forms of social grouping that are constituted not by eating and communion but by commercial exchange between autonomous individuals.

For Bakhtin, the openness of the mouth's wide entrance to the body and the excessive size and receptivity of the belly represent growth, procreation and celebration-living. Gaping jaws also represent the gates of hell; as ever, in Rabelais's writings, life and death are closely related, often in composite images. It is, however, the mouth which represents both the openness that is required for a body to live and the transgressing of inside/outside boundaries. For Bakhtin, the medieval grotesque body was a body open and receptive to food. None of the orifices of the body were closed or obstructed; openness was the body's life. Inside/outside boundaries are transgressed because the eater both assimilates nourishment and is assimilated into the eating-community. The eater both eats and is eaten by the corporate body of which they are part. The boundaries between the body and the outside world are permeable and shifting: 'The distinctive character of this body is its open unfinished nature, its interaction with the world.'[107] The body swallows and devours; it is 'enriched and grows at the world's expense', but is, as it were, simultaneously, eaten by the carnival.[108] In eating, the body is itself eaten. Carnival eating was not a private way of living but always social. The carnival-participant was actively part of a social event and ingested by the collective. Thus the physical body is not limited or something individual because, in eating, it belongs to the social body. In eating, it continually transgresses its physical and individual limits: 'The grotesque image displays not only the outward but also the inner features of the body: blood, bowels, heart and other organs. The outward and inward features are often merged into one.'[109] Each body is assimilative, giving and receiving of itself not only in words but by a change in body-surface and constitution. The individual as a separate, private entity does not exist. Instead, the eating body is part of an eating body-community; each body is open to the other.

A carnival-community centred around eating, the mouth and the belly, is no place for individualistic calculation of utility or autonomous separate persons, because the boundaries of bodies (both personal and social) are open and permeable. The grotesqueness of the open body is represented vividly by Rabelais with images of belching, farting, vomiting, excreting, etc. Such realism may be disagreeable or even offensive but makes the point that when the ethos of the community is approached via the activity of eating, and when the physical aspects of eating rather than mental representations are allowed to prompt theological reflection, the distinctions between the inside and outside of the body

---

107. Bakhtin, *Rabelais*, p. 281.
108. Bakhtin, *Rabelais*, p. 281.
109. Bakhtin, *Rabelais*, p. 318.

have to be thought about in different ways. Matthew records Jesus saying to his disciples: 'Take, eat; this is my body' (Matt. 26:26). Ignatius of Antioch writes: 'I desire the bread of God, the heavenly bread, the bread of life, which is the flesh of Jesus Christ . . . and I desire the drink of God, namely His blood, which is incorruptible love and eternal life.'[110] He wants the normal inside/outside distinction which separates his physical body from that of Christ to be transgressed and for Christ to become part of him, with anticipatable consequences for how what he takes into his body will affect both his mode of existence and what leaves his body, notably the outflow of speech and action. The body is not a closed structure in relationship to the world outside itself but a consuming body which ingests the body and blood of Christ, thereby enjoying mysterious communion with God through Christ who is 'the bread of life' (Jn 6:35).[111] In becoming one with Christ, the participant in the eucharist becomes part of a community whose ethos is based on eating, becoming one in body and blood with all who are united with Christ.

Eros and ascesis

Thus the ethos of the Christian community is one of thanksgiving, openness and the fullness of personal freedom. However, in our fallen condition this is a matter pervaded by paradox: healing is given in the shedding of Christ's blood; life in death. Despite some early Christian expectation that baptism was a protection against

---

110. Ignatius of Antioch, *The Epistle to the Romans*, ch. VII, *ANF*, Vol. I, pp. 76–77.

111. It does not serve our purpose here to recount the history of dialogue between eastern Orthodoxy and western Christianity, especially Protestantism, with regard to the sense in which the crucified Christ is present at the eucharist. See V. T. Istavridis, *Orthodoxy and Anglicanism* (London: SPCK, 1966); *The Greek Orthodox Theological Review*, XXX, 2 (1985), pp. 235–247. (This gives an account of discussion by Eastern Orthodox and Oriental churches of the 'Lima document', i.e., the statement of the Faith and Order Commission of the World Council of Churches on *Baptism, Eucharist and Ministry* (*BEM*).)

sin, it is 'natural' in our yet fallen condition that members of the church should fail to live up to their calling. Hence the importance of times of confession and repentance when we recognise failure and acknowledge the grip that sin still has upon us: 'Sin then is, as we have said, a fearful evil, but not incurable; fearful for him who clings to it, but easy of cure for him who by repentance puts it from him.'[112] To repent means to turn from sin and dedicate oneself to the amendment of one's life; it is an ascetic activity in so far as it often requires large measures of personal and spiritual discipline (Greek *askein*, meaning to work, practice or train). Asceticism does not tend to be popular in a culture where some (not all) forms of psychoanalytic counselling encourage the blaming of others rather than the changing of one's own behaviour. This is not to suggest, however, that asceticism is necessarily a harsh and demoralising experience. Ambrose writes that gentleness befits leaders in the church who preach the message of scripture that no one is free from sin:

> Moreover, it [gentleness] is the only virtue which has led to the increase of the Church which the Lord sought at the price of His own Blood, imitating the loving-kindness of heaven, and aiming at the redemption of all, [and] seeks this end with a gentleness which the ears of men can endure, in presence of which their hearts do not sink, nor their spirits quail.[113]

Ambrose wrote against the Novatians who favoured severity against the lapsed, and criticised them for putting on not the light yoke of Christ but a heavy burden of supposed sinlessness which Christians were not able to bear. By the grace of God, he argued,

---

112. Cyril of Jerusalem, *Catechetical Lectures*, No. II, 'On Repentance and Remission of Sins, and Concerning the Adversary', *NPNF* Second Series, Vol. VII, p. 8.

113. Ambrose, *Concerning Repentance*, Bk I, ch. I, §1, *NPNF* Second Series, Vol. X, p. 329.

the lapsed should not be shut out from pardon. Yet, he writes, repentance 'is not a single but a twofold grace'.[114] Whoever receives the grace of forgiveness also receives the grace of suffering. At a superficial level, this sounds odd, if not repulsive, to a culture which seeks to avoid suffering. It is easier to hear the words of the Dalai Lama: '[W]e all desire to be happy and to avoid suffering ... "How am I to be happy?"', than those of Ambrose, who suggests that suffering is to be welcomed as coming from the hands of God.[115]

Here we must be very careful not to imply that, of itself, suffering is good. Suffering is to be welcomed only in so far as it heals the person and brings spiritual profit. What suffers and dies is not our personhood, capacity for fulfilling relationship, or *joie de vivre*, but rather our selfishness that disrespects others, our lust that depersonalises sexual pleasure, and our deceitfulness that would defraud another of their due:

> Let, then, our flesh die to lusts, let it be captive, let it be subdued, and not war against the law of our mind, but die in subjection to a good service, as in Paul, who buffeted his body that he might bring it into subjection ...[116]

The sadness of Ambrose's teaching is that it reads so easily like abuse of the body. He seems sometimes to imply that that which hurts the body benefits the spirit.[117] This aspect of his work needs correction in the light of credal reminders about the resurrection of the body and biblical teaching about the body of Christ as a

---

114. Ambrose, *Concerning Repentance*, Bk II, ch. II, §8, *NPNF* Second Series, Vol. X, p. 346.

115. Dalai Lama, *Ancient Wisdom, Modern World* (London: Little, Brown & Company, 1999), p. 4.

116. Ambrose, *Concerning Repentance*, Bk I, ch. XIV, §75, *NPNF* Second Series, Vol. X, p. 341.

117. 'Do not then fear if your flesh be eaten away; the soul is not consumed.' Ambrose, *Concerning Repentance*, Bk I, ch. XIV, §77, *NPNF* Second Series, Vol. X, p. 341.

reality of communion and love. The answer to this problem, however, is not to alienate ourselves from the experience of repentance, or to confuse repentance with a sense of guilt at having transgressed a law. Far better to become attuned to the kind of ascesis that genuinely leads to personal fulfilment, communion with God and with one another.

Ascesis is disciplining of the body, not for the sake of discipline but for the sake of transfiguring natural impulses for self-preservation into occasions of relationship and love. It is not about subjection of the individual per se, or scorn for the substance of the body, but subjection of the impersonal aspects of one's mortal nature which drive towards egocentrism. Christos Yannaras helps us here with what he says about the ascetic realisation of true eros in marriage. While lamenting the bourgeois idea of the 'Christian family' – in which the institutionalised church uses the power of state authority to license conjugal life (rather than allowing the mystery of marriage to manifest the church's truth regarding the transcendence of individuality and entry into personal relationship) – Yannaras writes: 'In church life, marriage has always been an image and prefigurement of the perfect personal relationship and communion in love which forms the Kingdom of God, the eschatological realisation of salvation.'[118] Why does marriage prefigure the kingdom of God? Because autonomy, self-sufficiency, and biological individualism are transfigured to become a eucharistic relationship of thanksgiving one for the other. The couple reject separation, individualism and the state of being dual, and accept instead a oneness that is attainable only through love's grace. Sexual union is a realisation in the body of the grace of love, and, as is true of all acts of love, has the potential for new life. Nor is this act of love and way of living an isolating affair. Rather, it has the outward moving drive of love. In loving one person, one gains the capacity to love the whole of creation. It is not a matter of effort and result. Such love-making quickly

---

118. Yannaras, *Freedom*, p. 167.

descends into disappointment and frustration. Ascetic love resists the mindless sexual drive that equates with natural instinct, but seeks to affirm a mode of existence that is the movement of love. Ascetic love-making equates to eros, though eros should not be confined to the physical act of love-making. A virgin's life is erotic when free from the lusts of biological existence and given over to personal relationships that involve self-giving and the denial of individualism, and that have the potential for fruition. Indeed, the virgin witnesses, more clearly than is possible for the couple, to eros and asceticism being ecclesial and not individualistic way(s) of life.

The Authority of the Clown

I have argued that authority in the church should be understood according to a Chalcedonian way of thinking which turns worldly notions of authority upside down, mocks the narrow-mindedness of false piety, and is based on a eucharistic ethos of thanksgiving, openness and personal fulfilment. Using Bakhtin's ideas about carnival and the body in connection with Christian teaching about the eucharist, I have argued that we gain fresh insight into our bodily participation in the life of Christ. Linked to this, we have seen that the ascetic foolishness of a small number of saints of the church involved denial of the body – as witness to the denial of sin and of all that hinders spiritual life – and that, despite the problematic aspects of this witness, it is regarded by the church as a path to knowledge of the things of God. It is not the body per se that is the source of knowledge, but rather the body in relationship with Jesus Christ. As the church has taught for generations, human bodiliness will only ever be a shaky foundation for knowledge and the ordering of relationships between persons, because the body is subject to mortality and the necessities of natural existence. It is the body of Christ, not that of the individual, which forms the basis of the church, the body of Christ being broken symbolically and mystically at each sacrament of the eucharist (1 Cor. 10:16). But how is the ethos of the eucharistic community to be put into action? What are the implications of a eucharistic ethos for practical decision-making and church polity? Such questions are not easy for a host of reasons, not least the variations that pertain between different traditions and denominations, and the widely variant views within the church catholic regarding practices of pastoral leadership and co-ordination of the ministry and mission of the people of God. Hence, I confine my comments to ways in which the clown in carnival literature shakes us free from the false notions of authority through mockery, satire and popular-festive forms.

Before looking at Bakhtin's treatment of the subject, however, let us consider further the bodily knowledge implied in the eucharist as regards the structure of the church. Consider, in particular, the organically structured organisation of the church in so far as the body has a head. As a community of persons, the church is a visible body which exists variously in different times and places. Yet it is a body with a head. Christ is the head of the church (Eph. 1:22, 4:15, 5:23; Col. 1:18) and, even though the eucharist is celebrated in different times and places, there are not many bodies because Christ's headship unites them all. Cyprian (c. 200–258), Bishop of Carthage, wrote of Christ's headship of the church:

> She extends her branches over the whole earth in fruitful abundance; she extends her richly flowing streams far and wide; yet her head is one, and her source is one, and she is the one mother copious in the results of her fruitfulness.[119]

The unity of the church in Christ knows no division (Eph. 4:4). Indeed, this unity is to be asserted by believers and especially by bishops, who celebrate the sacrament of unity and live out the unity of the episcopate: 'The episcopate is one, each part of which

---

119. Cyprian, *The Unity of the Catholic Church*, ch. 5, *ANF*, Vol. V, p. 423.

is held by each one for the whole.'[120] It is worth pausing with Cyprian for a moment because he developed more clearly than any before him the doctrine of Christ's headship of the church in connection with the presidency of the bishops. He wrote in response to over-confident claims from those who had lapsed in the face of persecution that they should be readmitted to the church and, while he did not use the word 'hierarchy', his teaching gave rise to new understanding of orders of seniority in the church, and of the eucharist as a sacrifice offered to God by a priest, and unity of the episcopate.[121] The church catholic is united in Christ and the church local is established in its bishop so that 'The Church is founded upon the bishops, and every act of the Church is controlled by these same rulers . . . the Church is established in the bishop and the clergy. . . '[122] In other words, with Cyprian, the hierarchical structure of the church and its orders of bishops, priests and deacons began to be understood more clearly as representing the headship of Christ.

This notion that hierarchical orders of ministry represent Christ's headship of the church is notoriously problematic because it appears to run counter to the egalitarianism of the common priesthood of the faithful (Rom. 12:5; 1 Pet. 2:5). Thus Elisabeth Schüssler Fiorenza emphasises that her work is about a radical democratisation of the church such that all are equal in a congress of full decision-making members. She lambastes notions of the church as the 'hierarchology' of the threefold division of office

---

120. Cyprian, *The Unity of the Catholic Church*, ch. 5, *ANF*, Vol. V, p. 423.

121. 'For if Jesus Christ, our Lord and God, is Himself the chief priest of God the Father, and has first offered Himself a sacrifice to the Father, and has commanded this to be done in commemoration of Himself, certainly that priest truly discharges the office of Christ, who imitates that which Christ did; and he then offers a true and full sacrifice in the Church to God the Father, when he proceeds to offer it according to what he sees Christ Himself to have offered.' Cyprian, Letter LXII, §14, *ANF*, Vol. V, p. 362. See also Treatise I, *On the Unity of the Church*, §§4–5, *ANF*, Vol. V, pp. 422–423.

122. Cyprian, Epistle XXVI, *ANF*, Vol. V, p. 305.

because, when structures of ministry are ordered according to three 'grades' of authority – the orders of bishops, priests, and deacons – the message transmitted is that of exclusion from, rather than inclusion within, the exercise of priestly authority. The church ceases to be an 'ekklesialogy of liberation', or a house built by wisdom (Prov. 9:1–4, 6), because it has become a hierarchy which renders the laity objects of pastoral care.[123] This kind of criticism has been much needed in the church. However, we should be wary, I suggest, if/when it fails to take seriously the complex metaphor of headship and assumes automatically that hierarchy is to be abhorred. Such matters are not easy because Christian tradition abounds with examples of the metaphor of headship linked to ideas about the priest or pastor as rational and the 'flock' (Matt. 24:47) as irrational and lacking intellectual qualities. John Chrysostom writes: '[L]et the distinction between the pastor and his charge be as great as that between rational man and irrational creatures, not to say even greater, inasmuch as the risk is concerned with things of far greater importance.'[124] He does continue to talk about 'the rational flock of Christ' and about how the pastor-physician cannot cure the souls of those lacking the will for remedy. However, he states categorically that women must retire before the magnitude of the task because they have a propensity to sin and a tendency to disorder of the mind.[125] All this contributes to a justifiable aversion in the minds of many to the metaphors of headship and hierarchy, as does the fact that the metaphor of headship has been a dominant mode in the West of speaking about kingship.[126] I am arguing, however, that Christ's

---

123. Elisabeth Schüssler Fiorenza, *Sharing Her Word: Feminist Biblical Criticism in Context* (Edinburgh: T. & T. Clark, 1998), p. 112. See also *Discipleship of Equals: A Critical Feminist Ekklesialogy of Liberation* (New York: Crossroad, 1993), ch. 2.

124. John Chrysostom, *On the Priesthood*, Bk II, §2, *NPNF* First Series, Vol. IX, p. 40.

125. John Chrysostom, *On the Priesthood*, Bk VI, §1, *NPNF* First Series, Vol. IX, p. 75; Bk VI, §8, p. 78.

126. Bryan S. Turner, *Body and Society*, 2nd edn (London: Sage, 1996), p. 175.

headship of the church is the touchstone for testing the exercise of moral authority in the church, and that his headship both turns pietist moralising into nonsense and reminds us of the vital difference between will and desire.[127]

'Your King ... mounted on a donkey'

Matthew's gospel records the fulfilment of the prophecy that Israel's king would come triumphant but riding on a donkey (Zech. 9:9; Matt. 21:5). This passage precedes several direct challenges by Jesus to those abusing authority. In 'cleansing the temple' (Matt. 21:12–17), he challenged those who had allowed the centre of the nation's religious life to become a place of barter and double-dealing. In cursing the fig tree for not bearing fruit (Matt. 21:18–22), he challenged the leaders of the people for failing to exercise the kind of authority that is productive of good results. These passages are followed by an explicit discussion between Jesus and the chief priests and elders concerning the source of his authority (Matt. 21:23–27), placing Jesus' authority in stark contrast with that of officialdom: 'Therefore I tell you, the kingdom of God will be taken away from you and given to a people that produces the fruits of the kingdom' (Matt. 21:43). Methodius (260-c. 312), bishop in Lucia and later in Tyre, wrote in his 'Oration on the Psalms' that Jesus' colt-riding authority was marked by the restoring to health of many with infirmities, and by deeds of wonder and wise teaching.[128] Aphrahat (260–c. 345), a theologian belonging to the Semitic culture in the areas of Syria and Palestine, lists several paradoxes pertaining to Jesus' authority, including the

127. Etymologically, hierarchy means sacred or priestly government (Greek *hieros*, sacred and *archein*, to rule). Thus, for example, in the fifth century, Denys the Areopagite could speak of ecclesiastical hierarchy as a gift bestowed to ensure that we can be brought as far as we can be into union with God, because, as noted by Andrew Louth, he did not mean by hierarchy 'a rigid order of graded subordination', but a social patterning that reflects the radiance of God's glory (Louth, *Maximus the Confessor*, pp. 30–31).

128. Methodius, 'Oration on the Psalms', §1, *ANF*, Vol. VI, p. 395.

fact that he who will return on clouds of glory entered Jerusalem on a colt. He urges disciples of Christ to remember that he took the likeness of a servant: '[T]hough He was the fountain that quenches thirst, yet Himself thirsted and asked for water ... though He was the saviour of all mortals, He delivered Himself to the death of the cross.'[129] By implication, the king of kings mounted on a donkey is the criterion for determining the quality or genuineness of all authority in the church.

To use Bakhtin's words, Jesus' authority is that of the clown-king. Bakhtin does not write explicitly about Christology, but there is a dimension to his work that has application to our topic. In a carnival system, the king is the clown:

> He is elected by all the people and is mocked by all the people. He is abused and beaten when the time of his reign is over ... The abuse and thrashing are equivalent to a change of costume, to a metamorphosis. Abuse reveals the other, true face of the abused ... It is the king's uncrowning.[130]

The abuse and thrashing of the king are 'gay' and 'merry' because they represent the 'old authority' which is linked to that which must die. Thrashings are profoundly ambivalent because they kill old authorities while giving birth to the new: 'Every blow dealt to the old helps the new to be born.'[131] Thus the Catchpoles – inhabitants of an island who make their living by allowing others to thrash them – represent satirical attack against official feudal and ecclesial authorities of the day:

> The Catchpoles are ... the representatives of the old law, of the rights of a world that is dying and receding, but they are inseparable from the new world. ... The beating is a feast of

---

129. Aphrahat, *Demonstration* VI 'Of Monks', §9, *NPNF* Second Series, Vol. XIII, p. 369.
130. Bakhtin, *Rabelais*, p. 197.
131. Bakhtin, *Rabelais*, p. 206.

death and regeneration in the comic aspect. . . . The Catchpoles are beaten like kings.[132]

To Bakhtin's mind, there is obvious connection in Rabelais's mind
with the gospel stories of the mock crowning, uncrowning, and
scourging of Jesus, king of the Jews.[133] Given that Rabelais received
holy orders in the Franciscan convent of Gontenay-le-Comte and,
after leaving the order, was later received into the Benedictine
abbey of Maillezais, this is not unlikely. Indeed, it is against
this background that Bakhtin makes connections between the
uncrownings, thrashings and travesties of carnival and the
Christian gospel, and especially Jesus' riding into Jerusalem on a
donkey, 'the Gospel-symbol of debasement and humility'.[134] With
this in mind, let us consider what happens to an understanding
of moral authority, and especially to the metaphors of headship
and hierarchy, in this kind of interpretative context.

In carnival, writes Bakhtin, everything is done with laughter
and for laughter's sake. This laughter, however, is no mere passing
amusement but 'a powerful means of grasping reality'.[135] Thrashings and mockings are merry because they give way to life. Blood
is turned into wine. This is, of course, as nothing to us unless the
realism of which Bakhtin speaks is that witnessed to in the gospels.
As ever with both Bakhtin and Rabelais, there can be little certainty
about the intended theological allusions in their work. *The Catholic Encyclopaedia* says of Rabelais's work: 'As a whole it exercises
a baneful influence.'[136] If, however, we read their work in the light
of the blessing which Rabelais was reputed to have uttered during
his last illness, 'Blessed are those who die in the Lord', then
we can begin to understand the clown-king as representing the
uncrowning and debasement of authority based on social status

---

132. Bakhtin, *Rabelais*, p. 205.
133. Bakhtin, *Rabelais*, p. 198.
134. Bakhtin, *Rabelais*, p. 199.
135. Bakhtin, *Rabelais*, p. 211.
136. http://www.knight.org/advent/cathen/12619b.htm.

or wealth and cloaked in false moralism and pretentious piety.[137] The important question is the final aim as far as the thrashings and abusings etc., are concerned. In the story of the Catchpoles, the thrashings are ultimately in order that the inhabitants of the island can be free from the villainous Lord of Basché; the whole island is seeking a new laughter-filled existence. The beatings, blows, curses and dismemberings anticipate a new reality in which all pretensions to authority, law, virtue and self-control have been torn to pieces in the market place: 'In Rabelais abuse never assumes the character of merely personal invective; it is universal, and, when all is said and done, it always aims at the higher level.'[138] Little escapes his invective, including the church. Thus the bells from Notre Dame Cathedral are stolen by the young Gargantua and made into tinkling harness bells for his mare. What appears great in worldly eyes is uncrowned and degenerated/regenerated to ring in carnivalesque tones. They have a new mode of existence that is neither conventional nor linked to the practical piety recognised by social mores.

We must be careful not to give the impression that, in using Bakhtin's treatment of carnival, we seek to ridicule all moral authority associated with the church as institution. This is not the intention and, in any case, both Bakhtin and Rabelais ridicule only those aspects of church-life which deny the carnival spirit of the clown-king. We are alerted, however, to the pseudo-authority that corrupts the church and cloaks individual moral endeavour with pious religious feeling. Rather, the issues in question concern the kind of authority exercised by the church in the moral care of

---

137. This blessing is based on Rev. 14:13. Note, however, that accounts of Rabelais's death are varied. *The Catholic Encyclopaedia* records him as having said: 'Draw the curtain, the farce is played out.' Rabelais reputedly asked to be dressed at his death in a domino, i.e., a long loose hooded cloak usually worn with a half mask as a masquerade costume. It is unclear whether this travestied his citing of the biblical text or was intended in a carnival spirit, but I am tempted to opt for the latter.

138. Bakhtin, *Rabelais*, p. 212.

souls. Is it a clown-like authority which shares Jesus' humility and sorrow? Is it the kind of authority that the fires of carnival-satire would expose as truly sad and ridiculous? Gregory the Great put the matter plainly when he interprets Jesus' challenge to the temple authorities (Matt. 21:12): 'For to sell doves is to receive a temporal consideration for the Holy Spirit.'[139] When moral endeavour becomes a matter of individual advancement, religiosity, or a reward for good behaviour, then it is an abuse of God's gift of freedom and brings judgement on itself. This is the wisdom that comes from unexpected places: 'Have you never read, "Out of the mouths of babes and sucklings hast Thou perfected praise?" '[140] Children (and fools) utter the clear meaning of the gospel more readily than adults who teem with envy and frenzy.[141] The kind of authority exercised by Jesus is recognised only by faith and in prayer. It does not pander to people's natural desires for money, social recognition and sex, but sees sin for what it is and brings to the sinner the grace of God. In his homily on Matt. 21:12–13, John Chrysostom envisages Jesus' accusers asking him: 'Hast thou received the teacher's chair? Hast thou been ordained a priest, that thou didst display such authority?'[142] He notes that Jesus did not answer them directly because, if they had been willing to see his authority, then they would have perceived it. His authority lay in who he was, in his mode of existence, and was manifest indirectly.

The eucharist as a mode of existence

Bakhtin makes the following comment about Goethe's observations on the general world outlook expressed in popular-festive

---

139. Gregory the Great, Epistle LVII, *NPNF* Second Series, Vol. XII, p. 186.

140. Irenaeus cites Matt. 21:16 and Ps. 8:3 when commenting on Jesus' entry into Jerusalem as 'king in His sorrow of soul'. *Against Heresies*, Bk IV, ch. XI, §3, *ANF*, Vol. I, p. 475.

141. See also John Chrysostom, *The Gospel of Matthew*, Homily LXVII, *NPNF* Second Series, Vol. X, pp. 409–410.

142. John Chrysostom, *The Gospel of Matthew*, Homily LXVII, *NPNF* Second Series, Vol. X, pp. 411.

carnival forms: 'Goethe stresses the suspension of all hierarchic differences, of all ranks and status; carnivalesque revelry is marked by absolute familiarity.'[143] Carnival allowed for differences between 'superiors' and 'inferiors' to disappear, if only for a short while.[144] It allowed for the temporal authorities of officialdom, feudal and ecclesial, to be rendered temporarily inoperative, with the result that the indirect authority of the clown-king was more readily evident. Neither the authority of convention nor that of individual achievement were worthy of recognition by the people: 'The carnivalesque crowd . . . is outside of and contrary to all existing forms of the coercive socio-economic and political organisation, which is suspended for the time of the festivity.'[145] In our own day, it is difficult to imagine a carnival-event that could have such an effect. Yet Bakhtin challenges us to think about connections between authority and ethos that are radically different from those in secularised forms of authority. Judged by worldly standards, the kenotic authority of the incarnate God, and, consequently, of the church, is topsy-turvy and reverses normal concepts of what authority entails. When connected to the eucharist, every exercise of authority in the church is an expression of its truth and a way of living its reality, identifiable by the production of fruit in the life of the community. If kept apart from the eucharist, authority in the church inevitably ends up with variants of the inadequacies of individualism, pretension, false ideas about self-importance, and/or a lifeless amalgam of religious and conventional *mores majorum*, i.e., legalistic and social requirements.

Like the authority of God, the authority that marks a eucharistic mode of existence is the power (derivative from the power of God) to produce an increase over what had been there previously,

---

143. Bakhtin, *Rabelais*, p. 246.
144. See above (p. 213) on the limits of carnival as illustration of the Christian gospel because of the argument that it serves to protect the status quo.
145. Bakhtin, *Rabelais*, p. 255.

to initiate, to institute and establish, to nourish life and cause it to continue. Christ's body, says the liturgy, is broken and distributed. The free gift of life is available to all without discrimination (Gal. 3:28). This is the touchstone of the church's ethics and the end of its every exercise of authority. In contrast with the authority of individualism – which usually tends towards the autonomous right to choose, idealist notions which border on metaphysical absolutes, or rationally derived abstract principles which fail to account for personal distinctiveness – authority in the church is about manifesting and realising the life of Christ in hope of his coming reign. The Liturgy of John Chrysostom contains these words after the fraction of the sacred bread: 'The Lamb of God is broken and distributed; broken but not divided. He is forever eaten yet is never consumed, but He sanctifies those who partake of Him.' The church eats of forgiveness and freedom and its ethos is determined by this gospel reality. This ethos is not expressed necessarily by professionalised priesthoods, and has little to do with managerial efficiency. It does, however, have something to do with headship and hierarchy, albeit defined with reference to divine authority which takes no pleasure in sin or its consequences, but longs for each person to receive the blessings of heaven: 'O Thou who lovest mankind (*sic*) ... thou hast no pleasure in the death of a sinner, but rather that he should turn from his wickedness and live.'

Headship and hierarchy

'In the world of carnival ... established authority and truth are relative.'[146] 'Established' here means official relations in the social and political spheres of the day between inferiors and superiors. Carnival folly is opposed to the official, worldly wisdom of feudal relations and religious piety. Rabelais, says Bakhtin, praises folly as a form of unofficial truth: 'By "unofficial" is meant a peculiar conception free from selfish interests, norms, and appreciation of

---

146. Bakhtin, *Rabelais*, p. 256.

"this world" (that is, the established world, which it is always profitable to serve)."[147] Carnival represents the relativising of worldly wisdom and temporary existence according to festive wisdom. Like the clown, carnival participants are able briefly to look at the world with a simple lack of pretension and freedom from acquisitiveness and worry: 'On May Day eve one is permitted to look at the world fearlessly and impiously.'[148] Again, it is important to emphasise that not everything Bakhtin says about carnival casts light upon the task of Christian ethics. For instance, May Day celebrations were linked for Rabelais to ideas about the immorality of the people. Yet his comments about the wisdom of folly and the relativising of established authorities alert us to the dangers of separating authority in the church from the wisdom of its clown-king. Like the carnival, the church is no place for individual authority which undermines the ontological truth of its unified existence in Christ. Individual authority, which appropriates power and control to the self, denies the eucharistic mode of existence and is a compromised form of secularisation in the church. Headship in the church belongs to Christ; to have the mind of Christ (1 Cor. 2:16; Eph. 4:23) is to be transfigured from the authority that enforces obedience to that which engenders life. This, unlike the relationship between the authority of Jesus Christ and the social reality of organised ecclesial polity, is uncontroversial. The relationship of the authority of Jesus Christ to ecclesial hierarchy causes more dispute.

In Orthodoxy, the hierarchy (*hierosyne*) of the church equates to the ministry of bishops, presbyters and deacons, which is not simply a matter of organisation but part of the charismatic essence of the church.[149] In Roman Catholicism, the church is hierarchical in the sense that Christ the Lord set up a variety of offices, for

---

147. Bakhtin, *Rabelais*, p. 262.
148. Bakhtin, *Rabelais*, p. 262.
149. Georges Florovsky, *Ecumenism II: An Historical Approach*, Vol. 14 in his collected works (Vaduz: Büchervertriebsanstalt, 1989), pp. 29–33.

the good of the whole body, that are 'sacerdotal' or priestly in nature. The visible, organically structured organisation of the church was established by Christ, is vivified by the Spirit of Christ, and is governed by the successor of Peter and the bishops in communion with him.[150] Both traditions recall that the fathers witness to the fact and origin of the church's hierarchy, which includes deacons, priests and bishops. Both hold that bishops are the chief shepherds over the local churches, and that they are guided in their work but not controlled mechanically by the Holy Spirit. Protestant churches do not hold that hierarchy is of the essence of the church, though many value highly an understanding of *episcope*, by which is meant spiritual supervision. For example, the Lutheran church holds that spiritual supervision is present in each community of Christians gathered around word and sacrament: '[A]ll ordained ministries in the church, including the episcopal office of pastoral leadership and spiritual supervision (*episcope*) are founded in the mission of Jesus Christ.'[151]

Other Protestant churches or gatherings of Christians differ considerably in their attitude to the value of hierarchical organisation in living as Christ's body in the world. The Salvation Army is structured according to clear levels of command which comprise the General Commander, who is an international figure and has authority over whole army; the Territorial Commanders, who have authority over a country or part thereof; the Divisional Commanders, of which, for example, there are approximately twenty in the United Kingdom; and the Commanding Officers, who are in charge of individual Corps, hostels or 'eventide' homes. Each commander will be advised by a council, but authority rests

---

150. *Lumen Gentium* (21 November 1964), ch. III, 'The Church is Hierarchical' in *Vatican Council II*, ed. Austin Flannery OP (Dublin: Dominican Publications, 1992).

151. In this text we use throughout the terms 'episcopal ministry' and 'episcopal office' as referring to the task of pastoral leadership and spiritual supervision. Persons exercising this task in Lutheran churches are sometimes called bishops.

with them; there are also local census boards which have the authority to admit people onto the roll of the local corps as salvationists. These boards can recommend, but not effect, removal for disciplinary reasons (i.e., for reasons other than death, transfer or attendance at another place of worship). A soldier can only be removed for disciplinary reasons under the authority of a Divisional Commander.[152] Compare this structure with that of the Religious Society of Friends in Great Britain, who have no ordained clergy but who claim still to have leadership and ministry, both of which are given to them corporately by the Spirit. The Friends claim that 'the church can be so ordered that the guidance of the Holy Spirit can be known and followed without the need for a separated clergy'.[153] Moreover, they are 'disturbed at the linking of ordination with authority, for this can legitimise authoritarian leadership and limit the exercise of spiritual authority'. The Friends identify Elders who have a responsibility of the spiritual life of the Meetings, Overseers who have a responsibility for pastoral care within Meetings, and Clerks who serve administrative needs. The spiritual insights of members are tested by the group and the different insights of different groups are tested against one another through a series of area Monthly Meetings, county

---

152. Details of the duties of commanders are given in *Orders and Regulations for Corps Officers of the Salvation Army* (St Albans: Campfield Press, 1976). There it is stated, for example, that 'a Commanding Officer is responsible to God and his Salvation Army leaders – as represented by his Divisional Commander – for everybody and everything connected with the command'. The Commanding Officer is expected 'to strive for the substantial progress of his corps' and his/ her responsibilities include 'the conversion of the unsaved people of the district, irrespective of their attendance at Army meetings; the soldiers, recruits, adherents, junior soldiers and converts; the securing and developing of candidates for officership; and the effective visitation of both saved and unsaved'. A corps officer represents the Army in the locality and, except in special circumstances, should not appear out of uniform in the locality where he is stationed.

153. See *To Lima With Love: The Response from the Religious Society of Friends in Great Britain to the World Council of Churches Document* Baptism, Eucharist and Ministry (London: Quaker Home Service, 1987).

Quarterly Meetings, and national Yearly Meetings. The Friends reject the idea that the Twelve were the only apostles or that these apostles were the authority for ordained leadership. They do not equate the church's witness to apostolicity with the restoration of ancient systems but with life in the Spirit in which the apostles lived. They have, from their foundation, recognised the equality of women and men in the ministry of the people of God.

Thus, within different denominations and traditions, hierarchy is associated variously with the essence of the church, the demands of corporate relationship, and the authority of control (*potestas*). Such varied understanding and practice suggests that the inner structure of the church can be realised in many different ways.[154] Yet to some extent, this bypasses the feminist challenge that hierarchy is a 'bad thing' per se because it implies a ruling body of (usually male) clergy whose roles and responsibilities often mirror the worst aspects of the administrative, legislative and judicial patterns of the day. The challenge is an important one because hierarchy is commonly (and often justifiably) equated with a rigid order of graded subordination. It is not readily perceived as an inclusive and enabling concept even – and, at times, especially – within the church. Cultural conditions affect the semiotic significance conveyed by various forms of ecclesial polity and, at a time when hierarchy suggests a rigid, pyramidal, organisational structure comprising graded or ranked series, we need to think again about whether the concept can be used of the corporate organisation of the church. I suggest that it might remain of use if: (i) transposed from the context of individualism to that of corporate relations; (ii) ridded of association with pyramidal patterns of social relations; (iii) understood as expressing the ministry and ordination of all believers; (iv) lived as a practical expression of the love of God. On the other hand, the word 'hierarchy' might

---

154. Too much weight should not be placed on such an argument which is, of itself, liable to fall foul of the naturalistic fallacy.

now be so tainted by problematic associations that new language must be found.

This said, Bakhtin helps us with the first of these points because the hierarchy that carnival exposes as worldly folly is that of autonomous individuals seeking power to rule and graded into successively subordinate ranks. This is what Bakhtin refers to as 'the authority of the official realm' of church as well as state: authority void of divine grace or carnival spirit and regarded as something to be possessed and exercised by an individual.[155] At carnival time, however, normal worldly conventions vanish and respect for hierarchy among inferiors is cancelled for a short period.[156] Those living in the spirit of carnival anticipate a new utopian order rather than the usual world order. Instead of an atmosphere of sterility in which obstinate senility reigns, and in which a 'gloomy sacristan' jealously guards vestments for the clergy, carnival is 'merry play' in which all are free to participate and share the festivity.[157] As in some feminist criticism, the static and pyramidal hierarchies of individual claims to power are suspended in favour of new orders of relationship viewed from the perspective of corporate existence. This helps us to see that the church is not – unless it is distorted – hierarchical in the sense in which the 'old world' represented by the sacristan is hierarchical. The carnival logic of crownings and uncrownings exposed official claims to power as nonsensical; only the authority of the clown-king survived its fires of ridicule.

Bakhtin also helps us, initially at least, to consider why and how hierarchy expresses the ministry and ordination of all believers. For Bakhtin, carnival is the participation of the people in the festive spirit. He cites Goethe's perception of this truth:

Crowded together, its members are astonished at themselves.

---

155. Bakhtin, *Rabelais*, p. 259.
156. Bakhtin, *Rabelais*, p. 264.
157. Bakhtin, *Rabelais*, p. 268.

> They are accustomed at other times to seeing each other running hither and thither in confusion, bustling about without order or discipline. Now this many-headed, many-minded, fickle, blundering monster suddenly sees itself united as one noble assembly, welded into one mass, a single body animated by a single spirit.[158]

Everyday relationships which comprised individuals running to and fro contrast strongly with the carnival at which they were united by a 'single spirit'. At carnival time, the people were not *first* individuals who joined in festive activities and *then* participants. Rather, the carnival spirit was constitutive of their changed relationships one with the other. A lack of festive order and discipline was replaced by the kind of order and discipline that could unite a crowd of persons marked by an indefinite number of opinions and by lack of steadfastness, into a living entity that moved as one. This body was not homogeneous. It did not have a uniform structure or composition throughout: '[T]he unity did not have such a simple geometric character. It was more complex and differentiated; most important of all, it had an historic nature.'[159] The carnival body was not a static unity but a body in the process of becoming and growth. For Rabelais, this links with ideas of the immortality of the people. For our purposes, the unity and 'order' of the carnival body stimulates fresh consideration of unity and order in the church. It does so, however, from the perspective of the community as constituted by the Holy Spirit.

Christian Ethics and the Eucharist

From the earliest days of the church's existence, the Holy Spirit guided and formed its organisational existence as well as the discipleship of each member (Acts 6:1–6, 13:2, 15:28, 20:28). The

---

158. Bakhtin, *Rabelais*, p. 255.
159. Bakhtin, *Rabelais*, p. 255.

internal structure and sociology of the church was never isolated from its ministry and ethos, and it was in leading and building up each member that the Holy Spirit formed the church as the body of Christ. Of course, Christian attendance at the eucharist can be occasional, perfunctory, and characterised by boredom. Yet the eucharist provides assistance in the struggle against sin; its celebration of the resurrection of Christ relativises all earthly structures of power and witnesses to the final judgement of God. Its joy is a laugh in the face of death. Its ordinariness is a comfort in times of trial. Its egalitarianism exposes and condemns prideful claims to power and is efficacious for the building of just and peaceful communities. Its materiality affirms the significance and value of one's own material or physical existence, and teaches that care of oneself and one's body is integral to the respect and dignity due to someone created in the image of God. Moreover, there is a foundational interdependence between personal membership of the body of Christ and the ministry of the church as a whole; the church is a community of persons gathered and constituted by the Holy Spirit as a united, corporate existence (Eph. 4:15–16). The body is defined in terms of its head and its parts, each of which has a function to be performed in love. Paul writes of Christ's body as having identifiable members: the foot, hand, eye, ear etc., each of which has a particular ministry without which the whole would be impoverished. God has combined each part so that there might be no division in the body; an individual ministry cannot be understood without reference to the whole. Each member is assigned by God their place in the community. As John Zizioulas writes: 'Thus the Church becomes *hierarchical* in the sense in which the Holy Trinity is hierarchical: by reason of the *specificity of relationship*.'[160] Each body-part has its particular

---

160. Zizioulas, *Being as Communion*, p. 223. In explaining the notion of specificity, he cites Gregory of Nazianzus, *Oratio* 34, 10: '[T]he Son has everything in common with the Father and the Spirit except being the Father or Spirit and the Spirit possesses everything the Father and the Son possess except being the Father or Son.'

ordo within the community. Each is ordained at confirmation (i.e., appointed with the laying on of hands) to ministerial and priestly authority as a member of Christ's body; there is no such thing in the church as a non-ordained member.[161] The hierarchy of the church includes all its members, each of whom has a distinctive influence to exert and a particular function to perform. It remains arguable that, in today's society, use of the word hierarchy creates more problems than it solves. The temptation is always that authority is understood in terms of ascendancy, and when this happens – whether in ancient Israel, the time of the emperor Constantine, or the present day church – the forms of authority are present, but not the spiritual power.

---

161. Zizioulas, *Being as Communion*, pp. 215–216.

Chapter Five

Dimensions of the Christian Ethic: Priestly, Royal, Prophetic

Dimensions of the Ministry of Jesus Christ

Christian ethics is the study of the Christian ethos because it concerns the character and practice of life in Christ. So far, this has raised for us questions about why Christian ethics is life-affirming, dialogic and polyphonic, and why and how the church derives criteria for its actions from the moral image of the Word incarnate. In this chapter, we think further about living the faith in ethical relationship with oneself and society. This raises questions for us about holiness and the place of forgiveness in Christian ethics, and also about ethical relationships with one's body. In addition, it asks us to attend carefully to the semiotic significance of every exercise of authority in the church, and to consider why rooting ethics in the authority of God provides reasons for the defence of universal moral standards. The structure of the chapter is given by traditional perceptions of Jesus Christ's ministry as threefold: prophetic, priestly and kingly. Justin Martyr writes: 'It was foretold . . . He would suffer, would come in glory, and be Judge finally of all, and eternal King and Priest.'[1] Aquinas writes: 'Wherefore, as to others, one is a lawgiver, another is a priest, another is a king; but all these concur in Christ as the fount of

---

1. Justin Martyr, *Dialogue with Trypho, ANF*, Vol. I, p. 212. See also pp. 214 and 255.

all grace.'[2] Calvin thinks that to know the purpose for which
Christ was sent, we must 'look above all at three things in Him: the
prophetic office, kingship, and priesthood.'[3] I use this traditional
framework for thinking about Christ's ministry on the assumption
that all of these dimensions properly inform our understanding
of the genesis of Christian ethics.[4]

The Priestly Dimension

Let us think first about Christ's priestly ministry and its relationship to Christian ethics. The subject is difficult, not least because
one cannot in the current ecumenical climate arrive at a single
working definition or understanding of 'priest' or 'priestly'. The
Baptism, Eucharist and Ministry process, launched at Lima in 1982,
has left unresolved a mass of issues in this area, including: (i) the
interrelation between the calling of the whole people of God and
the service of the ordained ministry; (ii) the interrelation between
functional understandings of ministry and ministry as a special,
or sacramental, participation in the priesthood of Christ; (iii)
the ordination of women; and (iv) the normative character of the
threefold pattern of bishop, priest and deacon. *Called To Be One*
illustrates these difficulties by making plain that lay presidency of
the eucharist is one of the most sensitive issues in relationships
between Christian churches today.[5] Many tensions remain between
expressive or representative, ontological or functional, understand-

---

2. Thomas Aquinas, *Summa Theologiae*, Blackfriars edn (London: Eyre & Spottiswoode, 1963), 3a, 22, 1.
3. John Calvin, *Institutes of the Christian Religion* (Philadelphia: Westminster
Press, 1960), Bk II, ch. XV, §§1–6.
4. In this chapter, I draw on material presented to the meeting of the Society
for the Study of Theology, University of Manchester, 1998, and also to The British
and Irish Association of Practical Theology, University of Edinburgh, 1998.
5. *Called To Be One* (London: CTE Publications, 1996), appendices D and E.
Called To Be One points to the practical import of this difficulty regarding
authority and decision-making: 'Two questions still divide the churches: who ▷

ings of priestly authority. In what follows, and in light of the previous chapter, I draw a clear distinction between the priesthood of all believers and the presbyteral ministry of word and sacrament, and am concerned primarily with the former. I also hold fast to Luther's description of how Jesus Christ shows us 'in what manner all we Christians are kings and priests' in so far as all are called to pray for one another, to teach one another the things of God, and to come into the presence of God through faith in Christ.[6] These things, he says, are the duties of priests, and we are all equally priests by the grace of faith which allows each to claim the priesthood of Christ as their own.[7] They are 'figured' in the visible office of priesthood by those who minister and teach publicly, although the real challenge is to try to understand how Christ's priestly ministry and priestly authority is something that belongs to all, and can be exercised by all.

On corporateness and the call to holiness

What, then, characterises Christ's priestly ministry, and why do these characteristics provide foundational perspectives which inform Christian ethics? Let us begin by noting that Jesus does not refer to himself as 'priest', and it is only really the letter to the Hebrews that develops the theme of his priesthood, or, more accurately, his high-priesthood. It is clear, however, that in John 17, the evangelist links Jesus' authority with his forthcoming passion which is the means by which God's glory will be revealed. Jesus prays: '[G]lorify your Son so that the Son may glorify you, since you have given him authority over all people, to give eternal life to all whom you have given him' (Jn. 17:1b–2a). The *RSV*

---

in the churches have authority to interpret Christian teaching; and what is the level of authority to be attributed to such interpretation?' (p. 79).

6. Martin Luther, *Concerning Christian Liberty*, in *Luther's Primary Works: Together with His Shorter and Larger Catechisms*, trans. Henry Wace and C. A. Buchheim (London: Hodder & Stoughton, 1896), p. 271.

7. Luther, *Concerning Christian Liberty*, pp. 264–265.

rendered Jn 17:19 'And for their sake I consecrate myself, that they also may be consecrated in truth', conveying the sense that Jesus' priestly ministry and authority entailed the constant labour of displacement, in such a way that his own authority became diffracted in that of the disciples. Similarly, the writer to the Hebrews is adamant that, in his priestly role, Jesus did not glorify himself, but was subject to weakness, and made supplication for others who were in need of God's mercy and grace (Heb. 4:14–5:10). Jesus' priestly ministry consisted in his giving glory to God, and this is of vital importance to the ethic of the church: 'So . . . whatever you do, do everything for the glory of God' (1 Cor. 10:31). This injunction is expressed to the whole church and it refers to *everything*, i.e., not only liturgical practices but every aspect of its existence. Everything Jesus did was a manifestation of divine life and this is expected also of the church in its ministry.

As compared with most practices of priestly ministry, Jesus' ministry marks a quiet revolution. From his comparative sociological studies, Max Weber concluded that, typically, priests labour under pressure from both the unpredictability of prophecy, and the traditionalism and intellectualism of the laity and, in order to cope, take refuge in the niceties of casuistry, dogmatic formulations, pyramidal and/or rationalistic structures. He describes the many human pressures that militate in favour of the priesthood trying to control and sanitise the power of God, thus rendering the congregation a passive association.[8] Jesus' priestly ministry was very different. It was centred outside of himself in God the Father, and enabled others to discover new things about themselves. His priestly authority was marked by the heterogeneity of ministries that it evoked in others, and had no whiff of ascendancy or self-importance. Paul issues similar warnings when he warns believers not to put their 'I-ness' before living 'by faith in the Son of God' (Gal. 2:20), or to exercise gifts without striving for the building

---

8. Max Weber, *The Sociology of Religion*, trans. Talcott Parsons (Boston: Beacon Press, 1963; German edn 1922), pp. 63–73.

up of the church (1 Cor. 14), because then their spiritual authority would become an empty shell of self-gratification. He implies that priestly ministry is always inscribed in a complex network of communal interactions. Priestly ministry is always beyond the grasp of the individual; it is not an 'I-experience', because it is never something that belongs to an individual over against someone else. Nor is it a 'we-experience', when 'we' is a nebulous, undifferentiated herd that follows directions in a quasi-fatalist manner. Priestly ministry, like Christian ethics, is inherently corporate.

For ancient Israel, the corporate nature of its priestly ministry was linked to the call to be 'a holy nation'. This was an intensely political call which set them off as a people over against other peoples.[9] According to Deutero-Isaiah, it gave them a saving role to play amongst the nations: 'I have given you as a covenant to the people, a light to the nations' (Is. 42:6); Israel's redemption from Egypt prefigured new things that God would bring about, 'that my salvation may reach to the end of the earth' (Is. 49:6b). In the New Testament, the calling to be a holy nation of priests is no less political. Peter addresses the exiles of the dispersion as God's people who were to enable the Gentiles to 'glorify God when he comes to judge' (1 Pet. 2:10–12). The book of Revelation does not separate the kingdom of priests from world history, but expounds their calling with reference to the eschatological reality of the kingdom of God.[10] How then, we might ask, is the church called to be 'a holy nation' amidst the nations today? How is the mystery of the authority of the church as a 'holy nation' to be

---

9. Israel was called to be 'a priestly kingdom and a holy nation' (Ex. 19:6), distinct among the peoples of the earth. Deuteronomy requires all the people to love YHWH with all their heart, soul and might (Deut. 6:4–6), and urged none to worship him in ways that brought dishonour upon his name among the people in the land (Deut. 12:2–7).

10. This is argued by Elisabeth Schüssler Fiorenza, *The Book of Revelation: Justice and Judgement* (Philadelphia: Fortress Press, 1985), see esp. p. 56.

expressed in the public realm, without making it into a rhetoric of sanctity?

For Israel, holy nationhood reached beyond itself and looked for the establishment of justice in the earth (Is. 42:1, 4; 49:6). If similar authority attaches to the church as a holy nation of priests in the political realm, then the church is not a community outside of political history. There is a sense in which secular politics has its limits, and the church's life lies outside those limits, but there is another sense in which the church cannot be removed from the secular, political arena. Its influence is not that of an electoral minority, but of a more indirect kind that results from lives of holiness and godliness (1 Pet. 1:15–16; 2 Pet. 3:11–13). Unlike the prophetic task, the priestly task – and the priestly dimension of Christian ethics – is not to transform society, but to offer sacrifices of praise to God (1 Pet. 2:5), to engage in the ministry of prayer (Eph. 6:18; Col. 4:3), and to teach one another in all wisdom (Col. 3:16–17).[11] The prophetic task of the church is to preach repentance and transformation; its priestly task is more inward as, in its hagiophanic aspect, the church centres on the sacrifice of holy living. There is something self-authenticating that attaches to the authority of holy living, although there is little point wasting time in wondering how to be holy because this kind of authority is a by-product of service offered in imitation of the self-giving of Christ. It may be that the authority of the Christian church as institution is waning. However, its hidden life of priestly sacrifice will remain recognisable by its fruits; its nature is in Christ, and its high calling to manifest something of the holiness of God. This is at the heart of Christian ethics.

---

11. There are similarities of priestly functions here with those of ancient Israel that were allocated to specific persons and groups. These included the discernment of divine will (Deut. 33: 8), the teaching of torah (Deut. 33:10; Mal. 2:7), and the offering of sacrifices (Ex. 32: 26–29; Deut. 18:1ff). NB, sacrifice was not always a function restricted to the priests, and not all priests were Levites.

The priestly ministry of forgiveness

Christian ethics is characterised by the rigorous demands of the gospel, not least those concerning the forgiveness of sins. Jesus taught the disciples to pray: 'Give us this day our daily bread. And forgive us our debts, as we also have forgiven our debtors' (Matt. 6:11–12), thus urging an openness to both the giving and the receiving of forgiveness. Yet the matter is far from straightforward within Christian tradition where the understanding of forgiveness has been tied to discussions about the primacy of Peter and the nature of the power bestowed in 'the keys' (Matt. 16:18–19, 18:15–19; Jn. 20:22–23). A host of interpretations variously associate the power of the keys with exorcism, the determining of who goes to heaven and who to hell, whether or not a person's sins should be forgiven, and excommunication, so that talk about forgiveness is often associated negatively with the church's bringing of a wrong-doer to repentance and the use of sanctions.[12] The rigorous demands of penitential systems are frequently seen as expressions

---

12. In what follows, I assume Davies and Allison's conclusion, namely, that the gift to Peter of the keys of the kingdom of God (Matt. 16:18–19), given in connection with the power to bind and loose, both established his pre-eminent position and probably had to do with his teaching responsibility. The authority to bind and loose, as recounted in Matt. 18:15–19, is understood by them, and, I venture to posit, by the majority of New Testament scholars, as part of the community rules for dealing with disciplinary matters in the Christian community as a whole. (See W. D. Davies and Dale C. Allison, *A Critical and Exegetical Commentary on The Gospel According to Saint Matthew* (Edinburgh: T. & T. Clark, 1991), Vol. II, p. 635.) Günther Bornkamm, drawing on rabbinic senses of the phrases, reaches a similar conclusion, in so far as Peter, who is portrayed as a kind of 'supreme rabbi', is the guarantor and interpreter of Jesus' teachings. (Günther Bornkamm, 'The Authority to "Bind" and "Loose" in the Church in Matthew's Gospel: The Problem of Sources in Matthew's Gospel' in Graham N. Stanton (ed.), *The Interpretation of Matthew* (Edinburgh: T. & T. Clark, 1983/95), ch. 6.) The emphasis in Matt. 16:18–19 is on Peter and his teaching authority, whereas the emphasis in Matt. 18:15–19, where specific mention is not made of Peter, is on discipline.

of the legalism and authoritarianism of Christianity, and as having no relevance – or even being harmful – to situations of hatred and distress. 'Don't burden me with yet another reason to feel guilty,' cries the woman abused by her partner who is told that she ought to forgive.[13] All this suggests that there is much work to be done in understanding properly the place of forgiveness in Christian ethics, and also that failure to take seriously the place of forgiveness in Christian ethics leads to a diminishment of the church's ministry. With this in mind, I maintain that we might yet learn from traditional expressions of the Christian ministry of forgiveness, not least the traditions of penance. There are undoubtedly many problems associated with Christian traditions of penance, not least the structured systems which developed around the idea that God accorded reconciliation upon the pronouncement of the priest.[14] At best, however, they articulate the theological truth that the dynamic of forgiveness includes recognition of guilt, and that this dynamic might be aided by the person who has done wrong making some sort of restitution for their acts.

---

13. Cooper-White writes: 'All too often, survivors of violence are retraumatised by pastors and other well-meaning helpers who press forgiveness upon them as if it were something which, if they tried hard enough they could simply will into happening. If the survivor tries to forgive, she can only fail, and her failure will reinforce all the self-blame and shame of her original abuse'. (Pamela Cooper-White, *The Cry of Tamar* (Minneapolis: Fortress Press, 1995), p. 253. On the similar problem regarding child sexual abuse, see Sheila A. Redmond, 'Christian "Virtues" and Child Sexual Abuse' in J. C. Brown and C. R. Bohn (eds) *Christianity, Patriarchy and Abuse* (New York: Pilgrim Press, 1983). I am indebted to an ex-student Rachel Ker for her work on forgiveness in the context of violence against women in the home.) The image of the Christ as the suffering servant who silently accepts brutality and turns the other cheek can easily convey a sense that battered women should do the same.

14. The Council of Trent confirmed the reality of the effect of the priest's utterance of the formula 'I absolve you', and stated that faith without penance effected no remission of sins. Session XIV, November 1551, Canons on the Sacrament of Penance. See *The Council of Trent Canons and Decrees*, ed. J. Waterworth (Chicago, IL, 1848).

Christian tradition reveals a mixed history regarding whether, or in what sense, Jesus' gift to Peter conveyed the authority to remit and retain sins, and whether, or in what sense, this authority passed to the ordained priesthood. From the time of the *Shepherd of Hermas* there can be traced a system of penance in which forms of repentance came to be specified.[15] Clement of Alexandria, having made reference to the *Shepherd*, argues that the person who has received forgiveness ought to sin no more (Heb. 10:26). Sincere repentance, combined with regimen and special attention, should eradicate inbred sins.[16] For Tertullian, the baptism of repentance was a public means of the sign and seal of repentance, although it is difficult to determine from his writings how public the confessions were to be.[17] It is clear, however, that a structured system is developing around the idea that God accorded reconciliation upon the pronouncement of the priest. Cyprian, who was troubled by the laxity of some confessors, writes more explicitly about how the penitence of the lapsed should be fulfilled, making practical suggestions about how the people should be retained in ecclesiastical discipline, and when the public peace of the church should be given.[18] Augustine's *Sermon to the Catechumens* did not tell them that they would live without sin, but that their sins would be venial: 'For the sake of all sins was Baptism provided; for the sake of light sins, without which we cannot be, was prayer provided.'[19] Those whom the catechumens had seen doing

---

15. See *The Pastor of Hermas*, Bk 1, Vision III, *ANF*, Vol. II, pp. 12ff. This vision contains perhaps the first reference to penitential discipline: ' "Repentance", said she, "is yet possible, but in this tower they cannot find a suitable place. But in another and much inferior place they will be laid, and that, too, only when they have been tortured and completed the days of their sins" ' (p. 15).

16. Clement of Alexandria, *The Stromata, or Miscellanies*, Bk II, ch. XIII, *ANF*, Vol. II, pp. 360ff; *Salvation of the Rich Man, ANF*, Vol. II, p. 602.

17. Tertullian, *On Repentance, ANF*, Vol. III, pp. 657ff.

18. Cyprian, *Epistles*, XI, XII, XIII, *ANF*, Vol. V, pp. 292–294.

19. Augustine, *On the Creed: A Sermon to the Catechumens*, *NPNF*, Vol. III, p. 374.

penance, i.e., those required to make public show of their penance outside the doors of the church, had committed such serious sins as adultery or murder.

Between AD 451 and the emergence of scholasticism, the lingering challenge of Montanism pushed the church towards giving institutional form to the practices of penance. During this time, questions of the scale of penance became more pressing, with the rise of monasticism inaugurating practices of private confession. Priests were referred to as judges, with, for example, Alcuin of York (735–804) affirming that ordination bestowed the authority to bind or loose sin.[20] Abelard urged confession of sins among the faithful, whereas Thomas Aquinas insisted on the authoritative power of the church to forgive sins, arguing that the indicative formula 'I absolve you' shows the penitent to have been absolved not only symbolically but in fact.[21] John Wycliffe challenged the necessity of penance and confession, and was concerned that the pastoral consequences of the practice tormented rather than consoled the believer.[22] Luther, in his *Shorter Cat-*

---

20. For a detailed treatment of the subject see Oscar D. Watkins, *A History of Penance* (New York: Burt Franklin, 1961).

21. Thomas Aquinas, *Summa Theologiae*, Blackfriars edn (London: Eyre & Spottiswoode, 1963), 3a, 90,2. 'In Penance, however, the scales are righted in accord with the will of the sinner and the judgement of God against whom he sinned. For here not only is the restoration of the balance of justice sought, as in retributive justice, but above all reconciliation in friendship ... Hence on the part of a penitent there is required first, the intention of making amends, which is taken care of by contrition; secondly, that he submit himself to the judgement of the priest representing God, which is accomplished by confession, thirdly, that he make recompense according to the judgement of God's minister, which is done through satisfaction.'

22. See Anne Hudson (ed.), *Selections from English Wycliffite Writings* (Cambridge: CUP, 1978). Of particular relevance are 'The Ecclesiastical Hierarchy', which contrasts God's law and human laws, lines 136–138; 'The Duty of the Priesthood', which demonstrates pastoral concerns for penitents, and 'The Power of the Pope', which passes comment on the pope's power of absolution, lines 35ff.

echism, supported a method of confessing to the priest for the use of ordinary folk. Calvin placed more emphasis on James 5:16, and was convinced that there should be no special methods of confession, although a discipline involving penalties graded to the severity of the sin became operative in Geneva.

It is not possible to explore this varied history further. Suffice it to say that, of itself, the church has no authority to exercise a ministry of forgiveness: 'There is no ministry in the Church other than Christ's ministry.'[23] 'What could come forth', asks Calvin, 'from the defiled mouth of Isaiah and the foolish mouth of Jeremiah but filth and folly, if they spoke their own word?'[24] Yet Christ gave to the church the specific ministry of the binding or loosing of sin, i.e., the power and authority of 'the keys' (Matt. 16:18–19, 18:15–19; Jn 20:22–23), and it has often been expressed by the church in the proclamation of absolution and requiring of penance. Despite the many problematic aspects of ecclesial traditions associated with these verses, it is arguable that they witness to something important about the dynamics of human moral responsibility. The recitation of 'two Hail Mary's' does not automatically lead to absolution from sin. Such an interpretation trivialises the 'architectonics of answerability' to which the tradition bears witness. More important is the need for the kind of accountability before God and one another which opens the path to transformation.[25] Restitution is made for the sake of justice, and this allows the process of healing to begin. Arguably, Christian ethics has much to share with – as well as to learn from – the survivors of sexual abuse and domestic violence in this regard. A problem for both is that forgiveness is too often confused with passive acceptance of wrong, or the suppression of hurt and anger.

---

23. John D. Zizioulas, *Being as Communion* (Crestwood, NY: St Vladimir's Seminary Press, 1985), p. 210.

24. Calvin, *Institutes*, Bk IV, ch. VIII, §3.

25. M. M. Bakhtin, 'Introduction' in *Art and Answerability* (Austin, TX: University of Texas Press, 1990), p. x.

The supposed virtue of self-control, and the ideal of self-sacrifice or martyrdom, can lead women to believe that in accepting abuse and exploitation they are doing what Christianity – especially in its support for family values – requires. For neither, however, does forgiveness properly equate with sweeping wrong aside. Rather, it has regard for the specifics of a person's situation and never trivialises any suffering endured.[26] Anything less is what Bonhoeffer calls 'cheap grace', because there is no recognition of guilt and no call for genuine repentance.

On the healing of corporate memory

Yet the priestly ministry of forgiveness extends beyond the scope of personal relations to that of communities; distinction can be drawn between personal and corporate experiences of forgiveness. Both have their focus in the grace of God, but the subject matter is different. To talk of corporate experiences of forgiveness presupposes a body of people with a common identity, history and memory. The subject matter is not easy. If we ask: What, if anything, is corporate memory? 'Do we hunt it with a questionnaire, or are we supposed to use a butterfly net?'[27] the answers can be varied. A neurobiologist, who understands memory in

---

26. This is argued by L. Gregory Jones, *Embodying Forgiveness* (Michigan: William B. Eerdmans Publishing Co., 1995), p. 228. Arguably, the church also has much to learn from working with the survivors of sexual abuse and domestic violence regarding corporate responsibility for co-forming ecclesial and societal cultures that refuse to condone any form of abuse, express solidarity with the victims, and challenge the root causes of the problem(s). If the church's ministry of forgiveness involves praying for transformative change in those who have abused and battered, then this transformation might extend to the church's own responsibility for ensuring that the gospel message of Christ's once-for-all work of salvation is not distorted into a 'myth of redemptive violence' which encourages women to tolerate abuse. (This phrase is used by Walter Wink, *Engaging the Powers* (Minneapolis: Fortress Press, 1992), pp. 13–32.)

27. James Fentress and Chris Wickham, *Social Memory* (Oxford: Blackwell, 1992), p. 2.

terms of the complex biological functions of the individual nervous system, might be hesitant to talk of memory as social or corporate. An historian who studies the structuring and ordering of what is known of the past might talk of social memory in terms of oral and narrative traditions. Social memory is that which attaches to membership of certain groups, and manifests itself as collectively held ideas and experiences.[28] Some go so far as to argue that memory is always social because it is 'structured by language, by teaching and observing'.[29] They suggest that social memory is structured by group identities which change through time. It is not a storehouse of information, but a process that is active in calling information about the past to consciousness, recalling shared images of the historical past, and representing the past to the present. A company sales-manager might talk of the ethos of the company, perhaps as intended by its founding members. The phrase 'corporate memory' might also conjure up for them the problem of eliciting and storing knowledge held by an employee who is about to leave the firm. There are now consultancy firms that specialise in solutions to this problem. A Christian ethicist might answer the question in various ways, depending upon their denominational allegiance and/or theo-logical/philosophical/ideological leaning. More or less emphasis might be given to the apostolic and post-apostolic sources of Christian corporate memory, ecumenically agreed creeds as nor-mative content of corporate memory, the magisterium as bearer of corporate memory, or the primacy of the proclaimed word in keeping corporate memory alive.

Yet the subject has considerable practical significance. Consider

----

28. Fentress and Wickham study class- and group-memories in western societies, from the Middle Ages to the present day. They modify Maurice Halbwachs's development of Emile Durkheim's emphasis on the collective nature of social consciousness by giving more significance to the individual as member of a given social group, but continue to stress narrative and collective knowledge of the past. **29.** Fentress and Wickham, *Social Memory*, p. 7.

the relatively recent Commission of Truth and Reconciliation in South Africa. News reports are, perhaps, as near as one comes to one of the most astonishing processes in world history this century, as South Africa has, under the glare of the world's media, been working out how best to come to terms with its past and with the different narrative histories that have shaped it. After the Commission of Truth and Reconciliation was established by a bill in the South African Parliament on 21 October 1994, the world's press reported horrifying accounts of the crimes of the Afrikaner regime, as well as those of the African National Congress and other resistance groups.[30] This is not the place to reflect on a situation of which I have no direct experience. It is, however, an unprecedented example of a country seeking the healing of past wrongs though commitment to truthful confession and reconciliation.[31] Arguably, war-crimes tribunals in the Balkans serve(d) similar functions. Nor is the need to come to terms with the past and seek the healing of corporate memory exclusive to South Africa, Haiti, Kosovo, Northern Ireland and other places in the public eye. Most churches and local communities face similar needs for the healing of corporate memory and for increased awareness of corporate responsibility.

---

30. The Commission was charged with several tasks, including: (i) establishing as complete a picture as possible of the nature and extent of gross violations of human rights during the period from 1960 (the Sharpeville Massacre) to the end of 1993; (2) granting amnesty to persons who make full disclosure of all the facts relating to acts associated with a political objective; (iii) giving victims an opportunity to relate the violations they suffered; (iv) taking measures of reparation, rehabilitation and restoration of human and civil dignity to victims; (v) reporting its findings to the nation; (vi) making recommendations aimed at preventing violation of human rights in the future.

31. A similar process was carried out in Haiti, following the creation in December 1994 of its Truth and Justice Commission. Its mandate was to establish the truth concerning the most serious human rights violations between September 1991 and October 1994. Media coverage was less intense than in South Africa, perhaps because of the fear of reprisals against those testifying.

A vicar – whom for our purposes we can name Tom – told me about some of the difficulties that he was experiencing in his parish.[32] Tom's church is situated in the middle of a housing estate in which there are high levels of unemployment and low levels of literacy. The housing estate is a place that most inhabitants want to leave as the quality of housing, and the reputation of the estate in the area, is poor. The present church building is relatively new, having been rebuilt thirty years ago owing to structural problems with the old building, but it is already showing signs of ill-repair and has been the target of sustained vandalism. The congregation, says Tom, has little sense of corporate memory, because of the fact that few members know much about Christian tradition, or much about the history of the church in the estate. Tom senses a lack of corporate identity among the members. He finds it difficult to persuade members to take responsibility for routine tasks, and sums up the current ministry of the church in the estate as 'treading water'. Tom did not use the words 'corporate memory', but he linked the capacity of church members to develop a sense of Christian identity with the need to engender a sense of history, story, and belonging among the congregation. His practical response is to research the names and dates of service of previous priests appointed to serve in the parish. Far from wishing to promote clericalism, he hopes that this exercise in recollection will help to engender corporate memory and, thereby, to establish a sense of corporate identity. By ordering events of significance in the church's past into a history that can be recounted, he is enabling the church to trace its identity in the past, and to under-stand itself as part of a living tradition. This is Tom's way of getting the church to tell its own narrative history, even if in a partial and unsystematic fashion. The intention is not to recollect the past for the sake of preservation, but to awaken a sense of responsibility for being the body of Christ in that place. He cannot make the current congregation remember or be entirely

---

32. Names, and some details, have been changed in order to protect anonymity.

responsible for the actions of previous generations. That would be neither possible nor desirable. He believes, however, that if the church can project its identity into the past, then its members will gain a concomitant sense of the church's identity in the parish over a period of time, they will gain a sense of their irreplaceability in their own given time and place, and also a sense that what can be accomplished by them cannot be accomplished by another congregation. Tom links the establishing of corporate identity with the need to retrieve and recollect knowledge of past events, stories, biographies etc., even if only of previous vicars. 'We cannot afford to be wasteful,' he commented with a wry smile.

In taking seriously the notion of corporate memory as narrative history, Tom is recreating something of the same intellectual activity by which the people of Israel signified God's dealings with them through historical events. As in ancient Israel, the identity of his church is given over time by the grace of God, through the mediation of historical events. His experience is that corporate memory is both gift and task. It is gift because memory is, in some sense, time regained. At a personal level, memory enables us to see again, and to sense again, what had become lost to us. At a corporate level, memory does not bequeath to us the sensations of our forebears, or revive in us their dreams and fears. Instead, it involves some kind of acceptance of the past, and valuing of what is given, albeit critically. It turns the separation of time into a relationship that can be told and reinterpreted. This being said, there are reasons to be cautious. As a form of narrative history, corporate memory is always *a representation* of the social reality of the past in the present, and not its simple reflection.[33] An emphasis on narrativity can disguise the systems of values which structure discourse about the past. To think about collective memory in narrative terms can reinforce fiction and support role

---

33. This point is made by Bogumil Jewsiewicki, 'Collective Memory', *History in Africa*, 13 (1986), pp. 192–223.

and behaviour stereotypes.[34] Feminists are well aware that Christian corporate memory has not been socially neutral but has functioned to legitimise dominant power relationships, reconstructing supposedly authentic pasts in the present. At the very least, we must suspect that narrative histories are influenced by dominant power groups, and that these groups construe the factual and symbolic content of corporate memory to legitimise their control of the balance of power. Narrated history is always narrated by someone or some group, and there are usually vested interests at stake in the retelling.

So what of biblical testimony to the importance of corporate memory in the establishing of Israel's identity? The imperative 'remember' (*zakhor*) is a watchword for the people of Israel, and was often addressed not just to individuals but to the nation as a whole.[35] A glance at the Old Testament tells us that Israel's identity

---

34. Bogumil Jewsiewicki makes this point, and argues that collective memory should be thought of as a semantic code of memorisation in which hierarchies of values structure the codes by which events etc., are remembered.

35. The history of scholarship in this area can be traced in this century to H. Wheeler Robinson who, from 1911, described Israel in terms of corporate personality. He was influenced by contemporary anthropologists and sociologists, drawing on Durkheim's ideas about primitive peoples, and citing Levy-Bruhl's work on primitive mindsets that implied an inability of individuals to differentiate themselves from the tribe or clan. Powerful critiques have been levelled against the concept of corporate personality, notably by J. R. Porter and John W. Rogerson, both of whom dismiss its significance for Old Testament scholarship, and few scholars invoke the concept exactly as Robinson envisaged it. This information is given by Joel S. Kaminsky, who offers a useful review of the history of scholarship concerning the corporate features of Israel's life in *Corporate Responsibility in the Hebrew Bible*, JSOT Supplement Series 196 (Sheffield: Sheffield Academic Press, 1995), ch. 1. See also J. R. Rogerson, 'The Hebrew Conception of Corporate Personality: A Re-Examination', *JTS*, NS 21 (April 1970), pp. 1–16. The fact remains, however, that God frequently addressed the people of Israel as a whole. The Sinaitic covenant (Deut. 29:13–14) is made with all the people: 'The covenant is to constitute you his people this day . . . It is not with you alone that I am making this covenant and this oath, but with all those who stand here with us today before the Lord our God and also with those who ▷

did not arise automatically out of history but was formed through the retelling of the events of history as events of faith. In the Deuteronomic history especially, Moses constantly urges the people to remember God's faithfulness to their ancestors Abraham and Sarah, Isaac and Rebecca, Jacob and Rachel, and the rest. Israel is to remember of what narrative history they are a part. This is given graphic form in the Deuteronomic history when the males of the people of Israel are told to bind the commandments of Yahweh as a sign on their hands and wear them as pendants on their foreheads (Deut. 11:18). Both the content and the activity of shared memory become an outward and physical sign of corporate identity. Thus Moses reminds them: 'When *your forefathers* went down into Egypt they were only seventy strong, but now the Lord your God has made *you* as countless as the stars in the heavens' (Deut. 10:22 *REB*, emphasis added). Gerhard von Rad sums up the theological logic of Deuteronomy as follows: since Yahweh has shown Israel such faithfulness in all these matters, and will continue to do so, it is their duty to remember and to love him in return, and to keep his statutes and judgements.[36] By both inwardly accepting the commandments and publicly acknowledging love of Yahweh, Israel recognises its dependence on Yahweh: '[K]now that it is not because of any merit of yours that the Lord your God is giving you this good land to occupy; indeed, you are a stubborn people. Remember, and never forget, how you angered the Lord your God in the wilderness: from the day you left Egypt until you came to this place you have defied the Lord' (Deut. 9:6–7 *REB*). They should not be presumptuous

are not here with us today' (*REB*). The Davidic covenant (2 Sam. 7) is to be transgenerational in effect. Nathan the prophet is to say to David: 'This is the word of the Lord of Hosts: . . . I shall assign a place for my people Israel; there I shall plant them to dwell in their own land' (*REB*). David responded by asking the Lord God that his blessing might 'rest on your servant's house for ever' (2 Sam. 7:29).

36. This is a paraphrase of Gerhard von Rad, *Old Testament Theology*, Vol. 1 (Edinburgh and London: Oliver & Boyd, 1962; German edn 1957), pp. 225–226.

of a future, nor forget their past disobedience. The possibility of their own disobedience was always less ancient than that of their ancestors which they remembered. They had not known their ancestors in the wilderness, but their task is constantly to remember that they are not far away from knowing the same disobedience.

The theological axiom in operation is that faith renders historical events mediations of God's grace. It is clear from the Old Testament that Israel's corporate memory took shape in and through historical experience. Israel's corporate memory and sense of corporate identity did not exist without historical experience; there was nothing abstract or speculative about their faith. As Paul Ricoeur makes plain, the people of Israel accorded a primacy to history in multiple senses and at different levels, and respected 'the precedence of event over system'.[37] In a basic sense, all Yahweh's relations to Israel were signified through historical events. This is similar to what Ricoeur calls the level of 'founding events', e.g., the deliverance from the Red Sea, the revelation at Sinai, God's choosing of David, the exile and return. In a secondary sense, their theological reflection upon these events produced a theologically ordered history, or 'interpreting tradition'.[38] In a further sense, the work of interpreting tradition continues for each generation.[39] The intellectual activity that shaped Israel's corporate memory and identity was born of historical faith, and unfolded within a confessional framework. Ancient Hebrew theology presupposed the prevenient grace of God in the concrete events of history. Each

---

37. Paul Ricoeur, *The Conflict of Interpretations*, ed. Don Ihde (Evanston, IL: Northwestern University Press, 1974), p. 47.

38. Ricoeur dubs this the level of constituting traditions, referring to the ways in which the people of Israel are, time and again, called to remember certain events and to consider their significance.

39. This is what Ricoeur calls the level of constituted tradition, by which he means that each new generation was to take their significance to heart and, in so doing, to locate itself within a living tradition. Ricoeur, *Conflict of Interpretations*, p. 46.

new generation in Israel had the responsibility of becoming Israel. Each new generation is summoned to gratitude for what Yahweh has done, and is reminded not to forget his benefits: 'These commandments which I give you this day are to be remembered and taken to heart; repeat them to your children, and speak of them both indoors and out of doors, when you lie down and when you get up' (Deut. 6:6–7 *REB*). In urging the people to remember, Moses continually recreates the people of Israel as the unified subject of a narrative history. Yahweh's commandments to their forebears did not remain simply in the past, because memory brought them into play with the present and, in so doing, shaped their identity as a people in every generation.

Connections between healing and corporate responsibility

In Christian ethics, however, we need to take the study of corporate memory one step further in order to grasp the connection between healing and corporate responsibility. Consider the following scenario. A gospel meeting-house, on the outskirts of a national park, in a small village where there are building restrictions due to the exceptional natural beauty of the area, is due to close in the near future.[40] The meeting-house has had a strong family tradition, its members being largely drawn from two families, linked by marriage. In the 1970s, and subsequently, the strong family ethos detracted from any perceived need to build links with the wider community. Poor relationships with the village were compounded when the daughter of one family wanted to marry a non-meeting-house-going boy. Pressure from the family eventually persuaded her not to marry him, but the trauma of the experience resulted in her never going to the chapel again. Nearly forty years later, the number of members at the meeting-house is now so few that it has ceased to be viable, and the pastor is shortly to conduct the last service. Many factors have contributed to its decline, but the minister observes that the gradual dwindling of the

---

40. Again, details have been changed in order to protect anonymity.

congregation owes a lot to 'the meeting-house over against the community' ethos, and that this separateness of meeting-house from community life can be traced back over several generations. The members, he comments sadly, have not lived up to their corporate responsibility to confess the gospel in a credible way.

This scenario raises for us questions which are central to the task of Christian ethics. They are questions about the architectonics of corporate responsibility, by which I mean the way an understanding of corporate responsibility is put together, how members forge the kind of tentative wholeness that we call church in a given place.[41] What constitutes the inner connectedness of the members of a congregation and their unity of answerability?[42] What weakens or destroys the unity of answerability, given that bad or painful memories often block effective communication? In the above scenario, the memory of the relevant persons and families differed radically, and affected the ways in which they valued and evaluated events in the past. The family memory, and residual pain caused by the ill-fated romance, had become part of its corporate axiology, i.e., its assessment of values. For the meeting-house families, the painful memory of the supposed mistake and disaffection of one of their daughters altered how they valued contact with other families in the village. As the years passed, the memory became less immediate but was still silently invoked to make their responsibilities for ministry in the village easier. However, as the pastor and some members now realise, it will not do to invoke corporate memory, albeit painful, in order to justify want of answerability; any church, chapel, or meeting-house needs to be answerable through and through, at every stage of its life, although this is not easy, because answerability entails guilt, or liability to blame.[43] Nor will it do to ignore corporate memory, in

---

41. I draw on Bakhtin's ideas about the architectonics of answerability in *Art and Answerability*, pp. 1–3.

42. See Bakhtin, *Art and Answerability*, p. 1.

43. See again Bakhtin, *Art and Answerability*, p. 1.

the hope that it will cease to matter, or that the pain will go away. Only repentance and forgiveness enables both acceptance of guilt and freedom from the past. It has long been a tenet of the moral theology of penance that we cannot receive the forgiveness or friendship of God except on the condition of repentance, because it is repentance that strengthens the structures of responsible Christian action. The architectonics of corporate responsibility, just as much as the architectonics of personal responsibility, include readiness to be accountable, the need for healing of memories, and time for amendment. Unless the church lives this reality, it will be unable to preach it with conviction.

With this in mind, it is worth noting that the word memory has its source in the Indo-European root *smer* or *mer*, through which it is related to the root words for mourning. It is not linked (at least primarily) to the Indo-European root *men*, meaning to think, which is the source of mnemonic, amnesia, memento, reminiscence, mind and mental.[44] That memory is, to some extent, a work of mourning is evident in the bible. Consider the book of Ezekiel, where the prophet helps those in exile to mourn the loss of their homeland and all things familiar, and to come to terms with the past, before preparing for their return to Jerusalem. The scroll given to Ezekiel contained dirges, laments and words of woe (Ezek. 2:9–10). He was to be a prophet who mourned, although, when he opened his mouth to eat the scroll, it tasted as sweet as honey to him (Ezek. 3:1–3). Like many who minister to those who have suffered loss, Ezekiel knew that the people might harden their hearts and refuse to accept their need to face the truth (Ezek. 3:7). He knew the dangers of denial, in which persons suffering

---

44. This information is given in A. Charles Catania, *Learning* (New Jersey: Prentice-Hall, Inc., 1992), p. 302. It is supported by *Webster's Third New International Dictionary* (Chicago: Encyclopaedia Britannica, Inc., 1961) which traces a derivation for the word 'memory' from Greek *mermera*, meaning trouble resulting from anxious care, and links this derivation to ancient ceremonies for commemoration of the dead.

loss extinguish their grief by denying that the relationship had been of value to them.[45] Much of the book seems almost brutally forceful in urging the people accept what really happened in the past. He knew, however, that unless the truth of the past was confronted honestly, it would imprison or burden them. Thus he ties a large tile to himself and paints on it a picture of a city under siege, with battering-rams on every side. He lies under a heavy weight for 390 days because the sins of the past are like a burden that restricts movement of the body (Ezek. 4:1–8). In the chapters that follow, Ezekiel faces the people with the truth of what happened in their own and previous generations. He reviews the history of the nation, explains how God stayed his anger over many generations (Ezek. 20), and condemns them for having ceased to acknowledge the Lord as God and for having followed wicked ways. He calls the people to account (Ezek. 34:20) before the judgement of God, knowing that only God's acceptance and forgiveness will restore new life to them (Ezek. 37). The work of mourning, says Blanchot, is the inverse of dying.[46] Mourning becomes *poesis* or making, and can have healing effect. So too for Ezekiel, corporate memory, corporate mourning, corporate accountability and the healing of corporate memory, are integrally related.

But the connection between corporate memory, healing and corporate responsibility becomes yet more difficult. The Old Testament has more to say about their entanglement. Consider, for example, the several instances in which the community is held

---

45. Nussbaum describes the problems associated with this kind of mourning at a personal level. She says that a person can mourn in a way that cuts short or extinguishes the natural process of grief, and veers away from accepting the loss because it causes too much pain. This person restructures her memory or 'cognitive commitments', refusing to admit that she once valued someone supremely. See Martha Nussbaum, *The Therapy of Desire: Theory and Practice in Hellenistic Ethics* (New Jersey: Princeton, 1994), p. 385.
46. Noted by Gillian Rose, *Mourning Becomes the Law* (Cambridge, CUP, 1997), p. 104.

liable for actions committed by individual members. God often inflicts punishment on groups of people because an individual has erred, exacting retribution within and across generations. In Gen. 3, God curses humankind because of the deception of the serpent and the sin of Adam and Eve: 'To the woman he said: "I shall give you great labour in childbearing . . . You will desire your husband, and he will be your master." And to the man he said: " . . . on your account the earth will be cursed. You will get your food from it only by labour . . ." ' (Gen. 3:16b–17 *REB*). In Exod. 7 – 9, the people of Egypt suffer from foul water, swarms of flies, festering boils etc., because of Pharaoh's obstinacy. In Deut. 20:15–18, the people of Israel are to place six nations under solemn ban (Hittites, Amorites, Canaanites, Perizzites, Hivites, Jebusites), leaving not one soul alive, so that they may not teach the Israelites to imitate their abominable practices. In 2 Kgs 21:1–18, the Lord decided to bring disaster on all Judah because of the abominable things King Manasseh had done, the implication being that the exile is attributed to Manasseh's sin. There are, of course, form-historical, redactional and literary issues to be addressed in each of these instances. For example, what kind of aetiology is functioning in Gen. 3? Who wrote the Deuteronomic history, and is Manasseh the foil against whom to measure the achievements of Josiah?[47] We cannot evade the fact, however, that the Old Testament records many instances where God inflicts corporate punishment on a group because an individual errs (Josh. 7 tells of how Achan stole booty and was punished; 2 Kgs 5:27 recounts how Naaman's leprosy fastened on Gehazi and his descendants for ever; 1 Sam. 2:34 records Yahweh's vow that no one in Eli's house will attain to old age because of the sins of Hophni and Phinehas).

---

47. This is investigated by Kaminsky, *Corporate Responsibility in the Hebrew Bible*, ch. 3. See also his 'Retributional Chart', which lists forty-one Old Testament examples of punishment that either extend across several generations or spread across a single generation to include innocent people (pp. 190–191).

Similarly, God inflicts punishment on the people of Israel because their rulers or leaders err (2 Sam. 24).

To the modern, liberal eye, this makes uncomfortable reading. Our post-Enlightenment, individualist bias, leads us to assume the theological inferiority of passages in which God exacts punishment in uni- or trans-generational ways.[48] Is it possible, however, that we leap to this assumption too quickly, and that passages of scripture may yet have power to critique certain modern/post-modern assumptions about what corporate responsibility entails? Theologians of liberation answer this question with a resounding 'yes', having demonstrated time and again that sin deals death to people across and within generations. We, in the so-called First World, they argue, don't know how to handle the fact that our sin deals death to the innocent of the Two-Thirds world.[49] Such suffering, writes Jon Sobrino, is massive. It affects the majority of humanity, making it practically impossible for people to direct their own lives: 'For liberation theology, the major form of suffering in today's world is historical – suffering unjustly inflicted

---

48. We should also be aware of inner-biblical debates about sin and its consequences within and across the generations. Compare Ezek. 14:12–14: 'This word of the LORD came to me: "O man, when a country sins by breaking faith with me, I stretch out my hand and cut short its daily bread. I send famine on it and destroy all their inhabitants, along with their cattle. Even if these three men, Noah, Daniel, and Job, were there, they would by their righteousness save none but themselves" ' (*REB*) with Ezek. 18: 1–4: 'This word of the LORD came to me: "What do you all mean by repeating this proverb in the land of Israel: Parents eat sour grapes, and their children's teeth are set on edge? As I live, says the LORD God, this proverb will never again be used by you in Israel. Every living soul belongs to me; parent and child alike are mine. It is the person who sins that will die" ' (*REB*). There is debate going on within the Ezekiel tradition about whether or not God visits the sins of parents upon children. Nor is this kind of debate found only in Ezekiel. Compare Lev. 26:39–40 which asserts both that the Lord will punish those who survive the trials of the wilderness because of their forebears' iniquities, and that the Lord will remember the covenant with Israel if the people confess their own iniquities and those of their forebears.

49. See Jon Sobrino, *Principle of Mercy* (Maryknoll, NY: Orbis, 1994), p. 6.

on some by others.'[50] He suggests this is true on a micro as well as a macro scale. It is not only at global level that we need a nuanced practical theology that takes account of the individual's responsibility to the community. At a local level also, we need to grasp the connection between the healing of corporate memory and corporate responsibility.

In Christian ethics, however, corporate memory is never simply about the past but interplays with the present and the future. Jesus' command, 'do this in memory of me', is repeated at most, if not all, Christian celebrations of the eucharist. Christians cannot live without memory of Jesus Christ, but the eucharist draws us forwards into the future rather than backwards into the past. It receives meaning from the future. McPartlan encapsulates this nicely in his sense of the eucharist as 'memory of the future'.[51] By this he implies that only the future kingdom of God gives continuity to time; the memory of the church matters, not only because the significance of the past is carried into the present, but because the significance of the past is given to the church from the future. Celebration of the eucharist does not have a simple chronology because commemoration of Jesus Christ is bound up with the mystery of the coming kingdom. Memory matters eschatologically, and the remembrance of Jesus' death and resurrection is simultaneously the announcing of a sign of victory and the anticipation, or tasting, of the coming kingdom, as if it were already here. In the priestly ministry of the church, therefore, celebration of the eucharist does not have a simple chronology, because it brings present, past and future into intimate relation. Most eucharistic liturgies contain some form of the words, 'this is my blood of the new covenant ... Whenever you drink it, do this in memory of me' (paraphrasing 1 Cor. 11:25). Theologically, this connects every celebration of the eucharist with Jesus' last

---

50. Sobrino, *Principle of Mercy*, p. 29.
51. Paul McPartlan, *The Eucharist Makes the Church: Henri de Lubac and John Zizioulas in Dialogue* (Edinburgh: T. & T. Clark, 1993), pp. 220–221.

supper. John Chrysostom says people 'might be disposed now as if on that very evening, reclining on that very couch, and receiving this sacrifice from Christ himself'.[52] It joins the local church to the whole body of Christ, including the entire community of saints, living and departed. Most eucharistic liturgies contain some form of the words: 'For every time you eat this bread and drink the cup, you proclaim the death of the Lord, until he comes' (paraphrasing 1 Cor. 11:26).

This is important because, of itself, the church has no strength or authority to be such a witness or to exercise a priestly ministry. The church can only 'do this in memory' of Jesus because God has first remembered it. This answer is prefigured in the Old Testament which speaks of the memory of God, in relation to which all human memory is experienced as relative. Moses does not only exhort the people to remember Yahweh, but also prays that Yahweh would remember his servants Abraham, Isaac and Jacob, and for their sake overlook the wickedness of their descendants (Deut. 8:18, 9:6–7, 9:27). Yahweh, says Moses, will never forget the covenant made with their forebears. Therefore, they should not forget their covenant obligations (Deut. 4:31). The High Priest bore the names of the tribes of Israel on the shoulder-pieces of the ephod as reminders of the children of Israel before Yahweh (Exod. 28:12, 29–30; 39:6–7). The psalmist prays that the Lord will remember the offerings of David (Pss. 20:3, 109:14).[53] Israel is drawn into a dialectic of remembrance in which their remembrance of Yahweh's prior remembrance of them binds them into a community, and makes them conscious of corporate responsibility. That God has first remembered us is also implied in Jesus'

---

52. John Chrysostom, *Homilies on First Corinthians*, Homily XXVII, 3. Cited in Daniel J. Sheerin, *The Eucharist*, Messages of the Fathers of the Church 7 (Delaware: Michael Glazier, 1986), p. 214.

53. Gerhard von Rad makes the link between these passages in *Old Testament Theology*, Vol. 1, pp. 242–243. The context for these references is the cultic activity in which Yahweh decides whether Israel's sin is to be remembered or not.

eucharistic teaching in Jn 6, where he affirms it is God's will that none of those given to him by God should be lost (Jn 6:35–40), and states that none can come to him unless drawn by God (Jn 6:44). Paul speaks about holy communion as 'the Lord's supper' (1 Cor. 11:20), implying that he is the one who invites guests to eat and drink. This is the ultimate corrective to any fiction, or inauthentic legitimising of historical narratives in terms of privilege and power. It is a vital aspect of ecclesial Christian life which presupposes the ethical imitation of Christ by the community

The Royal Dimension

Imagery associated with royalty, like most words borrowed from human relations, is frequently problematic when speaking about God. The language of kingship or royalty has considerable capacity to alienate, not least because of unfortunate associations for women who feel excluded and for republicans who favour government in which the chief of state is not a monarch. How, then, are we to interpret this royal imagery in Christian ethics today? In what follows, I suggest that, despite its problematic nature, the ethico-theological principles to which it bears witness remain of significance to contemporary Christian ethics. In particular, we shall consider how royal imagery has functioned traditionally to speak both of freedom from the passions which destroy the health of body and soul, and of the virtue of discernment. In so doing, it is worth remembering that, when Pilate confused Jesus' royal authority with his own notions of empire and government, Jesus answered: ' "King" is your word. My task is to bear witness to the truth' (Jn 18:37b *REB*). Jesus' communication of his kingship was always indirect, being revealed pre-eminently at the cross: 'They put a reed in his right hand and knelt before him and mocked him, saying, "Hail, King of the Jews!" ' (Matt. 27:29b). His subversive truth was visible only to those who had eyes to see. Kierkegaard speaks in *Practice in Christianity* of Jesus being like a policeman in plain clothes, incognito, and not in the character of what he was. Likewise, he warns, the church should be wary of claiming or displaying the authority of kingship, not only because kingship and victory in the church only ever belong to Christ, but also because his royal authority manifests judgement on ungodliness.

Royal dignity? freedom from passions which destroy

How, then, are we to make sense of royal imagery in Christian ethics today? Gregory of Nyssa answers the question in terms of how the divine truth of kingship was known to humankind at creation:

> For seeing that man by the commission of the Divine blessing had been elevated to a lofty pre-eminence (for he was appointed king over the earth and all things on it; he was beautiful in his form, being created an image of the archetypal beauty; he was without passion in his nature, for he was an imitation of the unimpassioned; he was full of frankness, delighting in a face-to-face manifestation of the personal Deity), – all this was to the adversary the fuel to his passion of envy.[54]

God the Creator had blessed Adam and Eve with intellectual power in order that they might co-operate with God in the work of the garden, though Satan had persuaded them to turn these endowments towards vice and deceit. They were granted certain powers over the animal and plant life and were 'without passion' in their nature. In other words, they were not subject to the necessities of mortality relating to food, reproduction and death. John of Damascus likens the royal dignity of the first humans to that of God because they were made in God's image:

> Now when God was about to fashion man out of the visible

---

54. Gregory of Nyssa, *The Great Catechism*, ch. VI, *NPNF* Second Series, Vol. V, p. 481.

and invisible creation in His own image and likeness to reign as king and ruler over all the earth and all that it contains, He first made for him, so to speak, a kingdom in which he should live a life of happiness and prosperity.[55]

Eden's luxuriousness was 'fit for a king or queen'. Its air was sweet and the garden was flooded with light. Adam and Eve lived in a 'sensuous freshness and beauty' which transcends our imagination. Eden was a place divine; 'a meet home for him who was created in God's image'. They were free from the ascendancy of evil; their dispositions were not bound by any violent desires or passions. Moreover, this is the dignity restored to believers who, by virtue of God's grace, enjoy participation in Christ's kingship.

We must be careful here because the 'unimpassioned' existence which ancient writers equate with the royal dignity which the Christian gains in Christ can be easily misunderstood. It can be mistaken to mean that bodily existence is inferior to life of the soul, and that the royal dignity of the Christian involves a dualistic subordination of the former to the latter. Origen of Alexandria's (c. 185–254) anthropology suggested that the human body is essentially spirit, and that the soul's acquisition of a physical body represents a fall from an earlier perfection. Origen tends to ask more questions in his work than he answers definitively, and it is not always clear how and why the fifteen anathemas associated with the Second Council of Constantinople (AD 553) are targeted against his teaching. Yet De Principiis certainly leaves open the highly problematic suggestion that bodily existence represents a degradation from a purely spiritual state:

> If, however, it is impossible for this point to be at all main-tained, viz., that any other nature than the Father, Son, and Holy Spirit can live without a body, the necessity of logical reasoning compels us to understand that rational natures

---

55. John of Damascus, *An Exposition of the Orthodox Faith*, Bk II, ch. XI, 'Concerning Paradise', *NPNF* Second Series, Vol. IX, p. 29.

were indeed created at the beginning, but that material substance was separated from them only in thought and understanding, and appears to have been formed for them, or after them, and that they never have lived nor do live without it; for an incorporeal life will rightly be considered a prerogative of the Trinity alone. As we have remarked above, therefore, that material substance of this world, possessing a nature admitting of all possible transformations, is, when dragged down to beings of a lower order, moulded into the crasser and more solid condition of a body, so as to distinguish those visible and varying forms of the world; but when it becomes the servant of more perfect and more blessed beings, it shines in the splendour of celestial bodies, and adorns either the angels of God or the sons of the resurrection with the clothing of a spiritual body, out of all which will be filled up the diverse and varying state of the one world.[56]

He suggests that body and soul are created at different times, that beings fall into a state of material substance, and that they can return to their former glory when the 'corruptible puts on incorruption', i.e., at the resurrection of the dead when the resurrected body is clothed with the Wisdom and the Word of God. The resurrection of the dead is interpreted to be an incorporeal existence for which there will be no need of bodies: 'bodily matter returns to nothing, as formerly also it did not exist'.[57] Only then will the soul return to its rest, repaired and corrected, to regain its proper status and dignity.[58]

---

56. Origen, *De Principiis*, Bk II, ch. II, §1, *ANF*, Vol. IV, p. 270.

57. Origen, *De Principiis*, Bk II, ch. III, §3, *ANF*, Vol. IV, p. 272.

58. Origen, *De Principiis*, Bk II, ch. VIII, §3, *ANF*, Vol. IV, pp. 287–288. Origen's 'spiritualist' heresy has a modern counterpart in René Descartes's idea of the body as a machine. For Descartes, nature is discovered through thought. The nature of the body lay in its extension, the space it occupied. At creation, he argued, God formed the external shape of the body of man and configured its internal organs, but did not, at first, place in it a rational soul – nor a ▷

John Chrysostom does not succumb to Origen's 'spiritualist' heresy but offers a different answer to the question of how royal imagery might function in Christian ethics today which, arguably, speaks as much to the present day as to his own. The royal liberty of the Christian, he says, is to have a well-ordered mind and a body which is a Christ-bearing temple.[59] A well-ordered mind has authority over the body in so far as a person is not subject to the whims of preposterous passion which ruin their health, is not a slave of pleasure or in bondage to activities which corrupt the soul, is not oppressed by consciousness of evil deeds, is not cast down in despair amidst calamity, does not live at such a pitch of folly that they overlook the things that are important, is not plunged into the Satanic recklessness which often follows from indolence and contempt for one's fellows, and is not tossed about in the turmoils of life so that their life lacks direction. According to Chrysostom, authority over the body has nothing to do with its inferiority to the soul, because the body participates as much as the soul in the honours of royal splendour; the whole person bears the marks of the royal image with which they were born. The body can be the source of theoretical knowledge; personal experience of asceticism may encourage a person to trust in the power of repentance. Moreover, the body, like the soul will rise at the day of resurrection in like manner to Christ's resurrection body (Matt. 27:52–53; 1 Cor. 15:17–19):

> For the very same body [Christ's] which fell in death, and which lay in the sepulchre, did also rise again; (and it was) not so much Christ in the flesh, as the flesh in Christ. If,

---

vegetative or sensitive soul. It was wholly void of reason. Only after creation of the body did God create a rational soul and annex it to the body. (See *Discourse on the Method of Rightly Conducting the Reason, and Seeking Truth in the Sciences* (Yale: YUP, 1996), ch. 5, *passim*.

59. John Chrysostom, *Two Exhortations to Theodore after His Fall*, Letter I, §1, *NPNF* First Series, Vol. IX, p. 91. The following sentences paraphrase lines from these letters.

> therefore, we are to rise again after the example of Christ,
> who rose in the flesh, we shall certainly not rise according to
> that example, unless we also shall ourselves rise again in the
> flesh.[60]

The resurrection of the body is not an accidental afterthought;
the body is not dragged along on the skirts of the superior soul,
but will appear united with the soul before the throne of God.
Each without the other is useless. The physical body is mortal,
but will be raised in union with the soul to receive a crown of
blessing. Thus, authority over the body should be understood as
the mutual enabling of the other to grow. The body makes it
possible for the soul to grow in the likeness of God as the soul
makes it possible for the body to do the same. Each participates
in the other's deification as, together, united hypostatically, they
render service to God.

The royal dignity of Christians is thus manifest in freedom from
the kind of 'passions' which claim what John Cassian describes as
'dominion and a most horrible tyranny in our mortal body'.[61] He
lists eight evil passions which lead to principal faults in a person's
life, as follows:

> first, Gluttony or the pleasures of the palate; secondly, Forni-
> cation; thirdly, Covetousness, which means Avarice, or, as it
> may more properly be called, the love of money; fourthly,
> Anger; fifthly, Dejection; sixthly, 'Accidie', which is heaviness
> or weariness of heart; seventhly, *kenodoxa* which means
> foolish or vain Glory; eighthly, Pride.[62]

The exact composition of the list is less important than the sense
it conveys of how these passions can be recognised by everybody,

---

60. Tertullian, *On the Resurrection of the Flesh*, ch. XLVIII, *ANF*, Vol. III, p. 581.
61. John Cassian, *The Twelve Books of John Cassian on the Institutes of the Coenobia, and the Remedies for the Eight Principal Faults*, Bk V, ch. II, *NPNF* Second Series, Vol. XI, pp. 233–234.
62. Cassian, *Institutes and Remedies*, pp. 233–234.

how they inflame the mind and hinder right thinking. We should remember that John Cassian was an ascetic monk who wrote for his fellows; his specific recommendations may not be applicable directly to a present-day ethic. However, we may still learn from the way he distinguishes between the proper exercise of the desires of the body, and passions which are to be avoided because of their harmful effects. For example, hunger should be satisfied and the body cared for, according to specific needs, but gluttony should be avoided because it is an incentive to vice. Note the careful manner in which he attends to the differing needs of differing people while simultaneously specifying that harmful passions should not be indulged:

> The sickly food of moistened beans does not agree with everybody: nor does a sparing diet of fresh vegetables suit all, nor is a scanty meal of dry bread permitted to all alike. One man does not feel satisfied with two pounds, for another a meal of one pound, or six ounces, is too much; but there is one aim and object of continence in the case of all of these, viz.: that no one may be overburdened beyond the measure of his appetite, by gluttony.[63]

There is an appropriate care for the body and its nourishment which finds its fulfilment in good food, but this is not the same as eating 'according to the flesh', i.e., eating with unbounded licence rather than taking just what the body demands. The same principle holds true for the fathers in other matters also. Thus John Chrysostom recommends sensible but not expensive clothing; an excessively adorned woman was 'more unseemly than if she had been naked; for she had not modesty'.[64] Similarly with regard to the sexual relations of spouses. The sexual aspects of life are not to be devalued. Patristic writers repeatedly refer to Heb. 13:4,

---

63. Cassian, *Institutes and Remedies*, pp. 235.
64. John Chrysostom, *Homilies on Colossians*, Homily X, Commentary on Col. 4:3, *NPNF Second Series*, Vol. XIII, p. 308.

'Let marriage be held in honour by all, and let the marriage bed be kept undefiled; for God will judge fornicators and adulterers.'[65] Despite the belief held by some that abstinence from sex was an aid to spiritual growth, and that the ideal of virginity led to a 'mystique of continence', none debarred the married Christian from perfection.[66] In general, the lamentable lack of positive comments about sexual relations in the patristic writings is problematic for those seeking an adequate sexual ethic for our own day. The distinction, however, between appropriate and inappropriate exercise of the desires of the body, and the clear explanations as to why only the former belongs to the royal dignity of Christians, remain of vital significance in Christian ethics today.

On the virtue of discernment

Integral to the 'royal' dignity of Christian persons is the virtue of discernment (1 Kgs 3:16–28). Discernment (Greek *diakrisis*, *dia*, meaning through and *krisis* from *krinein*, to separate or to decide; Latin *discernere* from *dis* meaning thoroughly, and *cernere*, to sift or perceive) is something that few find easy in any kind of ethics. At a personal level, few are able, without considerable preparation, to give a well-reasoned account of how they make moral decisions. People use many different processes to come to what they think are appropriate decisions. 'I've a gut feeling . . .' 'I wouldn't like it

---

65. Clement of Alexandria, *The Stromata, or Miscellanies*, Book IV, ch. 20, *ANF*, Vol. II, p. 432.

66. John Chrysostom writes: 'For marriage and mixture of bodies is that wherein the communion consists.' John Chrysostom, *Homilies on First Corinthians*, Homily XIX on 1 Cor. 7:1–2, *NPNF* Second Series, Vol. XIII, p. 107. Clement of Alexandria writes: 'It becomes us who truly follow the Scripture to enjoy ourselves temperately, as in Paradise. We must regard the woman's crown to be her husband, and the husband's crown to be marriage; and the flowers of marriage the children of both, which the divine husbandman plucks from meadows of flesh. "Children's children are the crown of old men." ' *The Instructor*, Bk II, ch. VIII, *ANF*, Vol. II, p. 256.

if she did it, so I suppose . . .' 'I remember grandfather saying once . . .' 'The bible says . . .' are the sorts of phrases in common usage. Each could almost be described as a form of moral reasoning *in nuce*. Some are emotive. Some adopt a 'do as you would be done by' approach. Others appeal to traditionally received wisdom, which may or may not be religious. At a societal level, similar difficulties pertain, as in a plural society rival traditions vie for a validity that none can claim any longer prima facie. All of which means that the virtue of discernment is often reduced to 'making it up as we go along'. Nor is the exercise of discernment easy in Christian ethics. The accusation often thrown against the church is that discernment in Christian ethics means little more than learning to do what is required. Thus, in a letter to Dracontius, Bishop of Hermupolis Parva, Athanasius warns of the likely moral dangers that might be incurred in contradicting or denying an ordinance of the church.[67] Dracontius faces difficult decisions about how to act in the face of increasing political pressure and even persecution, and Athanasius urges him to walk by the standard of the saints and to imitate them without compromise while listening to his conscience. Is not your conscience 'a fire'? he asks. Does it not prick in your soul? Such teaching could easily be interpreted as Athanasius urging Dracontius to internalise external authority in blind obedience.

Like Dracontius, many Christian people find the exercise of discernment difficult. Tensions arise between personal 'royal' freedom in Christ and Christian formation according to the guidance of the church. How, then, are we to heed Jesus' words: 'Do not judge by appearances, but judge with right judgement' (Jn 7:24)? There are several ways in which this question can be approached. In what follows, I suggest that an important axiom around which to order an answer to this question is found in the biblical injunction: 'Choose life so that you and your descendants may live' (Deut. 30:19b). At a time when much contemporary

---

67. Athanasius, Letter XLIX, *NPNF* Second Series, Vol. IV, p. 558.

post-Christian feminism and 'New Spirituality' attempts to distinguish that which tends to death rather than life, I argue that this same concern is a characteristic of Christian ethics.[68] Christian ethics is life-affirming and health-giving, though much more realistically so than the ethics espoused by either of the above because only the former takes adequate account of the effects of sin and the reality of the human condition. So, what sense are we to make of the divine injunction 'choose life'? This injunction or command was given by God to ancient Israel though, as Walter Brueggemann acknowledges, Israel did not always choose well. Nor were its choices necessarily of the kind faced by liberally minded individuals in advanced capitalist societies. Significantly, however, they kept their testimony to the need to choose between life and death, blessing and curse: 'The choosing between construals of reality is something Israel always had to do again. And the choosing is not yet finished.'[69] Of itself the injunction 'choose life' does not provide terms or categories with which to adjudicate moral dilemmas. Arguably, however, it provides some guidance

---

68. 'New Spirituality' is the term given by Linda Woodhead to the multiple forms of spirituality that now pervade western culture. She writes: 'The New Spirituality has been given all sorts of different renderings – from Theosophy to Beat Zen, from the Advaita Vedanta of Vivekananda to the gentle mysticism of Tagore, from the political élitism of Hermann Keyserling to recent religious renderings of Deep Ecology. Yet this diversity should not be allowed to conceal an equally striking agreement between different manifestations of the New Spirituality. While the elements which usually unify a religion like community and cultus are fragmented in the New Spirituality, its underlying world-view or religio-philosophical scheme is remarkably (even mind-numbingly) consistent.' She lists five main consistencies: (i) all is one: this-worldly monism; (ii) one with the all: sacralisation of self and nature; (iii) the authority of individual experience and the rejection of institutional religion; (iv) religious universalism; and (v) radical evolutionary optimism. See Linda Woodhead, 'Sophia or Gnosis? Christianity and New Age Spirituality' in Stephen C. Barton, (ed.), *Where Shall Wisdom be Found?* (Edinburgh: T. & T. Clark, 1999), ch. 18, *passim*.

69. Walter Brueggemann, *Theology of the Old Testament: Testimony, Dispute, Advocacy* (Minneapolis: Fortress Press, 1997), p. 562.

for a Christian ethic with respect to the virtue of discernment in ways that are much more relevant to the human condition than the best efforts of post-Christian feminism, the many varieties of 'New Spirituality' or godless morality.

Choosing life

What, then, is required in order to clarify what is and is not right judgement in particular situations? Why and how is the virtue of discernment linked to the choosing of life? Such questions do not lend themselves to simple answers, not least because the injunction 'choose life' seems at one level to be overturned by Jesus' words:

> If any want to become my followers, let them deny themselves and take up their cross and follow me. For those who want to save their life will lose it, and those who lose their life for my sake, and for the sake of the gospel, will save it. (Mk 8:34–35)

Allegiance to Christ relativises all other commitments and concerns, even that for life itself, leaving no room for the pursuit of security, comfort and prestige. The radicalism of Jesus' teaching demands a disregard for physical well-being and the well-being of one's family (Matt. 10:34–39). How is this to be reconciled with the Old Testament injunction, 'choose life'? At first glance, one injunction seems to be cancelled out by the other. Upon closer inspection, the connections between the two are obvious and important and concern the different kinds of death to which humankind is subject. The death rejected in Deut. 30:19 is that of life bereft of the blessing of God (Deut. 11:26–28, 23:5, 28:1–68). Israel's choosing between life and death was not primarily about obedience to external laws but about a relationship with God which exceeded both the state of being compliant and the performance of duty. Similarly, the death rejected in Jesus' teaching is that which belongs to the fallen human condition and separates humankind from God:

'Very truly, I tell you, unless a grain of wheat falls into the earth and dies, it remains just a single grain; but if it dies, it bears much fruit. Those who love their life lose it, and those who hate their life in this world will keep it for eternal life.'

(Jn 12:24–25)

Many early Christians interpreted the radicalism of Jesus' words in concrete and specific ways.[70] Many monks and martyrs literally renounced family, wealth, security and social standing, for the sake of the coming kingdom. Today we might not imitate their practice, and, indeed, counsel against the extremes to which they drove themselves. Yet the theological principle that choosing life entails dying to death and sin remains both vital and valid.

Revisiting the canons of the early church

We need to be very clear at this point about what constitutes 'choosing life' and 'dying to death and sin' in the mind of the church. Too often the fact that 'choosing life' entails death to oneself as conditioned by sin is interpreted as self-abnegation and denial of the person. Many critics of Christianity accuse the church of preaching death, fear and gloom, and it is a desperately sad reflection upon the church when such criticisms carry credibility. All the more reason, therefore, for Christian testimony to be clear about the fact that to 'choose life' is to seek relationship with the Author of life, and that to die to death is not to negate one's authentic personal existence but to pass out of existence subject to the impulses of sin. In this regard, the ancient canons of the church, the regulations or dogmas decreed by a church council, may yet be of assistance to us.[71] There are many aspects of the

---

70. For examples, see Peter Brown, *The Body and Society: Men, Women and Sexual Renunciation in Early Christianity* (London and Boston: Faber & Faber, 1988), esp. ch. 11.

71. Yannaras suggests as much in *The Freedom of Morality* (Crestwood, NY: St Vladimir's Seminary Press, 1984), p. 182: 'We, perhaps, may see in these canons a system of law. But the Byzantines saw in them the preconditions and ▷

ancient canons that we might find very problematic today, not least the language of punishment and paternalism that suggests, at best, fatherly benevolence and, at worst, the kind of authoritarian oppression that results in psychologically damaged church members. We cannot simply ignore such language and convictions which border on the horrifying, nor be comfortable with the sometimes rigorist interpretations of the need for discipline and purity.[72] Nor should we place too much emphasis on regulations which confine their witness to Christ within culture-bound restrictions, e.g., canon XVIII of the Apostolic Canons states that whoever has married a widow, or a divorced woman, or an actress, cannot be a bishop, presbyter or deacon. Many strands of Christian tradition have not held this canon's standards to be binding. Similarly, the rule stated in canon LIV that a clergyman be excommunicated if found eating in a tavern, unless constrained by the necessity of a long journey, would leave most traditions and denominations very short of presbyteral leaders if it were to be applied to the letter today. However, it is arguable that if we jettison the canons utterly from the task of Christian ethics, then we risk losing important witnesses to relationships between bodily, mental and spiritual health, and to important criteria in the exercise of right judgement.

It is, perhaps, difficult for Christian persons schooled in western traditions to perceive the benefits that might still accrue from re-reading the ancient canons of the church. It might appear as if Christian ethics is being reduced to the learning of ecclesial regulations rather than being about the response of personal freedom to the grace of God, and as if Christian ethics comprises 'oughts' derived from a rigid formalism or legalism. This is most definitely

---

possibilities for an ascetic realisation of personal freedom and distinctiveness, for the real manifestation of the beauty of life.'

72. NB: rigorist positions tended to be held by western rather than eastern theologians. Tertullian argued the first duty of the church to fallen sinners was severity. See *On Repentance*, *ANF*, Vol. III, pp. 657ff.

not what is intended. Rather, what is of interest is how the ancient canons of the church have 'choosing life' at their heart. This is particularly evident in their concern for the cure of souls as, for example, in canon II of the so-called Quinisext council of AD 692 which explains that the canons of earlier councils had been handed down 'for the cure of souls and the healing of disorders'. Canon XII affirms that apostolic teaching was established 'for the health of the people', and canon CII speaks of applying medicine appropriate to the sickness of the person. The following advice is given:

> He who professes the science of spiritual medicine ought first of all to consider the disposition of him who has sinned, and to see whether he tends to health or (on the contrary) provokes to himself disease by his own behaviour, and to look how he can care for his manner of life during the interval. And if he does not resist the physician, and if the ulcer of the soul is increased by the application of the imposed medicaments, then let him mete out mercy to him according as he is worthy of it. For the whole account is between God and him to whom the pastoral rule has been delivered, to lead back the wandering sheep and to cure that which is wounded by the serpent; and that he may neither cast them down into the precipices of despair, nor loosen the bridle towards dissolution or contempt of life; but in some way or other, either by means of sternness and astringency, or by greater softness and mild medicines, to resist this sickness and exert himself for the healing of the ulcer, now examining the fruits of his repentance and wisely managing the man who is called to higher illumination. For we ought to know two things, to wit, the things which belong to strictness and those which belong to custom, and to follow the traditional form in the case of those who are not fitted for the highest things, as holy Basil teaches us.

All that is prescribed is to enable the sinner better to respond to God's immense love and enjoy a fuller human existence. Spiritual medicine is given to those in want and to persons as they can bear it.[73] The value of human life transcends material reality because its origin is in God, the implication being that to work together with God in the creating, healing, preserving, and protecting of all aspects of human life is integral to the Christian ethos.

Relatively few canons in the early centuries of the church's life dealt with moral sins, most being concerned with good order in the church's worship and polity. If, however, we look carefully at the canons which did deal with moral sins, then we see more clearly how they distinguish between that which tends to life and that which tends to death. Consider the connection that most have with the prohibitions stated in Acts 15:20, 28–29, concerning idolatry, sexual impurity, and bloodshed or lack of respect for life. These prohibitions derive from the first apostolic council of Jerusalem and the requirements placed on gentiles upon entry into the church 'to abstain only from things polluted by idols and from fornication and from whatever has been strangled and from blood'. They became the three headings, or themes, which featured most strongly in the canons of the early church as the most significant obstacles to the 'choosing of life' and the cure of souls. For example, the Council of Ancyra deals with idolatry in canons 4, 7, 8 and 12; with sexual purity in canons 11, 16, 17, 19, 20, 21 and 25; and with respect for life in 21, 22 and 23. (There are also canons which deal with general uprightness of life, e.g., 3 and 15; and with the practice of divination, e.g., 24.) There was, of course, a specific theological and ecclesiastical context for the council of Jerusalem, notably the need for unity in the church between Jews and Gentiles at a formative moment in its life. We must also distinguish between the meaning of the prohibitions in their orig-

---

73. This is reminiscent of Athanasius' concern that the requirements of the sufferers are not exceeded, because that would trouble the very persons that need God's help, and render God's appearance useless to them. Athanasius, *On the Incarnation*, §43, *NPNF* Second Series, Vol. IV, p. 59.

inal context and their meaning when read centuries later as scripture. Yet these prohibitions developed into the sins that were regarded as 'mortal', i.e., beyond the scope of the church to remit and therefore referred to God on the Great Day of Judgement.[74]

The instructions in Acts 15 concern the worship of a physical object as a god, sexual impurity, and bloodshed or lack of respect for life, and the majority of canons pertaining to morals assert that violation of these instructions obstruct the Christian's journey of moral freedom. Irenaeus speaks of instructions agreed by this council as the 'new covenant of liberty to those who had lately believed in God by the Holy Spirit'.[75] John Chrysostom remarks upon the continuity of the instructions with the teaching of Moses and Torah, noting how the apostles spoke of them as a burden.[76] For John Chrysostom, the burden of the instructions was their legal aspect: 'For these things the New Testament did not enjoin: we nowhere find that Christ discoursed about these matters; but these things they take from the Law.' Yet they were 'necessary things' commanded by the Spirit. They were not necessary in the sense of substituting for faith in Christ, but because they concerned matters relating to the body that caused great evil. This covenant of liberty contrasted with the covenant of circumcision given to Abraham and Isaac, and was linked to the fact that no persons should be dubbed common or unclean because God accepted all equally. The fact that the apostles thought it good to retain only certain requirements from the law (Torah) indicated freedom from its strictures. These requirements were retained in the ecclesial life of the 'new creation' only because they were necessary preconditions for participation in the life of Christ. They were necessary preconditions because they represented the mind

---

74. See Tertullian, *On Modesty*, chs III–V, *ANF*, Vol. IV, pp. 85–86.

75. Irenaeus, *Adversus Haereses*, Bk III, 12, §14, *ANF* Vol. I, p. 436.

76. John Chrysostom, *Homilies on the Acts of the Apostles*, Homily XXXIII, *NPNF* First Series, Vol. XI, pp. 207–208.

of the church regarding that which tended to death rather than life.

The question is whether these basic guidelines for the exercise of discernment, or right judgement, can or should be revisited by Christian ethics today. An argument against such a move is that the ancient canons represent the moralism of church leaders who think they 'know what's good for you' and use the concept of sin to secure compliance to their authority. Richard Holloway, for example, speaks of ecclesial traditions constructed by humans but linked to notions of divine disapproval which give them power over church members.[77] Evidence of this is found, he thinks, in the fact that the church continues to dictate who exactly may sleep with whom, and who may never sleep with anyone, in a 'strict rules morality' which requires subservience rather than freely given consent.[78] In a deliberate ousting of God from morality, he seeks to take morality to a 'level of arguability' in which it is not the traditions (or canons) of the church that shape decision-making but individual consent. Instead of specific guidance on moral matters, he urges liberal-minded people to apply a 'principle of harm' which requires tolerance and moderation and steers a relatively safe course in most situations of moral uncertainty. Each person is responsible for their own healing, preservation and protection, albeit with an eye to ensuring that no harm is done to others: 'We shall soon possess the dangerous freedom to shape our own future and the kind of society we want. It is this potentiality that is most frightening to people who are committed . . . to a fixed understanding of human nature and its possibilities.'[79] Within the constraints of the harm principle, each person's choice has an ultimacy of its own.

This kind of objection to revisiting the ancient canons involves

---

77. See Richard Holloway, *Godless Morality: Keeping Religion out of Ethics* (Edinburgh: Canongate, 1999), pp. 9, 18–19.

78. Holloway, *Godless Morality*, p. 158.

79. Holloway, *Godless Morality*, pp. 151–152.

a resistance at all costs to notions of divine and ecclesial authority in favour of a morality of consequences. The resistance to all absolutes requires each individual to decide for themselves. There is an obvious attraction to such a morality, providing as it does an affirmation of the principles of consent and refraining from doing harm. However, there are several problems to which such a morality is subject. Using Holloway's book as an example of this kind of approach, it is unclear as to whether morality can be sustained on the basis of mutually acceptable agreement; there are no clearly defined goals of moral judgement, no way of knowing what should move us to moral action, or of deciding how positive moral goods are to be defined. There are no clear reasons as to why a person should endeavour to refrain from harm for the sake of others. The positive suggestion is that morality is accomplished through persons agreeing one with the other.[80] But are consent and consensus sufficient criteria? What is to prevent the general will of those who have reached agreement from distortion if it functions always at a step removed from questions about what is good/evil, right/wrong? It is worth remembering that 'discourse' is a word derived from the Latin *discursus* which means running hither and thither, to-ing and fro-ing. Roland Barthes speaks of a lover's discourse as thoughts which run hither and thither, leaping about 'in a kind of lunatic sport' or gymnastics.[81] Chaos, or the threat of chaos, is never far away. In and of itself, such a morality is deficient. This said, Christian ethics recognises the importance of discourse and of doing no harm. Similarly, that discourse is embedded in Christian tradition is evidenced by Acts 15:28 which states: 'For it has seemed good to the Holy Spirit and to us to impose on you no further burden than these essentials.' The need to come to a common mind is evidenced by the long-established practice of synods and councils. Yet there are also ethical norms that provide sure guidance as to what is good/evil, right/wrong,

---

80. Holloway, *Godless Morality*, p. 34.
81. Roland Barthes, *A Lover's Discourse* (London: Jonathan Cape, 1979), p. 4.

fitting/unfitting in human life. Far from representing moralistic absolutes which override answerable self-activity, the ancient canons embody discursive norms into which is built the requirement that participants reach a common mind as befits those who abide in Christ (Jn 15: 5–15).

The term 'discursive norms' is somewhat paradoxical but expresses the kind of ethic which informs the ancient canons of the church. It describes a mutually informing relationship between the constant and clear principles which the canons express and their discursively experienced relativity to particular times and places. Of course, the principles expressed by the canons are humanly constructed, in the sense that they were agreed by the council of Jerusalem and transmitted by the church. They are normative, however, in so far as they accord with Christian confession that human beings are created by God and derive their true nature from being made in God's image. Thus the capacity to love and be in relationship is part of what it is to be human. Such principles are normative in so far as they express the mode of existence which Jesus Christ embodied. Thus agape-love and manifestations of all the other fruits of the Spirit described in Gal. 5:22 (joy, peace, patience, kindness, generosity, faithfulness, gentleness, self-control) are clear and unchanging categorisations of the behaviour appropriate to human beings. These positively expressed norms are at the centre of the Christian ethic and, arguably, are complemented by the negatively defined norms which inform the ancient canons. Yet the norms are discursive also, in the sense that their meaning and application for a given time and situation is subject to argumentation, as the common mind of the church is sought. For example, the Church of England teaches that marriage is 'indissoluble' in the sense that the promises are made unconditionally for life.[82] Yet it also recognises that, in some circumstances, a further marriage is possible after divorce,

---

82. See *Marriage: A Teaching Document* (London: Church House Publishing, 1999).

and recognises that some dioceses have drawn up experimental guidelines for consideration of whether such a marriage might be witnessed and solemnised in an act of worship. The 1999 document states that: 'the Church itself . . . has a part in deciding whether or not a marriage in such circumstances should take place in the context of church worship'. In other words, the Church of England recognises a certain amount of flexibility in response to changing pastoral needs. Christian ethics has unchanging norms regarding the importance of sexual purity, but allows for a certain openness as to what exactly this means in a given situation.[83]

Thus, it is possible to agree with Holloway that unless a moral 'ought' is rooted in answerable self-activity then it will be detached from a given person's life. To 'judge with right judgement' involves trying to ensure that judgement does not split into abstract theoretical validity versus personal conviction. This requires the judgement to be owned by a person and not to be just a moral 'ought' imposed from outside. As Bakhtin emphasises: 'It is not the content of an obligation that obligates me, but my signature below it – the fact that at one time I acknowledged or undersigned the given acknowledgement.'[84] That a judgement obligates a person wholly is more important than theoretical acknowledgement of

---

83. Under the heading 'idolatry' might belong a Christian critique of the many ideologies that pass for truth, e.g., the ideologies of ideal health, progress through technical advance, or the ideas of the dominant group in society at the time; exposure of the harm done to people when money, profit or sensual gratification are worshipped as gods. Under the heading 'sexual impurity' might belong Christian witness to the integrity of marriage, respect for personhood and the body, the differences between eroticism and pornography, contraception, appropriate sex-education for young people, support for the victims of domestic and sexual abuse, care for those suffering from sexually transmitted diseases, etc. Under the heading 'bloodshed or lack of respect for life' might belong issues relating to retributive justice, morality and the law, health-care, abortion and euthanasia, prenatal screening and diagnostic testing, and population expansion.
84. M. M. Bakhtin, *Toward a Philosophy of the Act*, trans. and notes by Vadim Liapunov, ed. Vadim Liapunov and Michael Holquist (Austin, TX: University of Texas Press, 1993), p. 38.

an abstract 'ought'. When an 'ought' is brought to the act of judgement from outside, as it were, and fastened on by duty and/or rationality, it lacks determinative content and is detached from the person's life: 'Content/sense abstracted from the act/deed ... is fundamentally and essentially alien to living historicity.'[85] If/when Christian ethics is reduced to theoretical acknowledgements of abstract norms or 'oughts', then it assumes a false naïveté in overemphasising the continuity between the bible, early Christianity and contemporary experience, only to repeat ever new forms of 'conservative antiquarianism'.[86] Yet in contrast to relativist and consequentialist positions, Christian ethics maintains that there will be 'better' or 'best', 'more fitting' or 'less wrong' courses of action in given situations. The purpose of ethical and moral judgements is to discern what these courses of action are. To this end, the canons of the church may yet be of assistance in warning us against that which is harmful to the human condition (Rom. 7:7).

The Prophetic Dimension

Consideration of the prophetic dimension of Christian ethics cannot start in a better place than the gospels where Jesus' authority communicates itself as charismatic and unique. Here one of the first things that we read is that people marvelled (Mk 1:22). Søren Kierkegaard could have been describing Jesus' prophetic authority when he wrote that authority is the 'recklessness of infinity': the fearless resolution to be willing to sacrifice oneself for one's cause.[87] He knew that true authority is present only when 'the truth is in the cause'. Hence, the Pharisees spoke

---

85. Bakhtin, *Toward a Philosophy of the Act*, p. 8.
86. Alasdair MacIntyre, *After Virtue: A Study in Moral Theory*, 2nd edition (London: Duckworth, 1981), p. 223.
87. Søren Kierkegaard, *Without Authority* (Princeton: Princeton University Press, 1997), pp. 211–212.

without authority, although they were institutionally authorised as teachers, whereas Jesus articulated the message of the reign of God in such a way that his identity was so bound up with this proclamation that he feared nothing. Jesus' prophetic authority was not comfortable, but disturbing. He challenged the religious institutions of his day to risk hearing God's word of judgement, and to stop sanitising their experience of divine authority by enshrining it within the minutiae of the law (Matt. 23:23–30). In reading this account, we are confronted with the question: could we be guilty, like the scribes and Pharisees, of diminishing the prophetic authority of God's word to that which we can manage? Are those of us who get paid for being theologians preoccupied with what Kierkegaard described as 'the perpetual rigmarole of Christian truth'?[88] God forbid! However, to be able to recognise the temptations to which the scribes and Pharisees were subject demands a willingness to be stimulated and provoked into critical reassessment by the field of energy released from the biblical text. The challenge here is the risk of interpretation: the conceptual necessity of staging the interaction of biblical text and present-day practice, in ways that allow the norms of authority, as defined by Jesus, to be seen and heard.

This is where the subject becomes difficult, because Jesus' pro-phetic authority was characterised by a radical givenness that exceeds human effort or imitation. Like the true prophets of the Old Testament, his prophetic authority was thrown up by the Spirit of God for specific tasks; it erupted without warning, and was characterised by charismatic and direct impact in crisis situations. Neither Jesus nor Elijah, for instance, could be controlled by institutional powers; they were 'loose cannons' who could not be relied upon by institutional organisers. Their power resided in a charisma that could not be controlled within any human organis-ation. Elijah, 'a figure of absolutely primeval force', demanded of the people: 'How long will you go limping with two different

---

88. Kierkegaard, *Without Authority*, p. 230.

opinions?' (1 Kgs 18:21), and his question was answered directly by Yahweh in unequivocal fashion.[89] Jesus challenged the established order with the reality of the reign of God, acting with authority because he was himself under authority: 'I do nothing on my own, but I speak these things as the Father instructed me' (Jn 8:28). Jesus did not acquire his authority through organisational or intellectual endeavour, but his words qualitatively asserted themselves because the Spirit of God rested upon him (Matt. 3:16–17; Mk 1:10; Lk. 3:22, 4:1) so that he spoke directly to the hearts of his hearers. The subject is a difficult one for the church today because we cannot organise for this kind of prophetic authority, only wait upon God for it. We might ask whether the church today is less equipped with prophetic authority or more equipped (cf. Lam. 2:9), but the power of prophetic authority is out of our control.

Once this is recognised, it means that prophetic authority cannot be regulated by the institution of the church; the tension between charisma and institution is no less real than when priests of the establishment were confronted on Mount Carmel with a seeming tin-pot idiot (1 Kgs 18:17–46).[90] Typically, the dynamic of prophetic authority risks breaks with the established order. If,

---

89. Von Rad, *Old Testament Theology*, Vol. I, p. 18.

90. Max Weber's work is still useful when dealing with this subject because he assists our reconstruction of how and why limitations of prophetic authority, and tensions between prophetic and priestly, come about. His *Sociology of Religion* relates an account of, among other things, human discomfort with prophetic authority, and the urge either to control or silence it. Weber warns that the unpredictability of prophetic authority produces a need for security that can contribute to a range of phenomena, including: hierarchical forms of organisation that contribute to the domestication of preaching; the rendering of the laity objects of pastoral care; the reservation of privileges 'for those charged with religious functions'; and, for movements past the first flush of youth, the need to struggle against indifference and stagnation by 'pushing distinctive criteria and differential doctrines to the foreground', so that codification, rituals and rubrics become the mechanisms of power. Weber, *Sociology of Religion*, pp. 61, 71–73.

however, Christ's authority is to be the norm and basis of authority in the ethical life of his body the church, then the church must continue to reckon with prophetic authority, not least because some are still called to prophesy (1 Cor. 12:28, 14:31–33; Eph. 4:11). *Lumen Gentium* is clear that the holy people of God 'shares also in Christ's prophetic office'.[91] If this is so, then the church must be wary not to undercut or delimit prophetic authority by, for example, becoming preoccupied with ensuring its economic existence, or by producing hierarchical and routinised institutions that try to 'manage' encounters with the divine, or by domesticating preaching.[92] In the Old Testament, true prophets rarely had popular appeal, announcing, as they did, God's judgement upon the kingly houses of Judah and Israel: 'Thus says the Lord: . . . put on sackcloth, and roll in ashes; . . . for suddenly the destroyer will come upon us' (Jer. 6:22–30). It is unlikely that they will be popular with those who exercise priestly and kingly and/or institutional power today. However, as Karl Barth explained of the Old Testament prophets: 'What makes their enquiries and declarations prophetic is that objectively and materially they are witnesses of Him who was still to come, i.e., of the grace now vouchsafed to Christians.'[93] Arguably, this is one criterion in the consideration of the Christian ethic that requires no modernisation.

This raises questions about how prophetic authority is to be exercised by the church as a whole. If the church is the bearer of Christ's prophetic authority in the world, then, in addition to being dependent upon individual figures raised up by God for particular tasks or situations, the responsibility to prophecy is in some sense universalised, and given to all. The prophets of the Old Testament were people raised by God in situations of crisis. Sometimes of a political nature, these crises required God's inter-

---

91. Vatican II, *Lumen Gentium* (2 November 1964) in *Vatican Council II*, ed. Austin Flannery OP (Dublin: Dominican Publications, 1975/1992), §12.

92. Weber, *Sociology of Religion*, pp. 71–73.

93. Karl Barth, *Church Dogmatics* (Edinburgh: T. & T. Clark), III.2, §2, p. 495.

vention through their hands and mouths in times of war, or other kinds of threat to Israel's well-being.[94] Thus, during a time of unrest and political ferment, 'a sword for the Lord and for Gideon' saved the Israelites from destruction at the hands of the Midianites (Jud. 6:1–7:25, esp. 7:20). The spirit of the Lord rushed on Samson and he was victorious over the men of Ashkelon, and the Philistines (Jud. 14:1–16:31). According to New Testament witness, some are still given the particular gift of prophecy (1 Cor. 12:28; Eph. 4:11). However, the church is the body of Christ in the world (Rom. 12:4; 1 Cor. 12:12ff; Eph. 4:4; Col. 1:18), and, as a whole, has been given this responsibility. The danger here is that when attention is focused less on one figure than on the whole body, instead of arousing the church to intense witness of the kind recounted in the bible, its prophetic authority becomes just another kind of pseudo-authority that translates into routine and bureaucracy rather than action that transforms lives for the better. The radical givenness of prophetic authority allows most believers to throw off the burden of exercising prophecy, because it is unlikely that the specific gift has been given to them. The corporate nature of prophetic authority in the Christian church similarly allows most believers to throw off the burden, because the gift has been given not only to them, but to every other believer as well. Two alternative fates? Or the dialectic that must be negotiated if the prophetic authority that accompanies proclamation of the gospel is to be realised today?

Signs of authority in the church

It is commonly acknowledged that the churches have less and less formally recognised authority in society, and that the Church of England will have even less in a fully reformed House of Lords. It is worth remembering that what marked out Jesus' ministry

---

94. Their authority resided both in their own persons and in what they did, including victories won in the name of YHWH, and actions performed in the name of the Lord (2 Kings 4:1–5:27).

as prophetic was not his links with the state, or the religious establishment, but his intense identification with the message he proclaimed.[95] His message, and that of the true prophets in ancient Israel, attracted opposition and hostility because what Weber dubbed their 'meaningful attitude towards life' conflicted with the perceived reality and wishful thinking of those in power.[96] His authority was, characteristically, outside of institutional control, all of which suggests that the proper mark of Christian prophetic authority lies not in political compromise with the establishment, but in uncompromising adherence to gospel concerns (Lk. 4:16–21). Yet far harder than ensuring that the churches and other religious organisations have adequate and formally recognised political representation is the actual exercise of prophetic authority in society, especially in connection with poverty, the realisation of human potential, and freedom from oppression. As a prophetic witness in society, however, the church is called to express divine authority in sociological terms. The subject is difficult because of problems associated with relating the ministry of the church to that of Christ. Yet as a sociologically distinct body, we need to consider how the ethos of church life affects its credibility as a figure of divine authority by virtue of participation in divine energies.

We are thus concerned with the ethos of church life. My working assumption is that structures of organisation in the church are not external supports or scaffolding, merely a technical means for the realisation of inner truth, which is the authority of Jesus Christ. Rather, every dimension of the church's ethos is the outgrowth of its imitation of Christ. How, then, are authority structures in the church to serve as icons of divine authority? How is the church's exercise of authority to move those who see it to glorify God? Such a question might seem farcical to many these days, not least because structures of authority in the church vary enormously

---

95. Weber, *Sociology of Religion*, p. 48.
96. Weber, *Sociology of Religion*, p. 59.

from one tradition or denomination to another. Enormous differences pertain between hierarchical and democratic structures among different denominations; each denomination has its own way of holding together theology and ecclesial sociology. Compare the Orthodox Catholic Church which claims to be 'aware of the identity of her teaching with the apostolic message and the tradition of the Ancient Church',[97] with the Baptist Church of Great Britain which holds: 'Pastoral oversight can never be a matter of requiring obedience; the only authority can be that of the winning of trust from others, through service offered in imitation of the self-giving of Christ.'[98] The former asks its teachers to submit to the divine law and to the sacred rules of the Holy Apostles and Holy Fathers, and holds that, in certain circumstances, submission to the will of the bishop is submission to the will of God.[99] The latter acknowledges that authority is nowadays accepted only where it proves itself. To ask: What is authority? is to ask about the criteria by which its exercise may be recognised.[100] What are we to make of these differences? Is there a tale to be told about the loss of the truth of authority as received? Is this just another example of the 'clashing symbols of Christian truth'?[101]

These tensions are not new. From the earliest days of the church,

---

97. Georges Florovsky, *Ecumenism 1: A Doctrinal Approach*, vol. 13 in his collected works (Vaduz: Büchervertriebsanstalt, 1989), pp. 139–140; Vladimir Lossky, *The Mystical Theology of the Eastern Church* (London: James Clarke, 1957), p. 188.

98. *Forms of Ministry Among Baptists: Towards an Understanding of Spiritual Leadership* by The Faith and Unity Executive Committee and the Doctrine and Worship Committee, 1994. Available from Baptist Union Publications, PO Box 44, 129 Broadway, Didcot, Oxon, OX11 8RT.

99. Taken from the consecration of a bishop, according to the *Service Book of the Holy Orthodox-Catholic Apostolic Church*, trans. Isabel Hapgood (New York: Syrian Antiochene Orthodox Archdiocese, 1922).

100. This wording is taken from the *Ecumenical Review* 21, pp. 150–166.

101. Hans Urs von Balthasar, 'The Gift of Joy', *Concilium* 39, ed. C. Duquoc (1968).

some have held that authority in the church is marked by discipleship and 'bottom-up' consensus, and others that it should be
marked by structured stability and 'top-down' direction.[102] How
then are the church's many institutional patterns, structures, and
disciplines to serve as prophetic witness to divine authority? Arguably, a variety of approach is to be expected if, as many have
argued, the New Testament gave direction but not directions
about the social forms that ministry should take.[103] The self-

---

102. A. C. Headlam traces these differences historically, and links them to differences in the late nineteenth and early twentieth centuries between F. J. A. Hort
and C. Gore. According to one view, it was of great significance that when Peter
preached first to the Gentiles he laid his actions before the apostles and believers
in Jerusalem, for their testing and approval (Acts 11:1–18). Similarly, it was because
of 'the consent of the whole church' that limited burdens only were to be placed
upon Gentile Christians: 'For it has seemed good to the Holy Spirit and to us . . .'
(Acts 15:22, 28). Among the early Fathers, Clement of Alexandria expounded the
priesthood of all, on account of the oblation of prayer made by the souls who
offer themselves to God. According to the other view, the apostles, prophets,
evangelists, teachers, pastors and others were appointed by Jesus himself, in no
way deriving their authority from the community of believers (1 Cor. 12:28; Eph.
4:11). (See Clement of Alexandria, *Comments on the First Epistle of Peter*, *ANF*,
Vol. II, p. 572.) Among the fathers, there are many witnesses to the fact and
growth of the church's hierarchy, and to the development of a sense of sacred
order in accordance with God's will. Cyprian, for example, wrote of Christ's
authority in the church 'as beginning from one'. Christ arranged that the origin
of authority in the church be found in Peter, whom he endowed with honour
and power (Cyprian, *On the Unity of the Church* §§4–5, *ANF*, Vol. V, pp. 421ff).
Augustine implied clear structures of authority, not only in the church on earth
but when believers rise from the dead (Eph. 5:14) and reign with Christ for a
thousand years, because 'this refers not to the bishops alone, and presbyters,
who are now specially called priests in the Church; but as we call all believers
Christians on account of the mystical chrism, so we call all priests because they
are members of the one Priest'. Augustine, *City of God*, Bk 20, ch. 10, *NPNF*
First Series, Vol. II, p. 432.
103. A. C. Headlam argues: 'The Apostles as the first rulers of the Church
gradually built up a ministry adapted to the conditions of the times, but they
gave no directions that have been preserved for us in any trustworthy or authoritative manner as to what should be the form of the society', *The Doctrine of* ▷

understanding of the church has always been varied. Yet it has always had an identity distinct from the society of which it is part and from the members who comprise it. This fact provides good socio-theological reasons for maintaining a harmonious diversity. Jesus prayed that his disciples 'may all be one' (Jn 17:21) – although it should be noted that unity is not sameness, in either a numerical or qualitative sense, but can be a differentiated unity which, by analogy to the unity of the Father and the Son, implies difference to such an intimate degree that unity and difference cannot be thought of without the other.[104] Space prevents a properly ecumenically informed study which would require an enormous amount of data about the differing ways in which different confessions derive forms of ecclesial polity from the basis of Christ's authority. The most that can be done is to keep open the question of how to evaluate the relationship between the authority of Jesus Christ, the social reality of organised ecclesial polity, and the semiotic quality of their interaction as expressed in language, liturgy and the diversity of callings to Christian ministry. Thus the question is a two-way one: how does the prophetic authority of Jesus Christ determine the signs and structures of authority in

---

the Church and Christian Reunion, being the Bampton Lectures for the year 1920 (London: John Murray, 1921), p. 242. Peter, for instance, implores exiles of the Diaspora: 'let yourselves be built into a spiritual house, to be a holy priesthood, to offer spiritual sacrifices acceptable to God through Jesus Christ' (1 Pet. 2:5), but refers in loose fashion only to elders (presbyters) and oversight (*episcope*) (1 Pet. 5:1–5). (Some authorities lack reference to the exercise of oversight.) He clearly intended a properly organised ministry, but no indication is given that any particular form should be essential. Paul speaks about gifts to be used in ministry (Eph. 4:11–13), and requires that all ministers of the word regard themselves as trustworthy stewards (1 Cor. 4:1). He made a unilateral decision that the Corinthians should hand over to Satan the man guilty of sexual immorality (1 Cor. 5:1–5), i.e., he exercised authority independent of the community of believers, but nowhere does he give directions about the future organisation of the church.

104. C. K. Barrett, *The Gospel According to St John* (London: SPCK, 1962), p. 427.

the church? And how do these signs and structures reflect and refract the authority of Jesus Christ?

All forms of authority in the church have the capacity to register, transmit, distort or pervert the sign of Jesus' authority, and should, for this reason, be tested continually against the witness of the gospels. Indeed, any reassessment of authority in church life must reckon with Luther's observation in 1531: 'there is no greater sinner that the Christian Church', and expect the human exercise of authority to fall into delinquency and tyranny.[105] Yet the whole church in its organisation, pastoral care and exercise of authority is productive of meaning as regards what it is to live as the body of Christ in the world. Signs of authority emerge in the process of interaction between one social grouping and another, and if we recognise that authority can arise only in relational territory, then questions about the exercise of authority and power cannot be divorced from the practical realities of who makes decisions, and who wields financial influence. Signs of authority, e.g., who is permitted to read the lectionary passage from the gospels in worship, who is permitted to pronounce words of absolution, the wearing of a bishop's mitre or a dog-collar, are aspects of the concrete forms of organised ecclesial intercourse. Each sign is more than a literary or physical artefact because it is accompanied by political refractions of power. Every sign of authority is a construct between socially organised persons, whether within local, national or international scope, and there are many temptations to acquire power instead of offering true worship to God (Matt. 4:8–10). How then are we to seek what Gillian Rose calls 'restitutive criticism', i.e., the giving back of every exercise of authority its proper source?

This question concerns nothing less than the nature of the body of Christ and its way of being in the world. If Christ is the head of his body the church, then what can be done to promote

---

105. Martin Luther, *Martin Luthers Werke*, Kritische Gesamtausgabe (Weimar, 1883–), 34/1.276.7f.

its growth so that the church becomes an icon of divine authority? What, if anything, distinguishes the Christian exercise of authority from the best-run private companies and public services? At a time when much uncertainty surrounds the relationship between lay and ordained ministries, the meaning of ordination, and the future direction of ecumenical dialogue about ministry, we need to avoid the familiar impasses and ecumenical introspection at the expense of missionary paralysis. As Luther was clear, it cannot, nor ought it, be the case that all should minister, teach, or speak the words of Jesus, publicly.[106] Some are called to act as stewards of God's mysteries (1 Cor. 4:1). For the sake of good order, there will be, as Luther accepts, some who exercise ministry on behalf of others. The laity are not, however, as Luther phrases it, 'something else than Christians', and if the exercise of authority in the church gives this impression, then we need to reconsider how the church as a body reflects and refracts the authority of Christ. To this end, Calvin reminds us that God uses human services only ever as a sort of delegated work, as a worker may make use of a tool.[107] God hides the treasure of his grace in earthen vessels, often using puny ministers as ambassadors of the Word and servants of the church.[108] What, then, will remind us that authority is not acquired by understanding doctrine or enforcing moral strictures, but is a quality that enters from elsewhere?[109]

To speak of the church as a prophetic witness to divine authority seems faintly ridiculous these days. Yet Christian ethics flows from belief in Christ, the sacraments, prayer and worship, and cannot therefore be separated from the exercise of authority in church life. Both need to be characterised by the giving back of every exercise of authority to its proper source. In the worshipping life of the church, one way of manifesting such a characteristic is by

---

106. Luther, *Concerning Christian Liberty*, p. 270.
107. Calvin, *Institutes*, Bk IV, ch. III, §1.
108. Calvin, *Institutes*, Bk IV, ch. I, §§5 and 8.
109. Kierkegaard, *Without Authority*, p. 98.

allowing, or indeed encouraging, all persons either ordained or commissioned by their church for the leading of public worship to report Jesus' words, 'your sins are forgiven'. I use the word 'report' advisedly to mean speech about speech or utterance about utterance.[110] According to Volosinov's Marxist studies in semiotics (Volosinov is argued by some to have been heavily influenced by Bakhtin, and by others to have signed his name to a work written by Bakhtin[111]), a reported utterance is never just a theme of speech but occurs as a constructional unit within another's speech. It is regarded by the speaker, and by the hearer, as belonging to someone else: '[I]t is from this independent existence that reported speech is transposed into an authorial context while retaining its own referential content . . . its original constructional independence.'[112] The speaker uses stabilised constructional patterns of language (e.g., for our purposes, liturgy) and, within these patterns, words react on words so that there is an active relationship of one message within and upon another. Importantly, if there is any dissolution of the reported utterance into the supposed autonomy of the speaker, then the integrity of the original utterance has been lost.

By using Volosinov's semiotic study of reported speech we can pursue this line of inquiry by focusing more specifically on the relationship between the 'what' of Jesus' words, 'your sins are forgiven,' and the 'how' or 'by what means' they come to be made real. Volosinov's concern is to explore how the dynamism of this relationship of the 'what' and the 'how' of reported speech can develop in different directions. There can be a tendency in reported speech, he says, to turn it into an isolated monologic

---

110. I draw on V. N. Volosinov, *Marxism and the Philosophy of Language*, trans. Ladislav Matejka and I. R. Titunik (Cambridge, MA: Harvard University Press, 1973/1996), ch. 2.

111. On this, see G. S. Morson and C. Emerson, *Mikhail Bakhtin: Creation of a Prosaics* (Stanford, CA: SUP, 1990), ch.3.

112. Volosinov, *Marxism and the Philosophy of Language*, p. 116.

utterance in which there is little active reception of the uttered words; utterance then becomes dogmatic and linear. Alternatively, there can be a tendency to abuse the integrity of the original speaker and to transpose the reported speech into a fluid movement between the hearers; utterance then becomes pictorial, and its external contours are lost amidst the individualism of many subjective appropriations. So, in Christian discussion of authority, as expressed in the proclamation of absolution, there can be a tendency towards the polarity of (a) confession made in the sacrament of penance, the efficacy of which depends upon the power of the keys, without regard to personal appropriation of its truth; and (b) confession made in the person's own conscience, the efficacy of which depends upon subjective desire for forgiveness.[113] Volosinov's semiotic studies review the syntactic patterns of direct speech, indirect speech and quasi-indirect speech, as modifications of how another person's utterances are conveyed and incorporated within given social contexts. For him, what is important is the dynamic relationship between reported speech and the reporting context.[114] He takes the problem of reported speech and postulates it as a problem from a sociological orientation. To do this socio-theologically helps us to recognise that the authority of Christ in the church can only come about within some kind of semiotic fabric; authority arises only in the material embodiment of the body of Christ in the world or ethos; every sign of authority is an act of reference between the authority that is in Jesus Christ and other already known patterns and forms of authority.

Present-day practices across the spectrum of Christian denominations are diverse. To take just three examples, the Roman Ritual includes rites for the reconciliation of individual penitents, for the reconciliation of several penitents with individual confession and

---

113. I draw here on Karl Rahner, 'The Church and the Sacraments' in *Theological Investigations*, Vol. 9 (London: Darton, Longman & Todd, 1975), pp. 202–211; 214–215.

114. See Volosinov, *Marxism and the Philosophy of Language*, p. 119.

absolution, and also for the reconciliation of several penitents with general confession and absolution.[115] *The Alternative Service Book 1980*, for use in the Church of England, requires that in the absence of a priest, 'us' and 'our' are said instead of 'you' and 'your' in all pronouncements of absolution.[116] The Methodist Church of Great Britain does not reserve the exercise of this authority to the ministry of the ordained. Its lay preachers can use the 'you' form, taking it for granted that a lay person, who has been commissioned for the leading of public worship and proclamation of the gospel, can quote the words of Jesus, 'Your sins are forgiven'. In each of these practices the semiotic significance of pronouncement of absolution is refracted in social and ecclesio-political conditions; every exercise of this form of priestly authority is an expressive sign which functions in given situations to convey different perspectives on the truth that priestly authority belongs to all, and can be exercised by all. It must be admitted at this point that autobiographical factors are probably affecting my theological judgement; I write as a member of the Methodist Church which holds to the fundamental principles of the Protestant Reformation with regard to the sacraments, and repudiates false distinctions between the ministry of bishops and priests, and the ministry of the rest of the people of God.[117] This said, if every ecclesial pronouncement of absolution is a reporting of the words of Jesus – speech within speech, utterance within utterance – and if, as has been argued above, the Christ's ministry belongs to all and can be exercised by all, then to encourage all persons either ordained or

---

115. *The Rite of Penance: The Roman Ritual revised by decree of the Second Vatican Ecumenical Council and published by the authority of Pope Paul VI* (Essex: Mayhew-McCrimmon, 1976).

116. *The Alternative Service Book 1980* (London: Hodder & Stoughton, 1980), note 4 re morning and evening prayer, p. 46.

117. This is the sense of The Deed of Union of the Methodist Church, in *Minutes of the Uniting Conference of the Methodist Church 1932* (London: Methodist Publishing House, 1932), Appendix II, §32, p. 302. It is alluded to in the 1985 response of the Methodist Church of Great Britain to *BEM*.

commissioned by their church for the leading of public worship to report Jesus' words, 'your sins are forgiven', is one way of giving back every act of pronouncing absolution to its proper source. Only in this way is it possible to evade the crisis in authority which visible ecumenical differences bring about.

Defending universal moral standards

But what of the exercise of prophetic authority in wider society? Christian ethics is not a sectarian discipline limited in scope to the life of the church. Rather, as John Chrysostom observes, it seeks pointers towards how all humankind is called to live in 'another country': 'He [Jesus] signifies to us obscurely that the fashion of the whole world is also being changed.'[118] How, then, does sharing in Christ's prophetic ministry have wider application? Answers to these questions can vary widely. John Milbank, for example, alerts us to the dangers of a Christology which indulges in metaphysical or speculist excess and which claims 'that Jesus's death is salvific because it somehow stands in an immediate causal relationship to all human beings, in a manner transcending normal historical processes'.[119] Don't play the liberal game, he urges, of pretending that the universal dimension of salvation in Christ can be translated into some notion of social universality that is simply a variant of the universalist emphases of the Enlightenment. Secular ethics has little, if any, integrity and is synonymous with nihilism. Hence Christian social theory 'must articulate Christian difference in such a fashion as to make it strange'.[120] Theologically, this requires us to take a position as

---

118. John Chrysostom, *Homilies on the Gospel of Matthew*, Homily XVI, §4, *NPNF* Second Series, Vol. V, p. 506.

119. John Milbank, *The Word Made Strange: Theology, Language, Culture* (Oxford: Blackwell, 1997), pp. 165 and 147.

120. John Milbank, *Theology and Social Theory* (Oxford: Blackwell, 1990), p. 381. As further illustration of Milbank's position, consider the essay 'Can Morality Be Christian?' in *The Word Made Strange*. The answer that he gives straightaway is 'No, morality cannot be Christian', the reason being that 'Christian moral- ▷

regards the effects of sin and evil upon human moral capabilities, and as regards the saving effects of the incarnation. At the risk of over-generalisation, neo-Augustinian strands within the western legacy tend to view general humanity pessimistically as cut off by nature from God.[121] The Christian ethos is a 'counter' or alterna-

---

ity is a thing *so* strange, that it must be declared immoral or amoral according to all other human norms and codes of morality' (Milbank, *The Word Made Strange*, ch. 9.) In brief, he takes five marks of general morality and contrasts with five notes of Christianity:

Five Marks of Morality	*Five Notes of Christianity*
Reaction	Gift
Sacrifice	End of Sacrifice
Complicity with Death	Resurrection
Scarcity	Plenitude
Generality	Confidence

For example, virtue, or morality, is complicit with death because, in seeking to oppose death, it must covertly celebrate it. Without death there would be no need to be good: 'So ethics must covertly celebrate death, for only our fragility elicits virtue' (p. 223). Ethics and/or morality which seeks knowledge of good and evil is, he says, a complicity with death. By contrast, Christianity opposes death because Christian ethics derives from the resurrection and not the dispensation of death. Similarly, morality (esp. Kantian and Aristotelian) as contemplation of the good, or concentration on teleological flourishing, is abstract and non-relational in form. In practice, it becomes a form of living under law, which is to be contrasted with Christian living in the confidence of grace. Thus, he concludes, faith is the first virtue and 'without the virtue of worship there can be no other virtue' (p. 230). Similarly, Michael Banner purported, in his 1996 inaugural address at King's College London, that Christian ethics is different from any other form because it centres around knowledge of the explicit commands of God.

121. Augustine, *City of God*, trans. Henry Bettenson (London: Penguin, 1972), Bk. XXI, ch. 13, p. 989. Augustine wrote with rhetorical flourish: 'We see then that the two cities were created by two kinds of love: the earthly city was created by self-love reaching the point of contempt for God, the Heavenly City by the love of God carried as far as contempt of self' (*City of God*, Bk XIV, ch. 28, p. 593). As interpreted by some, this results in a penchant for dramatic alternatives according to which God's grace is extrinsic to nature, or opposed to what is 'natural'.

tive way of life that is antagonistically at variance to the secular or neo-pagan. By contrast, the eastern legacy is more ready to view God's grace as infusing every created thing, so that every created thing has its point of contact with the divine. Vladimir Lossky writes: 'Eastern tradition . . . recognises no distinction, or rather division, save that between the created and the uncreated.'[122] Grace is not extrinsic to nature because the natural state of true humanity is conformation with the Word of God. In similarity with the neo-Augustinian position, Christian ethics is viewed as different from every other form of ethics because it refers everything to the revelation of God in Jesus Christ. However, there is an emphasis upon the fact that nothing lies outside the scope of the divine energies, and that all human beings have some knowledge of the good.

Are we to conclude, therefore, that there is, or at least should be, radical discontinuity between Christian and any other form of ethics because, to use Karl Barth's words, 'the general conception of ethics coincides exactly with the conception of sin'?[123] Is this radical discontinuity integral to the church's prophetic witness? Alternatively, are we to recognise no division between nature and grace because, to cite Gregory Nazianzen, the Word of God became truly human in order that 'the entire humanity fallen through sin might be created anew'?[124] Does the church's prophetic witness consist primarily in affirming its hope in the future which God has prepared for all humankind? The practical relevance of these questions lies in whether or not the church affirms universal moral standards. As noted in the Introduction, we live in a season of

---

122. Lossky, *Mystical Theology of the Eastern Church*, p. 88.
123. Barth, *Church Dogmatics* II/2, pp. 518–19, cited by Michael Banner in 'Turning the world upside down (and some other tasks for dogmatic Christian ethics' which was his inaugural lecture from the Department of Theology and Religious Studies, King's College London, delivered 16 October 1996.
124. Gregory Nazianzen, Epistle CI to Cledonius, *NPNF* Second Series, Vol. VII, pp. 439–443.

disenchantment as regards both the relevance of Christian ethics to societal concerns and the validity of universal moral standards. We need to recognise with the neo-Augustinians that human reason is often perverted and disturbed, and cannot reliably summon humanity to respond to the Word of God. How, then, is the prophetic dimension of Christian ethics to be realised in ways that fall neither into a ghetto mentality nor pretend that the world is restored in Christ when it manifestly is not?[125]

Such arguments are not new in Christian discourse and are found, in some similarity, in writings by the Ante-Nicene fathers who lived in pluralist societies which bear some similarity with our own. For example, Justin Martyr (c. 100–165) argued that all humans have the power to avoid evil and choose good by free choice: 'by free choice they both walk uprightly and stumble'.[126] Each person possesses the gift of free will, but this means neither that fate is the cause of good or evil, nor that virtue and vice are reckoned as such by opinion only. Justin developed this kind of argument by means of the concept of the spermatic logos, i.e., the presence in humans of rational powers which comprise seeds of truth. Thus he writes: '[T]here seem to be seeds of truth among all men; but they are charged with not accurately understanding [the truth] when they assert contradictories.'[127] His argument is that, in the beginning, God made the human race with the power of thought and of choosing the truth and doing right, so all are without excuse before God; 'for they have been born rational and contemplative'.[128] Human reason and moral responsibility is Christ in humanity. God's Word is not addressed to believers only because, as stated above, all human nature is included within the structure of divine address. Moreover, Christ and the power of the Holy Spirit in humanity is the ground of human capacity to

125. This point is made by Milbank, *The Word Made Strange*, pp. 165 and 147.
126. Justin Martyr, *The First Apology*, ch. XLIII, *ANF*, Vol. I, p. 177.
127. Justin Martyr, *The First Apology*, ch. XLIV, *ANF*, Vol. I, p. 177.
128. Justin Martyr, *The First Apology*, ch. XXVIII, *ANF*, Vol. I, p. 172.

be both rational and moral. Similarly, Clement of Alexandria regards reason as a preparation for faith, wherein it also finds perfection.[129] For Clement, Christ is Wisdom and because of this he can assert that philosophical knowledge is given by God and is fulfilled by contemplation of God. To live rationally, thought Clement, is to live according to the Word of God. To be rational is to be conformed to the will of God: '[A] rational work is accomplished through God.'[130] Human reason, as exercised by any person, is rational in so far as it is in harmony with God's will.

Arguably, such arguments give us preliminary reasons to maintain universal moral standards as essential for the existence of human life in society. For the Ante-Nicene fathers, these standards were designated the natural moral law and identified with prohibitions contained in the Decalogue.[131] Unfortunately, arguments about universal moral standards are often confused with the universalist emphases of the Enlightenment, even though they are clearly not identical because the object of faith is God and not human reason. This is not to say that there are no points of contact with philosophical projects to defend universal moral standards. It could be said that the arguments of Justin and Clement above provide warrant for a defence of universal moral standards in the face of the kind of cultural relativism which grounds ethical norms in social custom.[132] They ground a strong anti-relativism and concern for the proper exercise of human reason in natural moral

129. Clement of Alexandria, *The Stromata, or Miscellanies*, chs V–VIII, *ANF*, Vol. II, pp. 489–496.

130. Clement of Alexandria, *The Stromata, or Miscellanies*, *ANF*, Vol. II, pp. 310–311.

131. For an excellent study in this area, see Stanley S. Harakas, 'The Natural Law Teaching in the Ante-Nicene Fathers and in Modern Greek Orthodox Theology', Boston University School of Theology, doctoral thesis (1965), esp. p. 130.

132. Of interest in this regard is recent work by Martha Nussbaum in defence of universal values based on universalist accounts of central human functions. In *Women and Human Development* (Cambridge: CUP, 2000), she defends a 'capabilities approach' in which moral values are related to general human powers and their development.

law.[133] To pursue this even cursorily, we need to be clear about what is meant by the natural law. Briefly stated, the natural moral law – summed up in the Decalogue and other tenets of the Mosaic law, e.g., 'an eye for an eye, a tooth for a tooth' – supplies rules in ethics which can be regarded as functioning as a basic minimum or lowest common denominator. The natural moral law is referred to, albeit in passing, by Paul in Rom. 2:14–15. The passage suggests that Gentiles know what the law requires because it is written on their hearts, i.e., their consciences tell them that they have a law to which they are morally responsible. The general direction of his argument in Rom. 1–3 (which is to show that both gentile and Jew have sinned and are in need of God's grace) supports this interpretation, though, arguably, Paul's scanty treatment of the subject suggests either that he adopted widespread opinions of the day (Jewish or Stoic) or that he held the matter to be of little importance.[134] Whatever is the case, it seems clear in his mind that gentiles can acquire sufficient knowledge of the natural law to have no excuse for doing wrong (Rom. 2:12). This interpretation is supported strongly by John Chrysostom who argues that God gave humankind conscience and allowed them knowledge of good and bad so that they could become self-taught in matters of morality and the laws needed for peaceable existence: '[W]hen God formed man, he implanted within him from the beginning a natural law.'[135] Thus Adam could recognise sin in

---

133. I adopt Harakas's definition: 'a natural law teaching [is] any concept of ethical thinking which grounds morality in some kind of objective fashion to which human behaviour in general and positive laws in particular ought to conform and which is known by man through his natural faculties as distinguished from knowledge obtained through Divine Revelation' (Harakas, 'The Natural Law Teaching in the Ante-Nicene Fathers', p. 4).

134. For a useful summary of arguments in support of the former conclusion, see Stanley S. Harakas, *Toward Transfigured Life* (Minneapolis: Light and Life, 1983), pp. 120–127.

135. John Chrysostom, *Homilies on the Statues*, Homily XII, §9, *NPNF* First Series, Vol. IX, p. 421.

himself; Cain sought to conceal the wicked act of fratricide; legis-
lators – without connection to Judaism or Christianity – have, for
centuries, written laws concerning marriage, murder, wills, trusts,
abstinence from encroachments on another's property, etc.[136]
Moreover, there is considerable overlap in Chrysostom's mind
between the natural law and the moral (not ceremonial) Mosaic
law. For example:

> How was it then when He said, 'Thou shalt not kill', that He
> did not add, 'because murder is a wicked thing.' The reason
> was, that conscience had taught this beforehand; and He
> speaks thus, as to those who know and understand the
> point.[137]

There was no need for God to spell out in the Mosaic law the
reasons why murder was wrong because those receiving this law
for the first time knew the reason already. The natural law and
the Mosaic law overlap; everyone knows that societies would fall
apart if their members adopted maxims which urged murder,
adultery, stealing, lying, envy and seeking to deprive others of
what they have, dishonour of parents, etc.

Thus, as Stanley Harakas notes, Christian ethics should be
neither easily optimistic nor fatalistically pessimistic as regards
the consequences of sin and evil.[138] The prophetic ministry of the
church will point both against secular theorising and along with
it, depending upon its conformity with the natural moral law as
restored and fulfilled in Christ. Evil, to use Gregory of Nyssa's
phrase, still keeps company with destruction, and sin leads unwary

---

136. John Chrysostom, *Homilies on the Statues*, Homily XII, §§10–12, *NPNF* First
Series, Vol. IX, p. 422.
137. John Chrysostom, *Homilies on the Statues*, Homily XII, §9, *NPNF* First
Series, Vol. IX, p. 421.
138. Stanley S. Harakas, *Living the Faith: The Praxis of Eastern Orthodox Ethics*
(Minneapolis, MN: Light and Life Publishing Co., 1992), p. 13.

people away from what is good.[139] One need only read a newspaper to be convinced that the world is manifestly not united with God, and that we await the new creation. Yet if Christ assumed a human mind at the incarnation, and if human rational and moral powers are not utterly obliterated by sin, then we can affirm christologically the human capacity to be rational and moral. We can affirm the basic value and dignity of human life, including concern for the proper exercise of human reason. The problems of sin and death pervade our existence. Yet death no longer reigns because the Logos filled the world with divine presence and trampled death down in the victory of cross and resurrection; the cross was 'a healing of Creation'.[140] The incarnation happened in chronological time and cannot be repeated. In the ministry, death and resurrection of Jesus Christ, something conclusive has taken place. Yet this event is not closed to the present and finished, only to be retold as a tale about the past, because its application is universal.

The End of Ethics?

According to this way of thinking, the prophetic dimension of Christian ethics identifies the hope, or 'end', of Christian ethics with that of creation itself, anticipating the day when the Word of God 'pervades and works in the whole ... is in the whole Universe, and the whole is illumined and moved by Him'.[141] Christ's incarnation and resurrection relate to creation as a whole and include all human nature within the structure of divine address. The church lives in anticipation of the realisation of this reality and sees itself as experiencing a foretaste. At the eucharist, Christian people 'participate in immortality through association

---

139. Gregory of Nyssa, *On the Making of Man*, NPNF Second Series, Vol. V, p. 410.

140. Athanasius, *Against the Heathen* §4, NPNF Second Series, Vol. IV, p. 6.

141. Athanasius, *Incarnation of the Word*, §42, NPNF Second Series, Vol. IV, p. 59.

with that which is incorruptible'.[142] The ordinariness of bread and wine signifies that God assumed the fullness of humanity. Bread and wine are 'signs' of the incarnation: they are of the same material stuff as humanity (consubstantial with humanity), as was the incarnate Word of God. They are also signs of the eschaton which model or exemplify how humanity is changed and deified by participation in the humanity of Christ. In the eucharist, church life is conditioned eschatologically and caught up in the dynamics of Christian hope. Christian ethics is similarly conditioned because it is rooted eschatologically and points beyond history towards unbroken harmony on earth and in heaven. The implications for the prophetic dimension of Christian ethics include a refusal of moral relativism but also the defence of universal standards within an understanding of natural moral law. Here – somewhat para-doxically at the close of the book – is where an important aspect of the task of Christian ethics begins.

---

142. Gregory of Nyssa, *The Great Catechetical Oration*, ch. XXXVII, *NPNF* Second Series, Vol. V, p. 506.

Conclusion

We began this book by observing that few concepts are more controversial these days than that of authority, especially in ethics. We also noted the moral challenge from Friedrich Nietzsche, radical post-Christian feminists and others that confession of the authority of God is harmful to the human condition. Against this background, we have acknowledged that there is much to lament about the church's practical rendering of its vision of God. Any situation where power is concentrated in the hands of a few is oppressive. It is deplorable that the witness of the Christian church has, at times, fallen so far away from what is fitting that criticism of this kind carries such weight. The juxtaposition of the words 'authority' and 'God' has, in Christian history, licensed the harmful combination of ecclesial authoritarianism and destructive self-abnegation. Equally tragic is a situation where persons are devoid of the power of creative decision. Remember Nietzsche's jibe that faith in God is 'closing one's eyes to oneself once and for all, lest one suffer the sight of incurable falsehood'.[1] Christianity, he contends, breeds such weak human beings that they cannot live with themselves and are full of vengeance towards those who are happy and powerful. Against this background, only the most blatant self-delusion could blind us to the fact we are never far from temptation and failure when discussing authority and its relationship to ethics (1 Pet. 5:8). Yet we have argued that, far from being the problem of Christian ethics, the authority of God is its solution. What might be thought to be the most problematic,

---

1. Friedrich Nietzsche, *The Antichrist*, §§8–9 in Walter Kaufmann (trans. and ed.), *The Portable Nietzsche* (New York and London: Penguin, 1976), pp. 574–575.

unexpected and dangerous concept in Christian ethics has turned out to be essential to our task.

The task of Christian ethics is challenging in many ways. Advances in science and technology, the rampages of the market economy, new patterns of personal and social relationships, the aftermath of wars, all demand that we 'confront each new thing' in ways that are – to paraphrase Nussbaum's words – more 'finely aware' of and 'richly responsible' to the Christian message.[2] In this book, we have not engaged in the minutiae of moral reasoning in order to work out exactly, or in prescriptive detail, what such responsibility will entail. We have, however, considered the goals and norms of Christian ethics, and some resources that are likely to prove fruitful in decision-making within varying and changing contexts. Like the soon-to-be-sacked manager who is commended by Jesus for shrewd business practice – he is lauded for having acted more shrewdly in his dealings than do 'the children of light' (Lk. 16:8) – we need to use the resources available to provide for the future. As Søren Kierkegaard writes: '[A] human being lives in temporality, which goes on in time.'[3] We cannot go beyond the cognitive limits of human being. However, to want to prepare ourselves for the future is no indolent pastime, so long as we exercise discernment as to what it is important to learn. All human knowledge, says Kierkegaard, is subject to changeableness. Only the eternal is upbuilding at all times: '[O]nly the eternal applies at all times and is always, is always true, pertains to every human being of whatever age . . .'[4] Sometimes, however, learning *more* is less important than learning *anew*.[5] The priorities that matter are

2. Martha Nussbaum, *Love's Knowledge* (Oxford: OUP, 1990), pp. 3–10.

3. Søren Kierkegaard, 'On the Occasion of a Confession' in *Upbuilding Discourses in Various Spirits*, trans. Howard V. Hong and Edna H. Hong, *Kierkegaard's Writings* XV (Princeton, NJ: PUP, 1993), p. 16.

4. Kierkegaard, 'On the Occasion of a Confession', p. 9.

5. Kierkegaard, 'Sufferings Educate for Eternity' in *Upbuilding Discourses in Various Spirits*, p. 252.

those set by the eternal, in the vigilance of prayer. But how difficult it is to be vigilant.

Gillian Rose prefaced her book *Love's Work* with the words: 'Keep your mind in hell, and despair not.'[6] As part of her lyrical love song – to cite Michael Wood's tribute – the words inspire remembrance that 'to live, to love, is to be failed, to forgive, to have failed, to be forgiven, for ever and ever'. Members of the Christian church might feel that they fail constantly in their efforts to be the body of Christ; that they need forgiveness; that their life together is fallible and precarious; that Christian ethics is about the constant risk of glimpsing a way forward and then failing, and glimpsing and failing again. The 'new' is difficult to contemplate. Yet as Kierkegaard writes, 'the future is not utterly new, because there is nothing new under the sun', the implication being that the future can be prepared for in part by clothing ourselves in experiences of the past.[7] For this reason, we have drawn upon resources from throughout Christian tradition. Similarly, writes Kierkegaard, 'expectancy and the future are inseparable ideas'.[8] Expectancy, and the ability to live in anticipation of the future, is a sign of the greatness and nobility of human beings; to struggle with the future means that we are not in bondage to service of the moment.[9] For Kierkegaard, the life of prayer is part of the expectancy of faith. It is about facing the future boldly, and with adequate preparation. To struggle with the future in prayer is to be expectant in a way that cannot be disappointed, because it yields neither to superficiality or despair, for 'if you belong to Christ, then you are Abraham's offspring, heirs according to the

---

6. This is a quotation from Staretz Silouan. Cited in Rose, *Love's Work*, Preface.
7. Kierkegaard, 'The Expectancy of Faith' in *Eighteen Upbuilding Discourses*, trans. Howard V. Hong and Edna H. Hong, *Kierkegaard's Writings* V (Princeton, NJ: PUP, 1990), p. 18. The reference is to Eccl. 1:9.
8. Kierkegaard, 'The Expectancy of Faith', p. 17.
9. Kierkegaard, 'The Expectancy of Faith', p. 17.

promise'.[10] By what means, then, should we prepare ourselves, and what priorities should we set? How should we face the future? Kierkegaard writes metaphorically:

> When the sailor is out on the ocean, when everything is changing all around him, when the waves are born and die, he does not stare down into the waves, because they are changing. He looks at the stars. Why? Because they are faithful; they have the same location now that they had for our ancestors and will have for generations to come.[11]

---

10. Kierkegaard's reflections on the expectancy of faith are an exposition of Gal. 3:23–29.
11. Kierkegaard, 'The Expectancy of Faith', p. 19.

Index of Biblical References

Index of Subjects

hell 194, 207, 223, 228, 259, 325
henosis x, xxiii
heresy xiii, 14, 49, 76, 97, 103, 105, 106, 110, 159–166, 189, 242, 283, 284
heteroglossia xxvi, 53, 54, 122, 136, 151–153, 156, 157, 181
hierarchy 12, 130, 176, 196, 236–238, 240, 244, 245, 248, 249, 252, 262, 307
holiness 114, 181, 253, 255, 258
Holy Spirit xxv, 38, 39, 45, 61, 65, 66, 87, 91, 99, 102–104, 106, 109, 114, 117, 120–122, 126, 127, 134–136, 156, 158, 163, 166, 167, 171–173, 177, 180, 184, 185, 187, 188, 227, 242, 246, 247, 250, 282, 295, 297, 307, 317
hope xxiii, xxix, 4, 58, 78, 81, 84, 85, 179, 205, 214, 217, 244, 267, 274, 316, 321

icon 110, 111, 113, 114, 305, 310
iconography 108, 111, 113
ideology x, 6, 58, 154, 299
idol 129, 217, 294
idolatry 83, 164, 294, 299
image of God x, xxv, xxvii, 17, 46, 48, 55, 59, 61, 76, 81, 83, 89, 104, 105, 142, 151, 226
imagination 89, 137, 227, 282
imitation 95, 112, 115, 190–192, 211, 222, 226, 258, 280, 281, 301, 305
immortality 225, 250, 321
incarnation x, xxiii, xxv, 22, 48, 51, 75–79, 81, 83, 84, 86, 87, 90, 94, 95, 97, 104, 106, 108, 110, 115–117, 127, 151, 188, 190,

198, 199, 203, 208, 225, 226, 294, 315, 321
individualism xiv, xxv, 53, 54, 138, 153, 208, 216, 227, 233, 243, 244, 248, 312
infallibility 101, 134, 168, 170, 172, 173
intuitionism xix

joy 40, 44–46, 86, 207, 210, 222, 251, 298, 306
judgement x, xvii, xviii, 7–9, 25, 71, 89, 92, 96, 109, 116, 119, 131, 142, 154, 157, 166, 177, 178, 180–183, 242, 251, 257, 262, 270, 275, 281, 290, 292, 295–297, 299, 301, 303, 313
justice xvi, xix, 12, 65, 257, 258, 262, 263, 266, 299
justification xiv, xviii

kenosis xxiv, 3, 95, 208
kenotic 22, 67, 117, 147, 205, 208, 243
keys 259, 263, 312
kindness 55, 152, 298
knowledge x, xvii, xviii, xxi-xxviii, 4, 5, 17, 28, 41, 47, 64–66, 74, 84, 91, 95, 102, 137, 139, 146, 156, 157, 162, 169, 177, 181, 186, 198–200, 234, 235, 265, 268, 284, 315, 316, 318, 319, 324
kyriarchy 190

laughter 192, 193, 195, 196, 205–208, 222, 240
law xvi, xix, xx, xxiv, 8, 46, 60, 93, 98, 102, 121, 124, 127, 144, 161, 174, 180, 181, 185, 196, 232,

Index of Names